MW01101465

The Changing Face of War
Learning from History

One of the biggest problems facing military leaders is how to deal with situations that they have never confronted before. This collection of original essays, written by military professionals engaged in war studies at the Royal Military College of Canada, demonstrates the value of historical study. The essays examine the past, present, and future of war to find solutions for the problems of today and tomorrow.

Part I deals with the evolution of military strategy and doctrine, from the Napoleonic Wars to today. Contributors look at the influence of great military thinkers, such as Carl von Clausewitz, on the armed forces of the Western world and examine how previous military leaders dealt with issues similar to those faced today, such as the effects of technology on strategy, the significance of the operational level of war, and ways of restructuring the armed forces in times of uncertainty and change. Part II examines warfare at the end of this century. Examples of the development of revolutionary warfare in Asia from Mao to Giap are used to underscore the cultural and situational influences on doctrines of revolutionary war. Part III looks at the future of conflict in the twenty-first century. Contributors investigate diverse issues, including the impact of computers on warfare, the effect of media coverage on strategy, space policy, arms control in the post–Cold War era, political systems and their relationship to the probability of war, and the prospects of stealth technology.

In an era when armed forces around the world have come under increasing scrutiny and criticism, this collection of essays provides valuable lessons that may avert future military mistakes.

ALLAN D. ENGLISH teaches war studies and continuing education at the Royal Military College of Canada.

The Changing
Face of War

Learning from History

EDITED BY

ALLAN D. ENGLISH

Published for
The Royal Military College of Canada
by
McGill-Queen's University Press
Montreal & Kingston · London · Buffalo

© The Royal Military College of Canada 1998
ISBN 0-7735-1723-5

Legal deposit third quarter 1998
Bibliothèque nationale du Québec

Printed in Canada on acid-free paper

McGill-Queen's University Press acknowledges the support of
the Canada Council for the Arts for its publishing program.

Canadian Cataloguing in Publication Data

Main entry under title:
 The changing face of war: learning from history
 Includes bibliographical references and index.
 ISBN 0-7735-1723-5

 1. Military art and sciences–History. 2. Military history.
 3. War. I. English, Allan D. (Allan Douglas), 1949–
 II. Royal Military College of Canada.

 U21.2.C48 1998   355.02   C98-900075-3

This book was typeset by Typo Litho Composition Inc.
in 10/12 Times.

Contents

Foreword

It is a pleasure to write a few words of introduction to the first book of collected essays from the War Studies program at Royal Military College (RMC). The masters of arts degree in war studies was established nearly thirty years ago. It quickly established a reputation as a high-quality program. Yet for most of that time it had modest enrolments and was open only to full-time graduate students attending RMC. There seemed neither the resources nor the interest by defence authorities outside the college to invest in it. Unless one was fortunate enough to be in residence at RMC, most personnel had little access to it, a situation that was exacerbated by the demands of professional military life.

All of that changed in the early 1990s. In the confusing and dangerous post–Cold War world the need to provide continuous and higher learning without interrupting a normal military career was more and more evident. The RMC War Studies degree program responded by creating distance-learning centres wherever there was a critical mass of student interest. Part-time graduate courses in war studies were started in a variety of military centres. At the time of writing there are over 250 Armed Forces personnel studying for this master's degree.

And the quality of the program has remained high indeed. The following papers, written mostly by the students in the distance learning courses, are testimonial to that fact. This volume is meant to give expression to the quality of scholarship of Canadian Forces students and to provide for their comrades-in-arms an important tool in their professional development.

B. John Plant
Principal
Royal Military College of Canada

Foreword

Preface

When the military historian Vegetius wrote his *De re militaria* at the end of the third century AD, he was searching for answers to the monumental and dangerous changes taking place in the fortunes of the late Roman Empire, then under siege. He hoped that both civil and military Roman leaders would find guidance from the lessons of his military history. And for a while they did. So did subsequent generations over many hundreds of years. However, nearly two millennia later, in similarly dangerous and confusing times, we are still seeking to learn from the past. But the real issue in this volume is not only the use of the past as prologue, but the revelation of a tool that is not solely the domain of professional historians. Rather, the study of the military experience of the past is a legitimate device for all those who choose to use it. For military personnel, such studies are crucial because they give perspective and because their lessons can prevent us from making disastrous mistakes. They also teach us to anticipate and not be surprised; and they warn us against forging critical policy decisions in a vacuum.

RMC's War Studies program has always had these goals. And the papers that follow are excellent examples of the practice. The tradition of having the best research papers published goes back over twenty-five years, to the time when the first of a series of *War Studies Occasional Papers* appeared, and pieces continued to be published throughout the 1970s and early 1980s. The purpose then, like now, was not only to provide a forum for good scholarship beyond the seminar room, but to collect fine presentations under a common theme. A recent volume explored aspects of peacekeeping. It received a substantial distribution both in and out of military and academic circles. Its success pointed out another primary goal of the program: to be useful as well as informative for the practitioners of the military and civil craft. This book has all of the hallmarks of its predecessors.

But in the end, the greatest accolade is that the quality scholarship and long hours of editorial work in this present collection belong solely to the officers and civilian course members of RMC's War Studies program, who, under the tireless guidance of Dr Allan English, have put this fine volume together.

Ronald Haycock
Dean of Arts
Chairman of the War Studies Committee
Royal Military College of Canada

Editor's Preface

A project of this magnitude requires the support of many people. Among those who made a significant contribution were a number of students in the War Studies program. I am delighted to be able to acknowledge here some of those who made this book possible. First of all, the work of Lieutenant-Colonel Ronald Blank must be acknowledged. As administrative coordinator for this project, he ensured that all aspects were delegated, assigned, and completed on time. Next, the hard work of Lieutenant (N) Adrian Biafore in collating, organizing, and formatting the material was absolutely indispensable. He was ably assisted by a recent graduate of the War Studies program, Mr Bradley Runions.

For financial assistance in publication we are indebted to the Director-General, Manpower and Personnel, Brigadier-General Ernest Beno.

Those involved in the production of this book hope that its readers – professional military personnel, scholars, students, or casual enthusiasts – will gain insight through their examination and reflection on the essays presented here. If this occurs in any small measure, then our aim has been achieved.

Allan D. English
Editor

The Changing Face of War

Introduction

ALLAN D. ENGLISH

One of the most difficult problems faced by military leaders is how to solve problems that they have never before confronted. Some disciplines offer problem-solving models or methodologies grounded in simulations, based on the premise that people learn by experience, to help the leader cope with new situations. These methods are useful; however, as Bismarck once remarked, "Fools say they learn by experience. I prefer to profit by other people's experience."[1]

How to learn from the mistakes, and the successes, of others is the focus of this collection of essays. The essays are based on course work submitted for the Royal Military College of Canada's War Studies Program, War Studies 500: Theories of War from the 18th Century to the Present. The course began with an examination of Sir Basil Liddell Hart's classic essay *Why Don't We Learn from History?* This work, by one of the most controversial and respected military writers of the twentieth century, documented instances when military planners had been caught by surprise by changes in warfare and were forced to learn by bitter and costly ordeals the lessons their forebears had also learned the hard way. One reason for this failure to learn from the past, Liddell Hart argued, was that, given the amount of actual fighting most professional soldiers have experienced, especially in the second half of this century, "in a literal sense the profession of arms is not a profession at all, but merely 'casual employment.'" To remedy this situation Liddell Hart suggested that more effort be expended in institutions of higher learning on the study of all aspects of warfare. He advocated particularly the study of history because, done properly, it provides its students with a wide view of every aspect of life: "It lays the foundation of education by showing how mankind repeats its errors and what those errors are."[2]

Following Liddell Hart's advice, War Studies 500 students in the academic year 1995–96 undertook a broad study of the changing face of war. They observed these changes over time, from Machiavelli to Bernard Brodie, and over various cultures from the West to the Far East. In so doing, the students have attempted to draw lessons from the past to help the military leaders of today find solutions to problems with similar dimensions to ones found in the past. While recognizing that no current or future problem will be identical to those found in history, we should be aware of analogies and parallels that can provide valuable lessons for those who are faced with new problems to resolve. With the acceptance of chaos theory, even modern science has recognized that most important natural phenomena, like the weather, are, because of their complexity, nonlinear and nonrepetitive. This has led to a more widespread acceptance of historical method, which emphasizes the accurate collection of data about specific cases followed by the formulation of conclusions and generalizations that can be applied to other situations.[3]

Liddell Hart claimed that military history should form the basis of a military education because of its immense practical value; it contributes to the mental development of the military leader while at the same time providing a breadth of experience that would be impossible for anyone to encounter in a single lifetime. The essays presented here aim to provide the reader with some detailed case studies of problems in warfare from the last two hundred years. They have been selected to offer the reader not only a glimpse of the challenges faced by military leaders and strategists who have preceded us, but also to provide useful analogies from the past that can be applied to the problems of the present and the future.

The unique aspect of this work is that most of the essays have been written by serving military officers involved in postgraduate studies. Most have served in both operational and staff positions and so can bring a wide perspective to the issues they have investigated for the War Studies course. Some have been able to apply their academic findings to practical problems with which they have had to deal in their military careers. It is hoped that their insight will be useful to others engaged in studying warfare and especially to those who are practitioners of the art of war.

The first part of this collection focuses on how military strategy and doctrine have evolved from the time of the Napoleonic Wars to today. Like Machiavelli before him, Liddell Hart recognized that history has its cyclical aspects. He suggested that the only way to escape what he called the "cycle of familiar errors, endlessly recurring, which largely makes up the course of military history" was to scrutinize past experience candidly for the lessons it might yield.[4] The first six essays deal with our past military experience and examine, for example, how Clausewitz's ideas are still current among armed forces of the Western world, though not perhaps in forms that he would recognize. Other essays in this part consider how our predecessors have dealt with issues that face us today: the effects of technology on strategy, the significance of the operational level of war, and how to restructure armed forces in times of uncertainty and change.

The second part of this volume examines what for some is the latest face of war – unconventional warfare, or low-intensity conflict. Examples of the development of revolutionary warfare in Asia, from Mao to Giap, underscore the cultural and situational influences on doctrines of revolutionary war. An example of naval forces engaged in counterinsurgency operations is presented as a contrast. The final essay in this part deals with how the lessons learned fighting counter-revolutionary war might be applied, in some circumstances, to the newest forms of peacekeeping/peacemaking operations.

The last part of the collection attempts to use lessons from the past to look into some aspects of the future of conflict in the next century. Authors investigate issues as diverse as the impact of computers on war fighting, the effect of media coverage on strategy, space policy, arms control in the post–Cold War era, political systems and their relationship to the probability of war, and the prospects of stealth technology to see if analogies can be coaxed from the past to help us deal with future problems. In so doing we are attempting to avoid the pitfalls enumerated by Liddell Hart and to see if we really can learn from history.

NOTES

1 Cited in Liddell Hart, *Why Don't We Learn from History?* 15.
2 Ibid., 17.
3 Akenson, *God's Peoples*, 351–3.
4 Liddell Hart, *Why Don't We Learn from History?* 32.

PART I

The Evolution of Military Strategy and Doctrine

Clausewitz and His Influence on U.S. and Canadian Military Doctrine

LCOL RICHARD J. YOUNG

The writings of General Carl Philip Gottlieb von Clausewitz are well known to scholars, and a particular interest in Clausewitz has been evident in the military services of the United States since the war in Vietnam. Bernard Brodie, Henry Kissinger, Peter Paret, and the Princeton circle all have thought deeply and written seriously about the implications of Clausewitz's theories on the nature of war and its relationship to statecraft. The impact of this on U.S. military thinking would be clear to anyone who surveyed the official doctrines publications of any of the U.S. services from the late 1970s to the present. Clausewitz's influence is also apparent, albeit to a lesser extent, in the doctrines publications of Canada's other traditional allies, Great Britain, Australia, and New Zealand. Christopher Bassford, a prominent military historian, has gone so far as to say: "The ideas of Clausewitz run like a subterranean river through all of modern military thought."[1] What is particularly notable, however, is the conspicuous absence of any similar influence by Clausewitz on the doctrine of the Canadian Armed Forces.

This essay briefly explores Clausewitz and his theories, attempting to determine why they should be so influential. I will also examine the reception of his theories over the years, leading up to the reflection of his work in the military doctrines of the United States and elsewhere. Finally, I explore reasons why the "river" of Clausewitzian thought appears to have dried up short of the Canadian border. The strong influence of Clausewitz in the doctrine of the United States, in contrast to the apparent absence of it in Canada, is striking. While the reasons for this difference are undoubtedly complex, one important factor would appear to be the absence in Canada of a rigorous approach to the study of warfare in the professional military education system of the officer corps.

THE LIFE AND TIMES OF CLAUSEWITZ

To put this subject in context, it is important to examine the writings of Clausewitz, particularly *On War*, to understand why his ideas should be of such great significance. Since it appears that his influence has occurred as much through his many commentators as by the work itself, it is also necessary to appreciate the analysis of Clausewitz's writing by others.

Despite a successful military career, Clausewitz never attained a high command position; however, many of his appointments were as a highly placed staff officer, fighting against the French in both the Prussian and the Russian armies. Through these early experiences he was able to observe the conduct of war from all levels. His evolving theory of warfare was therefore heavily flavoured by direct experience and observation.

Clausewitz came to believe that it was important to be able to explain the nature of warfare both in the abstract and from an objective theoretical standpoint. He approached this undertaking with "ideas … borrowed from the philosophy of German Idealism and from the scientific thought of the time."[2] His expository technique was to use the dialectic approach of thesis, antithesis, and synthesis, mixed with notions from the German idealist philosophers Fichte and Hegel. The German idealists took the idea of "the will" from Kant and expanded upon it to equate individual free will to that of the state; further, they held that the state had its own will, a consciousness and a moral end of its own.[3] Clausewitz's formulation of the "remarkable trinity" of society, army, and state is clearly related to the propositions put forward by these philosophers.

Since he was not formally educated as a philosopher, Clausewitz's derivative application of the "science of knowledge" may explain the difficulty many found in clearly understanding his writings. Clausewitz's dialectic approach often spans widely separated sections of his immense work, so that an argument begun in one place would continue and evolve in another. A reader who reads only a selected portion of the text could miss the full development of his logical exposition. Additional potential for misunderstanding resulted from the fact that his theories were continually undergoing revision. He tested his hypotheses through analytical study of the history of conflict, initially centred around the French Revolution and the campaigns of Napoleon (with whom he had a special fascination), but later against a broader historical span, including "the seventeenth-century campaigns like those of Gustavus Adolphus and Turenne, the War of the Spanish Succession (1701–14), and east European wars with the Turks."[4] As he widened his historical database he would modify his theories accordingly. This evolution continued until his death.

His most important works were *Principles of War* (an embryonic version of his theories written for the crown prince in 1812), *On War* (the first three books of which appeared in 1832), and two historical studies, *The Campaign of 1812 in Russia* (written between 1814 and 1824) and *The Campaign of 1815 in France* (written 1827–30).[5] His earlier works show the progression of his ideas, but it is his final work, *On War,* that represents his lasting legacy.

Clausewitz started out as a commentator on the battles of Napoleon, whose politics and ambition he hated, but whose generalship he admired. He began to see, however, that underlying theories of warfare had different forms of expression, depending on the historic period and circumstances, and his views evolved accordingly: "Clausewitz's approach to history became increasingly historicist. That is, he saw history in relative terms, rejecting absolute categories, standards, and values. The past had to be accepted on its own terms. The historian must enter into the mind-sets and attitudes of any given period, the 'spirit of the age.' ... This historicism is particularly obvious in two key themes of *On War* that are missing in *Principles*. These are the famous notion that 'war is a continuation of policy with an admixture of other means' (i.e., organized violence) and the recognition that war can vary in its forms depending on the changing nature of policy and of the society within which it is waged."[6]

Clausewitz was still revising his manuscript of *On War* when he died, and he had expressed concern that he would be misunderstood if his works were published, incomplete as they were. None the less, his widow had the ten volumes of his works published between 1832 and 1837.[7]

There have been many interpreters and critics of Clausewitz, some of whom are discussed below, and those who have tried to summarize his work in a few pages. Attempts to explain Clausewitz in a few lines run the risk of *reductio ad absurdum*, as Bassford offers: "Although the commentaries of other writers are in some cases nearly indispensable to its interpretation, the reader who wants to gain a genuine understanding of Clausewitz cannot escape the task of actually reading *On War*."[8]

ON WAR

In its latest English translation, by Peter Paret and Michael Howard, published in 1976, *On War* is close to six hundred pages in length, and it is a dense, often difficult work. It is divided into eight books, each dealing with a different aspect of Clausewitz's theory of war: 1) On the Nature of War, 2) On the Theory of War, 3) On Strategy in General, 4) The Engagement, 5) Military Forces, 6) Defence, 7) The Attack, and 8) War Plans. Bassford contends that although books one, two, and eight are the most important as well as the most complete, a tendency to abridge the work by omitting books five, six, and seven, in a belief that they were obsolete, has contributed to many of the misunderstandings of Clausewitz's arguments.[9]

The opening chapter of Book One of *On War* is considered by Paret to embody the essential elements of what Clausewitz was attempting to accomplish: "It is the only chapter that Clausewitz regarded as complete. But he also expressed the confidence that it would 'at least serve the whole by indicating the direction I meant to follow everywhere.' In his eyes the opening chapter was the best introduction to his book, and thus it is also the best imaginable guide to his entire theoretical work." [10]

With this to recommend it, we can examine the opening chapter in some detail. Clausewitz titled the chapter "What Is War?" and began with a definition: "War, therefore, is an act of violence to compel our opponent to fulfil our will." [11] Clausewitz uses the analogy of two wrestlers, each attempting to render the other incapable of further resistance: the "immediate object of hostilities" is to "disarm" the enemy, thus rendering him powerless. [12]

He then expands on the aim of disarming the enemy; he observes that the enemy is not a passive object on which one's force is exerted, but is a thinking, reacting force trying to do to you what you are doing to him. Using the philosophical methods of his time, Clausewitz then takes his example to an extreme "ideal," or theoretical case. Clausewitz concludes this section with the observation that the enemy's power of resistance is composed not only of the "sum of available means" but also "the strength of the will," [13] concepts he also carried to their extreme or "ideal" state.

These extremes represent Clausewitz's theory of the absolute, or ideal state of war. He spends the rest of the chapter explaining that this ideal state is never actually achieved, for a variety of reasons. First, war is never an isolated act but takes place within a complex web of external factors. Second, war does not consist of one single, short blow, but is instead a series of connected contests, where each one influences the conduct of the next. Third, in war, the result is never final but is only a transitory state. These factors all combine to modify or to moderate the cases of interaction and prevent them from achieving the theoretical extreme state of absolute war. [14]

From these ideas, Clausewitz then turns to a discussion of the imponderables of warfare. Having established that the extremes do not occur in reality, he introduces the notion that "the probabilities of real life take the place of the extreme and the absolute." [15] He comes now to the central theme – that the political motive for the war will be a moderating factor that is aimed at the idea of matching means with ends: "Thus, therefore, the political object, as the original motive of the War, will be the standard for determining both the aim of the military force and also the amount of effort to be made." [16] In this important section, Clausewitz observes that there will be times when the political object and the military one coincide, and times when "the political object itself is not suitable for the aim of military action." [17] He concludes this section: "Thus it is explained how, without any contradiction in itself, there may be Wars of all degrees of importance and energy, from a War of extermination down to the mere use of an army of observation." [18]

After a series of discussions on the character of warfare, the attack versus the defence, and the fog of uncertainty that typifies warfare, Clausewitz arrives at another of his central concepts – the role of chance in deciding the outcome of battles: "There is no human affair which stands so constantly and so generally in close connection with chance as War." He continues this theme by focusing on what he terms the "moral" aspects of this very human activity. War, uniquely characterized by danger, makes everything difficult to accomplish, even the simplest of activities. Clausewitz maintains that courage, daring, boldness, and self-confidence are the qualities needed to counter the uncertainties he has just described: "Courage and self-reliance are, therefore, principles quite essential to War; consequently, theory must only set up such rules as allow ample scope for all degrees and varieties of these necessary and noblest of military virtues."[19]

Though not mentioned specifically in this chapter, all the factors he describes as taking war away from the absolute or theoretical ideal state will be rolled up into his concept of "friction," which creates the uncertainty and gives rise to the unpredictability of war. Hence, the conduct of war is seen to be more art than science; but, rather than choosing either of these descriptions, Clausewitz preferred the notion of "social intercourse," or politics.

The final sections of this introductory chapter refer to perhaps the most famous, most controversial, and most misunderstood concept in *On War* – the relationship of war to politics: "We see therefore, that War is not merely a political act, but also a real political instrument, a continuation of political commerce, a carrying out of the same by other means. ... That the tendencies and views of policy shall not be incompatible with these means, the Art of War in general and the commander in each particular case may demand ... But however powerfully this may react on political views in particular cases, still it must always be regarded as only a modification of them; for the political view is the object, War is the means, and the means must always include the object in our conception."[20]

Clausewitz then describes the different faces of war:

The greater and the more powerful the motives of a War, the more it affects the whole existence of a people. The more violent the excitement which precedes the War, by so much nearer will the War approach to its abstract concept, so much the more will it be directed to the destruction of the enemy, so much the nearer will the military and political ends coincide, so much the more purely military and less political the War appears to be; but the weaker the motives and the tensions, so much the less will the natural direction of the military element – that is, force – be coincident with the direction which the political element indicates; so much the more must, therefore, the War become diverted from its natural direction, the political object diverge from the aim of an ideal War, and the War appear to become political.[21]

Clausewitz completes the chapter with his conclusions on the understanding of military history: "We see, therefore, in the first place, that under all circumstances War is to be regarded not as an independent thing, but as a political instrument; and it is only by taking this point of view that we can avoid finding ourselves in opposition to all military history. ... Secondly, this view shows us how wars must differ in character according to the nature of the motives and circumstances from which they proceed." [22]

Finally, he states the consequences for the theory of war:

War is, therefore, ... a wonderful trinity, composed of the original violence of its elements, hatred and animosity, which may be looked upon as blind instinct; of the play of probabilities and chance, which make it a free activity of the soul; and of the subordinate nature of a political instrument, by which it belongs purely to the reason. The first of these three phases concerns more the people; the second, more the General and his Army; the third, more the government. The passions which break forth in war must already have a latent existence in the peoples. The range which the display of courage and talents shall get in the realm of probabilities and of chance depends on the particular characteristics of the General and his Army, but the political objects belong to the government alone. The problem is, therefore, that theory shall keep itself poised in a manner between these three tendencies, as between three points of attraction. [23]

HISTORICAL INTERPRETATIONS

It must be reiterated that the purpose of Clausewitz's theoretical writings was not to produce a book of instruction on the conduct of war, but to provide a theoretical backdrop and framework for the truer understanding of the phenomenon of war. Or as Peter Paret explains: "*On War* is, in short, an attempt both to penetrate to the essence of true war, to use Clausewitz's term – that is, ideal war – as well as to understand war in reality on the various levels of its existence; as a social and political phenomenon, and in its organizational, strategic, operational, and tactical aspects." [24] Gatzke summarizes the conclusions of many Clausewitz scholars when he observes: "The book is incomplete, and in many of its specific details and illustrations it has been outdated by the tremendous technical developments since Clausewitz'[s] time. Yet, inasmuch as it was not intended to be a specific instruction for the conduct of military operations but rather a philosophic appraisal of war, it possesses a timeless quality which makes it as vital today as ever." [25]

The direct influence of Clausewitz on military doctrine is difficult to assess, since he proposed a theory and explanation for the phenomenon of war rather than a prescription for its conduct. Thus it is not strictly correct to describe a strategy or doctrine as "Clausewitzian." However, the widely held acceptance of a basic explanation of war cannot help but have an effect on doctrine as it is being written.

There is no question that there has been a great deal of interest in Clause-witz in the past few decades, particularly in the United States, led primarily by the efforts of Peter Paret, Michael Howard, and Bernard Brodie. However, the serious study and appreciation of Clausewitz in the United States and Great Britain goes back many more years than is commonly appreciated. Christopher Bassford traced the passage of Clausewitz's work from Germany to England and the United States, and he showed that some interest in and discussion of the ideas of Clausewitz, particularly in Britain, took place almost from the time he began his writing: "A number of Clausewitz's works, both historical and theoretical, have been examined by British readers since the mid-1830s. Significant commentaries on Clausewitz were made in the 1840s by members of the Duke of Wellington's circle (including the Duke himself), by instructors at the British Army Staff College at Camberley after 1860, and by members of the 'Wolseley Ring,' the clique of military reformers surrounding General Sir Garnet Wolseley, from the 1870s on. Clausewitz was a significant and direct influence on British military thought in the period preceding World War I."[26]

Moltke's dramatic triumph over France during the Franco-Prussian War of 1870–71, and his subsequent praise of Clausewitz, followed by Colonel J.J. Graham's translation of *On War* into English in 1873, are often taken as signals of the beginning of what Bassford called the "first golden age" of Clausewitz, from 1874 to 1914.[27] European scholars who reflected on Clausewitz, such as Colmar von der Goltz, Rudolf von Caemmerer, and Hans Delbruck, were translated into English and widely read in both Britain and the United States. While many serious scholars, mostly reformers, such as Charles Chesney, G.F.R. Henderson, F.N. Maude, J.F. Maurice, Thomas Repington, and Spenser Wilkinson, were familiar with and wrote about Clausewitz, the writing and influence of Jomini was still far more prevalent in the military doctrines of both the United States and Britain during this period. However, the Boer War in South Africa (1899–1902) cleared the way for Clausewitz's rise to eminence, particularly in Britain, where its army had its reputation badly tarnished in South Africa.

Clausewitz would have likely entered into the mainstream of most military writing at this point were it not for the bloody experience of the First World War and the blame that was heaped on him for the immense squandering of human life in the "meat-grinder" of the trenches. The eclipse of Clausewitz after the war was brought about mainly by the writings of Captain Basil Liddell Hart and General J.F.C. Fuller –, especially Liddell Hart, according to Bassford: "Throughout his writing career, Liddell Hart was persistently and bitterly critical of Clausewitz, portraying him as the 'evil genius of military thought,' as the 'apostle of total war,' and as a relentless advocate of mass and the offensive. In his view, Clausewitz and/or his 'disciples' were responsible for the bloodbath on the Western Front, 1914–18."[28]

During the inter-war period, a small group of American uniformed scholars, including Joe Greene, George Meyer, Hoffman Nickerson, John Palmer,
and Oliver Robinson were aware of, and continued to write about, Clausewitz, but he was by no means in the mainstream of American military
thought. Hans Delbruck, writing in Germany during the first quarter of the
century with important new interpretations of Clausewitz, did not draw serious attention in the United States until the Second World War. [29] The steady
stream of German expatriates into the United States, both before and during
the war, are credited with bringing an increasing sophistication to the appreciation of Clausewitz. These included Hans Gatzke, Herbert Rosinski, Hans
Rothfels, and Alfred Vagts who came to dominate Clausewitz studies and
who collectively laid the groundwork for the post-1945 revival of the field.
The most notable American to have been influenced, by his own admission,
by Clausewitz was Dwight Eisenhower, though this influence applied more
to his two terms as president (1953–61) than to his years as a soldier. [30]

The immediate postwar period, dominated by the bi-polar Cold War and
the ever-present threat of a nuclear holocaust, set the stage for the re-
emergence of Clausewitz. The Korean conflict revealed problems with the
doctrine of massive retaliation and the notion of total war, and the conduct
of limited wars became a hot topic, with Clausewitz's writings on that subject becoming a focus for attention. The year 1957 marked a resurgence of
interest in Clausewitz, when three works published in that year, Henry Kissinger's *Nuclear Weapons and Foreign Policy*, Samuel Huntington's *The
Soldier and the State*, and Robert Osgood's *Limited War*, drew heavily on
Clausewitz. [31]

The post–Vietnam War period in the United States saw the kind of enthusiasm towards Clausewitz that had been evident in Britain after the Boer
War, giving rise to what now might be described as the "second golden age"
of Clausewitz. The focus on and the fascination with what had gone wrong
in Vietnam brought questions of strategy, policy, and war-fighting to the
forefront. A watershed in such studies, at least within the American military
itself, occurred with the publication of Colonel Harry Summers's *On Strategy: A Critical Analysis of the Vietnam War*, originally entitled *On Strategy:
The Vietnam War in Context* and first published by the Strategic Studies
Institute of the u.s. Army War College in 1981. Summers concluded that the
military objectives and the political aims for the war in Vietnam did not
match, something Clausewitz clearly identified as being entirely possible in
wars that are far from the theoretical ideal. [32] Rather than accepting that reality and deriving lessons for the army to deal with it, however, Summers concluded that such a situation must not be allowed to recur. [33]

The move towards using expressions and concepts taken from Clausewitz, at the highest military policy level, soon became striking. One particularly good example was the "Weinberger Doctrine" adopted by Secretary of

Defense Caspar Weinberger in 1984. Six conditions would need to be met before commitment of u.s. forces to combat. 1) The interest at stake must be vital. 2) The nation must intend to win. 3) The war must have clearly defined political and military objectives. 4) The forces must be sized appropriately for these objectives. 5) There must be reasonable assurance of public and congressional support. 6) All other means must have been exhausted – that is, force should be a last resort.[34]

The influence of Clausewitz runs through most, if not all, of the conditions listed, though in a curiously inverted manner. These conditions describe what Clausewitz would have viewed as nearly "ideal" conditions for going to war, which accurately reflects what the military envisions when war is being contemplated in the United States. Clausewitz himself would doubtless have observed that these conditions will occur rarely in limited warfare. Nevertheless, the Weinberger Doctrine has been fully embraced by the u.s. military, though it was a source of considerable concern to advocates of *Realpolitik*, such as Henry Kissinger and former Secretary of State George Schultz, who feared that the United States would thereby be constrained to fighting only popular, winnable wars.

THE IMPACT OF CLAUSEWITZ ON PROFESSIONAL OFFICER DEVELOPMENT IN THE UNITED STATES AND CANADA

Starting in the 1970s, Clausewitz begins to appear in the military doctrines of all the American services. *On War* was adopted as one of the primary textbooks at the Naval War College in 1976, the Air War College in 1978, and the Army War College in 1981. Since 1982, u.s. army doctrine in *FM 100-5 Operations* has contained numerous references to Clausewitz, as has its Marine Corps counterpart *FMFM-1*.[35] The 1992 version of the u.s. air force's (usaf) basic doctrinal publication, *AFM-1*, also has references to Clausewitz liberally strewn throughout.[36] The recently issued capstone doctrinal publication for the u.s. navy reflects Clausewitz in the description of naval warfare in chapter 3, and the short reading list includes *On War* among mostly naval warfare references.[37]

Harry Summers is quoted as observing, just before the Persian Gulf War in 1991: "Clausewitzian theory is going to define and determine the conflict in Iraq."[38] Colonel John Warden, chief architect of the Air Campaign Plan against Saddam Hussein, claimed to be applying Clausewitz's principle of centre of gravity in its design.[39] Therefore not only is the theory being taught, but practical lessons are apparently being drawn and applied.

Dr James J. Tritten, a civilian academic on the staff of the u.s. Navy Doctrine Command, observed that Clausewitz has been "thoroughly institutionalized" by all the major u.s. services.[40] It would appear that the study and appreciation of Clausewitz form the basis of the American professional military education system, particularly at the War College level, and provide the current foundation for u.s. doctrine. While not as obvious, the military doctrines of Britain and Australia reflect a similar appreciation. The introductory descriptions of war and its purpose in the doctrines of the air forces of both nations clearly mirror the concepts contained in *On War*.

In Canadian military doctrine, direct references to Clausewitz, or any indications of his influence, are difficult to discern. Particularly striking, in the first instance, is the lack of a formalized doctrinal structure of any kind. Because Canada has a supposedly unified armed force, one might expect to find a basic Canadian Forces doctrine publication as the capstone statement of fundamental principles. The closest to this ideal is the embryonic *Joint Doctrine for the Canadian Forces – Joint and Combined Operations*; however, it is not clear whether this document is intended to represent overarching, national-level doctrine, or simply an additional publication to be applied alongside others, when more than one environmental element is to be assigned to an operation. In any event, with its focus on joint operations, rather than the nature, purpose, and approach to war itself, the document shows little influence of Clausewitz.

As for the individual Canadian services, the maritime forces (navy) do not have any clearly identifiable doctrine, being content to utilize a series of mostly Allied publications, dealing primarily with tactical engagements at sea. The land and air forces have a somewhat more readily definable set of doctrinal publications, but these clearly reflect the influence of Jomini and Fuller in the recitation of principles of war as introductory to what is essentially tactical-level doctrine. The Canadian Forces Command and Staff College précis on aerospace doctrine contains an introductory exposition of the role and nature of warfare that is purely Clausewitzian, borrowed from the Australian air force doctrine publication, *The Air Power Manual*. However, the college is careful to point out that the document is for internal use by students and does not reflect the "official" view of the Canadian Forces. [41]

Canadian military historians have long commented on the absence of grand strategic thought in Canada, whether produced by individuals in uniform or by those outside the service. It may be that this logically results in doctrine that seems to start at the tactical level, without any extensive theoretical or higher strategical basis. If it is true that Canada does not have a clear national strategy of its own, but accepts the strategies of others (especially the United States and NATO), and sees its armed forces as merely plug-in units to larger foreign formations, always subordinate to foreign military direction, then perhaps there is no urgent need to decide what our own national view is on the larger issues raised by Clausewitz. Small units presumably need know only small-unit tactics; unfortunately, when Canada saw its forces grow during two world wars, there was not a similar expansion of its notions on their use. Canada was during those wars, and still is, basically ignored on larger questions of Alliance strategy. There are probably a variety of reasons for this, but chief among them must be Canada's failure to demonstrate the ability to articulate anything doctrinally sensible at the grand strategic level. But this failure may present major problems for the Canadian military in the future.

USAF Colonel Thomas A. Fabyanic, in a U.S. War College reading package article reprinted from the *Air University Review*, begins: "One cannot fight successfully a war for which one is not organizationally and doctrinally prepared."[42] His article made a strong case for the importance of a strong professional military education system for the USAF, reminding his readers of the statement by Bernard Brodie, from *War and Politics*, that "soldiers usually are close students of tactics, but only rarely are they students of strategy and practically never of war!"[43] Fabyanic argues that this failing must be corrected, particularly at the war college level, to the extent that the study of strategy and war should represent the culmination of an officer's professional development and preparation for the highest command assignments.

Fabyanic's article was originally published in 1986 and carried an extensive analysis of what he saw as the two competing schools or approaches to doctrine: the abstract-Jominian school (mechanistic, formulaic, principles of war) and the operational-Clausewitzian school (descriptive, realistic war as it unfolds amid chaos and friction). He argued strenuously for the latter approach and criticized the then-extant version of the *Basic Aerospace Doctrine* of the USAF. He also criticized the existing syllabus of the Air War College as representing too much of the former doctrinal school and suggested many remedies, most of which were subsequently incorporated: "If our tasks in the U.S. Air Force are to prepare for war, deter it if possible, and fight it successfully across a spectrum of conflict, then we must understand war, make war the basis for our doctrine, and teach war to our officers. If AWC [Air War College] wishes to be a war college in a meaningful sense, then it must teach the grammar and logic of war, conduct serious research on those issues, and attract a blend of soldiers and scholars who can teach. If it is willing to do those things, then it will produce graduates whom Clausewitz would recognize and with whom he would be satisfied. No greater compliment would be possible for a professional officer."[44]

Such a debate in Canada is hard to imagine, since the system for the professional development of the Canadian officer corps is stunted and incomplete. It is telling to observe that the formal, institutional approach to professional military education in the Canadian Forces essentially ends at the Command and Staff College (major/lieutenant-commander rank) level, which, in attempting to be unified, as well as presenting the unit command perspective for each of the environments, does a rather poor job of providing a solid academic approach to operational-level issues, let alone providing a basis for the study of warfare and strategy. Moreover, rather than representing the authoritative source of strategic thought and doctrine development, it must admit to the unofficial nature of its doctrine. Canada has never had a war college. The now-defunct National Defence College, supposedly the pinnacle of officers' professional development when it existed, was arguably the antithesis of a war college, subliminally transmitting the Canadian distaste for war-like topics, and inculcating a public service/administrative approach to national defence. Such an institution in a properly structured system of officer education might have been extremely useful, given officers who had first been properly educated in their own profession.

In the armed services of the United States, there is some indication of the beginning of a process of synthesis between the abstract-Jominian school and that of the operational-Clausewitzian school, while in Canada we have yet to fully appreciate that such approaches to doctrine exist, let alone know what to make of them. The study and understanding of warfare at all levels are a critical precondition to the development of a coherent national military strategy and accompanying levels of military doctrine. The quotation from Brodie about soldiers studying tactics but rarely strategy and practically never war seems pointed directly at the Canadian military.

The importance of Clausewitz, who provided the only fully realized theoretical baseline for the study of warfare, cannot be overstated. After years of commentary and debate over the validity and application of his ideas, most Western nations, particularly the United States, embraced and adopted Clausewitz as the key source for fundamental concepts regarding war. This is clearly reflected in their doctrine and their approach to the professional development of their officer corps. The notable exception is Canada, where doctrine development has lagged appreciably behind that of our closest ally, in part because of the abbreviated process for the professional development of our officer corps. Clausewitz must first be studied, and then he must be appreciated, before his influence can begin to take effect. And while the study of Clausewitz is no panacea for shortcomings in professional military education and doctrinal development, the study of his work is evidence of serious analysis of the problems of war. Much of this has yet to occur in Canada and in its professional military institutions.

NOTES

1 Bassford, *Clausewitz in English*, 5.
2 Paret, "Clausewitz," 194.
3 Curtis, *The Great Political Theories*, Vol. II, 88.
4 Bassford, *Clausewitz in English*, 13.

5 Ibid., 12.
6 Ibid., 13.
7 Clausewitz, "Principles of War," 309.
8 Bassford, *Clausewitz in English*, 7.
9 Ibid., 11.
10 Paret, *Clausewitz and the State*, 382.
11 Clausewitz, *On War*, ed. F.N. Maude, 2.
12 Ibid., 2.
13 Ibid., 5.
14 Ibid., 6–10.
15 Ibid., 10.
16 Ibid., 11.
17 Ibid., 12.
18 Ibid., 13.
19 Ibid., 19, 21.
20 Ibid., 23.
21 Ibid., 23–4.
22 Ibid., 25.
23 Ibid., 26.
24 Paret, *Clausewitz and the State*, 365.
25 Clausewitz, "Principles of War," 310.
26 Bassford, *Clausewitz in English*, 4.
27 Ibid., 67.
28 Ibid., 129.
29 Ibid., 177.
30 Ibid., 192.
31 Ibid., 201.
32 Summers, *On Strategy*, 70.
33 Ibid., 98.
34 Hartmann and Wendzel, *Defending America's Security*, 313.
35 Bassford, *Clausewitz in English*, 204.
36 *Air Force Manual 1–1*, Vol. I, *Basic Aerospace Doctrine*.
37 U.S. Department of the Navy, *Naval Doctrine Publication 1: Naval Warfare* (NDP-1), 31–41.
38 Bassford, *Clausewitz in English*, 208.
39 Telephone interview with Colonel John Warden, 18 May 1991.
40 Telephone interview with Dr James J. Tritten, 6 December 1995.
41 Air Command and Staff Program, *Aerospace Doctrine Manual*, 1.
42 Fabyanic, "War, Doctrine, and the Air War College," 31.
43 Ibid., 32.
44 Ibid., 46.

The Myth of Manoeuvre Warfare: Attrition in Military History

CAPT PAUL JOHNSTON

and the War won't end for at least two years;
But we've got stacks of men ... I'm blind with tears.

Siegfried Sassoon
"To Any Dead Officer"[1]

Attrition is not appreciated. This is true both in the sense of its being not well understood and in the sense of its being not well liked. At least since the first day of the Somme, when Britain famously lost 60,000 men to no apparent gain,[2] attrition in warfare has been seen as failure. Yet is that assessment entirely fair?

This essay alleges that – in point of fact – historically, attrition has been central to settling the outcome of virtually all major wars. Military historians may choose to decry this, but the pattern is strong enough that, if we are to learn anything from history, we ought not ignore it. Yet virtually all have. The only thoughtful analysis of attrition as a strategy ever written was produced by a turn-of-the-century German – Hans Delbruck. Unfortunately, his work seems to be not much quoted nowadays; attrition is almost never discussed, except as a failure. The English historian David French notes how the very word has become a pejorative.[3] Indeed, from the harsh criticisms of J.F.C. Fuller and B.H. Liddell Hart down to the present, most military theory has been a search for a "better way" – a way to avoid the horrors of attrition.

In the 1920s and 1930s this quest led to the development of both armoured warfare and the concept of the war-winning bomber offensive. More recently it has led to something of a renaissance of thought devoted to "manoeuvre warfare" and an infatuation with so-called precision guided munitions (PGMs). In any event, dislike of attrition remains strong. The American historian David Palmer has even gone so far as to write: "Attrition is not a strategy. It is, in fact, irrefutable proof of the absence of any strategy. A commander who resorts to attrition admits his failure to conceive of any alternative."[4]

Any perusal of recent military journals reveals the same attitude. This viewpoint is not necessarily bad – it would be hard, after all, to argue in favour of attrition – but it is at best incomplete. Incomplete, because, as this essay endeavours to show, in the end it has been attrition that has determined the outcome of virtually all major wars. This need not mean that the tactics of an attritional war must necessarily be wasteful of lives and material. Indeed, the actual fighting of an attritional war can and should draw on as many clever and artful stratagems as possible – but that cannot gloss over the fact that it is almost always the exhaustion of attrition that brings the loser down. It would be disingenuous to conclude otherwise.

ATTRITION CONSIDERED

The first issue to be addressed is to consider what exactly we mean by "attritional warfare." Significantly, the only definitions have been advanced by those wishing to set it up as a straw man and then argue against it. Typical of these is the "manoeuvre warfare" theorist Robert Leonhard, an American soldier-scholar, who defines attritional theory as an approach that seeks "to defeat an enemy through the destruction of the enemy's mass." [5] "Manoeuvrists," as we see below, would rather destroy something else – usually the enemy's morale, or at least its command and control. "Attritionists," in contrast, are portrayed as seeking merely to grind down the enemy's fighting forces – in other words, their main strength.

However, manoeuvrists such as Leonhard burden the term "attrition" with more pejorative connotations than this simple definition might imply. Leonhard writes: "Attrition theory is a 'bottoms-up' approach to war, because it focuses first upon bringing the enemy to battle and then seeks to defeat him in that battle or in follow-on battles ... 'Addicts of attrition' ... generally cannot think beyond the battle." [6]

Another manoeuvre theorist (and soldier-scholar), Richard Simpkin, adds a further dimension to his definition of attrition theory – he equates it explicitly with "positional warfare": "[A]ttrition theory (also known as 'position theory') is about fighting and primarily about casualties ... An adherent of this approach to war simply seeks to achieve a shift of relative strengths in his favour ... To achieve the shift of relative strength, the addict of attrition seizes and holds a piece of ground ... The process is repeated until one side has gained overwhelming strength (Second World War) or becomes exhausted (First World War)." [7]

As indicated by Leonhard's remarks about a "bottoms-up approach" and Simpkin's equation of attrition theory with "positional warfare," there is a tendency to assume that attritional warfare is characterized by the tactically inept throwing of soldiers and material at the enemy, in the hope of eventually grinding it down. While that may well have been the approach of the

British army in the First World War,[8] attritional warfare need not necessarily be like that. In order to realize why, we need to consider the various "levels of war" – tactical, operational, and strategic.[9]

This essay asserts that virtually all major wars have been attritional at the strategic level. The fighting at the lower operational and tactical levels may or may not have been so. For instance, the Napoleonic Wars involved many campaigns and climactic battles that – at least for a time – were victorious for France. Yet ultimately France decisively lost the conflict. Despite many brilliant tactical and operational victories, France was eventually exhausted strategically.

ATTRITION'S HISTORY IN WARFARE

France's eventual defeat in the Napoleonic Wars hints at a larger historical pattern. Quite simply, with very few exceptions, it has been attrition that has decided the outcome of major wars. Consider the record.

The modern military era is often dated from the Revolutionary/Napoleonic wars, and so too is Napoleon generally considered one of the greatest commanders of history. The British historian Robert Epstein notes that the early French victories of 1805–07 "dazzled Jomini, Clausewitz, and others … All believed that the short decisive victory was an attainable goal."[10]

Yet all those who admire the genius of Napoleon's brilliant victories seem to forget that in the end it was cruel attrition that brought down the French.[11] Epstein goes on to note that, starting with Wagram in 1809, "victory was a product of successive battles and engagements. The War of 1809 became the model for the future. Warfare became protracted. Victory was won by first mobilizing greater resources and then crushing an opponent in a series of battles."[12]

In other words, ultimately Napoleonic warfare was attritional. Furthermore, this was true despite a long series of dramatic French victories, all of which had seemed brilliantly decisive. As we see below, this is a recurrent pattern – apparently decisive victories based on superior military art, which are ultimately reversed by attrition.

The mid-nineteenth century saw three major wars: the Crimean War, the U.S. Civil War, and the wars of German unification. The Crimean was a bitter campaign, centred mostly around a protracted siege of Sevastopol. Few would challenge its attritional nature; after all, it was this war that gave us Tennyson's immortal lines about the charge of the Light Brigade.[13] Similarly, the U.S. Civil War is famous for the way in which superior Northern numbers and industrial might slowly ground down an apparently more gifted and deft Southern military effort. Indeed, in the civil war we once again see the pattern of early military success based on manoeuvre and craft (in this case, the early Confederate victories, such as First Bull Run) reversed by slow grinding attrition.[14]

The German wars of unification are so interesting because they are so different. In a series of wars, each of which was measured in mere months, Bismark's Prussia managed decisively to defeat the Austrians and then the French and establish a new German Reich. It was this dazzling success that so captivated the turn-of-the-century German military mind and led to what the military historian Jehuda Wallach calls the "dogma of the battle of annihilation."[15]

This dogma, of course, got its come-uppance in the First World War, famously a contest of attrition.[16] What is less often appreciated is that the Second World War was equally attritional. As the American military historian Earl Ziemke noted: "Paradoxically, the restoration of manoeuvre [during the Second World War] to the battlefield ... did not eliminate the problem that had been thought of as peculiar to trench warfare – attrition."[17]

More recently, the American historian John Ellis has devoted an entire book to demonstrating that the Allies won by the sheer, attritional weight of numbers.[18] Since 1945 too, most major conflicts have been attritional: the Revolutionary War in China, the Korean War, Vietnam's several wars, and the Iran–Iraq War. The one exception is the Israeli success over the Arabs, particularly in the 1967 Six Day War.[19] In all the Arab–Israeli wars, smaller Israeli forces used manoeuvre warfare repeatedly to defeat larger Arab armies. Indeed, they have no choice – if the Arab–Israeli conflict had ever become attritional, the Israelis would certainly have ceased to exist.

This has been a quick overview of two centuries' worth of military history – and the examples selected to illustrate the point can be debated – but the overall pattern should be clear. With only rare exceptions, it has been attrition that ultimately decided the outcomes. And one of the notable exceptions – the Israeli successes in the Arab–Israeli wars – is instructive. Despite repeated Israeli victories over the Arabs, Israel has been chronically unable to establish her security decisively in the Middle East. The dramatic Israeli victory in the Six Day War was followed only seven years later by the Yom Kippur war, an Arab attack that once again almost succeeded in wiping Israel from the map. Those rare non-attritional victories may be less costly, but they often seem to be less decisive. Does this make attrition an attractive strategy?

HANS DELBRUCK

Perhaps the first prominent theorist to consider the role of attrition, and advance it as a coherent strategic theory, was Hans Delbruck, a German military historian of the turn of the century. The German officer corps of the time was strongly wedded to the concept of the "battle of annihilation," which it believed Clausewitz had explained and the German wars of unification had conclusively proved. This view held that the aim of strategy was to concentrate an overwhelming force rapidly at the decisive point, and there crush the enemy in a single battle of annihilation.[20] Succinctly expressing this view, one of its major proponents, Chief of the Greater General Staff Alfred von Schlieffen, once wrote of the "emphatic accentuation of the annihilation-idea ... The destruction of the hostile forces is the most commanding purpose among those which may be pursued by war. This is the doctrine which led us to Koniggratz and Sedan."[21]

Delbruck challenged this dogma, arguing that there was not merely one correct approach to war, or "strategy," as he put it, but two. The first he called the *Niederwerfungsstrategie*, or strategy of annihilation. This, of course, was the conventional approach to warfare so prominent in Wilhelmine Germany. However, Delbruck's exhaustive study of military history convinced him that it was not the only possible approach to war and that it had not always been appropriate to circumstances. Delbruck believed that he had discerned another approach – the *Ermattungsstrategie*, or strategy of exhaustion.

Delbruck saw history as being comprised of differing eras, each with different fundamental characteristics. In particular, he believed that the French Revolution marked a transition from one era to another. For a variety of reasons, he argued, the French Revolutionary armies were able, as Napoleon showed everyone, to force battles of annihilation on their foes. However, Delbruck continued, this was most expressly not the case prior to the French Revolution. Because of the nature of armies of that time – their mercenary character and dependence on magazines for supply, for instance – for practical reasons it was simply not possible for their commanders to launch them on campaigns of annihilation. This meant, Delbruck concluded, not that there was no art of strategy in that period, but merely that the strategy was different – that commanders sought victory not by annihilating the enemy but by advantage in manoeuvre and attrition. This alternative method – the strategy of exhaustion – was not, Delbruck emphasized, derivative from annihilation or inferior to it. It was merely different and appropriate for different circumstances. It too had its great masters, and into this category Delbruck nominated Frederick the Great.

It was this conclusion that embroiled Delbruck in a fierce and long-lived debate with the German officer corps. Frederick the Great was revered as the saviour of Prussia and a greater commander than Napoleon. Unshakeably imbued with the dogma of the strategy of annihilation, the German officer corps interpreted Delbruck's assertion that Frederick had been a master of the strategy of exhaustion as an unforgivable slight on the Prussian king, and reaction was fierce and unforgiving.

Whatever the truth of the matter,[22] Delbruck's theorizing on limited war has limitations of its own. He seemed to see history as sharply divided into eras – some in which material circumstances made exhaustion the only workable strategy, and some in which material circumstances allowed for annihilation. Delbruck did not dispute that the nineteenth century had been a time for annihilation, just as the Schlieffen school maintained it was. This stance would seem to imply that a state can fight only a war of annihilation or a war of exhaustion, depending on what sort of era it is in. It would appear, from Delbruck's analysis, that if a state is living in a time of wars of annihilation, it cannot choose to avoid them. Is this necessarily true?

ATTRITION VERSUS ANNIHILATION OR ATTRITION VERSUS MANOEUVRE?

It may or may not be true that Frederick the Great's era did not permit of a strategy of annihilation, but Delbruck's theorizing creates two "poles" (as he put it) in strategic theory – annihilation on the one hand and attrition on the other. However, the great annihilations of history – the Napoleonic Wars and the two world wars – have all been the products of years of attritional fighting. Those rare non-attritional victories – the Prussians at Konnigratz and Sedan, the Germans in France in 1940, the Israelis over the Arabs – have often been described (lauded even) as decisive "battles of annihilation," but the casualties and destruction they each produced were trivial compared to attritional wars. So perhaps attrition and annihilation are not the "poles" that Delbruck saw them as being.

The modern trend has been to take a somewhat different tack. Rather with tongue in cheek, the irreverent American military commentator James Dunnigan remarked in his book *How to Make War* that there are fundamentally "two ways to fight a war: plain (attrition) and fancy (manoeuvre)." [23] Indeed, in recent years a considerable body of literature has developed touting the concept of "manoeuvre warfare."

One of the leading writers of this school, Robert Leonhard, has written of what he calls "manoeuver theory" as the attempt "to defeat the enemy through means other than simple destruction of his mass." [24] As the quote indicates, the term "manoeuvre" is actually a poor, or at least incomplete, description of the style of warfare being discussed. "Manoeuvre theory" is about more than manoeuvre; it actually describes an entire approach to fighting that is flexible and agile. Leonard writes that manoeuvre theory seeks, in descending order: "1) Preemption: defeating or neutralizing the enemy before the fight has begun; 2) Dislocation: rendering the enemy's strength irrelevant by removing the enemy from the decisive point, or – preferably – by removing the decisive point from them; and 3) Disruption: neutralizing the enemy by successfully attacking or threatening his center of gravity." [25]

In order to effect these actions, manoeuvrists stress a variety of cardinal precepts. The first of these is attacking enemy weakness rather than strength, and reinforcing success rather than failure. By these means, a breakthrough of the enemy's lines is to be achieved. [26] Second, manoeuvrists stress tempo

– that is, speed of operations.[27] If a manoeuvre-based force can act faster than a more ponderous enemy can react, it can seize and hold the initiative – to considerable advantage. Furthermore, manoeuvrists generally advocate a command style that is "directive" rather than rigidly detailed – what the Germans, who practised it so well, called *Auftragstaktik*.[28] This approach is held to be necessary in order to achieve the flexibility and pace necessary for manoeuvre warfare. Of course, when manoeuvrists write about these concepts they are not simply plucking ideas from the air – they have historical precedents in mind. Indeed, while they may cite examples widely from the history of warfare,[29] they generally have one, very specific example in mind – the German victory over France in 1940.

The American strategist Edward Luttwak has even written an eight-page description of an allegedly generic manoeuvre-based attack, in which: "We might observe a long column of tanks, infantry carriers, and trucks moving in single file deep within enemy territory, advancing almost unresisted."[30] This mobile column has broken into the enemy rear, Luttwak explains, through a "break" made in the defender's line, "by an infantry assault supported by both artillery and air strikes. But the breach is no more than a narrow passage. On either side of it, strong forces of the defensive front remain. … [P]enetrations are segmenting the territory of the defense as so many slices in a cake. Then we see how the defense is reacting and we encounter the crucial and determining fact: those forces of the defense still so strong on either side of each breach are not converging one toward the other to close the gaps. Instead, they have been ordered to withdraw as rapidly as they can, in order to reconstitute an entirely new front … [C]learly the [defenders'] intention is to cope with those advancing [attackers'] columns by confronting them with solid strength [in a new line much farther back]." [31]

This is clearly not a generic description at all, but a retelling of the manoeuvrists' favourite story: the German victory over France in 1940. Yet there is a great irony in this – eventually the Germans lost the war. The serving American officer John Antal examined this argument in an article entitled "Manoeuvre versus Attrition": "Fans of manoeuvre warfare theory argue that the Germans had the right idea in their concept of Auftragstaktik. 'Manoeuverists' call opponents of manoeuvre theory 'attritionists.' A manoeuvre-oriented military analyst may argue that manoeuvre versus attrition is the primary argument in styles of warfare; that manoeuvre warfare offers cheap victories; and that Operation Desert Storm vindicated manoeuvre theory concepts. Others, who seldom call themselves 'attritionists,' argue that each military situation is unique; that Desert Storm vindicated the decisive, attrition role of firepower."[32]

Manoeuvrists, as Antal put it, promise rapid and decisive results without long attritional struggles. It is only manoeuvre, they argue, that can avoid the carnage of attrition. Indeed, most of the military reformers of the 1920s and

1930s (Fuller, Liddell Hart, and others) took this as a given – their aim was to restore manoeuvre to warfare so that it could again be decisive. Yet, as Antal sardonically notes, the Germans did ultimately lose the Second World War.[33] And as we saw above, the historical record would seem to indicate that non-attritional victories are prone to reversal in the higher court of attrition. What does this say about the oft-claimed "decisiveness" of manoeuvre warfare?

DECISIVENESS IN WAR

Unfortunately, the very concept of "decisiveness" in war is somewhat slippery. Decisiveness would seem to have at least two very different aspects to it. The first is temporal: decisive wars are wars that are brought to a close quickly. The fighting in the First World War is often called "indecisive" because it dragged on and on, whereas the Six Day War is often labelled as "decisive" because the Israelis so quickly smashed the Arab armies.

The second aspect of "decisiveness" is the "finality" of the result, or the extent to which the war settles the issue at hand. For instance, the Battle of Waterloo was "decisive" because it finally ended Napoleon's career – yet it came only at the end of a very long series of wars that could be described only as attritional. As this example makes clear, often wars are "decisive" in one of these two senses but not the other.

Russell Weigley in *The Age of Battles*, his masterful survey of conflict from the Thirty Years War to the Battle of Waterloo, comes to the ultimate conclusion that "the possibility of waging a grand, climactic battle provided at least a hope [during the era he was studying] of deciding the outcome of war promptly and at a cost that might not appear exorbitant."[34] This was certainly the hope of Napoleon and the outlook of Clausewitz and Jomini. Nevertheless, as Weigley points out, decisiveness was actually elusive. Even the great Napoleon's wars dragged on for years, as one climatic victory after another proved unable to secure his continental system. In the end he lost after a decade and a half of gruelling attrition that left France exhausted. "The age of battles proved to be an age of prolonged, indecisive wars, sufficiently interminable that again and again the toll in lives, not to mention the costs in material resources, rose grotesquely out of proportion to anything their authors could hope to gain from them."[35]

It need scarcely be added that this pattern has persisted since Waterloo. The reason is probably that it is simply too hard to force large states to do what they do not want to do – which is precisely the classic aim of war. "An act of violence intended to compel our opponent to fulfil our will," as Clausewitz put it. Yet for every action there is usually an equal and opposite counter-action. Napoleon's very successes drove the other states of Europe into alliance against him. So long as states are committed to the struggle they will continue to resist, until finally exhausted and beaten down in a long, attritional struggle. This explains why attritional wars are so common and why those rare non-attritional victories are of such transitory impact. Speaking of this phenomenon in the First World War, and the heavy criticism that its generals have come in for, the American theorist Colin S. Gray has pointed out: "Could it be that there was no clever way to win the war on the ground by inspired operational art? ... The central problem in 1914–18 was not, as too often alleged, with the incompetence of the military systems engaged, but rather with the character of the policy goals which governments obliged their generals and admirals to serve. The belligerents suffered as heavily as they did because they sought total victory in a great war between very mighty coalitions." [36]

CONCLUSION

It would be hard to argue in favour of attrition as an approach to war. However, we should admit that with almost no exceptions, in any major war between roughly evenly matched opponents, the final result has, in the end, been determined by attrition. But does this doom militaries to campaigns such as the Somme, simply throwing men and materiel at the enemy until it is eventually swamped? Not necessarily. Major wars may be decided by attrition at the strategic level, but it does not necessarily follow that the battles and campaigns that make up the war at the tactical and operational levels need be attritional. If a great power (or coalition of great powers) can be worn down only over time, best that the wearing down be effected by a series of manoeuvre-based campaigns that do not rely solely on the blunt instrument of sheer weight in numbers.

This, in essence, appears to have been Delbruck's argument. A smaller power such as Frederick the Great's Prussia can fight a nimble series of campaigns that are very much nonattritional and manoeuvre-based in their actual execution, but are meant to exhaust the enemy at the strategic level. The result has been manoeuvre at the tactical and operational levels and attrition at the strategic level.

Britain's effort in the Napoleonic Wars can be seen in that light – a series of campaigns fought with relatively limited armies that capitalized on manoeuvre (particularly the mobility that came from the Royal Navy's command of the sea) to eventually wear down the French. [37] Similarly, it was a series of campaigns that swept across continents that eventually wore Germany down in the Second World War.

Manoeuvre-based fighting, the employment of PGMs, or any other stratagem designed to make fighting less costly is clearly something to be pursued at the tactical and operational levels of war. However, we should not allow ourselves or our statesmen to be deluded into thinking that these are panaceas that can bring difficult victories cheaply. When solid, evenly matched opponents are determined to have their way with each other, there is no easy way to victory – attritional warfare is virtually inevitable. As the Duke of Wellington is reputed to have said at Waterloo: "Hard pounding this, gentlemen; let us see who will pound longest."

NOTES

1 Sassoon, *Counter-Attack and Other Poems*, 42.
2 Actually only some 20,000 of these were fatal casualties. See Middlebrook, *The First Day of the Somme*, 263.
3 French, "The Meaning of Attrition," 385.
4 Palmer, *Summons of the Trumpet*, 117.
5 Leonhard, *The Art of Maneuver*, 19.
6 Ibid.
7 Simpkin, *Race to the Swift*, 21–2.
8 For instance, the British Expeditionary Force's director of military operations, Brigadier F.B. Maurice, wrote in a letter in 1915: "We must keep hammering away and to do that we must have more and more men and more and more ammunition. If we can only keep our attacks going we shall wear Germany out." Quoted in French, "The Meaning of Attrition," 396.
9 Consideration of the "levels of war" has often become hackneyed, but it is still a useful concept. Leonard gives a good discussion of them in *The Art of Maneuver*, 5–10.
10 Epstein, "Patterns of Change and Continuity," 377.
11 For the standard account of the Napoleonic Wars, see Chandler, *The Campaigns of Napoleon*.
12 Epstein "Patterns of Change and Continuity," 381.
13 On the general nature of the Crimean War, see Seaton, *The Crimean War*. A more recent revisionist work opens with a bold claim: "The intention of this book is to demonstrate that the 'Crimean War' so familiar to twentieth century historians has no factual reality," but even it does not challenge the ultimately attritional nature of the conflict. Lambert, *The Crimean War: British Grand Strategy*.
14 On this theme, see Beringer et al., *Why the South Lost the Civil War*.
15 Wallach, *The Dogma of the Battle of Annihilation*.
16 No one seriously disputes the attritional nature of the First World War. The debate instead centres on when, precisely, it became attritional and on the extent to which this may or may not have been avoidable. On the former issue, see, for instance, Dewar and Boraston, *Sir Douglas Haig's Command*; or French, "The Meaning of Attrition," 385–405. On the latter, see any of J.F.C. Fuller's or B.H. Liddell Hart's fulminations against the war, or more recent reassessments such as Winter's *Haig's Command: A Reassessment*.

17 Ziemke, "Annihilation, Attrition and the Short War," 28.
18 Ellis, *Brute Force*.
19 For an excellent overview of the various wars in general, and the Six Day War in particular, see Herzog, *The Arab–Israeli Wars*.
20 See, for example, Wallach, *The Dogma of the Battle of Annihilation*.
21 Quoted in ibid., 69.
22 History has been kind to Delbruck; the German obsession with the dogma of the battle of annihilation as the one and only true strategy of war is now almost universally excoriated.
23 Dunnigan, *How to Make War*, 428.
24 Leonhard, *The Art of Maneuver*, 19.
25 Ibid., 79–80.
26 Perhaps the first writer to stress this idea explicitly was B.H. Liddell Hart, with his "expanding torrent" metaphor.
27 Simpkin discusses this at some length in *Race to the Swift*, 145–50.
28 See Leonnard, *The Art of Maneuver*, 113–21; or Simpkin, *Race to the Swift*, 226–55.
29 Genghis Khan is popular for some reason.
30 Luttwak, *Strategy: The Logic of Peace and War*, 99.
31 Ibid., 100–1.
32 Antal, "Maneuver versus Attrition," 21.
33 Ibid., 19–23.
34 Weigley, *The Age of Battles*, xiii.
35 Ibid., xii.
36 Gray, *War, Peace and Victory*, 176.
37 On this theme see Liddell Hart's *The British Way in Warfare* and the more recent reappraisal by French, *The British Way in Warfare*.

Strategy and Technology in Transition: Moltke and the Prussian General Staff

LCOL KENNETH M. NESBITT

In the mid-nineteenth century, the art of warfare in the Western world was in a state of transition, which would significantly alter how armies moved, communicated, and fought. Strategy affecting the battlefield was being irreversibly changed by an unprecedented wave of new technology spawned by the industrial revolution. The expansion of railways in Europe was revolutionizing military concepts of transportation, allowing rapid mobilization, deployment, and redeployment of large forces. Also, and equally important, the newly invented telegraph permitted long-distance communication, enabling commanders at the strategic, and to a limited extent even the tactical, level to communicate with and control large, dispersed formations. Further, new weapons, such as breechloading rifles and steel breechloading cannons, were drastically affecting firepower in battle and the tactical employment of troops. The emergence of these technological factors required a reappraisal of traditional methods of warfare.

Rising to pre-eminence in this rapidly changing military environment was the Prussian general Helmuth von Moltke (1800–1891). Because of his striking successes while chief of the Prussian General Staff in the war with Denmark (1864), the Seven Weeks War with Austria (1866), and the Franco-Prussian War (1870–71), Moltke has earned a reputation as one of the great European strategists between the Napoleonic era and the First World War.

The new railway technology, telegraph communication, and advances in weaponry were not unique to Prussia during this period. However, Moltke proved himself to be the most successful in Europe in exploiting the advantages of the modern technologies and combining them with the existing elements of the professional Prussian army. Moltke was a product of the

German General Staff system, and he concentrated on military education as the foundation for professional officers. At the core of Prussian military education was the study of military history. The lessons of history, Moltke contended, if properly taught, could provide commanders and staff with the basis of mutual experience on which to build a common doctrine. Professional military training and thorough planning, combined with flexible tactical execution, were Moltke's means to achieve overall strategic victory. This essay focuses on Moltke's unique ability to meld the new technology with the Prussian military system to form a single, efficient war-fighting system, and seeks to show how in doing so he created a military machine that would, in a few short years, change the balance of power in Europe and affect the overall strategy of warfare for ever.

Assuming command of the Prussian Army General Staff in 1857, von Moltke inherited a modernized military with several unique characteristics; the army's staff and its staff-training system, its procedure for conscription and raising reserves, and its mobilization plans were all highly evolved, and would soon become the standard for all Western militaries. Within this solid organizational foundation, Moltke, who during his thirty years as a staff officer developed a thorough understanding of Prussian theories of war, exerted his special talents for strategic thinking, organization, and detail. [1]

Moltke started his military career in the Danish army, becoming a lieutenant in 1819. But limited prospects for advancement prompted him to apply for a commission in the Prussian army. [2] To become a Prussian officer he was tested in French, German, mathematics, field fortifications, geography, statistics, and German and world history. He passed his examinations and was enrolled as a cavalry squadron lieutenant. [3] Promotion was slow initially, but his talents were soon recognized and he was selected to attend the three-year War Academy course. The War Academy was under the direction of Clausewitz during this period, though Moltke would not become familiar with Clausewitz's works until after the latter's death. [4] Following his three years as a student at the War Academy, Moltke was appointed to the Prussian General Staff in 1826.

The scholarly Moltke was dedicated to his profession of soldiering and made his way steadily up through the ranks of the peacetime Prussian army, augmenting his experience with an assignment to the Turkish army as an adviser. [5] While working for the General Staff his primary employment was as a surveyor and cartographer. He planned war games, participated in the staff rides, trained divisional staff officers, gave lectures, wrote essays, and made maps. His most comprehensive cartographical project was the development of new detailed tactical maps of Silesia and Bohemia, exactly the same terrain over which he would fight the Austrians in 1866. [6]

To appreciate Moltke's success, it is important to understand the military environment in which he operated; how he integrated the new technologies in transportation, communications, and weapons into his campaign strategies; and how they became key factors in his successes in war. The particular tools he put to such effective use had actually been around for some time. Elements of the General Staff, the system of mass conscription, and a large, well-trained reserve had been in place since their creation by the influential Prussian generals Scharnhorst and Gneisenau before 1815.[7] Preparing detailed war plans in advance had been advocated by many great military thinkers and was already a key feature of the Prussian General Staff training and philosophy. The use of railways for transporting armies and communications by telegraph was vitally important in the American Civil War.[8] As early as 1857, all these elements were in place within the Prussian system, and von Moltke, a devoted product of Prussian General Staff training and philosophy, clearly demonstrated the ability to use the advantages of organization in combination with the evolving technology not just more effectively than his opponents, but with devastating impact. Moltke's success, however, was not the result of any single stratagem, event, or action on the battlefield; his genius is revealed rather in his flexibility in planning and execution, and in his integration of the various elements of military art, science, and new technology to achieve a decisive result in battle.[9]

MOLTKE AND THE PRUSSIAN GENERAL STAFF

An evaluation of Moltke's success based on his strategy and his use of new technologies certainly begins with the General Staff system. The Prussian General Staff of 1866 was the result of many years of evolution. The system had arisen with the reforms of the Prussian army during and following the Napoleonic Wars. Essentially the role of the staff was to provide each level of command – army, corps, and division – with its own permanent body of officers who were involved in planning and operations. At the top the Great General Staff, headquartered in Berlin, provided national-level planning and direction.[10] The General Staff was independent of the War Ministry, and the Chief of the General Staff was effectively the head of the armed forces. What made the German staff system in particular so effective was the fact that it existed both in war and in peace. Other nations' military staffs were not permanent and were not founded on the Prussian principles of professional education and standardized training, but were instead formed only in wartime.[11]

The business of the General Staff in peacetime was the gathering of information on possible adversaries and theatres of war and the drafting of detailed plans for mobilization and deployment. Also the staff prepared regulations, conducted war games, and participated in the annual staff ride to familiarize officers with each other and with the terrain they might be required to fight over.[12] Thorough planning in advance and common doctrinal training, focusing on military history, mathematics, logistics, and maps, were at the core of the General Staff's success. In the crucial opening moves of a campaign, the Prussians, through the preparations of the staff, had their plans already laid out in detail, while their opponents would still be organizing. In wartime, the staff officers assisted commanders in the field with planning and by providing advice. Moltke's General Staff, by contemporary standards, was a highly specialized organization that combined flexibility and initiative on the battlefield with conformity to common operational doctrine. [13] His system institutionalized coherency and combat efficiency through common training by ensuring that in a given situation different staff officers would arrive at approximately the same solution. The common doctrine was imparted through attendance at the War Academy, which was a prerequisite for selection to the staff and for more advanced professional training. [14] Meticulous planning, rapid mobilization, timely concentration of forces, concentric turning movements for envelopment of the enemy by armies converging from different directions, and a high degree of tactical independence were the essence of Moltke's strategy and of his success in the application of force.

From each graduating class at the War Academy, Moltke recruited a dozen of the most outstanding officers and employed them with the staff, on probation under his supervision. Those who were successful remained with the General Staff; the others were returned to regimental duty. After a period with the Great General Staff; the officers would rotate to the Troop General Staff at corps or division level, and, later, back again. This method ensured an intermingling of line and staff perspectives, which kept staff officers aware of life with the troops and disseminated Moltke's ideas and standards throughout the army. Eventually, there were staff officers at each army and corps headquarters who had been trained under this system. [15]

With huge forces in the field (350,000 in three widely separated armies in 1866), Moltke was unable to use the Napoleonic "directed telescope" (i.e., the ability to survey and influence the entire battlefield) method of command and control, but had rather to use staff officers at the front as his eyes and messengers. These staff officers were attached to the operations headquarters for army, corps, and often division levels. [16] With use of telegraph communications and with deployed staff officers guiding the field commanders, Moltke and his staff were able to take a somewhat detached view of events and concentrate on strategic objectives. Information flow was critical to operations, but Moltke understood the realities of warfare and remained calm even if news from the front failed to arrive in a timely manner, as was often the case. [17]

The position of the General Staff in the Prussian army of 1866 was not strong. The staff was relatively small – around 120 officers – though certainly some of its success can be attributed to its compactness, as the corporate vision was easier to impart and maintain within a smaller, homogeneous group. [18] The feeling among the regular army officers towards the staff, however, was not generally positive. The activities of the General Staff were not well understood and were viewed with some suspicion by the average line officer. Moltke himself, who by 1866 had spent nine years as chief of staff of the army, was not well known. One Prussian officer, during the Austrian campaign, was handed a staff directive and remarked: "This is all very well, but who is General Moltke?" Another officer, called to the staff headquarters at the beginning of the Koniggratz campaign, commented: "A mass of do-nothings trying to look important is always repulsive, especially when they act friendly, wish you success, appear to agree with everything, yet feel duty-bound to comment on things they know nothing about." [19] The importance of the General Staff and the notoriety of Moltke were much less in doubt after the successful war with Austria. Very soon afterward, service with the staff became a coveted assignment in the army, and the wine-red trouser stripe of General Staff officers became the symbol for a new elite within the officer corps. [20] The Prussian General Staff system had been studied with interest by other nations, but even after the war with Austria no one had felt compelled to copy it.

The results of the Franco-Prussian War, however, served as a wake-up call to Western militaries. It was obvious that the incredible Prussian success could not be attributed to the needle-gun or some quirk of fate, but that the superior planning and leadership of the Prussian army had made short work of what was reputed to be the best army in Europe. The secret of the Prussians' success, according to a contemporary British source cited by Samuel Huntington, was that it depended more on "the professional education of the officers than to any other cause to which it can be ascribed. Neither gallantry nor heroism will avail much without professional training." [21]

The Prussian army of the mid-nineteenth century had another distinct advantage over its opponents in its system of conscription, regular forces training, and reserves. The Prussian foreign minister, von Roon, and Moltke worked together in reforming their army on a new model in 1861. This was based primarily on a system of universal military service, with which the Prussians conscripted 63,000 men per year, who then served an active duty enlistment of three years. After their active army time, the men would serve in the reserves for five years, and then they were assigned to the *Landswehr* (local militia). In this manner, Prussia had redefined its manpower base and became pre-eminent in the application of this system of reserves on such a large scale and with such effectiveness. [22]

By way of comparison, the French in 1870 had a very different system of conscription and reserve service. Most French soldiers were long-term professionals with a minimum tour of duty being five years. Backing up the regular army were the *Garde mobile* and the *Garde national*. These reserve and militia organizations were formed by men who had not been conscripted into the regular army, and their training and preparedness were not of a high standard, primarily because some in the French government feared that a Prussian-style system would over-militarize the populace. The French had no permanent staff system. Instead, they had adopted the "we'll muddle through somehow" philosophy and believed that, instead of professional officer training or extensive planning ahead of time, they could rely on the élan of their officers and their ability to improvise success. [23]

MOLTKE'S STRATEGIC THOUGHT

Moltke was a keen student of military history and had studied the campaigns of Napoleon in great detail. He believed deeply in the utility of history in the development of a military leader. Historical study, he argued, had great value in acquainting future commanders with the complexities of the circumstances under which military action could and would take place, and it was the most effective means for peacetime teaching of warfighting. No staff exercises or army manoeuvres, important as they were for training, could place before the commander the sort of realistic picture of the significant aspects of war as history did. [24] History had always been central to Prussian military education, and a separate history bureau was created within the General Staff officer training system. [25]

The lessons of history, however, did not require blind obedience, and Moltke recognized that, though strategy could benefit from the lessons of history, history was not identical to strategy. Moltke wrote: "Strategy is a system of ad hoc expedients; it is more than knowledge, it is the application of knowledge to practical life; the development of an original idea in accordance with continually changing circumstances. It is the art of action under the pressure of the most difficult conditions." [26] The "ad hoc expedients" that Moltke described were plans or actions, formal, informal, or improvised, but flexible enough to be adapted to a given situation, and that allowed an officer to take any available advantage to achieve the desired result.

Aware that one was unable to plan for every eventuality and convinced that history showed the futility of even trying to do so, Moltke designed a decentralized system stressing individual initiative inside an overall strategic design. Therefore he placed his confidence in his training system, which was intended to guide the commanders and staffs in common operating principles, because he believed that if the basic strategic objectives of an operation were known, commanders and their staffs could employ the tactical method that would work best to arrive at the common goal. [27] While Moltke wanted to extend the ideas of science, reason, and control over warfare as much as possible, he also believed that war was as much art as science. Crucial to understanding Moltke is his notion that planning can only do so much. His adage "No plan survives the first collision with the main enemy body" may sound simplistic, but in the confusion of battle, Moltke knew, detailed plans seldom survive, and the training, experience, intellect, and initiative of the individual commander must be relied on. [28]

The idea of freedom of tactical action on the part of the field commanders directed to achieving an operational goal is embodied in Moltke's philosophy of *Auftragstaktik* (mission-oriented tactics).[29] This concept was central to Moltke's strategy on the battlefield, wherein staff headquarters decided the strategic objectives and directed the movement of forces at the operational level. But when the higher headquarters was out of contact with its formations, or when the units were engaged with the enemy, the commander's initiative to seize opportunities as they occurred was vital, and, in the heat of combat, strategy was seen as secondary to tactical victory.[30] "A favourable situation," Moltke wrote, "will never be exploited if commanders wait for orders. The highest commander and the youngest soldier must always be conscious of the fact that omission and inactivity are worse than resorting to the wrong expedient."[31] For many of his concepts Moltke relied on historical example, especially on his interpretations and adaptations of a past master of strategy, Napoleon.[32] For example, Napoleon had organized his armies into self-supporting, self-contained corps, and, using separate roads and carefully coordinating his routes of march, he could move his armies faster than had previously been possible. Napoleon used his speed and dispersion of forces to compel his opponent to fight; the strategic turning movement was now possible, and an enemy army could be forced to choose between fighting or being flanked in retreat.

Moltke would use the same concepts, but adapted for his time. In the 1860s the technological innovations of railways and the telegraph became available on a large scale, and Moltke, mindful of Napoleon's principles, recognized how these new inventions could increase the dispersion and speed of his armies while still retaining his overall strategic control and direction.[33] This was even more important, given the extremely large size of the field armies being developed by all the great European powers. At Sedowa in 1866, the Prussian and Austrian armies together totalled 460,000 troops, in one of the largest battles ever fought until that time. Four years later, in the Franco-Prussian War, both sides together mustered more than 1.5 million men.[34]

Moltke's vision was to take Napoleon's strategy and adapt it to the modern situation of larger, dispersed armies, with new transportation and communication means. As Moltke put it: "The essence of strategy is the organization of separate marches, but so as to provide for concentration at the right moment ... It is even better if the forces can be moved on the day of the battle from separate points against the battlefield itself. In other words, if the operations can be directed in such a manner that a last brief march from different directions leads to the front and the flank of the enemy."[35]

Moltke demonstrated great flexibility of thought and was continually revising and improving his planning and methods – he was essentially an innovator and an improviser. Schlieffen summarized Moltke's philosophy as "not one method, one means, one makeshift, but many." Because of his application of technology, Moltke's methods were a synthesis of strategic and tactical doctrine, and speed was the key: rapid mobilization and rapid concentration, through the use of the rail and telegraph, and then if possible to force the enemy into an engagement before it is fully prepared.

RAILWAYS

Moltke was one of the first military leaders to appreciate the central role that railways could play in the deployment, movement, and supply of armies on a great scale.[36] In an essay published in 1843, Moltke described the importance of railways and the opportunities for their future development.[37] After taking charge of the General Staff in 1857, Moltke set about correcting the chaos that had existed in the mobilizations of the early 1850s, by focusing on transportation and communications. In 1858, the General Staff conducted the first-ever large-scale railway troop movement exercise in peacetime, involving 16,000 troops, 650 horses, and 78 fully loaded wagons. The exercise revealed both that railways had much greater capacity than previously thought and that much more preparatory work was required for smooth operations.[38] Moltke's early establishment of a permanent railway branch of the General Staff reflected his foresight and keen interest in the new technology. Railways were of little use in moving troops into the actual combat area, but they allowed a new kind of offensive based on movement of widely separated forces and their concentration near the battlefield at the right moment.

Railways clearly offered new strategic opportunities. Troops could be transported six times as fast as the armies of Napoleon's era could march.[39] Therefore countries such as Prussia, which possessed a highly developed rail system and a central position in Europe, gained important, even decisive, advantages in war. The speed of mobilization and the concentration of armies soon became essential factors in strategic calculations. Moltke and his staff, working with detailed plans and timetables, were far ahead of their European adversaries, and as early as 1859 Moltke asked the War Ministry for more track to be built, especially double-track lines, to speed deployment.

TELEGRAPH

The introduction of railway technology was accompanied by the rapid expansion of another revolutionary invention, the electric telegraph. The trains could provide the mobility to change the time and space context of war, but it was the communications capabilities of the telegraph that made smooth mobilizations and deployments possible. In the military campaigns of the mid-nineteenth century, the telegraph was critical in the planning and deployment stages, but as one approached the enemy the telegraph, because of its limitations in mobility, played an increasingly smaller role. By the mid-1850s, most important European cities were linked by wire, and a rapid expansion of the Prussian army's Telegraphic Institute (an early attempt to put telegraph equipment into wagons for field use) was under way. By 1866, the Prussian civilian and military telegraph service and infrastructure were roughly equal to that of other European countries, but they had the distinct advantage of the peacetime planning attentions of the General Staff, which drew up detailed plans for the telegraph's use in initiating mobilization and for controlling the first concentration of troops, along with procedures for sending, receiving, and acknowledging messages.

The telegraph was soon to prove its importance to many aspects of military communications, but it was not without significant limitations. First, of course, it was dependent on wire, and stations had to be fixed locations. The telegraph in these circumstances was generally more useful in coordinating a defence than an attack, because of the difficulty in keeping up with advancing troops. Telegraph lines ran primarily along railways and greatly aided in planning and mobilization, but once armies were away from the rail lines, the problems associated with the medium's lack of mobility were evident.[40] With the armies on the move during the Austrian campaign of 1866, the time it took for messages from Moltke's headquarters in Berlin to reach the army headquarters in the field varied from as little as four hours to as much as three days. As well, Moltke's written supplements travelled by rail and courier and sometimes arrived before the telegraphic message, leading to misunderstandings.[41]

The telegraph was not instantly accepted, either. The excitement about the new technology was tempered by awareness of its limitations and concern about the change it represented from the accepted and traditional methods of command and control in war. In 1861, an Austrian officer wrote: "A commander who is tied down in this way is really to be pitied; he has two enemies to defeat, one in the front and another in the rear ... [E]verything combines to rob the commander of his force and independence, partly by accident, partly by design."[42]

Many of the concerns about the telegraph, its limitations, and its place in the exercise of command and control over armies in the field were valid. The telegraph had utility in linking the major field army headquarters with the general headquarters, but its ability to influence the corps and divisional levels was extremely limited. Telegraph lines could be constructed only at the rate of two or three miles per hour in good conditions, and so keeping up with mobile formations was almost impossible. In fact in the Austrian campaign of 1866, characterized by its short duration and relative mobility, almost none of the major engagements was fought with any control or direction from the army commanders.[43] Given the limitations inherent in the telegraph, the success of Moltke's campaigns against Austria and France are testimony to his ability to recognize the capabilities of the new device and to blend it into the existing command system. The telegraph was a new and important tool, but it had its drawbacks, especially in effecting command and control at the tactical level.

Under the Napoleonic system, armies marched to the scene of the battle, then spent up to an entire day making the transition from marching to battle formation. This required concentration and assembly of the army well before the start of the battle.[44] Moltke recognized that with railways and telegraph a continuous strategic sequence was possible – mobilization, movement, concentration – and that the side which put these new tools to the best use would have the decisive advantage. If properly handled, numerically superior forces converging from different directions could be concentrated before the enemy could react. With armies formed as independent, self-sustaining forces, but deployed within supporting distance of one another, once initial contact was made they could engage the front and flanks of the enemy and manoeuvre for complete or partial envelopment. This interaction of movement and convergence of armies for envelopment in a single, decisive battle became Moltke's trademark. Moltke's philosophies would have their decisive proving ground in two short but significant wars, first with Austria and then with France.

THE SEVEN WEEKS' WAR

In 1866, the Prussian chancellor, Otto von Bismarck, ignored the objections of Emperor Wilhelm I and provoked a war with Austria by occupying the duchy of Holstein, which had been under Austrian administration since 1864. This deliberate move by Bismarck was but one of a series of steps to overcome Austrian dominance of the German Confederation and to unite the German states under Prussian hegemony.[45] The war would be the first test of the Prussian army on a large scale since the peace of Vienna fifty years earlier. A larger military, more experienced commanders, and a favourable strategic position all seemed to ensure Austrian success once the fighting started. Conversely, Prussia had the sixty-six year old Moltke as the head of the General Staff. Moltke had been an officer since 1819 but had never commanded anything larger than a battalion, and that only in peacetime. Further, Moltke had no large campaign experience, unlike some of his Austrian opponents.[46] Yet in seven weeks the war with Austria was over, as Moltke's swift success and devastating application of Prussian strategy had stunned the world.

The well-trained Prussian staff had planned skilfully, and the mobilization of the reserves, as well as the initial concentration of the armies, went smoothly, with the help of the railway and the telegraph. For the initial deployment, Moltke, unaware of the exact intentions of the numerically superior

Austrian army under the capable command of General Benedek, spread his forces across a 200-mile front to cover the possible avenues of Austrian advance. It seems that Moltke's strategic intentions were not well understood even by the Prussians, and the opening disposition of forces caused great consternation among the army leaders. It was felt that the Austrians, operating from interior lines, could engage the individually smaller, dispersed Prussian armies and destroy them piecemeal in the famous Napoleonic manner.[47] Moltke, however, had confidence that if the main enemy force was contacted, any of the individual Prussian armies could hold on until the adjacent forces could turn, converge, and support them.

Once the Austrian intention to move east towards Silesia was confirmed, Moltke ordered a concentration of forces around the central town of Gitschin. On 2 July, the Prussian 1st Army finally located the main Austrian force, dug into defensive positions around the town of Sadowa (near the fortress of Koniggratz). Moltke's overall plan was to use his converging armies to trap the Austrians, but his independent-minded commanders did not seem to grasp their roles, and the opportunity for complete encirclement was lost.[48] Even Moltke's plan to have the Prussian 2nd Army, under the command of the crown prince, crush the Austrian right was growing tenuous.

By midday of the battle the Prussians had made little headway against stubborn Austrian resistance and well-placed artillery. The Prussian emperor, who was with Moltke, turned to his chief of staff and said, "Moltke, Moltke, we are losing the battle."[49] Moltke appeared unperturbed, however, and answered that not merely the battle but the campaign was as good as won. Moltke must have had some trepidation, because the 2nd Army was very late arriving, but finally, at around 1500 hours, the first of its units were moving in on the Austrian right. The Austrians, realizing the danger of their outflanked position, covered their retreat by fighting a brilliant rearguard action and saved the bulk of their army. The Prussian victory was decisive, and Benedek had suffered numerous casualties, but the Austrian forces withdrew to Vienna in good order. The war might have continued except that internal political difficulties and the initial defeat at Sedowa prompted the Austrian emperor to accept the limited concessions sought by the Prussians.

Though railways and telegraphs had aided Moltke in the disposition and control of forces, another technological innovation also affected the battlefield at Sedowa. The new Prussian Dreyse "Needle-Gun" breechloading rifles had proved their worth in the war. Though badly outranged by the Austrian muzzle-loading rifle, and with an inefficient seal at the breech that sometimes emitted a flash which could blind a man, the high rate of fire of the Dreyse was decisive. In the Napoleonic Wars, because of the inaccuracy of the muskets and the slow rates of fire and loading procedures, entire companies and battalions relied on tight formations standing upright to fire salvos on command into the enemy ranks. Breechloading weapons made firing from a crouching or prone position possible, and with increased rates of fire troops could spread out, seek cover, and still deliver effective offensive and particularly defensive firepower. For the first time large numbers of troops could fight effectively while not standing upright in full view of their enemy or their commanders. This led to a rapid decrease in the direct control that senior and junior commanders could exert over the troops. Previously disciplined formations were turned into the equivalent of massed skirmishers, particularly on the attack.[50]

Describing the impact of technological advances on the art of warfare in the mid-nineteenth century, William McElwee had this view of the Austrian campaign: "This is what makes 1866 from the technological standpoint a turning point in the history of the art of warfare. For centuries … victory had depended on the ability of the generals and the morale of the troops they commanded. Now, for the first time the outcome of battles came to depend on the performance of new weapons."[51]

The effectiveness of the new Prussian rifles in the first engagements of the war was not overlooked by the Austrian commanders. Their difficulty was an inability to adapt their tactics and operational doctrine quickly enough to account for this tactical shift on the battlefield, which technology had brought. Much of the Austrian infantry had been trained almost exclusively in the use of the bayonet, at the expense of musketry practice.[52] The true extent of the Austrian casualty rates was not revealed until after the war. In most engagements the individual Austrian units had performed very well, but with triple the casualties of the Prussians. The needle-gun's high rate of fire, coupled with the ability of the soldier to remain under cover or prone while loading and firing, had established its predominance over the muzzle loader.[53] While the breechloading rifles themselves may not have been the deciding factor in the Austrian campaign, and their advantage was partially offset by the excellent Austrian artillery, the rapid-fire rifle had given a new dimension to infantry tactics and had rendered the bayonet charge largely obsolete.

In a quick and decisive campaign, Moltke had put to excellent use the new inventions of the industrial age. With thorough staff planning in advance and the advantage of five rail lines to the theatre of operations, as opposed to only one for the Austrians, Moltke had ensured a rapid, orderly mobilization and deployment.[54] Despite misunderstandings and Moltke's difficulties with his commanders during the operations, an overall strategy was directed and managed via the telegraph for command (though still backed up by courier messages). The needle-gun, with its high rate of fire, though limited in range, was lethal at close quarters, and the Austrian infantry had suffered enormous casualties. The war was won by pre-planning, efficient execution of the mobilization, flexible command, and some good fortune. However, the lesson of the superior Austrian artillery, and the effective role it played at

Sadowa, was not lost on Moltke, and he was immediately planning for the next campaign.

Four years after Sadowa, the Prussian army was massed on the borders of Alsace and Lorraine, mobilized and positioned for war with France. This time it was the French who possessed the superior rifle – the Chassepot. Patterned after the Prussian Dreyse breechloader, the Chassepot had an improved design, with a better seal at the breech, which solved the flash problem and nearly doubled the range, providing increased defensive power against infantry and cavalry attacks.[55] The French advantage in rifles was offset, however, by the newer Prussian, Krupp steel, breechloading, rifled cannon. The Prussian artillery gained an increased role in the offence by operating outside the range of the rifle fire. The Prussian artillery also fired a new type of percussion-fused shell that exploded on impact, and, given as well the increased range and accuracy of the rifled barrels, the Prussians quickly silenced the French guns and inflicted serious casualties on the French infantry.[56]

However, as in the Austrian campaign, the advantages in weaponry, on either side, while significant to the local tactics and even the outcomes of certain engagements, were not the deciding factor. The real difference came in the organization, mobilization, and execution as carried out by the Prussian General Staff and its army. While the war was not without problems for the Prussians, in comparison to the dismal French performance the Prussian campaign was a model of efficiency. Since 1866, Moltke and his staff had reworked the mobilization plans a dozen times to perfect the timetables and to maximize the rail transportation and concentration of troops to any theatre, and the General Staff had often "war gamed" the Western Front problem. In November 1867, the army was mobilized and in position to march in thirty-two days. In 1868 the time had been reduced to twenty-four days, and by January 1870 it was down to twenty days.[57] Thus, when hostilities broke out in July 1870, the Prussians were at the frontier with 450,000 troops and France was only halfway through its mobilization.

An ailing Napoleon III, without an effective staff or a brilliant general to lead his forces, put his faith in the Chassepot rifle and the legendary élan of the French soldier. Concentrating his forces near Metz, Napoleon III found his supply situation in disarray and his army unready to take the offensive, and so he waited for the Prussians. Moltke, expecting the French to attack, had deployed roughly as he had in Austria and was ready to hold the enemy in place with the central army and envelop it with the other two. The first battle was initiated without Moltke's orders by an overly aggressive General Steinmetz and the small 1st Army on the right. The Prussians suffered heavy casualties, but the French were forced to withdraw or be outflanked. [58] This, and four other lost battles in the next two weeks, demoralized the French, but they also gave huge confidence to the Prussians. In all these engagements, the tactical power of the rapid-firing breechloader was reconfirmed, especially on the defence, and the Prussian rifled artillery, with percussion-fused ammunition, found a significant new role in the offensive.

Reeling under Prussian pressure, the French 1st Army under Marshal Bazine retreated into the fortifications at Metz, where they were immediately besieged by the Prussians. The French 2nd Army, under Marshal MacMahon, retreated to the nearest railhead and moved back nearly 240 km to Chalons. However, not everything went the Prussians' way. During one battle near Metz, the elite Prussian Guard of 30,000 infantry advanced on the French, who were occupying good defensive positions. The Prussians, attacking in Napoleonic style against the dug-in French, lost 8,000 killed and wounded in a little over twenty minutes. [59] The commanders on both sides were slow to learn the lessons of attacking with formed infantry against an entrenched enemy with rapid-firing weapons. The troops were learning, however, and increasingly the tendency was to disperse, seek cover, or go to the prone position to return fire.

Blockading Bazine and his 170,000 troops in Metz, Moltke sent the rest of the army towards Chalons in pursuit of MacMahon. Under government and public pressure to relieve the Metz garrison, MacMahon's army, with Napoleon III now in personal command, marched north and east, trying to evade the main Prussian forces and link up with Bazaine at Metz. Moltke received word of MacMahon's intentions and, exploiting his interior lines, manoeuvred to catch the French in a pincer movement, cutting them off on three sides, with their backs to the Belgian frontier. On 1 September 1870, the Prussians, with a numerical advantage of 90,000 and with their far superior and well-placed artillery, finally forced the surrender of Napoleon III, taking 104,000 prisoners. Bazaine, holding out in Metz, surrendered in October 1870, with 170,000 troops. The Franco-Prussian War lasted until the end of January 1871, culminating with the fall of Paris. The French had lost their main combat armies in the first four months of the war and were unable to continue effective resistance. [60] The war, which had been carried on with such huge expenditure of forces on both sides, had lasted seven months.

Moltke's success against the French was as astonishing to most observers as it was spectacular. The French had been considered the best army in Europe because of their large professional forces and their relative success in recent military engagements, both with Austria and in their colonies abroad. Their modern infantry weapons, telegraphs, and railways, and their large manpower pool of reserves, seemed formidable. But in fact it was to be a contest of the well-trained and organized against the grossly incompetent. The meticulous planning of the Prussian General Staff, the stunning speed of the Prussian mobilization, and the carefully practised command carried out by telegraph and transport by railway set the stage for strategic victory. Though the French had numerous opportunities for localized successes, and the individual soldiers performed well, their commanders and their staff failed them. Moltke's ability to plan and to control the rough strategic direction of his huge forces, and yet be flexible enough, through the concept of the *Auftragstaktik*, to allow his commanders the tactical freedom to pursue their local objectives as the situation dictated, was the key to success.[61]

CONCLUSION

In his last years in office, Moltke continued to struggle with the growing operational and strategic dilemma of a two-front war for Germany. As both the French and Russian armies became more powerful and better organized, the need to attain a rapid and decisive victory over one, and then turn to deal with the other, became a planning imperative. Unfortunately for Germany, with the rise of ever-larger armies and the increasing geographical scale of conflict, Moltke had difficulty in seeing a way to achieve the quick victory he required to avoid a long, destructive war of attrition.

In his last public statement to the Reichstag in 1890, Moltke provided a grave warning to his successors on the future of European warfare. Any war, he said, even one ending in victory, would be a misfortune for the nation. It was inevitable, he warned, that if another European war should break out, then its end could not be foreseen, for the strongest and best-equipped powers of the world would be fighting in it. None of these powers could be crushed in a single campaign. The next war might last for seven, perhaps twenty years, and become a continuous meat grinder, destroying the manpower and economy of the nations involved. Woe be to him that sets fire to Europe. Moltke offered a bleak view of the future and a grave warning to the German leadership, but he had no advice to offer on how to avoid what was coming.

Helmuth von Moltke left behind an incredible military legacy. For Prussia he fulfilled the role of the right man at the right time. He reshaped the definition of professionalism in the military through his influence on the General Staff and by reinforcing the concepts of a professional officer corps, highly trained in a common operating doctrine, dedicated to detailed planning and flexible in the execution of strategy and tactics. At the War Academy, emphasis was placed on the study of historical examples, which, if correctly interpreted, could form the basis of a winning strategy. While Moltke's own military training was grounded in Napoleonic methods, he demonstrated great personal flexibility of thought by readily grasping the advantages of new technologies and their application to warfare. Moltke recognized the advantage of railways very early and prepared intricate plans to exploit their capabilities. The telegraph permitted centralized command and direction of large forces on an unprecedented scale, and Moltke used it to enact his strategy of rapid concentration, movement, and envelopment to achieve decisive victory in battle.

Through his successes, Moltke proved that the greatest military virtues are flexibility of thought and the ability to learn from the experience of others. Through the combination of his campaign strategy, his command philosophy of freedom of tactical execution for his subordinates, and his unequalled application of new technology, Moltke became one of the most incisive and influential military leaders in the last half of the nineteenth century. His accomplishments provide a signal example for modern military planners faced with the task of adapting strategy and doctrine to technologies in transition.

NOTES

1 Bucholz, *Moltke, Schlieffen, and Prussian War Planning*, 39–41.
2 Holborn, "The Prusso-German School," 284.
3 Bucholz, *Moltke*, 39.
4 Ibid., 284.
5 Holborn, "The Prusso-German School," 284–5.
6 Bucholz, *Moltke*, 32–3.
7 Holborn, "The Prusso-German School," 282.
8 Bucholz, *Moltke*, 43.
9 McElwee, *The Art of War*, 107–8.
10 Rothenberg, "Moltke, Schlieffen, and the Doctrine of Strategic Envelopment," 301–2.
11 Miranda, "The Franco Prussian War," 6.
12 Bucholz, *Moltke*, 34–5.
13 Holborn, "The Prusso-German School," 289.
14 Bucholz, *Moltke*, 22–3.
15 Ibid., 49.
16 van Creveld, *Command in War*, 111.
17 Ibid., 123–4.
18 Rothenberg, "Moltke," 301.
19 K. von Blumenthal, *Tagebucher* (Stuttgart, 1902), entry for 6 July 1866, cited in van Creveld, *Command in War*, 112.
20 Huntington, *The Soldier and the State*, 51.
21 Ibid., 47.
22 A. Jones, *The Art of War in the Western World*, 395.
23 Miranda, "The Franco Prussian War," 10.
24 Holborn, "The Prusso-German School," 290.
25 Bucholz, *Moltke*, 23.

26 Holborn, "The Prusso-German School," 290.

27 Ibid., 289–90.

28 Rothenberg, "Moltke," 301.

29 Ibid., 296.

30 Holborn, "The Prusso-German School," 291.

31 Rothenberg, "Moltke," 299.

32 Holborn, "The Prusso-German School," 288.

33 Rothenberg, "Moltke," 301.

34 van Creveld, *Command in War*, 105.

35 Holborn, "The Prusso-German School," 288.

36 Pearton, *Diplomacy, War and Technology*, 69.

37 von Moltke, *Essays, Speeches, and Memoirs*, 228–60.

38 Bucholz, *Moltke*, 39–40.

39 Ibid., 287.

40 McElwee, *The Art of War*, 118–19.

41 van Creveld, *Command in War,* 124.

42 "Oesterreichische Militarische Zeitschrift," Vol. 2, 1861, no. 2, cited in van Creveld, *Command in War,* 129.

43 van Creveld, *Command in War,* 131.

44 Holborn, "The Prusso-German School," 288.

45 Flenley, *Modern German History,* 216–17.

46 Ibid., 175.

47 McElwee, *The Art of War,* 107–8.

48 Holborn, "The Prusso-German School," 184.

49 van Creveld, *Command in War,* 137–8.

50 Ibid., 106–7.

51 McElwee, *The Art of War,* 241.

52 Ibid., 128.

53 A. Jones, *The Art of War,* 397–8.

54 Bucholz, *Moltke,* 46.

55 A. Jones, *The Art of War,* 398.

56 Ibid., 401.

57 Bucholz, *Moltke,* 51–2.

58 Ibid., 400.

59 Ibid., 405.

60 Ibid., 407.

61 Holborn, "The Prusso-German School," 289.

A Study in Operational Command: Byng and the Canadian Corps

LCOL IAN MCCULLOCH

The Canadian Forces have yet to develop or adopt military doctrine which reflects the concepts of campaigns and campaign planning, even though such concepts are fundamental to the practise of the operational level of war, and despite the fact that all our Allies, with whom we are likely to cooperate in any future conflict, now have done so ... This reason alone compels the military profession to develop an understanding of and competence in the operational level of war. Without training at this level, the Canadian Forces will be ill-prepared, should it ever be necessary to plan or even cooperate in the planning or conduct of campaigns and major operations. Even the planning and execution of relatively simple strategic level actions or raids may indeed be beyond our ability without a better doctrinal basis than currently exists.[1]

So wrote a serving Canadian officer in 1992. As late as 1995 an article in the *Infantry Journal* bemoaned the absence of a formal General Staff system within the Canadian Forces command and control structure to ensure "the efficiency of the military as a whole by supplying a body of officers who, for their commanders, manage the training, planning, operating and evaluation of military activities." It went on to suggest that the Canadian Forces have neither "a coherent philosophy for command and control" nor "systematic opportunities for self criticism and doctrinal consistency," both essential ingredients for any armed forces that hope to achieve consistent and effective command and control at the operational and tactical levels.[2] Given the recent events in Somalia, Bosnia, and Haiti, one might conclude that the writer has a point.

Earlier this century, however, Canadians were operational innovators in one of the most cataclysmic occurrences in human history – the First World

War. And, though the operational level of war did not exist in the military lexicons of the day (it was recognized in some circles as "grand tactics"), a means was required to bridge the sometimes-huge gap between the enuncia-tion of strategy and the practical means of winning the battles to achieve strategic objectives. Allan Millett and Williamson Murray, in differentiating between what constitutes operational military activity and tactical activity, posit that the former is marked by the analysis, selection, and development of institutional doctrines and concepts to ensure success at the tactical level.[3] This essay considers the early operational history of the Canadian army and, by means of a study in command, shows that Canadian operational doctrine was developed in the crucible of the First World War. Many of those opera-tional foundations were put in place by a British general and his staff, but they now are largely forgotten.

The history and reputation of the Canadian Corps in the trench warfare that characterized the Great War has an important niche in the national psyche. The Corps was *the* well-tuned instrument of war – well trained, well equipped, and well led – that captured the heavily defended Vimy Ridge from the German army during the Easter of 1917. In Canadian historiogra-phy, this event has been hailed as "both a great military achievement and a supreme and defining moment of Canadian nationalism." Desmond Morton called it "a nation-building experience." C.P. Stacey declared that the "cre-ation of the Canadian Corps was the greatest thing Canada had ever done" until that point in history.[4]

The accolades are often accompanied with claims that, for example, "the history of the Canadian Corps in World War I is inseparably linked with the name of General Sir Arthur Currie who rose to its command fol-lowing the capture of Vimy Ridge in the great battles of April, 1917,"[5] or "the corps' role in the remaining year-and-a-half of war, led for most of that time by Lieutenant-General Sir Arthur Currie ... and the victories of 'The Last Hundred Days' from the attack on 8 August 1918 to the triumphant entry into Mons on 11 November, demonstrated that Canadian soldiers and Canadian generals were the peers of those in any country."[6]

This nationalistic approach has somewhat impeded proper understanding of how the Canadian Corps developed its attack doctrine and its concepts of campaign planning, which became fundamental to its practice of the opera-tional level of war and the key to its subsequent tactical successes. That the development was not uniquely Canadian and occurred largely through the influence and direction of an unorthodox British general, assisted by a very able, and predominantly British professional staff, does not, it would ap-pear, sit comfortably within the nationalistic theme. Even if the fact that almost half of the Canadian Corps's soldiery was British-born can be easily overlooked by Canadian historians, the fact that the Corps's operational command and leadership concepts were developed within the Corps by professional British regular force officers is something that deserves to be examined.

This lack of acknowledgment (except in books dealing specifically with Vimy) of the contributions of the Corp's second British commander, Lieutenant-General Sir Julian Byng, and his British staff, in bringing the Canadian Corps to its high level of operational effectiveness, is understandable from a nationalistic point of view.[7] But it was Byng, in his detailed analysis of the problems that faced his Corps in the taking of Vimy Ridge, who saw the need to create a vigorous training program specific to the Corps, to reorganize staffs, to establish new operating procedures, and to oversee the development of new tactics and units in order to defeat the challenges of trench warfare.

The bravery of individual Canadian soldiers and the fighting spirit of the veteran Canadian battalions would have gone for nought at Vimy, and in battles thereafter, but for the professionalism and operational expertise instilled in the Corps by Sir Julian Byng. The first section of this essay examines the formative years of Byng's professional military career, especially factors that helped shape him as a commander. It also identifies some particular personal traits that Byng brought with him to the Canadian Corps which proved conducive to his being the leader that the Canadians needed and wanted in 1916 – a commander in the right place at the right time. The second section looks at the measures that Byng implemented once in command of the Corps, instilling his military organization with a strong sense of *esprit de corps*, professionalism, and operational expertise. Finally, it examines the staff organization that Byng trained and put in place to breathe life into his operational orders and to act as the lubricant for the excellent fighting arms and support services that had been placed at his disposal. Any attempt to understand the operational effectiveness and functioning of the Canadian Corps in the Great War must take into account Byng's staff, which converted his ideas and direction into orders. By working out all details related to their execution, the staff freed Byng to deal with other important matters. Byng's staff became his legacy to Currie and one of the underpinnings of the Canadian Corps's ability to excel at the operational level of war.

Brigadier-General "Ox" Webber, one of Byng's able British staff officers, commenting after the war, stated that most men of the Corps of the British Expeditionary Force (BEF) "did not have a life" and were mere machines organized to supply their necessary formations. By contrast, "the Canadian Corps was an organization. It had a life; there was family feeling present!"[8] We can now explore the phenomenon known during *and* after the war as "The Byng Boys."

BYNG: THE EVOLUTION OF A COMMANDER

"General Byng was ready to make an inspection today and the parade was ready in the proper place; but he came into the horse lines through a hedge, jumping the ditch as unaffectedly as a farmer would come on a neighbour's place to look at his crops. This is a soldier – large, strong, lithe – with worn boots and frayed puttees."[9] The common view of First World War battles is one of long lines of soldiers advancing towards the enemy in slow waves that shudder and falter as machine-guns mow them down, lambs sent to the slaughter by red-tabbed, red-hatted, and red-faced generals ensconced in their chateaux well behind the lines and far from the action. The classic, apocryphal narrative of the bankruptcy of British generalship is the one offered in almost all accounts of the protracted, mud-sodden attack on Passchendaele in 1917.

This stereotypic image of all British generals as incompetent, uninformed, and unimaginative "donkeys" has been perpetuated by historians such as Alan Clark and Denis Winter, but it does not do justice to the many senior officers of the British army who were considerate, competent, and innovative commanders who desperately sought ways of breaking out of the offensive mind-set and developing a professional approach to the challenges and stalemate of trench warfare.[10] Names such as Edmund Allenby, Charles Harington, Claud Jacob, Louis Lipsett, Ivor Maxse, Herbert Plumer, and Horace Smith-Dorrien may come to mind.

Hundreds of thousands of Canadians, after the Great War, would have readily attested that at least one other British general could be placed in such talented company. According to biographer Jeffery Williams, Sir Julian Byng was the "inspiring, tough, competent and sympathetic" commander who transformed the Canadian Corps "into a superb fighting force and set them on the road to victory." In doing so, Williams claims, he won "not only their trust and admiration, but their devotion."[11]

A cultured cavalryman born into the British aristocracy, however, was a most unlikely leader of the rough and ready Canadians. Byng himself questioned the appointment, but he was clearly not just any other spit-and-polish British general of the Great War. He was casual in his dress, spartan in his habits, affable with all ranks, and, above all, extremely unorthodox. Among the formative events and circumstances that shaped this commander and imbued him with a flexible mind and a professional devotion to his men's training and welfare were a number of command and administrative posts in the pre-war British army. He was appointed adjutant of his regiment, the 10th Royal Hussars, in October 1886[12] and distinguished himself by maintaining good order and discipline and by providing sport and canteen facilities for the men.[13] Byng attended the Army Staff College at Camberley in 1893 with many officers whose names would become well-known during the First World War – Haldane, Kiggell, Rawlinson, Snow, and Wilson. After a stint as squadron commander in his regiment, Byng became a staff major at Aldershot, working under General Redvers Buller. There, Byng was heavily involved in the administration and training of the command that traditionally formed the basis of any expeditionary force sent from Britain. [14]

When war broke out in Africa in 1899, he was appointed deputy assistant provost-marshal of Buller's Corps, and he was active in staffing the force's immediate embarkation. When it arrived in South Africa, the Boers had the upper hand, and Buller was forced to divide his expeditionary force into relief columns rather than using it as a cohesive army in a quick overland thrust to Bloemfontein to win the war. [15] Byng was ordered to take command of a new regiment of colonial irregulars at Cape Town, to be called the South African Light Horse. Its rank and file were mainly loyal South African colonists, but other colonials and foreigners were in its ranks. In all, eight squadrons, about 600 men, were under Byng's command.

Byng's irregulars were organized as cavalry, but their main arm was the rifle. While they might carry out traditional cavalry roles such as reconnaissance, they were not designed for mounted combat. They would fight on foot. [16] The regiment took part in some of the hardest fighting in Natal, leading his commanding officer to observe: "Colonel Byng was not only a good soldier but was possessed of that inestimable quality, *clear common sense*; he and his fine regiment, I soon found, could always be absolutely depended upon." [17] Byng took valuable lessons away from the Boer War. As a regimental officer, there was nothing he could do about the shortage and inadequacy of maps, the lack of artillery or poor generalship, but he took stock, and stored the lessons away for use at a future time and place where he might find himself in command.

On his return to England after the war, Byng's star was ascending, and he found himself appointed to the command of his own regiment, the 10th Royal Hussars, by the new king and colonel-in-chief, Edward VII. By the spring of 1905, Byng was promoted to brigadier-general and given command of the Second Cavalry, "superseding some 31 cavalry officers senior to him." [18]

Byng used his experience in South Africa to propose changes to cavalry's traditional roles of screening, reconnaissance, and attacking enemy cavalry with the sword and lance. Byng proposed that cavalry be trained to fight dismounted as infantry, using rifles and machine-guns. It could also act, he believed, as a mobile reserve that could move its firepower rapidly to threatened sectors of the field, or it could defend (as opposed to just observing) a flank, or it could seize and hold a distant objective until infantry could arrive. [19]

However, Byng's divisional commander was Sir John French, a proponent of traditional cavalry roles, and it was not until the latter's departure from Aldershot in 1909 that cavalry troopers were allotted enough rifle ammunition to permit them to train up to the infantry's standard of shooting. That same year, Byng was promoted to major-general (bypassing twenty-four places on the seniority list) and given command of the East Anglian Territorial Division in August 1910. Two years later, Byng was commanding the British forces in Egypt, the "youngest general on the staff of His Majesty's Regular Forces."[20]

At the outbreak of the First World War, he returned to command the 3rd Cavalry Division, which had a crucial role in stemming the German tide at the battle of First Ypres, his cavalry troopers plugging the gap in a threatened sector at Hooge, fighting it out with their rifles and machine-guns as dismounted infantry. Kitchener and Winston Churchill brought him belatedly to Gallipoli in August 1915 to try and help salvage a dying operation, which Byng immediately saw was hopeless. Within a week of arrival, Byng had instructed his staff to prepare a secret contingency plan for evacuating Suvla Bay. The orders to evacuate Gallipoli were reluctantly signed by Kitchener, and the British began a withdrawal in the face of the enemy, one of the most difficult and dangerous operations of war. That it was operationally successful was due, in no small part, to Byng and his staff. One of his aides wrote that "the General is in great form and jolly glad to get out of that bloody Suvla. There has not been much mention of his name as he does not advertise ... I hope he gets all the credit he deserves."[21] The evacuation of Gallipoli roused the admiration of professional soldiers everywhere, even in Germany, where one commented, with perhaps a touch of irony: "As long as wars exist, their evacuation of (Gallipoli) will stand before the eyes of all strategists of retreat as a hitherto unattained masterpiece."[22]

In February 1916, Byng was back in France, commanding the new 17th Corps, which he found entrenched opposite the infamous, whale-shaped Vimy Ridge. It was here that he became "fascinated" by the ridge, according to his biographer, and "spent hours reconnoitring it until he knew every contour."[23] It was also here that he encountered, for the first time, a new type of combat – tunnelling, counter-tunnelling, and mine warfare – and he made himself an expert on this new and deadly approach to solving the riddle of the trenches. After only three months in command of the 17th Corps, he was ordered to report to Headquarters Canadian Corps at Ypres by 28 May to take command. Little did he know that he would be returning to the Vimy sector before the year was out in order to plan one of the most successful operations of the war.

"BUNGO" AND "THE BYNG BOYS": OPERATIONAL COMMAND

One of Byng's immediate problems in the Canadian Corps was a political one – sorting out the controversy that had developed between the Corps and the

Militia Department in Ottawa, headed by the irrepressible Sam Hughes. Within days of Byng's taking over, the commander of the 3rd Divsion was killed during a German attack. Byng received a message shortly afterward that read: "Give Garnet 3rd Division – Sam." Garnet was Hughes's son, commanding a brigade in the 1st Division. Byng ignored the message and appointed Brigadier-General L.J. Lipsett, an ex-British regular whom he considered better qualified, to the vacant divisional command position. Byng wrote to a friend that he had "presented an ultimatum the other day saying that I do not think I could carry on unless promotions and appointments were in my hands." To him, the Canadians "were too good to be led by politicians and dollar magnates, and if the credit of the Corps is to be augmented, the men must be led by leaders." After Sam Hughes's resignation three months later, Byng no longer had to worry about political interference and could devote himself solely to training his "splendid men" for whatever operation might arise.

Byng rapidly deduced that his was a unique command. Having commanded two British Corps already, he knew that they were "hollow horses" compared to the Canadian Corps. Normally a BEF corps controlled a sector and planned battles for whatever divisions passed in and out of its control. Byng realized that he had his own small army, which he could train and influence without the continual "top-down" interference from the BEF command structure "that paralysed open discussion, made innovation difficult and allowed faulty decisions to stand when subordinates knew of serious problems."[24] Because superior headquarters "offered little more than grand directives and windy principles [during the Great War], corps and divisions had to develop specific tactics for the tough problems the Germans regularly created." In this regard, Byng was not shy and "had the brains and courage to experiment."[25] He would rebuild the Canadian Expeditionary Force (CEF) from the "bottom-up."

E.L.M. Burns, a brigade signals officer in the Great War, recalled the importance of the homogeneity of the four Canadian divisions. Byng, in his opinion, "stood in the first rank of the higher British commanders," and, though many British divisions "were as good or better than any of the Canadian divisions, and ... British soldiers were just as brave as the Canadians," the Canadian Corps believed itself "to be the spearhead of the army," with "a guid [good] conceit" of itself. The homogeneity of the Canadian divisions was "a great advantage to the Canadians, at Vimy and in later battles, [and meant] that they always operated together, under a corps commander and staff whom they could trust, and whose methods and abilities they knew and understood. In contrast, British divisions moved about from one corps to another, and sometimes suffered from misunderstandings arising from different operational and administrative practises in the different corps, and personality clashes between officers on the divisional and corps staffs."[26]

How did Byng build and win that trust? From the first day of his command, he made it apparent to the Canadians that he was thorough. Having drained his staff of all pertinent information, he proceeded to visit every unit of the 2nd Division, which had recently been very roughly handled by the Germans at the battle of the St Eloi craters. One of the battalion officers, D.E. McIntyre – later the first Canadian staff officer to be a divisional General Staff Officer (GSO) I in the war – recalled: "It took but a short time for his personality to make a favourable impression on the officers and men of the Corps. He showed us in his quiet unassuming manner, that he was an able soldier who had learned his trade thoroughly and could teach it to others. Heaven knows we had plenty to learn. Unlike some high-ranking officers whose minds functioned in a more rarefied atmosphere, Byng had the common touch and could take a rifle from an infantryman and show him more about it than the man ever knew. He understood and respected the average private and NCO. A soldier to him was not just a statistic or 'other rank,' but an individual."[27]

Byng's links with the common soldier were thus forged early in his command, and the Canadians came to know their fifty-four–year-old Corps commander by sight. He seemed to be everywhere at once, usually on foot, dressed in frayed soldier's trousers, puttees, and unshone boots, chatting, questioning, and observing the ordinary Canadian soldier at work and rest. He preferred to live like the rank and file as much as was practicable. Because the troops got so little leave, he took very little himself. In four years of war, his wife saw him only five times. Food at Corps Headquarters during his tenure was deemed "execrable." He was content to eat whatever was on offer and usually packed sandwiches wherever he went.

After the Battle of Mount Sorrel, in June 1916, fought five days after he took over command of the Corps, Byng realized that a major overhaul of his staff and extensive staff and formation training were necessary to make his Corps more operationally effective. The Germans' successful surprise attack and capture of three small hills heightened his resolve that his troops would be better prepared in the future.

The lessons that Byng and his staff learned at Mount Sorrel – thorough preparation, attention to detail, and overwhelming artillery support – would become the trademarks that Byng would imprint on the Canadian Corps staff for all future operations, though at the Somme he and his Corps were not given much scope for manoeuvre. Suffering 24,019 casualties there, they had been confined by very narrow boundaries and given no tactical latitude for innovation by General Sir Hubert Gough's headquarters. Byng's biographer notes that "from Corps Commander down to private soldier, they carried away a sense of frustration at the way in which they had been employed ... For Byng and his Canadians, it was the first experience of sustained offensive operations under the intimate control of a higher headquarters. Their first instinctive conclusion was that there must be a better way to win battles." [28]

The task given Byng and the Canadian Corps – to capture Vimy Ridge – was a defining moment in the operational history of the Canadian army. This ridge, generally considered "the most dominant and tactically important feature on the whole of the Western Front," was for the Germans "the lynch pin joining their northern defensive line, which ran through Belgium to the sea, to the new Hindenburg system in the south. To them it was not only of tactical importance. As long as they held it, they could operate the Lens coalfields which were [strategically] important to their war effort." [29] Vimy Ridge thus acted as a catalyst on Byng and his staff to rework corps tactics and organization completely. Immediately after the Somme, Byng ordered his staff and each division to make detailed studies of every aspect of the offensive battle and to analyse the recent actions fought by the Corps. A new attack doctrine specific to the Canadian Corps was in the making.

Byng gave Major-General Currie, GOC 1st Division, the job of coordinating the lessons learned on the Somme battles and asked him to recommend applications for the infantry tactics and training to be conducted prior to Vimy. On completion of a detailed report, Currie went to Verdun in January 1917 for further study of the lessons learned by the French army. On his return, he recommended to Byng that the policy of attacking in waves be discontinued and that the smaller, less vulnerable, platoon be established as the basic manoeuvre unit and used to spearhead attacks. He further advocated that platoons and sections be assigned easily recognizable objectives in the attack and that fire and movement drills be used to attain them. [30]

Byng agreed, and battalions organized four platoons per company on a permanent basis, each with four sections. Instead of companies advancing in line, halting until flanks were safe or the artillery had dealt with a problem, attacking infantry could now manoeuvre against an enemy post that held them up by using fire and manoeuvre. An infantry company would have four platoon teams, each capable of fighting its own small battle. "Leaders and men would know each other and, through briefings and rehearsals, all would know what to do," claimed Morton. "It had taken a long time, but Canadian infantry would be organized and trained to fight their own battles and not to be patriotic automata." [31]

The adoption of these tactics, and their dissemination through the Corps and divisional battle schools that were set up, demonstrated the operational level of war at work. The developing tactics had a catalytic effect at the next level of war – the operational – with Byng actually laying down measures to coordinate how his divisions and brigades were to fight themselves forward in the Corps operations order. His instructions parallelled the German *stormtruppen* tactics of exploiting the weakest points and reinforcing success. Written at the Corps level, they constitute a definite awareness of operational manoeuvre. His revolutionary operational paragraph reads: "In the event of any Division or Brigade being held up, the units on the flanks will on no account check their advance, but will form defensive flanks in that direction and press forward themselves so as to envelop the strong point or centre of resistance which is preventing the advance. With this object in view reserves will be pushed in behind those portions of the line that are successful rather than those that are held up."[32]

Byng reshaped his artillery as much as the infantry. One of the main problems at the Somme had been the failure of the artillery to cut the wire, destroy trenches, or provide counter-bombardment fire on German guns. McNaughton, who would command the Corps Heavy Artillery by the end of the war, wrote:

General Byng was one of the first to grasp the significance of the lessons of the Somme and, with Major-General Edward Morrison, set about perfecting our artillery organization. As the number of guns available began to increase, the existing artillery units had to be expanded and new ones raised. Technical skill had to be developed and previous lessons and teachings modified to suit the changing conditions. The field and horse gunners, accustomed to fighting under circumstances which enabled them to observe every round, had to cease [in] scoffing at corrections for temperature, barometric pressure, velocity and direction of wind, wear of guns and type of shell and fuse. And the heavy artillery, used to the utmost deliberation, had to learn speed. Accuracy of fire on unseen targets, and the ability to shoot close over the heads of our own infantry, had to be acquired, and an organization built up which could effectively handle large masses of artillery.[33]

Byng was tireless also in the development of an extensive intelligence-gathering network within the Corps. "Byng's intelligence organization was unique in the British armies," claims Williams. "Under the personal control of his own intelligence officer were air photo interpreters, interrogators, scouts, snipers, observers and collators. Working closely with the counter-battery organization, they assembled a detailed picture of the German defences on the Ridge and of the strength and habits of the garrisons who manned them."[34] Trench raids and patrolling were conducted extensively before Vimy and brought in much useful intelligence, as well as ensuring that the Corps dominated no man's land and denied German patrols any accurate intelligence indicating a build-up of forces in front of the ridge.

No function that contributed to the Corps's effectiveness – engineers, signals, supplies, medical, and transportation – escaped Byng's eagle eye, and his staff were the executors of his will. All services improved and, in doing so, inspired confidence in themselves and pride in the Corps. The main key to operational effectiveness, Byng knew, would be training, and he allocated each of his four divisions three weeks to master the new tactics.

Everything possible was done to promote realism. Mounted officers moved forward with flags to simulate the pace and movement forward of the rolling barrage. Everyone carried exactly the loads that they would have to carry into battle. An area near the French town of Servins was taped to scale to represent the prospective battlefield, detailing every jumping-off trench, enemy strong points, and the successive lines of enemy trenches they were to capture. Almost daily, Byng was there to watch, patiently accompanying battalions over the ground and pointing out the salient features. He exhorted officers to "make sure that every man knows his task. Explain to him again and again; encourage him to ask you questions. Remember also, that no matter what sort of fix you get into, you mustn't just sit down and hope that things will work themselves out. You must do something. In a crisis the man who does something may occasionally be wrong; but the man who does nothing is always wrong."[35]

A large plasticine model of the ridge was made, showing in minute detail every known enemy trench, pillbox, and dugout. Officers and NCOs from all the assaulting battalions were given ample time to study it and work out plans in detail to deal with the problems they would soon have to face. Often Byng himself took part in their discussions, not only to guide them, but to discover any weaknesses in his plans that he could remedy. He went to extreme lengths to train company and battalion commanders, as he believed that they would play crucial roles in the upcoming battle, and he invited them over the winter months to stay for a week at his headquarters. Much of this time was spent with Corps staff on the study of tactical problems or required administration for their units. Byng himself was often present and attempted to talk, at least once, with each officer informally in his mess. As Byng's biographer reports, "the surroundings were far from luxurious, but the atmosphere was cheerful and relaxed."[36]

Perhaps the ultimate gesture of trust and confidence by Byng, from the viewpoint of the Canadians, was his insistence that everyone be fully knowledgable on the plans for the attack. Williams wrote: "A wide-scale issue of maps of the battlefield had a psychological impact on the soldiers quite separate from their satisfaction at receiving a useful tool. Formerly, maps were for officers; marked maps were protected and rarely seen by the men. Now they were being given to corporals. It meant that they were trusted and had been given a share in the responsibility for the enterprise ... By taking these men into his confidence Byng inspired them in a way which could never have been achieved by rhetoric or any other shallow device."[37]

When Vimy Ridge was taken in April 1917, it cost the Corps 10,602 casualties, 3,598 of them dead.[38] For their pain, however, they had taken what the Germans regarded as an impregnable position, over-running it, from their own frontline trenches to the German supporting trenches, in a single day. They had then advanced a further five miles. "The great lesson to be learned from these operations," read a 1st Division after-action report, "is this: If the lessons of the war have been thoroughly mastered; if the artillery preparations and the support are good; if our Intelligence is properly appreciated; there is no position that cannot be wrested from the enemy by well-disciplined, well-trained and well-led troops attacking on a sound plan." [39]

McNaughton summed up the feelings of Canadian soldiers towards Byng when he spoke of him as the "wonderful commander who did so much to establish our identity, our unity of purpose and our general attitude towards life and our mission in it. He was, in fact, literally adored by all the Canadians who were in France." [40] That love became mutual as the new commander formed a deep fondness for his "Canucks." Twice, Sir Douglas Haig tried to remove him from command of the Canadian Corps in order to give him an army, but Byng resisted. The third time, however, Byng had no choice and received a peremptory order to hand over the Corps in three days and take command of the 3rd Army.

BYNG'S STAFF LEGACY

Even though Byng had departed, his staff system, which historian Michael Howard described as "a nervous system animating the lumbering body of the army, making possible that articulation and flexibility which alone render it an effective military force," survived. [41] Vimy destroyed the naive assumptions that Canadians had an innate talent to wage war and therefore needed neither professional military education nor experience on the modern battlefield to do a good job. A "new sense of professional awareness had been born within the Canadian Corps." [42]

That professional staff was necessitated by the sheer size and complexity of the improvised mass army of the BEF, of which the Canadian Corps was an integral part. Staff-trained officers in Canada's small pre-war Regular Force were few and far between and not necessarily of top ability. The 1914 Militia List shows only eight serving officers as having passed the Camberley Staff College. These, plus the four officers then actually at the college, were a very small cadre indeed from which to staff the large force that the CEF was to be in the field by the end of the war. Of these dozen Camberley-trained officers, several were not even used as staff officers. One became a divisional commander, and three rose to brigade commands. [43]

Though the officer corps was never less than 70 per cent Canadian-born for much of the war, most of the key General Staff appointments within the Canadian field formations were filled by British officers. These were the first-grade appointments at divisional and Corps headquarters and the senior General Staff and administrative appointments at Corps. Byng was blessed with a cast of high-calibre British regular staff officers who were well connected to the rest of the BEF. C.P. Stacey observed that the British War Office in the Great War was clearly "more intelligent than it is given credit for," as it "had sent the Canadian Corps the very best (staff) officers it had."[44] Lieutenant-Colonel D.E. McIntyre concurred and wrote in his autobiography that Canada "should be forever grateful" for the services of these senior British officers:

They were top-level men who went on to higher appointments in their own service later. Three of them, Sir John Dill, Lord Alanbrook and General "Tiny" Ironside were of such calibre that they became Field Marshals. Prominent among such officers were men like Major General C.H. Harington, Brigadier General P. De B. Radcliffe, [Brigadier General] N.W. "Ox" Webber, Brigadier General G.N. Farmar and many others of outstanding ability. They felt that in us they had good raw material but it was necessary to spell things out for us in more detailed form than it would have been for professionals ... and so we came to be a well-forged weapon in the hands of the Commander ... In time, these staff officers, with the exception of a few excellent men who remained with us to the end, retired to make way for Canadians trained at staff courses and in the hard school of war.[45]

At first, Canadian officers provided by the units to higher-formation headquarters as "staff learners" were the misfits and cast-offs that their commanding officers wished to get rid of, but the system eventually produced competent Canadian staff officers, so that "by the summer of 1917 in the Canadian field formations, there were 14 Canadian General Staff officers, and 12 Imperial; there were 18 Canadian administrative staff officers and only one Imperial; there were nine Canadian brigade majors, and five Imperial."[46] Burns adds that a doubling of establishment put in place "in the early days of the CEF when nearly all staff appointments were held by British officers" unintentionally became an excellent arrangement, contributing "to the efficiency of Canadian staff work." The second positions were for the "staff-learners" to mirror their British colleagues, but when the British officer left and the learner moved into his vacancy, the double establishment was left, and most staff positions then had two experienced and fully-trained staff officers. Burns note that this arrangement was to be found only in the Canadian Corps and gave formation staffs a twenty-four–hour capability and distinct advantage over other hard-pressed and smaller staffs in the BEF.[47]

Even the most hard-bitten and hypercritical of soldiers, such as Private Fraser, were able to realize that things had changed for the better after the Battle of Vimy. His training and briefings were crucial, for "when the actual test came, I had absolutely no difficulty in making for my objective without the least deviation. Everything loomed up as clear as crystal – the wire, the roads, the village, the cemetery." Morton acknowledged that the staff officers of the Great War were not the stereotypical blunderers that they have been made out to be. On the contrary, they were the operational keys to tactical

success. "In fact, the staff officers shaped the course of the war in its gran-
deur, its misery and outcome," he claims. "Their plans moved the millions of
men and the mountain of shells around Europe to create the stalemate on the
Western Front and, in the end, they devised the techniques and tactics that
broke that stalemate in 1918."[48]

CONCLUSION

[A]lthough the Official Historians understood how the staff worked, what the duties
in a headquarters were, the routine of his commander and his relations with his staff,
and how these structural details affected the conduct of battles, [the official histories]
were written for the cognoscenti and [the historians] did not see a need to include this
information in [their work] ... Consequently, later generations of unofficial historians
have had to waste a lot of time trying to figure out exactly what much of the official
writing implies, regarding these functions at the [operational and tactical] levels of
war.[49]

As historian Dominick Graham has astutely noted above, there is cause
to believe that Byng's contribution at the operational level of war has been
partially obscured by problems generated by the British official history and
Canadian official histories (the latter not being produced until 1939 and
1962). There are many Canadian historians who have rightly noted that the
Canadian Corps became a superb fighting machine by the end of the Great
War, an organization imbued with a strong sense of professionalism and
esprit de corps, but these accounts invariably fail to give Byng, and the staff
he put in place behind the scenes, their due credit. This oversight stems partially from a misunderstanding of or ignorance about how the four levels of
war (tactics, operations, strategy, and politics) interact.

We have seen how Sir Julian Byng and his staff's role established the
foundations for the Canadian Corps's operational effectiveness. The many
subsequent tactical successes of the Canadians in the war were really a function of the proper application of the operational level of war, made possible
largely by Byng's efforts to rebuild the Corps from the "bottom-up" and,
after the Somme battles, to hand over an operationally effective Corps to his
protégé, Currie. Currie in turn refined and implemented some clever innovations of his own, especially prior to the Last 100 Days' battles, which
required a more open, manoeuvre style of warfare. Byng personally picked
Currie as his replacement and groomed him for the day he knew political
exigencies would demand that a Canadian general officer commanded the
Corps. Currie would learn much from the patient British cavalryman, a natural leader and thoroughly dedicated professional. Lieutenant-Colonel A.
Frith, Currie's divisional staff officer in charge of administration, wrote after
the war that "Byng's methods of command, his determination to extirpate

the canker of politics, to crush inter-divisional jealousies and develop *esprit de corps* appealed at once to Currie and elicited his whole-hearted support. There can be no doubt that Byng's influence over Currie was great and had much to do in developing and moulding Currie as a commander."[50]

The image of the Corps reaching its peak of performance under Currie, however, has tended to overshadow the debt owed to Byng, who, through his professionalism and mastery of the operational art, gave rise to the fighting machine the troops proudly called "The Byng Boys" during and *after* the war, despite the leadership and accomplishments of Byng's replacement. Colonel G.W. Nicholson has stated that the Canadian Corps was fortunate in its leaders: "To Sir Julian Byng must go much of the credit for laying the foundations of the Corps *esprit de corps* and its splendid fighting efficiency."[51]

Indeed, one might go a step further and rightly claim that Byng was the father of the operational doctrine of the Canadian army, as many of his innovations and procedures developed before Vimy in patrolling, intelligence-gathering, sound-ranging, logistical preparation, small-unit fire, and movement and training techniques are still with us today. The context in which operational doctrine was first driven and developed for the Canadian army was the lethal environment of the First World War. However, lack of any "operational" history of the Corps after the war, encapsulating its experiences and lessons learned, fettered the intellectual growth of the Canadian military and prevented any real understanding of what it had achieved in the crucible of war.[52]

Today, it is hard to convince Canadians that a well-defined doctrine must be in place to ensure that the Canadian Forces are capable of planning and cooperating with allies at the operational level of war. Some success has been realized in the formation of the Joint Staff, as well as the continuing interest of the staff colleges in fostering an understanding and competence in the operational level of war. But much remains to be learned from Canada's military history. The accomplishments of the Canadian Corps in the First World War, a time when Canadians were not just practitioners of the operational art, but innovators as well, is one shining example of this. We can profit a great deal from the experiences of Sir Julian Byng and his beloved Canadian Corps.

NOTES

1 Eddy, "Canadian Forces and the Operational Level of War," 21.

2 Wyatt, "Into the Loop: A Canadian General Staff Corps," 17.

3 Millett et al., "The Effectiveness of Military Organizations," 12.

4 Granatstein, *The Generals*, 5; Morton, *When Your Number's Up*, 169; and Stacey, *Canada and the Age of Conflict*, Vol. 1, 238.

5 McNaughton, cited in "Foreword" in Swettenham, *To Seize the Victory*, 238.

6 Granatstein, *The Generals*, 5.

7 Swettenham, *To Seize the Victory*, passim; and Marteinson et al., *We Stand on Guard*, 95–210.

8 Brigadier General N.W. Webber in Colonel Hugh Urquhart Papers, Acc. No. 393, McGill University Archives.

9 Macphail, *The Medical Services*, 57.

10 Winter, *Haig's Command*, passim; and Clark, *The Donkeys*, passim. John Terraine stated that the latter book symbolized "the bloody fools' interpretation of British generalship." Clark's view was that most officers above the rank of captain were grossly incompetent. No less a personage than Liddell Hart vetted the drafts of Clark's irreverent history of British generals – the same man who openly admired Wolff's Grecian rendering of Passchendaele and went on the record denouncing John Terraine for his presumption in daring to defend Haig.

11 Williams, *Byng of Vimy*, vii.

12 Ibid., 4–15.

13 Williams, *Byng of Vimy*, 15; and Brander, *The Tenth Royal Hussars*, 111.

14 Williams, *Byng of Vimy*, 24.

15 Ibid., 26–8.

16 Ibid., 29.

17 Dundonald, *My Army Life*, 201.

18 Williams, *Byng of Vimy*, 51.

19 Ibid., 54.

20 Ibid., 57.

21 Ibid., 109.

22 Ibid., 108.

23 Ibid., 112.

24 Travers, *How the War Was Won*, 176. Travers notes that British armies, corps, and divisions were forced to "produce their own ideas and tactics."

25 Morton, *When Your Number's Up*, 162.

26 Burns, *General Mud*, 35.

27 Macintyre, *Canada at Vimy*, 73–4.

28 Williams, *Byng of Vimy*, 141.

29 Ibid., 143.

30 For an excellent discussion see Rawling, *Surviving Trench Warfare*, 87–102.

31 Morton, *When Your Number's Up*, 163–4.

32 Williams, *Byng of Vimy*, 152.

33 Cited in ibid., 144.

34 Williams, *Byng of Vimy*, 146.

35 Byng, cited by W.W. Murray in Swettenham, *To Seize the Victory*, 155.

36 Williams, *Byng of Vimy*, 147.

37 Ibid., 153.

38 Morton, *When Your Number's Up*, 168.

39 Cited in ibid., 169.

40 Cited in ibid., 169.
41 Michael Howard, cited in English, *The Canadian Army and the Normandy Campaign*, 89.
42 Harris, "The Canadian General Staff and the Higher Organization of Defence," 70.
43 Stacey, "The Staff Officer," 47.
44 Ibid., 47–8.
45 McIntyre, *Canada at Vimy*, 113.
46 Stacey, "The Staff Officer," 47.
47 Burns, *General Mud*, 76.
48 Reginald Roy, *Journal of Private Fraser*, 261.
49 Morton, *When Your Number's Up*, 113.
50 Undated letter transcript from Major-General A. Frith to Colonel H.M. Urquhart in Urquhart Papers.
51 Nicholson, *Official History of the Canadian Army in the First World War*, 534.
52 Schreiber, "The Orchestra of Victory," xv.

An Example of Force Development: Tukhachevsky and the Soviet Art of Deep Battle

MAJOR DUNCAN C.D. MILNE

Oh yes, one of the generals killed by Stalin.
> – Remark attributed to a Soviet citizen
> on being asked who Tukhachevsky was.[1]

It is August 1945; the Soviet Far East Command is poised to strike at the Japanese defending Manchuria. Three fronts – the Trans Baikal, the First and Second Far Eastern, comprising over one and a half million men, organized as eleven combined, one tank, and three air armies – have been given the tasks to "secure Manchuria and to destroy a large portion of the Japanese Kwantung Army."[2] The plan relies on speed, surprise, mobility, and overwhelming combat power, with planned rates of advance of seventy kilometres per day for tank units and twenty-three kilometres for the remainder.[3] D-Day is set for 9 August, and STAVKA, the Soviet High Command, estimates that one month will be required for the overall campaign. It lasts seven days. The Japanese were totally unprepared to fight the kind of battle waged by the Soviet veterans of the war against Hitler; Soviet spearheads advanced rapidly, preventing the Japanese from forming any cohesive defence, and, though individual units fought with their usual Bushido bravery, the Japanese High Command was paralysed by the Soviet performance.

In his historiography of the Second World War, *The Battle for History,* John Keegan observed that "the eastern war itself has been less well served by the historical profession"[4] and that most of the works concentrate on the main Russo-German front. As a consequence, the campaign in Manchuria has been largely relegated to minor reference in histories of the war. In part, this may be because of the Western tendency to credit Soviet success principally to the admitted weak and parlous state of the Kwantung army, which had been drained of both personnel and equipment during the Pacific war.[5] Yet, despite these deficiencies, as David Glantz notes, "the combat record of units ... dismisses that charge."[6] This is not the case in Russia, where the "scope, magnitude, complexity, timing and marked success have made the Manchurian offensive a continuing topic of study for the Soviets, who see it as a textbook case of how to begin war and quickly bring it to a successful conclusion."[7] Recent American studies are now also acknowledging that a large amount of credit must also be given to a campaign plan that "relied on maneuver to envelop large segments of the Kwantung Army and to incapacitate the remainder."[8]

The operational concepts key to this campaign's success are now called Deep Operations (*glubokaia operatsiia*), and they were developed principally by Mikhail N. Tukhachevsky.[9] This essay examines the development of the underlying Soviet concepts of war and the forces to execute them, which enabled this campaign, waged over an area larger than western Europe, to be fought and won so decisively.

Tukhachevsky, an ex-tsarist officer, rose to prominence during the Russian Civil War; he is generally remembered for leading the catastrophic 1920 drive on Warsaw and in being the most prominent victim of Stalin's purges. His real significance, however, is found in his work in the development of equipment and doctrine for the Red Army. Unlike other "apostles of mobility" in the interwar years, Tukhachevsky was not a voice crying in the wilderness but a practitioner of war, able to incorporate the concepts of combined arms operations, airborne operations, and deep operations into Soviet military doctrine and regulations. In Canada, the linkage of policy, equipment requirements, and doctrine is known as the "force development process." An examination of Tukhachevsky's work within a comparable Soviet process provides a remarkable success story. In their recent book *Clash of Titans*, David Glantz and Jonathan House commented: "What was unprecedented about the Soviet concept was the official sanction it received from ... Stalin, who geared a large proportion of his five year economic development plans to provide the industrial capacity and production needed to implement that concept."[10]

However, as Tukhachevsky is not generally well known, I first establish some basic background on this Soviet theorist of war.

MIKHAIL NIKOLAEVICH TUKHACHEVSKY

Characterized by J.F.C. Fuller as an autocratic, superstitious, romantic, and ruthless barbarian, with the soul of Genghis Khan,[11] Tukhachevsky was born on 16 February 1893, near Smolensk, in the twilight of the Romanov empire. He came from mixed aristocratic and peasant roots and early in life decided on a military career. Enrolling first in a cadet corps and then in the Alexandrovsky Military Academy, he completed his studies and was in 1914 "gazetted a junior lieutenant in the élite Semyonovsky Guards,"[12] where, with the outbreak of war, "his future prospects did not seem great to anyone but himself."[13] The war ended for the young guards officer in February 1915, when he was knocked unconscious by German shell-fire, captured, and sent to prison camp. He was a far-from-model prisoner, and his defiance and repeated escape attempts eventually saw him "moved up the scale of escape-proof prisons ... to Ingolstadt IX, Germany's ultimate repository for troublesome escapers."[14] In one of the strange coincidences of history, Charles de Gaulle was also a prisoner in Ingolstadt; it is reported that they had many discussions on "military tactics and the future of warfare."[15] Near the end of the war, laxer supervision by the German guards allowed Tukhachevsky to escape, and he negotiated the eleven hundred kilometres back to Russia. Largely motivated by personal ambition, he became "a committed soldier of the Bolshevik revolution."[16]

Initially employed in the training of new units in the fledgling Red Army, in June 1918 Tukhachevsky was given command of the First Army on the Eastern Front. He was twenty-five years of age. Despite his youth and inexperience, Tukhachevsky prospered in the Civil War, where he became known as a relentless and innovative commander and came to the attention of Mikhail Frunze, a veteran Bolshevik and leader on the Eastern Front.[17] Tukhachevsky is credited with the development of the campaign plan used to defeat Admiral Alexander Kolchak, the White commander on the Eastern Front. The plan relied on the surprise generated by using an extremely difficult route to break into the White rear area and required coordination of several armies scattered over a 200-kilometre front.[18] Even at this early stage in his career Tukhachevsky was thinking on a large scale, and his success solidified his position as a rising star in the Bolshevik stable of generals.

On the Southern Front, Anton Denikin, a former chief of staff to General Brusilov, had launched an offensive in the summer of 1919 and posed the greatest threat to the survival of the revolution. Fortunately for the Red Army, Tukhachevsky was available, cooling his heels in Moscow in temporary disgrace and out of favour over an incident involving his wife, who had been caught smuggling food to her family and who had later committed suicide.[19] Posted to take over the 13th Army, he was promoted instead to take over the Caucasus Front, responsible for the area from Kursk to the Caspian Sea, and by February he had developed a new campaign plan for the five armies under his command. His plan "was marked by deliberation, precision and stern discipline"[20] and envisaged the use of large sweeping manoeuvres to encircle and to destroy Denikin's forces. By mid-March the White forces were in full retreat, and, with the capture of Novorossisk on 27 March, Denikin was defeated. Tukhachevsky's report to Lenin claimed the capture of 12,000 officers, 100,000 men, 300 guns, 500 machine-guns, and 200,000 rifles. And, according to J.F.C. Fuller, "the skillful execution of the final offensive against Denikin had placed Tukhachevsky on a new level among the Bolshevik military commanders. Where the impetuous pursuit of Kolchak through Siberia and the Urals had seemed to be the deed of a reckless but lucky youth, the cool deliberation of the mass assault against the Whites in the South seemed to promise a genuinely great military talent."[21]

The successful defence of the revolution now permitted the Bolshevik leadership to address another question – Poland, whose re-emergence was one of the byproducts of the final days of the First World War. Dreaming of a Baltic-to–Black Sea federation of Poland, the Baltic states, and Ukraine, the Polish leader, Marshal Piłsudski, had attacked Russia in 1919, occupying Vilna and Minsk, and had entered into an alliance with the anti-Bolshevik Ukrainian leader, Semyon Petlura. The Poles invaded Ukraine in 1920, and by May they had seized Kiev and installed Petlura as leader of an independent Ukraine.[22]

During this turmoil in the western reaches of Russia, a great debate was raging amongst the Bolshevik leaders. To many, the revolution could not survive unless the benefits of Marxism could be exported to other countries. Political uncertainty in the aftermath of the Great War had led to the establishment of a short-lived "Soviet Republic" in Saxony, and revolutionary activity elsewhere in central Europe indicated that circumstances were favourable for the export of revolution.[23] For many of those who wanted to export the revolution, Germany was the key, because it was seen as Europe's centre of gravity. In J.F.C. Fuller's words, "once she was won, the rest of Europe would become untenable and could be conquered."[24] And the route to Germany lay through Poland. Lenin was enthusiastic about fighting Poland, while Trotsky was opposed, on the grounds that success was dependent on an uprising by the Polish workers in support of the Red Army, a condition that was unlikely to be fulfilled.[25] The main individual in a fight with Poland would be Tukhachevsky, who was appointed to the command of the Western Front on 29 April 1920. The basic plan was for the bulk of the forces, concentrated under Tukhachevsky, to attack the Polish left wing and move on Warsaw. The South West Front under Yegerov (with Stalin as commissar) would launch a supporting attack. Though Tukhachevsky was making reasonable progress, it soon became apparent that he needed more forces. Lenin determined that the 1st Cavalry Army, from the South West Front, should move to the assistance of Tukhachevsky, but Yegorov and Stalin stalled. Thus when Tukhachevsky launched his final drive on 6 July and moved over almost 500 kilometres towards Warsaw, a gap was created on his left flank. This opened the door for the Poles. Pilsudski, aided by French advisers, including Tukhachevsky's companion from Ingolstadt, Charles de Gaulle, was able to create a reserve from those forces facing the South West

Front and use it to drive in the exposed flank of Tukhachevsky, forcing an armistice on 12 October 1920.[26] This defeat at the gates of Warsaw marked the end of the Russo-Polish war, and, in the Soviet Union, created great bitterness between the principal players in the two fronts that would have consequences in the future.

Tukhachevsky's next employment was in the birthplace of the revolution – Petrograd. Sailors at the naval base of Kronstadt, dissatisfied with the turn taken by the revolution, issued a set of demands on 21 February 1921, calling for, among other things, new elections, free speech, and an end to communist control of the military. The situation quickly deteriorated to the point where the government demanded that "Kronstadt and the rebellious ships must immediately submit to the authority of the Soviet Republic"[27] and gave them twenty-four hours to comply. They refused. Tukhachevsky was the military commander in Petrograd, and he was responsible for the preparation of the plan to bring the recalcitrant sailors to heel. The first assault went in during the early hours of 7 March, but it failed, with heavy casualties. Reinforcements were brought in, and ten days later another assault was launched with 50,000 troops. This time they succeeded, with casualty estimates ranging from 3,200 (the official total) to 10,000. This marked Tukhachevsky's last major combat operation, and it "cemented his position as a loyalist who put the welfare of the Communist regime above all else."[28]

The next stage of Tukhachevsky's career[29] brought him to the highest councils of the Red Army. With the Bolshevik revolution now seemingly secure, debate began to focus on the type of military forces that the Soviets would continue to maintain. This debate was heavily influenced by the formative experiences of the Civil War. In contrast to the struggle on the Western Front of 1914–18, the Civil War in Russia was characterized by what the Soviets termed manoeuvrability, mobility, activeness, offensive action, and surprise.[30] A principal feature of this style of warfare was the use of strategic cavalry raids, accompanied by horse-drawn carts (*tachanka*) carrying machine-guns, light artillery, and armoured cars. These experiences would be the foundations on which Soviet military theories on the strategic, operational, and tactical levels of war were developed, particularly some of Tukhachevsky's ideas on what would become deep battle.[31] The significance of this era is also acknowledged by the Soviets. Savkin's view of the Civil War era was that "Red Army operations, based on the revolutionary enthusiasm of the labouring masses, were distinguished from operations during the period of World War I by the decisiveness of goals, low operational and tactical densities, great scope and creative application of the principles of massing, activeness, surprise and mobility."[32] But before examining this question in detail, we should first look at the Soviet art of war.

THE SOVIET ART OF WAR

Modern Russian military tradition has its foundations, like so much of modern Russia, in the reign of Peter the Great.[33] This applies to concepts of "deep battle" as well. Duffy notes that Peter formed a *korvolan*, or "flying corps," a self-sufficient, all-arms mobile force of some 6,000–7,000 men, in his pursuit of King Charles XII of Sweden to Poltava and that the Berlin raid of 1760 marked a further application of a distinctively Russian technique still found today in the Operational Manoeuvre Group.[34] The main influence on Russian development, however, was geography. The vast distances of Russia encouraged its military leaders to think on a large scale; the most direct influence on them was the wars waged against the Ottoman Turks in Ukraine and the Crimea. However, the first major test for the Russian army came during the Seven Years' War against Prussia. Russian soldiers proved stoic and hard fighting, if hindered by poor organization and treason by some of their commanders.[35] Just as the post-Napoleonic period led to the development of theories of war in the West by Clausewitz and Jomini, so too did the Russians seek to understand the basic theories of war. Savkin lists an extensive number of military intellectuals, among whom Kutosov (1745–1813), Leyer (1829–1904), and Miknevich (1849–1922) are credited as being the major figures.[36]

The works of these theorists would have been used in the education of Tukhachevsky, and thus they were probably among his formative influences. Leyer's basic principles – simultaneity of actions; concentration of forces on the decisive point; hitting the enemy at its most sensitive point; surprise; developing the after-effects of victory through energetic pursuit; and being strong where the enemy is weak[37] – permeate Tukhachevsky's works. Miknevich's contribution was in recognizing that technology would force an adaptation in tactics and procedures to incorporate the benefits of technology. This determination foreshadowed the process by which Tukhachevsky would develop his theory of "deep battle." Though the basic organizational structure of the Imperial Russian Army may have been subject to the inefficiencies and failings of the Romanov empire, the intellectual underpinnings of military art and science were strong and provided the doctrinal basis from which a relatively obscure tsarist lieutenant was able to become one of the foremost military thinkers in the Soviet Union. Indeed, the emphasis on a firm doctrinal foundation in military art and science continued into the Soviet era, with contemporary authors noting that the Soviet Union "has a well developed theoretical framework and body of knowledge appertaining to war in all its respects."[38]

The major figures in the early days of the Red Army were Leon Trotsky and Mikhail Frunze. Trotsky, as commissar for war, was the architect of the Red Army. He had been forced by the demands of the revolution to employ a large number of ex-tsarist officers as "military specialists" along with ex-tsarist NCOs and many of the better-educated and politically reliable conscripts in the Red Army to provide leadership in a rapidly expanding force. The Red Army peaked at five and a half million personnel by the close of the Civil War and, having ensured the survival of the Bolshevik regime, now came under attack as a wasteful economic drain on the economy of the Soviet Union.[39] The stage was now set for the debate that would determine the future organizational precepts of the Red Army.

When examining the development of the Red Army in its early years, one must first dismiss the myth of a monolithic military philosophy, because the debate over the future force structure of the post–Civil War Red Army was quite lively. From the earliest days of the revolution the Bolsheviks had been ambivalent about the need for an army, which they had traditionally viewed as an oppressive instrument of the tsarist regime. The Bolsheviks had effectively destroyed the combat effectiveness of the imperial army by undermining its will to fight, through the promotion of disobedience and the spread of pacifistic ideas and simple but emotive slogans such as "Peace, Land and Bread," and yet now they needed an army to resist counter-revolution. At the Third All Russian Congress in January 1918, the party "accepted the idea of a professional class-based army,"[40] as opposed to a revolutionary army. Pragmatically, Trotsky envisioned developing the Red Army in two stages. First, ideology would be played down and a military capable of defending the Soviet state would be created. Second, once the security of the state was ensured, a revolutionary army guided by communist ideology would be created.[41] At the end of the Civil War, Trotsky was ready to embark on his second stage, but he was challenged by other factions within the Red Army.

The first and smallest group was composed of ex-tsarist senior officers who had allied themselves with the Bolsheviks for a variety of reasons. This group, of whom the most prominent member was Major-General Aleksandr Svechin, advocated a professional standing army, on the lines of the old imperial army, as the preferred solution. This approach found little support within the party apparatus.[42] Trotsky's plan was to "convert the army to a militia system in which the troops would simultaneously provide labour, support themselves, contribute to the economy and perform military service."[43] This stance was essentially defensive in nature and envisaged the Red Army as protecting the motherland. Part of the army would, of necessity, remain composed of regular forces to guard the frontiers, but the bulk of the force would be converted into a militia that would be recruited, stationed, and trained largely in industrial areas, with leadership coming from the industrial management. The factory manager in peace would become the battalion commander in war.[44]

The opposing school to Trotsky, made up largely of the "self-made" men of the revolution, was headed by Mikhail Vasilyevich Frunze, a Bolshevik party stalwart who was self-educated in military affairs. In direct contrast to Trotsky, Frunze "emphasized that the Red Army operations should be permeated with active offensive zeal, have a decisive nature and not be limited to repelling enemy attacks."[45] Frunze believed that there was a unique communist doctrine of war, and he was supported by the 'Young Turks' of the Red Army, among whom Tukhachevsky was the most prominent. To them "trench warfare, static defences and fortifications were a thing of the past. Moreover, Communism could provide the inspiration for a doctrine rooted in the spirit of the offensive, upon which all training and development of the Red Army should be based."[46] Future war would be total war and thus would require a large army with a significant permanent cadre. This army was to be technologically up-to-date and emphasize manoeuvre warfare, as opposed to attrition warfare.[47]

The final solution adopted by Lenin was a compromise between the two dominant factions. Accordingly, by 1924 the army had been reduced to forty-two militia divisions and twenty-nine regular divisions, so that emphasis could be placed on the economic revival and strengthening of the state through Lenin's New Economic Policy and the later five-year plans.

In the turmoil surrounding the death of Lenin and the emergence of Stalin, Trotsky was replaced by Frunze, and on 18 July 1924 Tukhachevsky was named Frunze's deputy, becoming the "intellectual fount of the Red Army."[48] Between them, Frunze and Tukhachevsky embarked on an ambitious plan to modernize and expand the Red Army. The displacement of Trotsky enabled Frunze to emerge as the de facto winner and to mould the Red Army in his image. In his eighteen-month tenure as head of the Red Army, Frunze's principal legacy was the development of a doctrine that was "based on imaginative thought, aggressive political will, a careful study of experience and the incorporation of the latest technology." [49] (Soviet military doctrinal framework "serves to determine the size and shape of the armed forces and through the constituent elements of 'military science' ensures the integration of organization, tactics, training and equipment." [50] This definition can help us understand Tukhachevsky's actions.)

As a consequence of the stress during this hectic period, Frunze fell ill with ulcers and was ordered by the Central Committee to undergo surgery. Unfortunately for Frunze, he died on the operating table. To what extent this was a Stalinist plot, as claimed by Trotsky, or merely the consequences of the fateful combination of a weak heart and an anaesthetic that his doctors had warned against, may never be known, but Frunze's death signified a further consolidation of power for Stalin, as Frunze's successor was not his deputy, Tukhachevsky, but Voroshilov, one of Stalin's cronies from the Civil War. Stalin had not forgotten Tukhachevsky's criticisms of the South West Front's campaign in Poland, and Tukhachevsky was relegated to the sidelines as commander of the Leningrad Military District.

Despite his reputation as a "yes" man and his mediocre performance in the Great Patriotic War, Voroshilov's tenure was instrumental in bringing many of the ideas of Frunze and Tukhachevsky to fruition. To Voroshilov, the way to impart mobility to the Red Army was through mechanization, which would be achieved through the five-year plans. The emphasis on industrial output was not related merely to achieving "economic competitiveness" but was vital to the creation of an arms industry that would ensure survival of the "crucible of world revolution" – a focus that marked the Soviet economy until the fall of communism in 1989. By 1932, Russia was producing over 2,600 planes and 3,300 tanks annually, and the figures were rising.[51]

With Frunze's death, Tukhachevsky became the foremost Soviet military theorist, and he entered into a period of intense writing, becoming the Soviet authority on technological warfare and pioneering the development of airborne forces.[52] In 1931, he was sent to Moscow to become Voroshilov's deputy (the same position he had held under Frunze) and to supervise the technological reconstruction of the Red Army.[53] From this return until his death at the start of Stalin's purges against the military, Tukhachevsky would develop and shepherd the basic organizational, doctrinal, and equipment issues that would ultimately win the Great Patriotic War.

TUKHACHEVSKY AND THE FORCE DEVELOPMENT PROCESS IN ACTION

Canadian doctrine defines the "Defence Planning and Force Development" process[54] as the methodology that translates "government policy, direction and resources into a capable and affordable force structure." In its broader sense it ensures that the appropriate links and relationships are set out between policy, doctrine, and capabilities and that the right equipment is introduced into service to meet government direction and policy aims.[55] Tukhachevsky's position, at what Butson terms the "pinnacle of power," allowed him to control the Soviet equivalent of the force development process and to implement sweeping changes to the Soviet style of war. The first step – determination of government policy – had been achieved during the Trotsky–Frunze debates over the future shape of the Red Army.

Malcolm Mackintosh has noted that, during this dynamic period, the Red Army was able to conduct significant experimentation in doctrine and continually adapted its force structure and training requirements to meet the demands of the new doctrine. Tukhachevsky was at the forefront of this process, experimenting with airborne forces, air-to-ground coordination, and combined arms tactics and structures.[56] He directed the establishment of the first mechanized brigades, containing an equal mix of tank and motorized infantry supported by artillery and reconnaissance units, and by 1933, during the Kiev manoeuvres, mechanized, cavalry, and airborne forces "practised Tukhachevsky's concept of a major offensive operation."[57]

The specific operational concept – deep battle – that was generated to give the Red Army the doctrinal basis that would enable it to fight successfully was developed by three men: Tukhachevsky, the conceptualizer and man of action; V.K. Triandafillov, the thinker who translated concepts into instructions; and G. Isserson, the editor and partial author of the Field Service Regulations. Following force development methodology, "they did not develop their thinking in the wake of changing historical conditions but forecast the possibilities of new technological instruments of war."[58]

The roots of deep battle go back to Peter the Great's *korvolan*, General Gurko's operations in the Russo-Turkish War of 1877, and General Mischenko's raid in the Russo-Japanese War.[59] Despite this long flirtation with concepts of strategic penetration, the immediate origins derive from Soviet (and Tukhachevsky's) experience with the manoeuvre-based campaigns of the Civil War. The Soviets were quick to appreciate that tanks and aircraft had emerged as effective weapons, and they had a long tradition of excellence in field artillery. This led them to believe that a mobile combined arms force based on tanks, aircraft, and artillery could punch through defensive systems and wage a decisive war of manoeuvre in rear areas.[60]

In contrast to the western European and American armies of this era, the Soviet Union wholeheartedly embraced concepts of mobile warfare, designed its vehicles specifically for this purpose, and developed the necessary supporting doctrine. Whereas Voroshilov had envisaged the mechanization of the army, Tukhachevsky went even further, advocating creation of special mechanized forces, based on long-range tank groups whose role was to penetrate deeply into the defensive layout of the enemy and to destroy its reserves and headquarters.[61] The principal equipment to carry out this function would be the Fast Tank, or BT series, based on the American Christie designs. When fielded, this tank gave the Soviets a weapon that was unmatched for its combination of range, speed, and main armament, as noted by the British tank expert Colonel Giffard Martel on seeing it in action during the Kiev manoeuvres of 1935 and 1936.[62]

As director of armaments, Tukhachevsky was uniquely placed to put his ideas into practice, and he ensured that tanks and aircraft continued to roll off the assembly line to support his operational philosophy. This coordinated production enabled him to move beyond the initial mechanized brigades and establish the "shock troops" required to support the concept of deep battle. In 1932, two mechanized corps were established,[63] each containing 500 tanks and more than 200 other armoured vehicles, which, in conjunction with airborne attacks and deep bombing raids, would provide the means to penetrate and strike deep in the enemy's rear.[64]

To establish the doctrinal basis for his theories, Tukhachevsky issued a new set of orders entitled "Temporary Instructions on the Organization of Deep Battle" in 1933 and superseded them in 1936 with *Vremennyi Polevi Ustav*, or "Provisional Field Service Regulations (PU 36)." The basic premise of these "deep operations" was that positional warfare was to be replaced by a war of manoeuvre characterized by "annihilating strikes and swift tempo," based on deeply echeloned masses of infantry, tanks, and artillery, supported by aviation.[65] Thus the main tenets of operations were to be surprise, close control of combined arms, and manoeuvre, with the object being to "break the enemy's defence throughout its entire depth."[66]

As part of the educational process of the Red Army, Tukhachevsky published an article in *Red Star* on 6 May 1937 and sought to explain the key points of difference between the new and the old Field Service Regulations. This extract captures the essence of Tukhachevsky's philosophy on deep operations:

If the enemy keeps his flanks closed and it is not possible to envelop them, the enemy battle formation must be crushed by a deep strike from the front.

Technically, we use tanks for direct infantry support and for long range objectives.

Our technical equipment enables us to put pressure on the enemy not only directly on the line of the front, but also to break through his disposition and attack to the full depth of the battle formation ... [M]odern means of combat permit us to organize the attack in such a way that the enemy is simultaneously hit to the full depth, and his reserves can be contained on their approach to the threatened sector. We now have such means as aviation and tank assault parties. The Field Service Regulations say "the enemy should be immobilized to the full depth of his disposition, surrounded and destroyed" (Article 164). "Groups of DD (long range) tanks have the mission of breaking through to the rear of the main forces of defence, crushing reserves and headquarters, destroying the primary artillery grouping, and cutting off the routes of withdrawal for main enemy forces" (Article 181).

Thus, according to the requirements of the new Field Service Regulations, long-range tanks supported by artillery fire should pass through the enemy front and capture his routes of withdrawal. This is the main difference between the 1936 Field Service Regulations and the 1929 Regulations.[67]

Tukhachevsky had completed the "force development" cycle. His initial concepts, based on his Civil War experiences, were developed in response to the strategic posture adopted by the government. These ideas envisaged use of powerful mechanized forces, operating in conjunction with air support and parachute forces, striking deep at the nerve centres of the enemy, and they came to be known as "deep battle." To carry out this concept required the development and acquisition of specific equipment – most notably, a tank with long-range and adequate firepower and protection to meet what are termed in Canada as "capability deficiencies" and to achieve the operational parameters required by concept of deep battle. To provide the doctrinal component of "force development," he had introduced a set of temporary instructions, and following the validation of his theories at the Kiev manoeuvres he had produced new Field Service Regulations to implement these concepts throughout the Red Army.

Tukhachevsky was still in the process of revising PU-36 when the end came. One of the first, and certainly one of the most prominent, victims of Stalin's purge against the military, he was arrested on 26 May 1937, tried in camera on 11 June, found guilty, and sentenced to death the same day. The sentence was carried out that night, and his body was disposed of in a mass grave in a mine shaft.[68] His fall marked the start of the great purge that decimated the leadership of the Red Army.

The loss of Tukhachevsky and so many of the leadership cadre of the army was bad enough, but it did not satisfy Stalin. Tukhachevsky's theories were discredited; most of his theoretical writings were removed from circulation and destroyed, except for a few copies that survived in archives.[69] A new set of Field Service Regulations (PU-39) were introduced. Henceforth, the infantry would be the dominant arm, and all others would be subsidiary, with tanks now having the basic mission of supporting the infantry. Both of the special mechanized corps with their deep-strike mission were broken up. As a consequence, the Red Army entered its epic struggle for survival against Germany with outmoded operational and tactical concepts and bereft of leadership. It would take a long and bitter struggle to remake the Red Army in the mould of Tukhachevsky.

CONCLUSION

What then are we to make of Tukhachevsky as a theorist of war? Why should we study his influence and theories? Tukhachevsky represented the school of military thought that shaped the Red Army in the crucial period between the Civil War and the Second World War. His influence was also central in the development of the postwar Red Army and in the Russian army today.

To the Soviets, the key to defending the Soviet Union and to exporting world revolution was a mechanized army. Tukhachevsky was not only an enthusiastic supporter of this viewpoint, but also one of the principal architects in its development and the author of a specific operational concept – deep battle – in support of it. Deep battle has been described by one author as one of "the most advanced ideas ever attained in the history of military theory."[70] Unlike other "apostles of mobility" in the 1920s and 1930s, Tukhachevsky was uniquely placed to do more than espouse theories, for he could implement them. That his theories did not survive his demise should not diminish them, because, as Glantz notes, many of the Soviet commanders left after the purges were reluctant to embrace the concepts of Tukhachevsky, a "traitor" to the motherland. The trial of war against Germany gave momentum to the revival of his methods, and by the summer of 1942 the Soviets were using deep-battle techniques again.[71] One of the most successful practitioners was one of Tukhachevsky's disciples – Marshal Zhukov.[72] In future years, deep battle became the basis for the Operational Manoeuvre Group concept that posed such a dilemma for NATO in the 1980s. More recently, Naveh credits the formulation of the Allied coalition attack plan against Iraq in the Gulf War to the influence of Tukhachevsky.[73] While this assessment may be controversial, the basic premises of deep battle have proved remarkably enduring, especially within Russia, where they still form the basis for strategy at the operational level of war.

Tukhachevsky's premature death created one of the great "what ifs?" of the Second World War, and there has been a great deal of speculation as to how the Red Army would have fared in 1941, had it been commanded by the leadership that had been educated by Tukhachevsky in the concepts of deep battle, trained for five years under the aegis of the 1936 Field Service Regulations, and equipped with the incomparable T-34. As it was, the Red Army managed to hang on in the face of adversity and gained the time to relearn the methods of Tukhachevsky. When these operational concepts were introduced on the Eastern Front, the Germans had to adapt, and though they were able to develop counters to the limited thrusts that were launched initially, they ultimately failed as time passed and the Soviets were able to marshal more combat power. The Soviet way of warfare imposed respect on all who encountered it and, in the immediate postwar period, inspired a series of U.S. military monographs on various aspects of the war, including one entitled *German Defense Tactics against Russian Break Throughs.*[74]

We military professionals have all experienced upheavals in military organization resulting in doctrinal change, though less dramatic and violent than that experienced by Tukhachevsky and his Soviet contemporaries. Nevertheless, as a major influence on the development of the Soviet art of war and its operational concepts, which are still influential in modern strategic thought, the professional career and theories of Mikhail Tukhachevsky provide us with valuable insights in dealing with issues of force development and restructuring.

NOTES

1 Butson, *The Tsar's Lieutenant,* 239.
2 Glantz, *August Storm,* 71.

3 Ibid., 73.

4 Keegan, *The Battle for History*, 71.

5 See Coox, "The Effectiveness of the Japanese Military Establishment in the Second World War," 19; and Glantz, *August Storm*, 28–32.

6 Glantz, *August Storm*, 155.

7 Ibid., xiv.

8 Ibid., 157.

9 There are various spellings of Tukhachevsky's name; Tukhachevski, Tukhachevskiy, and Tukhachevskii are used as well. I have adopted the most prevalent.

10 Glantz and House, *When Titans Clashed*, 9.

11 Fuller, *The Decisive Battles of the Western World*, Vol. III, 339.

12 Butson, *The Tsar's Lieutenant*, 10–11. The Semyonovsky were the second most senior regiment in the imperial army, occupying the same relative status as the Coldstream Guards in Britain.

13 Ibid.

14 Ibid., 18.

15 Ibid., 20.

16 Ibid., 23.

17 Ibid., 27–8.

18 Ibid., 49–50.

19 Ibid., 66.

20 Ibid., 73.

21 Ibid., 78.

22 Ibid., 82–4.

23 Ziemke, "Strategy for Class War," 505–6.

24 Fuller, *Decisive Battles*, Vol. III, 335.

25 Butson, *The Tsar's Lieutenant*, 86.

26 For a full account of the Battle for Warsaw, one of the "Decisive Battles of History," see Fuller, *Decisive Battles*, vol. III, chap. 9.

27 Quoted in Butson, *The Tsar's Lieutenant*, 121.

28 Ibid., 131.

29 Tukhachevsky also suppressed the peasant uprising in the Tambov area, but this was not as significant as the Kronstadt rebellion.

30 Savkin, *The Basic Principles*, 40–1.

31 Bellamy, *The Evolution of Modern Land Warfare*, 156.

32 Savkin, *The Basic Principles*, 40.

33 See Duffy, *Russia's Military Way to the West*, for a detailed description of the evolution of the Russian military in the eighteenth century.

34 Ibid., 30.

35 Ibid., 124.

36 Savkin, *The Basic Principles*, 28–36.

37 Ibid., 31.

38 Donnelly, *Red Banner*, 102.

39 Ziemke, "Strategy for Class War," 507.

40 Kolkowicz, *The Soviet Military and the Communist Party*, 37–8.

41 Ibid, 39.

42 Malcolm Mackintosh, "The Red Army," 53.

43 Ibid.

44 See Deutscher, *The Prophet Armed*, 477–85, for an explanatory note that expands on Trotsky's military views.

45 Gareev, *M.V. Frunze*, 157.

46 J.M. Mackintosh, "The Development of Soviet Military Doctrine," 251.

47 Scott and Scott, *Soviet Military Doctrine*, 6–7.

48 Butson, *The Tsar's Lieutenant*, 160.

49 Donnelly, *Red Banner*, 72.

50 Ibid., 106. A detailed chart showing the "Theoretical Framework for the Study of War" is found on page 103.

51 Strachan, *European Armies and the Conduct of War*, 158.

52 Glantz, *The Soviet Airborne Experience*.

53 Ziemke, "Strategy for Class War," 513–15.

54 The major steps in this process are concept development, including identification of capability deficiencies; validation; and doctrine promulgation.

55 Canada, Department of National Defence, *Defence Development Plan 1993*, 1–2.

56 Tukhachevsky always appreciated the requirement for combined arms formations as opposed to an all-tank force, as espoused by some Western theorists, especially J.F.C. Fuller.

57 Malcolm Mackintosh, *Juggernaut*, 68–71.

58 Simpkin, *Deep Battle*, 32–3.

59 Bellamy, "Antecedents of the Modern Soviet Operational Manoeuvre Group," 50–59.

60 Scott and Scott, *Soviet Military Doctrine*, 13.

61 Milsom, *AFV Weapons Profile 37: Russian BT Series*, 2.

62 Ibid., 15. Comparative data for other armoured vehicles of this period can be found in White's *Tanks and Other Armoured Fighting Vehicles of World War II*, 155–6.

63 These "corps" were roughly equivalent in size to the first German Panzer divisions but antedated them by three years.

64 Simpkin, *Deep Battle*, 40.

65 Scott and Scott, *The Soviet Art of War*, 19–20.

66 Ziemke, "Strategy for Class War," 517.

67 Scott and Scott, *The Soviet Art of War*, 58–9.

68 See Alexandrov, *The Tukhachevsky Affair*, for a dramatized account of the circumstances surrounding his fall.

69 Glantz and House, *When Titans Clashed*, 12.

70 Naveh, "Tukhachevsky," 270.

71 Glantz, "Soviet Operational Formation for Battle," 5–7.

72 Butson, *The Tsar's Lieutenant*, 235.

73 Naveh, "Tukhachevsky," 270.

74 These monographs are still available from the u.s. Government Printing Office. They were written by former German senior officers to provide the u.s. army with an understanding of Soviet tactics in the early days of the Cold War. Originally classified and intended for a military audience, the entire series was reprinted as a special series in 1979 by Garland Publishing as *World War II German Military Studies.* The particular volume mentioned was recommended reading when I attended Canadian Forces Land Forces Command and Staff College.

The Problem of Army Renewal: Seeckt and the *Reichswehr*

MAJOR ROBERT POIRIER

All three stages [of action] are governed by the will. The will is rooted in character, and for the man of action character is of more critical importance than intellect. Intellect without will is worthless, will without intellect is dangerous.[1]

Hans von Seeckt

The German army of early 1919 was a shambles, broken in battle and disintegrating. Twenty-two years later the *Wehrmacht* sat astride much of Europe, having demonstrated its superior leadership, training, tactics, and operational art. That the rebirth of this army occurred during a time of economic and social upheaval in a Germany under the limitations of the Versailles Treaty was a stunning demonstration of military reform in turbulent times. The basis of the victorious *Wehrmacht* of 1941 lay in the new *Reichswehr* that emerged in 1919 and existed until 1933.

The parallels between the German problem in 1919 and the current Canadian military problem are instructive. Both forces face an apathetic electorate whose interests lie with internal economic matters, both have just emerged from a war (the First World War and the Cold War) whose lessons must be learned, both lack the resources to accomplish all they wish, and both face internal lack of faith in the military leadership. It would be dangerous to suggest that the *Reichswehr*'s example be followed exactly. It would be useful, however, to examine its experience in its formative years, to see how its chief, General Hans von Seeckt, dealt with the challenge of building a small yet modern and effective army.

PRELUDE

The *Reichswehr* had its roots in the *Kaiserheer* of Moltke and Schlieffen, an army with a history of success and of excellence. To be a commissioned or a non-commissioned officer signified a prestigious career in Wilhelmine Germany, and such officers were carefully selected and well educated and enjoyed considerable social standing. The army followed a sensible doctrine, which allowed for intellectual flexibility. Moltke's dictum – "in war as in art there is no general rule"[2] – was reflected in the 1869 version of the "Regulations for the Higher Troop Commanders," which stressed the use of combinations of manoeuvre and fire and the desirability of encirclement yet were not too prescriptive.[3] At the top sat the Great General Staff, composed of officers selected in their late twenties for their character and intellect and then carefully educated to become collectively the "brains of the army." The German army that entered the First World War in 1914 was a good one.

The quality of the *Kaiserheer* was recognized by the Allies, and a portion of the Versailles Treaty was devoted to ensuring that the German army could never again menace its neighbours. First, army strength was reduced to 100,000 of all ranks, to ensure that Germany's professional army remained small. Second, the army was to be one of long service – officers to serve twenty-five years, other ranks twelve years – to prevent the building up of a large reserve of trained soldiers. Third, heavy artillery, tanks, aircraft, poison gas, and certain other armaments were prohibited or limited, and arms imports forbidden. Fourth, the Great General Staff was ordered disbanded.

In addition to these restrictions, the army and German society faced severe economic problems. The demands for reparations, the impact of the Allied blockade on Germany in the war, and the postwar demobilization of war industry led to unemployment and hyperinflation.[4] This economic hardship spawned serious political upheaval. Most important among the political changes was Germany's sudden transformation from a monarchy, with the kaiser as commander-in-chief of the armed forces, to a republic, with the consequent changes of ruling elite. The army's traditional supporters were monarchist and conservative, and the *Reichswehr*, a republican creation, lost this traditional backing. At the same time, it was viewed with intense suspicion and even hostility by the newly empowered socialist republicans.[5]

The *Reichswehr* was born into a Germany that bordered on anarchy, and the army was of necessity involved in the sometimes-bloody political struggle. The army as an institution effectively fell apart in December 1918, with most of the rank-and-file soldiers deserting as army formations returned to Germany.[6] However, the demands made by revolution and unrest on the eastern borders and beyond for combat-ready units led to the creation of numerous semi-official *Freikorps* (armed groups of ex-soldiers), battling communists and others both inside and outside the country. Officers moved freely back and forth between the *Reichswehr* and the *Freikorps* for some time, and elements of the army were involved in some of the political unrest, most notably a coup attempt in 1920. All in all, the *Reichswehr* was created in a climate of fear, confusion, and conflicting loyalties, and it would take someone with a strong personality to master it.

VON SEECKT

The needed strength was provided by General Hans von Seeckt. Field Marshal Erich von Manstein wrote of Seeckt that "everyone had sensed the inner fire that inspired him and the iron will which made him a leader of men." [7] He had the drive and intellect to bring order out of the chaos in which he began his work. Like most Germans, he wanted to see his country regain its status as a great power, and he was prepared to violate the Versailles Treaty to help accomplish this aim.

Seeckt was sixty-four years old in 1920, when he was appointed chief of Army Command. He had had a "good war," and he was respected within the army. He had been a chief of staff on the Eastern Front, first of a corps, then an army, then two army groups in succession, and finally of the Turkish army. Following Versailles, he became chairman of the Commission for the Peacetime Army Organization, head of the *Truppenamt* (the illegal successor to the Great General Staff), and finally, in March 1920, chief of Army Command. He was well travelled, spoke several languages, and, unusually, held the *Abitur* (high school matriculation) from a civilian *Gymnasium* rather than from a cadet school. [8]

Despite being the son of a Prussian general, he was an acceptable army chief to the republican politicians of the day, because as a strict constitutionalist he supported the Weimar Republic, and he was politically astute. [9] One possible reason he preferred a small professional army was the relative ease of ensuring the political neutrality of such a force compared to a larger one. However, he felt a deep attachment to the monarchy (which would lead to the ending of his career in 1926), and he was personally "cold," "irritable," and "icy"; his nickname was "The Sphinx." [10] Overall, he possessed an overpowering personality, and "Seeckt came to the Reichswehr convinced that the new Army must reflect traditional Prussian virtues and learn from the experiences of modern warfare." [11] He was open-minded in matters of detail, and his preferred focus was at the operational level of war. [12] However, he was not a theorist, and he expressed his hostility to military theorists with these words: "There are three things against which the human mind struggles in vain: stupidity, bureaucracy and catchwords." [13]

Seeckt did believe in an empirical approach to army restructuring, but it was based on wide practical experience, especially on his plans for the successful mobile campaigns fought on the Eastern Front. He abhorred the 1914–18 stalemate on the Western Front, and he "doubted that giant armies of the traditional type could ever be manoeuvred in accordance with a strategy that sought a rapid decision" [14] and believed in a small, long-service, professionally trained, mobile army. [15]

A small, professional army, as he saw it, must meet four demands. First, it must be highly mobile, through the use of motor transport. Second, it must be effectively armed, with the most modern weapons available. Third, it must have a motorized logistics system capable of continuously replacing men and materiel at the front. Fourth, it must be fully employable without use of reserves, so that it could seize the operational initiative without the usual pause for mobilization.[16] The reserves, in his concept, were only slightly trained and equipped to conduct home defence and perhaps provide a few reinforcements to the field army.[17]

Seeckt saw his army as comprised of two fundamental aspects: technology and man. He believed that every form of modern technology must be employed, but to do this, he needed educated officers, each with both a technical and a general education. The value of the former is obvious in a modern army, while the latter both developed the intellect and ensured that the officer did not lose touch with society.[18] Putting together the new army was largely a function of training, and Seeckt was above all else a trainer. He delegated almost all responsibilities to his very capable staff except that for training, which he personally supervised.[19]

Despite his forward-looking views in many areas, he retained a rather odd affection for horsed cavalry to the end of his days and has been accused of being rather blinkered in his outlook.[20] In addition, Seeckt never fully appreciated the power of massed armour operating in conjunction with other arms and with air power. His major weakness turned out to be his monarchist views. In early fall 1926, he allowed a member of the Hohenzollern (Prussian royal) family to attend the annual army manoeuvres in uniform. This was specifically forbidden by Versailles and also clashed with an upsurge of republican feeling in Germany at the time.[21] Seeckt was forced to resign, and he died in 1938. From April 1920 to October 1926, then, this was the man who built and trained the *Reichswehr*. This essay examines key aspects of the army that he built.

LEARNING THE LESSONS OF THE WAR

There were five fundamental problems facing the *Reichswehr*'s leadership following Versailles. The army had to be reconstructed, the continuing effectiveness of the General Staff ensured, the government supported, the eastern border defended, and the lessons learned in the war evaluated. All issues were tackled successfully by 1926. From the point of view of forming an effective army, the last problem – learning the lessons – was the most critical.

In Germany it was widely held that leftists and defeatists had brought on the 1918 defeat by stabbing the army in the back. The army itself, with typical General Staff objectivity, did not institutionally subscribe to the "stab-in-the-back" theory. The General Staff began to deal with the lessons of the war even before the war ended, and indeed had arrived at a broad consensus on some issues by November 1918, including the value of the attack coupled with a clear operational-level goal, and the bankruptcy of an attritionalist strategy.[22]

Seeckt initiated a formal study of the lessons of the war in November 1919, just one week after taking charge of the *Truppenamt*. A total of eighty-six separate army committees were eventually formed to examine various aspects of the war, subsequently joined by further air service studies. The studies at their peak involved over five hundred officers, out of four thousand in the army, during a time of political, economic, and organizational turbulence. Each committee was charged with examining its particular subject area in relation to four fundamental questions. What new situations arose in the war that had not been foreseen before the war? How effective was pre-war doctrine? What new doctrine emerged during the war? Which of the newly identified problems has not yet been solved?[23]

So many industrious officers produced considerable material, and some of their observations remain valid today. Their findings included the following major conclusions. Technology had to be better understood than it had been in the First World War by the German army. There had been few technically trained officers in the *Kaiserheer*, and therefore technical education became an important part of *Reichswehr* officer and General Staff training.[24] Tactical lessons of import included the value of general directives (*Auftragstaktik*; see below) to help overcome friction on the battlefield; use of the General Staff as the conduit for ideas from the front to be turned into doctrine, equipment, and training; the value of all-arms cooperation; the value of the "storm trooper" tactics of infiltration and attacking objectives in the enemy's operational rear while disregarding flanks; and finally the potential of the tank.[25] The need for better logistics support in the advance was also understood.[26] And the air force was seen as most valuable in what would now be called the roles of close air support and battlefield air interdiction. Organizationally, these lessons translated into the adoption of motorization as far as possible, both for logistics troops and to transport the combat arms; adoption of smaller divisions with three manoeuvre formations rather than the previous four; emphasis on all-arms cooperation; and centralized control of the air forces to allow concentration at the decisive point.[27]

Seeckt himself saw the lessons of the war as falling into five major areas. The provisions for the mobilization of the economy and of manpower were inadequate. The *levée en masse* "has outlived its usefulness." Man is still pre-eminent. The new technology requires better training and a higher quality of soldier. Air power is an entirely new dimension of war.[28]

Now the study results had to be translated into action. Seeckt initiated, and wrote part of, Army Regulation 487 – "Leadership and Battle with Combined Arms" – in two parts, in 1921 and 1923. Based on all arms, services, and weapons, not just the ones allowed by Versailles, these two books became the basis for *Reichswehr* training until the 1930s, when they were amended into the famous Army Regulation 300 – *Truppenführung* – which remained in use until 1945.[29]

MEN

The basis of the *Reichswehr* was the soldiery, and more effort and staff time were expended on recruiting and training than on other aspects of the army. This was the result partly of the German humanist tradition and partly of Seeckt's decision to form a *Führerheer* – a leader's army – in which selection and training aimed to ensure that a soldier of any given rank was fit to do a job one or two ranks higher.[30]

Soldiers were recruited by sub-unit commanders, each of whom was assigned a geographical recruiting area and carefully checked character by means of inquiries made of police, teachers, and local officials. Norms were established by the General Staff, but the final decision to enlist a given soldier was left to the sub-unit commander. This officer also decided on the soldier's occupation – rifleman, gunner, and so on.[31] While getting the desired standard of new soldiers was obviously important, considerable effort was also spent to ensure acceptable living standards and that the men were prepared for civilian life after discharge. Officer-soldier relations were relaxed relative to the Imperial Army's standard, and by 1928 (a time of economic prosperity in Germany) there were fifteen applicants for each noncommissioned vacancy.[32]

Officer selection was even more rigorous, and with only 250 officers per year being brought into the *Reichswehr* extremely high standards were imposed. Seeckt directed that officers be selected based on character, according to the old pre-war criteria, and he kept striving for ever higher standards.[33] However, character seems not to have been explicitly defined but was rather left to the opinion of the rating officer. And even today, character is still a primary means of assessing officers in today's *Bundeswehr*.[34] Candidates had to be approved for enrolment by their prospective regimental commander, who looked for "character and general suitability," such as being graduates of a sports or youth movement.[35] Applicants were preferred if they possessed the *Abitur*, or high-school matriculation, a relatively high level of academic achievement at that time. To Seeckt, the "*Abitur* was a mark of social maturity as well as educational accomplishment," and it was a sound basis on which to add later technical training.[36]

The *Reichswehr* was quite ruthless in its drive for quality. At first, many of its young officers were those who had received battlefield commissions during the war. However, as a group, they were considered to lack the intellect to excel in the army; therefore, they were subjected to several rigorous screenings and made to achieve the *Abitur* on their own time. Many who did not measure up were released before their term of service ended.[37] Officer quality remained a concern of the German army through to 1945. A compelling case has been made that this factor, above all others, ensured the cohesion and the frequent tactical successes of the *Wehrmacht* right up to the end by guaranteeing that officers remained competent and therefore were obeyed even in times of great adversity.[38] The German army allowed the ratio of officers to other ranks to fall from a low of 4 per cent in the *Reichswehr* to an incredible 2½ per cent during the expansion prior to the Second World War and did not change the length of training from the existing four years.[39] Such a small officer cadre was made possible through Seeckt's foresight in forming leaders, including NCOs, who could be promoted into higher leadership positions.

Once enrolled, the officer could not breathe easy, for promotion was hard to come by, and the *Reichswehr* had what would seem to us a vicious policy of releasing officers for below-average performance. Quotas were set for annual separations – high under von Seeckt and even higher under his successors.[40] In addition to performance, character was always assessed and was the first element cited in evaluations.[41] Pay was quite low, though this must be examined against the high jobless rate in Germany at the time. All in all, the system discouraged place seekers, while it encouraged bright officers who liked to soldier and who were ambitious, but not excessively so, for such officers would be terminated by their character assessments.

As mentioned above, Seeckt placed the highest stress on training. He spent about one-third of his time visiting units and issued annual "Observations," which heavily favoured training matters. He emphasized such items as combined arms cooperation, mobility, speed of reaction and thought, shortness of the orders process, and simplicity.[42] These things may seem self-evident, though perhaps more in the breach than in the observance, but Seeckt's training of his generals was new. He recognized that the pre-war reliance on the staff officers to provide the doctrinal unity of operations was weakened by the tendency of the generals to operate in isolation. Therefore he used annual "leader's staff rides," beginning in 1921, to ensure doctrinal commonality among the army's commanders and to impose a uniform pattern of thought "at all levels and ranks."[43]

The training of soldiers and NCOs was straightforward and based on basic infantry skills, on sport, and on tactical training in the field. Typically, four days per week would be spent out of garrison in a training area. NCOs were "taught to be independent-thinking and acting men," and they were customarily trained as platoon commanders, as most *Reichswehr* platoon commanders were NCOs.[44] Promotion was by merit, not seniority, and relations with officers were good. A huge proportion of the army was of NCO rank, such that in 1926 19,000 were senior NCOs and another 19,000 corporals. In the 1930s the demand for officers from a rapidly expanding army was met mostly by promotion of NCOs into company-grade officer positions.

Officer training was seen by Seeckt as taking priority over all other train-ing goals.[45] It took four years, alternating unit service as a soldier and NCO and time at arms schools and focused on leadership and combined arms war-fare. The attrition rate on such training, even after the rigorous selection pro-cedures applied to officer aspirants, was 50 per cent.[46] Once an officer was commissioned, training did not stop. In addition to training the troops, offic-ers were expected to take part in a heavy officer-training schedule, which included evening lectures, staff rides, and study for the compulsory staff-selection exams.

Individual training within units was generally accomplished between November and March each year. The period between April and October was devoted to collective training, beginning at regimental level in 1923 and rising to corps level by 1926. The largest manoeuvres were each September, after harvest. Seeckt aimed to eliminate the trench mentality of the previous war, and by 1926 he was satisfied that he had been success-ful.[47] His emphasis throughout in the design of collective training was on mobility coupled with firepower, realism, and mastery of technology.[48] All existing weapons systems were brought into play, even those (such as tanks and aircraft) forbidden by Versailles. These prohibited systems were repre-sented either by the umpires or by mock-ups. Aircraft could not be easily simulated, but air officers were present at all levels to ensure that non air-minded actions were noted and punished by the umpires.[49] Above all else, the *Reichswehr* stressed the leader's character and will to succeed in execut-ing collective training. In the words of Seeckt, "it is the man who decides ... the battle," and he fought hard against the "mental formalism" of the First World War in favour of simple tactical doctrines, quickly executed.[50] The major disadvantage of such an aggressive collective training schedule was the chronic tension between unit training and individual training courses for officers and NCOs, which led to even more responsibility being given to NCOs.[51]

Individual training was provided in the branch schools, of which there were four – infantry, cavalry, artillery, pioneers. These schools provided all officer training, especially the infantry school, which gave all officers, regardless of branch, one year's training. Unlike many other armies, the *Reichswehr* conferred a high status on instructors, and these officers tended to be the best in the army. Augmenting the schools were three illegal training installations, for armoured, aerial, and chemical warfare, in the Soviet Union.

The major weakness in the entire training process was the lack of techni-cal awareness at many levels – rather surprising, given Seeckt's declared pri-orities. While modern technology was readily introduced into service or at least into the illegal centres in Russia, and while technically trained officers such as Guderian prospered, the individual officer was not really technically minded.[52]

At the heart of the *Reichswehr* lay the (prohibited) General Staff. The *Reichswehr* from its inception included the *Truppenamt* (Troop Office), which was a camouflaged Great General Staff,[53] and the *Truppenamt* was the heart of the decision-making machinery of the army. Some functions previously carried out by the General Staff were farmed out to other government departments – for example, the cartography section, the historical section, and parts of the intelligence function. However, supervision of these functions was still provided by the *Truppenamt*.

Prior to the First World War, approximately 160 officers per year were selected to attend the *Kriegsakademie* at Potsdam for a three-year course, which stressed history, tactics, logistics, and operations.[54] During the war, the *Kriegsakademie* was closed, and after some experimentation a combination of apprenticeships and a nine-month course at Sedan was used to produce staff officers.[55] This system was acceptable for the war but was widely seen as too incoherent for peace and a common doctrine. The conduct of general staff training was ripe for redesign when Seeckt became chief of the Army Command; however, the prohibitions of Versailles meant that staff training had to be hidden.

All young officers had to take an annual examination conducted at the military-district level, requiring approximately five months of intense individual preparation, on their own time. The examination was based on "Leadership and Battle with Combined Arms" manual and heavily stressed applied tactics, in addition to branch knowledge. The written examination, a physical ordeal in itself because of its eight-hour length and vast range of content, was accompanied by an oral examination; a typical pass rate was thirty-seven of 270 (about 14 per cent).[56] The best of the graduates of this examination were selected, after a review of their files, for staff training. They were usually from twenty-five to thirty years of age, with three to nine years of commissioned service, and their branch of service was immaterial.[57] Favouritism was evidently quite limited in the selection process.[58] Finally, ten officers were accepted into the General Staff – 4 per cent of those who wrote the district exam.[59]

The selected officers were now trained for between four and five and one-half years to become an officer who "was primarily expected to display a command of tactical operations involving division-level forces."[60] The training involved two years of academic training at the district headquarters, followed by a year more in Berlin, and lastly one to two years of practical experience as a troop staff officer. Officers were released at any stage of this training if they failed to meet the standard. The thrust of the training was to produce a tactically proficient officer, who could think independently, but within the broad limits of approved doctrine. This sort of approach – *Auftragstaktik*, or mission command – is currently in vogue in Western armies. Officers faced with a problem were to react in the prescribed sequence of estimate, selection of option, production of plan, and action. Emphasis was on action, and, as a consequence, character was always heavily emphasized in assessments.[61] To prevent the absence of orders being an excuse for inaction, stress was laid on the need to understand the concept of operations of the commander two levels up, so that action could proceed in accordance with this concept despite a lack of orders. Most of the course focused on tactical studies and the estimate process, but other subjects taught included military history, the study of specific branches, logistics (as a component of tactics), and some technology. All of this was brought together by frequent command post and map exercises, war games, and staff rides.

General staff training did not stress technology, but technically proficient officers were required for the modernization of the army. This requirement was met by a weapons staff composed of specially selected officers who obtained engineering schooling at civilian institutions and then worked alternately in the Weapons Office and with troops.[62]

Because Seeckt was actively involved in selection and training, he frequently took the opportunity to discourage conformity of thought and of method in the process. For example, some examination questions, to be passed, required the officer to disobey orders.[63] Seeckt also ensured that staff officers did their command tours with line units, in reaction to the criticisms made during the war that staff officers did not face the same dangers as the *frontschwein*.[64]

The highly structured German training of staff officers has been criticized for two principal reasons. First, it is alleged that it engendered conformist thinking and a lack of originality. However, the standard of German generalship and staff work, compared to the Allied equivalents, would suggest that this is a difficult criticism to substantiate. Second, and more telling, the focus on the operational level of war led to officers with little strategic or grand strategic vision.[65]

Overall, the German General Staff provided a small, highly motivated cadre to direct the rest of the central staff and the formations. Its worth was shown during the period 1933–40, when the *Wehrmacht* increased fifty-fold while simultaneously perfecting its mobile war doctrine. During the Second World War most General Staff alumni, as troop staff or commanders, performed excellently at the operational level.

ORGANIZATION

The *Reichswehr* was organized in accordance with the Armed Forces Law of March 1919. At the top stood the president, as commander-in-chief. Parliamentary control was exercised through the Ministry of Defence, which supervised the army and navy. Under the minister stood the chief of Army Command, to whom all elements of the army were answerable.[66] Von Seeckt totally dominated the defence minister through force of personality and, during his tenure, had his own way with "his" army, with little constructive involvement by the politicians of the Weimar Republic. [67]

Seeckt's army of seven infantry and three cavalry divisions was organized into two group commands, and each infantry division was also assigned a geographical district for recruiting and other administrative purposes. The army headquarters was subdivided into a series of "offices" – Personnel Office, Administration Office (for the civilian side of the ministry), Weapons Office, and, first among equals, the *Truppenamt*. All major decisions were made by or through the *Truppenamt*. [68] It in turn was divided into four sections: T1 – Army Section, responsible for operations and plans; T2 – Organization, which also included the air staff; T3 – Statistics (Intelligence); and T4 – Training. Later, section T7 – Transportation – was also formed. The *Truppenamt* secured close control over the weapons directorates by placing a small detachment from the T1 section into each of the weapons directorates, to approve specifications and contracts and to ensure that weapons development matched official doctrine. [69] The total strength of the General Staff in 1926 was about two hundred, which included those General Staff officers who were serving with formations.

When the first plan to expand the army illegally was drawn up in 1926, the *Reichswehr* organization was used to form the mobilization base, as it was to do for the future *Wehrmacht*, and secret budgets were used to accumulate mobilization stocks of equipment. [70] By 1930, the expansion plan had been refined to accommodate a twenty-one–division army, later increased to thirty-six divisions once Hitler took power in 1933. At that time, two differently equipped and organized armies were created within the *Wehrmacht*, roughly consistently with Seeckt's plans. Most of the *Reichswehr* was used as the core of a relatively small, mechanized army, with the remainder forming the framework of a mass, infantry army. [71] The *Reichswehr* expanded with little help from reserve forces because of the limitations of Versailles, and also because of Seeckt's desire for a long-service army.

METHOD

The doctrine of the *Reichswehr* sprang from the lessons learned discussed above. The most notable parts of that doctrine concerned armoured warfare and its integration with air power. The development of armoured warfare must be seen as a reaction to the perceived technical failures of the First World War. These were seen as failure to stop the French mobilization, failure to prevent the redeployment of French troops, and failure to recognize the limits that nature placed upon foot-borne and horse-drawn armies. [72] This led, in Army Regulation 487, to an emphasis on the attack supported by combined arms theory – using each weapon to offset the weakness of another, with the infantry as the focus of all effort.[73] Seeckt preferred the strategy of annihilation, as opposed to the strategy of attrition, but he acknowledged that under some circumstances attrition was all that was left to the weaker combatant.[74] Above all, he emphasized movement. His training orders were headed with the slogan "Operation Is Movement." There was a continuing insistence that commanders command from well forward to ensure that they understood the situation and could react quickly to changes.[75]

While most professional officers would agree with this doctrine, where the Germans differed was in their realization that the outcome of battle rested on the individual fighting man, especially the junior leader. Seeckt sought strength at all levels of leadership,[76] and Army Regulation 487 provided for the tactical independence of junior leaders, on the principle that the man on the spot knew best what was required. As later refined by the *Truppenführung,* the role of the junior leader was expressed in six rules of soldiering: develop individual initiative and responsibility; never follow orders blindly; develop proper discipline; develop cohesive primary fighting groups (sections, platoons); develop an unremitting attack philosophy; and the "golden rule": it is better to do something wrong but decisively than to wait for orders that may never arrive.[77] Coupled with the valuing of junior leaders was the emphasis on small staffs. German formation staffs were approximately 40 per cent of the size of the equivalent American army formations and therefore had no option but to delegate authority and responsibility.[78]

The man may have been the backbone of the *Reichswehr,* but machines were needed to fight. Two machines in particular emerged from the First World War that were seen as essential to German doctrine – tanks and aircraft. In the German case, equipment followed doctrine, though there was considerable feedback from the Weapons Office into doctrine.[79] For example, Guderian describes in detail how the decision to use tanks in mass and in depth led to demands being placed on weapons staff to provide the communications and optical equipment that would make the envisaged tank doctrine practicable.[80]

From the beginning, Seeckt saw the tank as something special, though he never fully grasped the power of mechanized warfare. He saw tanks developing into a "special arm" additional to the three conventional combat arms of artillery, infantry, and cavalry.[81] But he was unsure as to how to proceed exactly, and experimentation marked his term of command. Early experiments in motorized transportation led to work with an all-arms grouping based on tanks, and by 1927 large field-training exercises included "tanks" (simulated ones, due to Versailles). Also in 1927, the chief of section T1 (operations) of the *Truppenamt* would write: "Armoured, quickly moving tanks most probably will become the operationally decisive offensive weapon. From an operational perspective this weapon will be most effective, if concentrated in independent units like tank brigades."[82] Two years later Guderian formed an armoured battalion from a supply battalion![83]

The result of Guderian and others' experimentation was a synthesis of the continental mass-army model and von Seeckt's "depreciation of mass." It developed into an army within an army – a small, well-equipped armoured force within a largely horse-drawn infantry army. Within the mechanized army, the Germans developed the storm trooper tactics of the First World War into mechanized all-arms doctrine. One writer has gone so far as to state that German successes in the Second World War "rested almost entirely on the exploitation doctrine of 1918 infantry tactics."[84] Tanks were to work in conjunction with motorized infantry, field artillery, air defence artillery, and engineers on the ground, intimately supported by the air force and pulled together by very sophisticated communications equipment. The aim of this force was less to win the breakthrough battle than to exploit a breakthrough won by infantry divisions.[85]

The main equipment itself – the tanks – had to be developed in secret because of Versailles, as did aircraft and chemical warfare materiel. To allow for this, von Seeckt, from early in his command, pushed for an arrangement with the Soviet Union, trading training assistance to the Red Army for secluded training areas in the USSR. Prototype tanks were built secretly in Germany, smuggled to the USSR, and tried there. In addition, young officers took the last two-thirds of a year-long armour course there. The significance of the training in the Soviet Union should not be exaggerated, but it did help to further German armoured warfare doctrine and equipment.[86]

It is possible that Seeckt did not approach the problems of armoured warfare with his wonted vigour because he liked the horse too much. His initial thoughts on motorization involved motorizing the supporting arms of the cavalry – artillery, armoured cars, some infantry, and so on.[87] However, stories about gallant young officers (notably Guderian) fighting entrenched conservative generals are much exaggerated. Resistance was expressed in terms of the speed of change and development, not in terms of opposing change.[88]

Seeckt recognized the revolutionary nature of air warfare, probably with more comprehension than he did armoured warfare. He retained in the nascent *Reichswehr* 180 air service officers – out of 4,000 officers total – and advocated the air force as a third service. Prohibited from actually doing this by Versailles, he formed a shadow air force. *Truppenamt* directorate T2 was responsible for air matters, and each military district got an air officer on staff. Air input was required for all exercises and was extensively umpired. As a mark of how seriously Seeckt took air matters, he devoted approximately 10 per cent of his annual "Remarks" to air-related matters, particularly air training. An air-training facility was established in the Soviet Union, attended by up to thirty officers a year.[89] Doctrine for the air arm centred on support to ground forces, preceded by obtaining air superiority. Unlike Britain and the United States, Germany would use bombers for what is now called battlefield air interdiction. To this end, the Germans concentrated on building fighters first, followed by ground attack aircraft, and finally medium bombers.[90]

A harsh criticism of the *Reichswehr*'s isolation from political realities has been made by Michael Geyer.[91] He suggested that, following failure of the Schlieffen Plan in 1914, there were continuing efforts "to rebuild a semblance of ... a coherent military practice that would unify strategy, operations, and tactics" and that these efforts resulted in tension between those seeking unifying principles (management-of-arms approach) and those aiming at a new practice of war (ideological approach).[92] This tension led to a fusion of ideologues and technocrats that propelled Germany into the Second World War and catastrophe. Seeckt's place in this debate, according to Geyer, was on the side of the technocrats, in that he favoured a "professional approach" to remaking the German army.[93] Seeckt was interested in the army as an instrument complete in and of itself, and thus he "moved to the very fringes of domestic and international affairs in order to reconstitute the autonomy and unequivocal identity of the army."[94] This approach was consistent with von Schlieffen's concept of an army that would be allowed to fight a battle of annihilation on its own, without political interference, in exchange for a quick, decisive end to military action. This concept in turn led to German focus on the operational art, with a view to obtaining quick decisions in war in return for military control over the waging of war.[95]

This separation of the soldiers (the practitioners of war) from the politicians (the strategists) led, in the Second World War, to many German operational successes with no lasting strategic impact, and, according to Geyer, the German army was remiss in not taking more account of national strategy. Geyer's critique is in line with the Western notion that strategy is the purview of the government, especially the politicians. None the less, Geyer succeeds in illustrating the dangers of an army that tries to exist independent of the political structure, and he clearly shows that technical brilliance by itself is a hollow shell.

THE RESULTS

The full impact of Seeckt's methods on the *Reichswehr* becomes visible through the lens of the will to succeed, in that training, organization, and doctrine were all means to an end – victory. The "Foreword" to the 1921 Army Regulation 487 stated: "The leader's will to victory must be communicated to the lowest-ranking soldier,"[96] and this attitude was transferred into Hitler's *Wehrmacht*.

There were a number of faults, however, in the *Wehrmacht*; the rearmament effort was economically incoherent and largely ignored German economic weaknesses.[97] The *Luftwaffe* was not capable of any level of strategic operation, as shown by its lack of success in the Battle of Britain. For some, the non-political focus of Seeckt's army allowed the excesses of Hitler, because the General Staff declined to intervene in the political life of the country, even though many of its members found Hitler repugnant.[98] A strong criticism of von Seeckt's army is that the military view of the General Staff was too narrow. In 1934, the Chief of General Staff narrowed the focus of the *Kriegsakademie* to the tactical (division and corps) from the operational level of strategy, leading to the neglect of subjects such as logistics and intelligence.[99] As Albert Seaton wrote, "the activities of the army general staff rarely rose above the level of grand tactics, so many of its members being content to '*operien*' as if in a vacuum, with strategic appreciations being kept within a radius of 200 miles and always halting at the salt water's edge."[100] This led to a "bankruptcy of professional strategy," where operational successes led nowhere.[101] The most telling criticism is that of a German scholar, who wrote: "German feelings of superiority in will and leadership were responsible for consistently shortsighted evaluations of the capabilities of potential adversaries."[102]

None the less, the machine worked reasonably well. In 1940, a slashing seven-week offensive destroyed the French army; the lessons of the First World War had clearly been learned. Later, the *Wehrmacht* went on to further tactical and operational successes in North Africa, in the Balkans, and especially in Russia. Towards the end of the war, the German army's leadership and doctrine were sufficient to delay the destruction of Hitler's state, despite overwhelming Allied superiority in materiel. General Frido von Senger und Etterlin, a successful commander at the operational level, was to write of the *Reichswehr*, "I was struck by the foresight of General von Seeckt ... Seeckt visualized the future of war as taking the form of battle between small professional armies ... Compared to them, the people's army, mass-organized as infantry, would play a subordinate role. The course of this war proved Seeckt to be quite right."[103]

But are Seeckt's experiences of any use to the Canadian Forces of today? I believe that there are a number of lessons that can be drawn from the *Reichswehr*'s experience to guide Canadian planners now. First, there must be a close integration of political authorities with military planning staffs, admittedly something not easily done. None the less, the military has a professional obligation to ensure that the responsibility for strategic-level doctrine and plans lies with the government. In a democratic society, this may best be achieved through an open policy-making process – for example, by giving greater prominence to the parliamentary standing committee on defence. Without some widely accepted structure for intimate political supervision over high-level doctrine and plans, the military will inevitably fill the resulting vacuum, but not always in ways the government would wish.

Second, the soldier is crucial in the success of the army. At every level in the *Reichswehr*, from the operational to the rifle-section tactical level, consistent efforts were made to train independent-thinking leaders with a common doctrine and with the personal skills and the equipment they needed to accomplish the mission. Above all, the training and personnel systems ensured that those with both the necessary intellect and the will to succeed rose to the top. The corollary to such a system is that the continual demands for action inevitably lead to mistakes being made, but in the German case this was always acceptable, provided that the mistakes made were those of commission, not of omission. This acceptance of human error is evidence of a wider, humanist approach to manning the army; selection of recruits was decentralized, and even the selection of officer candidates was done at regimental level. It is unlikely that the *Reichswehr* would have accepted the Canadian Forces' centralized, overly bureaucratic system, where administrative duty performed without error carries as much weight in advancement as regimental soldiering. The German experience argues strongly in favour of the greatest possible decentralization of recruiting, training, career management, and professional development. It also urges concentration on character and intellect, as opposed to error-free performance of duty, as criteria for advancement.

A third lesson lies in the proper development of a staff system. The *Reichswehr* put enormous effort into the selection, training, and professional development of staff officers. These officers formed a small, close-knit body that shared a common ethos and doctrine and directed the army without undue attention to the details of execution on the battlefield. The elite nature of the members of the staff, and the intense demands placed on them, led to a high standard of personal and corporate performance. There was room for independent thought and objectivity, perhaps because the collegial nature of the staff allowed all its members to see the "big picture," and the control exercised by the staff ensured that the *Reichswehr* was an instrument responsive to its commander. Without such control in the Canadian army, many competing power centres detract from its main mission. The creation of some sort of staff system (preferably a joint staff), while clearly elitist and contrary to recent Canadian practice, is one possible solution to the problems that plague us today.

A final lesson is the need to develop doctrine in an effective manner. The responsibility for this task in the German army lay with the central staff, but thinking and debate were spread widely, and independent thought and action were encouraged and publicized in an active, professional press. Not only were competing theories welcomed, but the existence of a General Staff, independent of the competing regiments, helped to minimize the effects of the tribal nature of military organizations. Development of doctrine was a key duty of the *Truppenamt* and was not relegated to the status of relatively minor staff function, as is the case in the Canadian Forces. Once developed, doctrine, in so far as this is possible, became the driving force for organization, training, and equipment. Because of the encouragement of debate on doctrinal matters, doctrine was continually challenged and refined and was not, as some claim is the case in today's Canadian army, merely the opinion of the senior officer present.

There are many other lessons that could be drawn from the *Reichswehr*. However, the most salient are the close integration of political leadership and policy, the primacy of the soldier, proper staff systems, and correct doctrine. Because it paid attention to these things, the *Reichswehr* of Hans von Seeckt, tiny but nearly flawless, was one of the outstanding military machines of history – its methods bear careful scrutiny.

NOTES

1 Von Seeckt, *Thoughts of a Soldier*, 123.
2 Ibid., 9.
3 Addington, *The Blitzkrieg Era and the German General Staff*, 6; and Corum, *The Roots of Blitzkrieg*, 30.
4 Craig, *Germany*, 439–40; Corum, *The Roots of Blitzkrieg*, 68–9; and Dupuy, *A Genius for War*, 216–19.
5 Spires, *Image and Reality*, viii.
6 Corum, *The Roots of Blitzkrieg*, 25.
7 Von Manstein, *Lost Victories*, 76.
8 Corum, *The Roots of Blitzkrieg*, 25–7.
9 Messerschmidt, "German Military Effectiveness," 220–1.
10 The sketch of Seeckt's personality is drawn from a variety of sources, including Liddell Hart, *The Other Side of the Hill*, 25; Seaton, *The German Army 1933–1945*, 6, 9; von Manstein, *Lost Victories*, 76; von Senger and Etterlin, *Neither Fear Nor Hope*, 43; Corum, *The Roots of Blitzkrieg*, 30, 52, 54; and Dupuy, *A Genius for War*, 225, 345.
11 Spires, *Image and Reality*, viii.
12 Corum, *The Roots of Blitzkrieg*, 53. See von Seeckt, *Thoughts of a Soldier*, 10–12, for a sketchy discussion of the operational art vis-à-vis tactics.
13 Von Seeckt, *Thoughts of a Soldier*, 3. His biographer, General von Rabenau, suggested that he was a theorist (quoted in Wallach, *The Dogma of the Battle of Annihilation*, 229.) However, Wallach was out to prove the importance of theory, while nothing in Seeckt's own book suggests that he held to any particular theories.
14 Addington, *The Blitzkrieg Era*, 29. See also von Seeckt, *Thoughts of a Soldier*, 55.
15 Corum, *The Roots of Blitzkrieg*, 29.
16 Von Seeckt, *Thoughts of a Soldier*, 63–6.
17 Addington, *The Blitzkrieg Era*, 30; and Wallach, *The Dogma*, 231.

18 Addington, *The Blitzkrieg Era*, 2.

19 Seaton, *The German Army*, 6.

20 O'Neill, "Doctrine and Training in the German Army," 146. Von Seeckt, *Thoughts of a Soldier*, 81–107, is a rather long essay on the value of cavalry in war.

21 Dupuy, *A Genius for War*, 220–1, has the best treatment of his resignation.

22 Corum, *The Roots of Blitzkrieg*, 1–4.

23 Ibid., 37–8, has a good discussion of Seeckt's approach.

24 Ibid., 23–4.

25 Ibid., 5–9. Corum discusses tank lessons learned at 122–4.

26 Addington, *The Blitzkrieg Era*, 19, 26.

27 Ibid., 24–5; and Corum, *The Roots of Blitzkrieg*, 13–18.

28 Von Seeckt, *Thoughts of a Soldier*, 51–62.

29 Corum, *The Roots of Blitzkrieg*, 39–40, 49.

30 Ibid., 69.

31 Van Creveld, *Fighting Power*, 67; and Seaton, *The German Army*, 12–13.

32 Corum, *The Roots of Blitzkrieg*, 69–70.

33 Ibid., 2.

34 Personal discussions of the author with three *Führungsakademie* graduates during the 1994 course at British Army Staff College, Camberley, England. Further, those selected to attend the *Führungsakademie* are given a rigorous battery of psychological tests, designed to estimate their suitability for the training and subsequent employment.

35 Spires, *Image and Reality*, 3.

36 Ibid., 4, 8.

37 Ibid., 12.

38 Notably in van Creveld, *Fighting Power*, and in Dupuy, *A Genius for War*, for both of whom officers' quality and the related aspects of training and leadership form the central concern of their books.

39 Van Creveld, *Fighting Power*, 151–3; Corum, *The Roots of Blitzkrieg*, 200–2; and Addington, *The Blitzkrieg Era*, 40.

40 Addington, *The Blitzkrieg Era*, 90–1.

41 Spires, *Image and Reality*, 69.

42 Corum, *The Roots of Blitzkrieg*, 74–6.

43 Wallach, *The Dogma*, 237–8; and O'Neill, "Doctrine and Training," 146–7. See also Corum, *The Roots of Blitzkrieg*, 89.

44 Corum, *The Roots of Blitzkrieg*, 71–3 and 76–7.

45 Spires, *Image and Reality*, 17.

46 Ibid., 17–20.

47 Corum, *The Roots of Blitzkrieg*, 72, 184–6.

48 Spires, *Image and Reality*, 106.

49 Corum, *The Roots of Blitzkrieg*, 163–5.

50 Spires, *Image and Reality*, 105.

51 Ibid., 21–3, 108–9, 115–6.
52 Corum, *The Roots of Blitzkrieg*, 33 and 95.
53 Spires, *Image and Reality*, 30.
54 Corum, *The Roots of Blitzkrieg*, 11.
55 Dupuy, *A Genius for War*, 187.
56 Spires, *Image and Reality*, 31–3, 37.
57 Ibid., 35.
58 Ibid., 39.
59 Corum, *The Roots of Blitzkrieg*, 89–90.
60 Spires, *Image and Reality*, 46.
61 Ibid., 47.
62 Corum, *The Roots of Blitzkrieg*, 93.
63 Spires, *Image and Reality*, 34–6.
64 Ibid., 59.
65 Ibid., 41.
66 Corum, *The Roots of Blitzkrieg*, 35.
67 Dupuy, *A Genius for War*, 220.
68 Corum, *The Roots of Blitzkrieg*, 35–6.
69 Ibid., 100–1.
70 Seaton, *The German Army*, 27; and Corum, *The Roots of Blitzkrieg*, 174–6.
71 Dupuy, *A Genius for War*, 237–40; and Addington, *The Blitzkrieg Era*, 37.
72 Addington, *The Blitzkrieg Era*, 29.
73 Corum, *The Roots of Blitzkrieg*, 40, 42.
74 Von Seeckt, *Thoughts of a Soldier*, 14–16.
75 Wallach, *The Dogma*, 233–4.
76 Corum, *The Roots of Blitzkrieg*, 33.
77 Kooistria, "The Six Rules of Soldiering," 10–12.
78 Corum, *The Roots of Blitzkrieg*, 47.
79 Ibid., 102.
80 Guderian, *Panzer Leader*, 16–18.
81 Macksey, *Guderian*, 58.
82 Werner von Fritsch, quoted in Corum, *The Roots of Blitzkrieg*, 130–1.
83 Guderian, *Panzer Leader*, 10–11; and O'Neill, "Doctrine and Training," 147–50.
84 Coox, "Military Effectiveness of Armed Forces," 263.
85 Addington, *The Blitzkrieg Era*, 34.
86 Corum, *The Roots of Blitzkrieg*, 190–7.
87 Ibid., 31–2.
88 Ibid., 140. Guderian's praise of Liddell Hart is found only in the English translation of *Panzer Leader*, which Liddell Hart edited.
89 Corum, *The Roots of Blitzkrieg*, 147–50.
90 Ibid., 145–6.
91 Geyer, "German Strategy in the Age of Machine Warfare."
92 Ibid., 528.

93 Ibid., 555.
94 Ibid., 556.
95 Ibid., 554.
96 Corum, *The Roots of Blitzkrieg*, 40.
97 Messerschmidt, "German Military Effectiveness," 227.
98 Spires, *Image and Reality*, 127–8; and Geyer, "German Strategy," 564–5.
99 Messerschmidt, "German Military Effectiveness," 244.
100 Seaton, *The German Army*, xxii.
101 Geyer, "German Strategy," 572.
102 Messerschmidt, "German Military Effectiveness," 219.
103 Von Senger, *Neither Fear Nor Hope*, 27.

PART II

Unconventional Warfare

Mao Zedong: A Peasant Who Learned from History

CDR ROSS STRUTHERS

A recent movie purported to record the events surrounding "The Last Emperor" of China, but the person the movie depicted was not the last emperor, and neither is there a "last emperor." Until February 1987, Deng Xiaoping (Teng Hsiao-ping[1]), the successor to Mao Zedong (Mao Tse-tung) who preceded him, was de facto emperor, and another emperor will follow him. Harrison Salisbury, an author who has spent his life studying China, pointed out that to be emperor in China, bloodlines do not count, but power.[2] In those terms, it is clear that Mao, like some emperors before him, had led a peasant revolt to assume the "Mandate of Heaven" and to rule China from the Forbidden City.

The story of how a peasant from rural China could move from the fields to the "Dragon Throne" is one that has unfolded many times in Chinese history. Mao studied and reflected on these aspects of history as a young man, and in his early adulthood he was thrust into the conditions that led to dynastic change in China. When Mao entered his twenties, he lived in a land ruled by a corrupt regime no longer able, or willing, to care for its starving people. China was a country that had been partitioned by foreign powers, which were pursuing their own national interests, to the detriment of those of the Chinese people. At that time, Mao recognized the opportunity inherent in the existing chaos (*luan* in Chinese) and recognized that the power to effect change lay in the masses of peasants, of whom he was one.

Armed with a broad education and an unswerving belief that he, and he alone, possessed the intellect and leadership to rule China, Mao started on the path from Changsha to a mausoleum in Tiananmen Square. On the way, he created a mode of revolutionary warfare that was distinctly Chinese, yet many of its elements served as the foundation for strategies used by revolutionary leaders throughout the world. This essay traces the origins of Mao's way of war in order to clarify the origins not only of his strategic thought but also of the strategies employed by his imitators, some of whom are discussed in other essays in this book. The origins of Mao's way of war are important because Mao's strategy of a "people's war" would clash directly with the doctrine of Western-style armies commanded by his opponents, and in the end Mao's Chinese way of war would prevail.

To understand how Mao's victory came about, it is necessary to be acquainted with Chinese history and with Mao's education. From this foundation, it is easier to understand how Mao developed his theories on revolutionary warfare in China. Mao was a product of Chinese history, religion, and culture, with which he mixed the new religion of communism. Following Chinese historical precedent, Mao seized the opportunities presented in times of chaos, and, as other peasant leaders had before him, he mounted the Dragon Throne.

A BRIEF HISTORY OF CHINA AND CHINESE PHILOSOPHY

China is an ancient culture with a recorded history reaching back over two thousand years. This rich history forms an indivisible part of the Chinese character and gives rise to many concepts still held in modern China. As is discussed below, Mao was a scholar of history and believed that the ancient Chinese texts on government were valid guides to governing. Throughout his rise to power, and later as ruler, Mao would demonstrate an understanding of the dynamics of Chinese history.

Pre-Confucian Chinese history is a mixture of myth, legend, and fact. The Chinese believe that they are the inventors of civilization, notwithstanding the lack of an archaeological basis on which to lay this claim. [3] It was during these times that the five classics of Chinese literature, the *I ching* (Book of Changes), the *Shu ching* (Book of History), the *Shih ching* (Book of Poetry), the *Li chi* (Book of Rites), and the *Ch'un-ch'iu* (Spring and Autumn Annals) are believed to have been written. Confucius (551 BC–479 BC) himself is believed to be both the transmitter and the commentator to these books. The classics, taken together, provide not only a record of the government and institutions but also models of good governance for all later rulers. Confucius is believed to have used the Annals, in particular, "to suggest to men certain moral laws and principles which would guide them in the management of their affairs." [4]

Confucian philosophy was a philosophy of human relationships. Confucius taught that subordinates should be reverent and obedient to superiors and, in turn, superiors needed to be benevolent and just in their dealings with subordinates. He saw history as the model for society's behaviour and held that customs and traditions were invaluable. He also argued that a ruler must exercise his power in a humane fashion and that it is necessary to educate leaders in the proper way of using power. Mao would study the five Confucian classics as part of the body of knowledge of every educated Chinese.

Daoism (Taoism, or the Way) was next to Confucianism as the most highly regarded native Chinese philosophy. Daoism argued that harmony with the forces of nature was central. Daoists rejected positions of power and argued that a wise man would mind his own business, ignore the government, and hope that the government would ignore him. "To the solemn, rather pompous gravity and burden of social responsibility of Confucianism, Daoism opposes a carefree flight from respectability and the conventional duties of society; in place of the stubborn Confucian concern for things human and mundane it holds out a vision of other, transcendental worlds of the spirit."[5] Daoist philosophy would later intermingle with medicine and other elements of folk culture to produce a religion with numerous deities.

Standing in contrast to Confucian philosophy, with its belief in the importance of the group, and to Daoism, with its belief in the individual, was Legalism. Legalism was described by the philosopher Han Fei Zi (Han Fei Tzu, d. 233 BC) as a way of life that preached self-interest; it was probably an outgrowth of a need for a more rational organizational structure in society and a means to strengthen the state against its rivals. Legalism was concerned with the solution of immediate problems and provided specific mechanisms of control. Legalists believed that people were amoral and therefore needed a strong system of rules to compel correct behaviour through rewards and punishment. By ruthlessly punishing minor infractions, Legalists believed, one could deter serious crime. In legalistic thought, the ruler need not take into account the views of his subjects, as Legalists believed generally that the people were too stupid to recognize either good or bad government. Under Legalism, an emperor was expected to use the empire for his own pleasure. Legalists completely rejected ethical values, emphasized government by law rather than individual leadership, and, on the whole, represented the antithesis of Confucian thinking.[6] The harshness of this philosophy led to the overthrow of the Legalist Qin dynasty (221–207 BC) by a peasant, Liu Chi, who founded the Han dynasty.

Liu Chi's overthrow of the Qin conformed to the model of dynastic change, which was a constant from China's early history on. Both the *Book of Poetry* and the *Book of History* explained that Heaven commanded certain men to be rulers over the tribes of the world,[7] through the bestowal of the "Mandate of Heaven" (t'ien-ming). Dynasties started with competent and vigorous leaders, who were concerned with the welfare of their subjects. However, the vigour of the emperors and then bureaucracy would eventually decay. In the countryside this would be paralleled in the manner in which land was owned. At the start of a dynasty, land was held by the peasants, since the great landowners usually lost their land holdings in the break-up of the previous dynasty. As time went on, the landowners would gain control of great portions of land, suppress the peasantry, and learn to evade taxes, usually by corrupting the emperor's bureaucrats. This caused the tax burden to be shifted to the peasants, who, when unable to pay the taxes, were driven to banditry. Hunger and anarchy brought on by the decaying regime would cause the emperor to lose the "Mandate of Heaven," and a new, vigorous dynasty would rise to replace the old. In this manner, China saw power pass from the Qin to the Han, the Han to the Sui (581 BC),[8] the Sui to the Tang (618 BC), and the Tang to the Song (Sung) (960 BC).

Pre-modern China had a remarkably strong culture, one which was able to absorb invaders and integrate the invaders into Chinese society. During the late Song period, China came under increasing pressure from northern nomads. The Mongols under Kublai Khan conquered all of China in 1279, but the Mongols did not change Chinese civilization – they were changed by it. They became the Yuan dynasty and remained in power until they were expelled by the Ming a century later. One legacy, however, of the experience of a foreign dynasty was that China as a nation became more isolationist.[9]

This isolationism existed in China as Western merchants began to arrive in significant numbers in the sixteenth century. In the early years of trade with China, the balance of payments favoured China. European merchants bought tea, silk, and porcelain and paid in gold and silver.[10] As commerce grew over the centuries, the British sought to redress this inequality in trade. They began exporting to China opium, which they had acquired from their possessions in India in tremendous quantities. Soon the balance of payments was reversed, and China was suffering from tremendous drug abuse. This situation became untenable to the Chinese government and reinforced its belief in isolationist policies. In 1839, China moved firmly to suppress the opium trade, confiscating and destroying the drug supplies held by the European merchants in Guangzhou (Canton). This act of nationalism started the Opium War, which was to last until 1842. The end of the conflict saw China submitting to British demands for treaty ports and the islands of Hong Kong, and also allowing Western missionaries and merchants freer access to China.

The situation in China now paralleled historic periods of dynastic change. The Qing had a weakened and ineffective military and a corrupt bureaucracy. Peasants, to survive, were driven to banditry, and local leaders had to raise their own militias to protect their interests against both internal and Western enemies. In this climate, a group of Buddhists started an uprising – the Taiping Rebellion. Unable to suppress the revolt with imperial troops, the emperor permitted the conversion of local militias into real armies controlled by the gentry. These forces, working with Western troops and sometimes under the leadership of Western officers, firmly put down the rebellion. The fact that support from Western barbarians was needed to defeat the rebels caused the Chinese to rethink the value of Western technology and military doctrine and created a schism within society. People who wanted to reform China to Western ways were opposed by the conservative court, led by the Dowager Empress.

The tension created by this dichotomy in Chinese society led to the outbreak of the Boxer Rebellion. Though initially opposed to the Dowager Empress, the Boxers were co-opted by the Qing court in an effort to drive the "foreign devils" from China.[11] The fighting was limited largely to northern China; in the south, local officials understood the power of the Europeans better and maintained the fiction that the rebels were fighting against the dynasty, thereby permitting them to ignore the empress's orders to support the Boxers. The Western armies in China joined together to defeat the Boxers and then extracted a huge payment from the Chinese government.

The defeat of the Boxers by the Western powers had a profound influence on the imperial court. The Qing started a massive program of modernization, based on a Western model. The Confucian civil service exams were abolished, the education system was Westernized, students were sent abroad to study, and an army made up of educated men, organized on Western lines, was created. The court even announced plans to form a constitutional government, convening a national assembly in 1909, but this program backfired. Progress, once started, was not fast enough for most people; real political power was slow in coming, and an educated army was more responsive to revolutionary propaganda than previous armies had been.

It was in this environment that a nationalist revolutionary named Sun Yat-sen gained prominence. This Western-educated Christian formed the Revolutionary Alliance with the intention of overthrowing the Qing dynasty. Though not immediately successful, he persisted and, in 1911, started a rebellion in Sichuan province; despite being weakly organized, the revolution gathered momentum rapidly because of local dissatisfaction with the central government.[12] The Qing, lacking an army capable of stopping the insurrection, turned to a powerful warlord, Yuan Shikai, who, rather than fighting them, made a deal with the revolutionaries. In return for the presidency, Yuan supported the formation of a republic, and the Qing dynasty effectively ended. Sun Yat-sen lacked a power base strong enough to oppose Yuan, so he joined forces with him, and in 1913 an elected parliament was convened. The most powerful party was the Guomindang, or Nationalist party, a derivative of Sun Yat-sen's Revolutionary Alliance. Sun Yat-sen, however, lacking the skills of a politician, was not a central figure, preferring to accept a nominal post in the Guomindang and to devote his time to planning a modern railway for China.

Yuan, however, never effectively took control of China, and power still rested with various military factions. In 1914, Yuan dissolved parliament and declared himself emperor, but his dynasty was short-lived. With Yuan's death in 1916, central authority in China collapsed and the country entered a decade of warlord rule. Notwithstanding the lack of a central government, China continued to modernize and Westernize. However, the poor suffered terribly, since they were severely overtaxed by the landowners and brutalized by the warlords. The absence of a competent central authority and the vacuum left in former German-held areas following the First World War permitted the Japanese to expand their sphere of influence into what had been the German treaty area of Shangdong province.[13] As well, the Japanese demanded a substantial degree of control over China as a whole.

The combination of Western education and foreign encroachment encouraged the continued rise of nationalism in China, but the nationalists lacked an organizational structure with which to oversee modernization. Russia's Communist party provided one organizational model, and in 1921 the Chinese Communist party was founded. To survive, the Communists formed an alliance with the Goumindang; the alliance, operating under a nationalistic banner, grew rapidly, and by 1927 it controlled a substantial portion of China. However, before the Japanese could be driven from China, this alliance collapsed, and in the midst of the nationalistic war against the Japanese, a civil war between the Communists and Goumindang, now controlled by Chiang Kai-shek, broke out.

Mao Zedong grew up in a period of Chinese history, like many before it, when the old dynasty had become corrupt and was decaying and the people were oppressed. Mao had read Western philosophy, but, unlike the other major leaders in China in his time, he had never lived or been educated in the West. Mao was sensitive to the Chinese belief that rulers needed the "Mandate of Heaven" in order to rule, and once that mandate was lost, so too would the emperor fall. He was also aware of the importance of an education (Confucianism) and the dangers of brutalizing the peasantry (Legalism). Mao would blend his knowledge of Chinese history and philosophy with the revolutionary ideas of Marx to create a distinctively Chinese strategy for revolution. Mao believed that after the overthrow of foreign domination, the strength of the Chinese revolution would come from the peasantry, rather than the Russian model, based on industrial workers. This belief would set Mao clearly against the Chinese Communist party's Central Committee and its Russian mentors.[14] To help us understand how Mao came to these beliefs, a biographical sketch is necessary.

MAO'S EDUCATION

Even as a child, Mao was clearly different than his peers. He was both a scholar and a dreamer in a society that put children to work in the fields as soon as they could walk. As Mao matured, these differences would manifest themselves in severe disagreements with his father. His father was an ordinary peasant of modest means, who, in typical Chinese fashion, regarded his sons as his retirement plan. Mao's drive for knowledge permitted him to break out of the model of a Chinese peasant's child and to acquire a broad education while making friends with influential scholars. His academic foundation would launch him as the major theorist of the Chinese Communist party and gave him the intellectual tools to challenge the Russian model of revolutionary warfare.

Mao was born in the clan village of Shaoshan, Hunan, in which everyone's name was Mao. In December 1893, only paths connected Shaoshan to the provincial capital Changsha, seventy kilometres away. As a peasant child, Mao started work in the fields at age four, but he left them at seven to begin school. It was at the village school that Mao studied the *Analects* of Confucius and the five classics of Chinese literature. [15] During this time, he borrowed a book called *Heroes and Great Men of the World* and learned about George Washington, Benjamin Franklin, Napoleon Bonaparte, Abraham Lincoln, and others. Washington's protracted struggle against the British, in particular, was to strike a chord with Mao. [16]

At eighteen, Mao had the good fortune to be accepted into one of China's finest schools, the Changsha Normal School Number One. There he continued his study of such classical Chinese works as *The Three Kingdoms* and *Outlaws of the Marshes* (also known as *The Water Margin*). *The Three Kingdoms* is a somewhat fictionalized version of Chinese history, while *Outlaws* is a Chinese version of the Robin Hood Story. Mao would later comment on them repeatedly as textbooks for guerrilla warfare. Mao also read Sun Wu Zi's (Sun Tse) *The Art of War*, the classic work on military strategy, written about four centuries before Christ. Mao was also influenced strongly by his professor, Yang Changji, a man known as the "Confucius of Changsha." At the normal school, Mao became associated with a number of teachers and students who, with him, would join the newly created Communist movement. [17]

In 1917, Mao and a friend, Siao Yu, went begging – an honourable profession in China, in which Siao had some experience. This trip, which was to take Mao through the contryside, gave Mao his first deep insights into the life of the ordinary peasant. [18] The friends spent six weeks on the land, walked some five hundred kilometres, and depended on the charity of peasants for their survival. Later, Mao's affinity for the peasant class would lead him to break with traditional Marxist dogma, which called for a revolution to come from the urban proletariat, and instead call for a revolution led by the masses of peasants.

Mao was not to read Marx until after he went to join Professor Yang in Beijing, where he worked at the Beijing University Library and joined the leading young radicals. In later years, when Mao was to cite Marx, the quotations would be from *The Communist Manifesto* and would focus on class struggle. *Das Kapital*, the other communist classic, was not published in China until 1938, by which time Mao was in Yunan, and there is no reason to believe that Mao ever read it.[19] However, Professor Yang was a dedicated Marxist, and most of the elite in the Chinese Communist party had trained in Russia, so it is likely that Mao would have been familiar with its main themes. During this period many of China's future leaders were heading to Europe on work exchanges, but not Mao. In fact, Mao was to leave the "Middle Kingdom" only twice, after he had gained power, and both trips were to the Soviet Union.

Over the years in Shaoshan, Changsa, and Beijing, Mao had acquired a broad education in both classical Chinese philosophy and strategy and in Western history and philosophy. He also gained valuable leadership experience and was exposed to major Chinese Communist scholars, while keeping his peasant roots and his Oriental view of warfare, which is substantially different from the Occidental view. These contrasts would result in a cultural clash in styles of warfare during China's revolution, which would parallel the ideological clash and change the way in which revolutionary war was perceived by Western scholars of warfare.

STRATEGIC THOUGHT IN ANCIENT CHINA

Gérard Chaliand writes in his *Anthologie mondiale de la stratégie*: "Our Western orientation, in the military sphere, considered other societies to be negligible. It needed the unexpected victory of Mao Zedong in order to rediscover Sun Zi."[20] Sun Zi's *The Art of War* is reputed to have been written more than two thousand years ago and is considered the oldest work on military strategy. Sun Zi posits (like Clausewitz many years later): "The art of war is of vital importance to the state. It is a matter of life and death, a road either to safety or to ruin. Hence under no circumstances can it be neglected."[21]

Sun Zi states a series of general principles that can guide the conduct of conflict, starting with the need for the ruler to be in harmony with his people. Next, Sun Zi emphasizes the need to know one's enemy, because by knowing the enemy one can develop a strategy most able to defeat him. Sun Zi saw victory as overcoming the enemy, and he believed that this could be accomplished, at times, without resorting to battle. Sun Zi was an early exponent of an indirect strategy: "To fight and conquer in all your battles is not supreme excellence; supreme excellence consists in breaking the enemy's resistance without fighting. In the practical art of war, the best thing of all is to take the enemy's country whole and intact; to shatter and destroy it is not so good."[22]

Mao was to share many of Sun Zi's principles in his vision of revolutionary war. In places, Mao's vision and Sun Zi's would be so close that Eric Chou would observe in his biography of Mao: "Undoubtably he was good at absorbing other people's ideas and summing them up in his own words.

If one is well versed in Chinese classics, one would have no difficulty in detecting that his strategic thought is basically a hotchpotch of General Sun Wu's [Sun Zi] Military Strategy, *Romance of the Three Kingdoms* and *The Water Margins* [Outlaws of the Marsh]."[23]

Opinions differ, however, concerning Sun Zi's view of protracted warfare. John Keegan, in *A History of Warfare*, argued that Sun Zi's philosophy of "gradualism" – wearing an enemy down over time – is the source of Mao's protracted struggle strategy.[24] However, Sun Zi also states that wars should be short, so that the peasants can return home before they lose their enthusiasm. "When you engage in actual fighting, if victory is long in coming, the men's weapons will grow dull and their ardor will be dampened ... Never forget: When your weapons are dulled, your ardor dampened, your strength exhausted, and your treasure spent, other chieftains will spring up to take advantage of your extremity."[25]

The theory that the use of peasant armies demands short wars to permit the peasants to return to farm their land appears to be common logic in theories of war. Mao was a chieftain who recognized that you could borrow from both Confucius and Marx and use education as a means to ensure that your army's ardour was maintained through its belief in the revolution and ultimate victory. He believed that this ardour for victory could supplant the peasant's natural desire to return to his home. In this fashion, Mao created a Chinese revolution with a peasant army able to sustain a prolonged struggle against more powerful forces. As Keegan put it, "Primitive tactics become effective if the warrior is inspired by a belief in the certainty of victory and is always willing to return to the struggle, however often he disengages when a particular fight goes against him."[26]

THE RUSSIAN MODEL

Chinese Communists had a model for creating revolution in the example shown by the Soviet Union; however, revolution did not come easily to Russia. As early as 1872, just as *Das Kapital* was being translated into Russian, a group of revolutionaries was trying to mobilize the peasant masses. "Several thousand men and women – the forerunners of the Narodniks – discovered to their dismay that peasant ignorance, drunkenness, apathy, and misplaced faith in the Czar, not to mention the size of Russia, poor communications, and powerful secret police and army made revolution by persuasion a difficult task."[27] The difficulty in arousing the peasant masses was to become a recurring theme in Russian revolutionary activity.

Though Marx and Engels, through their study of the German peasant war, clearly saw that the support of the peasantry was critical to revolutionary success, Lenin did not exploit the support of the peasant masses to the degree that Marx and Engels envisioned.[28] In order to feed his army, Lenin endangered peasant support by forcing distribution of grain without adequate payment.[29] He also reintroduced conscription, a measure that was most un-popular among the peasants, who depended on the manpower of their families to generate a living.

The difficulty of mobilizing Russian peasants, in comparison to workers and the army, led Lenin to stress the building of a revolutionary foundation in the cities. Walter Laqueur recognizes that motivating revolutionary fervour in the peasant class is a problem: "The difficulty facing the guerrilla leaders has always been to harness this revolutionary potential on a nation-wide basis in view of the traditional reluctance of peasants to fight outside their neighbourhood."[30] Notwithstanding the theoretical views of Marx and Engels, Lenin was able to overthrow the power structure in Russia and bring about the first communist state without depending on the active support of the peasant class.

Besides the issue of class struggle, Marx and Engels were concerned also with the relationship between the military and society, particularly the role of the army in a revolutionary state: "They realized that the army itself could serve as a social agency of the first order; in fact, it could serve as the major channel through which a democratic society might emerge."[31] Whether Mao was influenced by Marx, or if Mao arrived at the same conclusion independently, is not known. However, within the Chinese Communist party, the education of the army and of the peasant class, from which it was primarily drawn, would become a major tenet of the doctrine of protracted struggle. "The Red Army fights not merely for the sake of fighting, but in order to conduct propaganda among the masses, organize them, arm them, and help them to establish revolutionary political power."[32]

Of the young Chinese communist leaders who went to Russia for training, most returned to China with the belief that the exploited urban workers were the foundation of a revolution. As a result, these young, foreign-educated Bolsheviks concentrated their energies in major cities such as Shanghai. In an attempt to sideline the outspoken Mao, these same leaders sent him away from the cities to investigate the revolutionary potential of the peasants in Hunan, where he would find that the Russian model was not necessarily applicable to China and that the peasants could be educated and aroused. Ironically, Chang Kai-shek unknowingly abetted Mao's rise to power by slaughtering the communists in Shanghai, driving the entire leadership into the countryside, from which it would slowly learn the Chinese lesson that it was the peasants who constituted the masses, not the urban proletariat.

MAO'S STRATEGIC VISION

Guerrilla warfare is not new. As Gérard Chaliand points out in his introduction to *Stratégies de la Guérilla*, examples can be found in ancient China and Egypt. Chaliand goes on to explain that such warfare is particularly common during wars of resistance to foreign occupation.[33] Mao, however, integrated guerrilla warfare, which harasses an enemy, into revolutionary warfare, which overthrows the political order. Mao saw revolutionary warfare as a combination of using regular forces and employing guerrilla forces alone in the field, or attached to regular units, depending on circumstances. Putting revolutionary war in a Chinese perspective, Mao broke with the Leninist model of revolution and recognized the peasant, rather than the worker, as the strength of China's revolution.

Mao in 1930 laid out his prescription for the strategy that he would follow in conducting revolutionary war. In "A Single Spark Can Start a Prairie Fire," he wrote: "Ours are guerrilla tactics. They consist mainly of the following points: Divide our forces to arouse the masses, concentrate our forces to deal with the enemy. The enemy advances, we retreat; the enemy camps, we harass; the enemy tires, we attack; the enemy retreats, we pursue. To extend stable base areas, employ the policy of advancing in waves; when pursued by a powerful enemy, employ the policy of circling around. Arouse the largest numbers of the masses in the shortest possible time and by the best possible methods. These tactics are just like casting a net; at any moment we should be able to cast it or draw it in. We cast it wide to win over the masses and draw it in to deal with the enemy."[34]

Mao followed these precepts. Pressured by the Goumindang in his base area of Kiangsi, Mao retreated into the mountains on the Hunan border, there making peace with the bandits. Chiang Kai-shek's Fifth Encirclement Campaign drove the Communist forces from the south of China and precipitated the Long March in October 1934. Mao's First Front Army, 86,000 strong, left Hunan and headed east to disengage from the Nationalist forces.[35] Turning north near Loushankuan, it was blocked from crossing the Yangtze River by another powerful Nationalist force. Rather than fighting on unfavourable terms, it again retreated to the south and east, turning north once again after making a feint towards Kumming. The First Front Army made its way through some of the most difficult terrain in China, but in doing so it avoided the main concentrations of Nationalist forces. The First Front Army fought when it had to, but when negotiation with Nationalist warlords could permit unhindered passage, its leaders did not hesitate to negotiate. During the Long March some of the Communist forces died in battle, others died from the hardship, and some left for home. New soldiers were recruited to fill out the ranks, but one year and over nine thousand kilometres after the Long March began, 4,000 soldiers remained to join with the Fourth Front Army and establish a base in Yenan.

While in the caves of Yenan, Mao wrote a large number of essays to prescribe the form revolutionary warfare should take in China. From a strategic perspective perhaps the most important was *Yu Chi Chan* (On Guerrilla Warfare), written in 1937. In it, he lays out the fundamental steps necessary to gain the complete emancipation of the Chinese people: 1) arousing and organizing the people; 2) achieving internal unification politically; 3) establishing bases; 4) equipping forces; 5) recovering national strength; 6) destroying the enemy's national strength; and 7) regaining lost territory.[36] After the Long March, Mao had programs in place to educate and arouse the masses, he had consolidated power, and he had found a secure base. From Yenan, he was to recover strength while harassing the Japanese. Finally, he would embark on regaining lost territory.

THE STRATEGY OF ETHICAL BEHAVIOUR

As discussed above in the section on Mao's education, Mao had studied *The Analects*, the classical works on Confucianism. One of the precepts of Confucius was that the ruler had to behave in a good and humane manner towards his subjects.[37] However, the reality in China in the late 1929 was quite different. Peasants were starving in the streets; young girls were trucked into cities in cattle cars to be sold into brothels and human meat was for sale in the bazaars.[38] Unlike the warlords, the Communists took the moral high ground in their fight for the cooperation of the masses.

Mao condensed the rules for his soldiers into three commands that his peasant army could remember. (Two contrasting translations illustrate the different approaches translators take in rendering Chinese into English. Chinese characters are independent of dialect, so it is not significant which Chinese dialect the speaker used.) One translation of the rules reads: "Obey orders in all your actions. Don't take a needle or a piece of thread from the people. Turn in everything you capture." Another states: "All actions are subject to command. Do not steal from the people. Be neither selfish nor unjust."

The three commands were further elaborated as follows: "Speak politely. Pay fairly for what you buy. Return everything you borrow. Pay for any damage. Don't strike or swear at people. Don't damage the crops. Don't take liberties with women. Don't mistreat captives."[39] Also: "Replace the doors when you leave the house. Roll up the bedding on which you have slept. Be courteous. Be honest in your transactions. Return what you borrow. Replace what you break. Do not bathe in the presence of women. Do not, without authority, search the pocketbooks of those you arrest."[40]

Mao's insistence that his army be indoctrinated in the laws of war ensured that discipline was strong, so much so that it was able to win the support of the peasant farmers in most areas in which it moved. Mao's dictums echoed Sun Zi's of two thousand years earlier. Sun Zi tells the story of a general who gave strict orders to his army not to molest the inhabitants. When one of the general's own comrades misappropriated a bamboo hat belonging to one of the people, the general had his friend beheaded, "and from that time forth even articles dropped in the highway were not picked up."[41]

This image of a disciplined force fighting for a China free of foreign domination was important in the Communists' war against the Nationalists. "The Red Army was not – like its enemies – a conventional army of professional soldiers or mercenaries, but of men imbued with a sense of mission."[42] The Communists' propaganda was able to sway the masses to the extent that they were welcomed into formerly Nationalist strongholds in the south without significant resistance. Conversely, in the north, Nationalist forces were constantly harassed by guerrillas following Mao's principles of operations, which emphasized attacking dispersed, isolated enemy forces.[43]

Mao did not see a disjunction between the ethical behaviour he espoused for the army and the killing of landlords and rich peasants in order to redistribute the wealth. To Mao and the peasants in his army, the two concepts were complementary. After all, "Our enemies are all those in league with imperialism – the warlords, the bureaucrats, the comprador class, the big landlord class and the reactionary section of the intelligentsia attached to them."[44] Overall, however, the behaviour of the Communist troops constituted a radical departure from that of both Nationalist and Japanese soldiers, who were justly detested throughout China for rapine and brutality.[45]

Salisbury points out: "In old China it was said that you did not use good iron to make nails or good men to make soldiers. The Red Army completely reversed that adage, and [the] moral conduct [of its soldiers] won the peasantry and won China."[46] It is a particularly Chinese twist of fate that a man who would be responsible for killing millions through the "Great Leap Forward" and the "Cultural Revolution" would have gained power in part because he led an ethical army.

CONCLUSION

Traditional Occidental wisdom characterizes the Chinese as devious and inscrutable. However, as Keegan observes: "Long before any Western society had arrived at a philosophy of war, the Chinese had devised one. The Confucian ideal of rationality, continuity and maintenance of institutions led them to seek means of subordinating the warrior impulse to the constraints of law and custom."[47] Only later, through the writings of Liddell Hart and others, would Westerners realize that this was the expression of an "indirect" strategy that was at the base of Chinese strategic thinking. Mao closely followed the precepts of the strategists who had gone before him – particularly Sun Zi and the heroes of *The Three Kingdoms*. Like Sun Zi, Mao was challenged on the battlefield and was able to demonstrate that his strategy was the correct one for him at that time.

Mao wrote extensively concerning the manner of conducting a Marxist-style revolutionary war. However, the bulk of his writings on this subject were composed in the caves in Yunan and were designed to establish him as

the pre-eminent Chinese communist scholar in order to consolidate his position as chairman of the Chinese Communist party. Mao is perhaps better
remembered for his more popular *Quotations of Chairman Mao Zedong*,
which is made up of the prescriptive elements of his strategic writings on
revolutionary warfare, designed to train cadres and peasants in the conduct
of war. Its slogans encouraged nationalistic ardour and emphasized ethical
behaviour.

Even though authors such as Eric Chou may deprecate Mao's work as a
mélange of ideas from Chinese literature and history, the same thing can be
said of many famous strategists. Mao was able to take ideas from diverse
sources and synthesize them into a strategy that was rooted in Chinese history and accepted the peasants' nationalism. Using the power of the masses,
he brought China from a divided, feudal nation to a major modern power.
Mao's uniquely Chinese revolutionary strategy would ultimately catapult
him to leadership of the most populous nation on earth and provide a widely
imitated model for revolutionary leaders everywhere.

NOTES

1 In this essay the *pinyin* spellings for Chinese are used, but the first time a word
   appears, the older, Wade-Giles spelling is given in parentheses. A few names,
   such as Sun Yat-sen, which are embedded in English under the Wade-Giles
   system, have retained their old spelling.
2 Salisbury, *The New Emperors*, xii.
3 De Bary, *Sources of Chinese Tradition*, 1.
4 Ibid., 4.
5 Ibid., 48.
6 Ibid., 123.
7 Ibid., 6.
8 Central government collapsed in China in AD 220, with the fall of the Han, and
   was not reinstated until 581, with the arrival of the Sui. During this period, however, the nation did not fall into barbarism. When the Sui restored central authority, it controlled a civilization at the same level that had existed when the Han
   dynasty disintegrated.
9 Moise, *Modern China*, 20.
10 The origins of this wealth were the Spanish conquest and subsequent plundering
    of Latin America.
11 Moise, *Modern China*, 37.
12 The rebellion was so weakly organized that the revolutionaries in Wuhan, de-
    prived of their leadership by police raids, captured an army officer, Li Yuanhong
    and convinced him, on threat of execution, to be their leader. Li Yuanhong rose
    over the next five years to be the nominal president of the republic of China.
    Moise, *Modern China*, 42.

13 Asprey, *War in the Shadows*, 338, stated that Japan took advantage of the German defeat in the First World War to replace the German presence in Shantung province.

14 Keegan, *A History of Warfare*, 51.

15 Salisbury, *The Long March*, 72.

16 Salisbury, *China,* 46.

17 These descriptions on Mao's education are taken from Salisbury, *The Long March*, 72–6, and Chou, *Mao Tse-tung*, 9–29.

18 Salisbury, *China*, 48.

19 Salisbury, *The New Emperors*, 133.

20 Chaliand, *Anthologie mondiale de la stratégie*, xxv.

21 Sun Zi, *The Art of War*, 9.

22 Ibid., 15.

23 Chou, *Mao Tse-tung*, 85.

24 Keegan, *A History of Warfare*, 202.

25 Sun Zi, 13.

26 Keegan, *A History of Warfare*, 96.

27 Asprey, *War in the Shadows*, 286.

28 Neumann and Hagen, "Engels and Marx," 268.

29 Asprey, *War in the Shadows*, 307.

30 Laqueur, "The Character of Guerrilla Warfare," 325.

31 Neumann and von Hagen, "Engels and Marx," 277.

32 Mao Zedong, *Quotations from Chairman Mao Tse-tung*, 54.

33 Chaliand, *Stratégies de la guérilla*, 28.

34 Mao Zedong, *Chairman Mao Tse-Tung on People's War*, 32.

35 Salisbury, *The Long March*, 2.

36 Mao Zedong, *On Guerrilla Warfare*, 41.

37 Moise, *Modern China*, 6.

38 Salisbury, *China*, 21.

39 Salisbury, *The Long March*, 117.

40 Asprey, *War in the Shadows*, 360.

41 Sun Zi, *The Art of War*, 55.

42 Girling, *People's War*, 54.

43 Mao, *Chairman Mao Tse-tung on People's War*, 33.

44 Mao Zedong, *Quotations from Chairman Mao Tse-tung*, 8.

45 Asprey, *War in the Shadows*, 360.

46 Salisbury, *The New Emperors*, 76.

47 Keegan, *A History of Warfare*, 388.

Revolutionary War: The Viet Minh and the First Indo-Chinese War

CAPT NEAL ATTFIELD

The First Indo-Chinese War (1946–54) was one of a number of conflicts that arose after the Second World War, challenging previous Western notions of war. Addressing an alarmed Senate Foreign Relations Committee in May 1966, U.S. Secretary of Defense Robert McNamara, noted that the number of "armed insurgencies" had risen from twenty-three in 1958 to forty in 1966.[1] These were conflicts in which generally ill-armed forces arose, seemingly from nowhere, to threaten the previously irresistible power of colonial states. Such a force arose in wartime Vietnam and within eight years shattered French forces in Indo-China, forcing them to retreat in disgrace from Southeast Asia. This defeat challenged the latent chauvinism of European strategic thinkers and plunged strategic thought into a crisis of understanding.

"Why did the French lose?" is a question that has been asked many times in different forms, right up to and after the capitulation of Soviet forces in Afghanistan. The First Indo-Chinese War provides an excellent venue for examining the roots of the dilemma that revolutionary and guerrilla war presents for Western strategists in the post–Cold War era. But the debate on revolutionary warfare has really barely begun; even its definition is not generally agreed on. For the purposes of this essay, I have adopted a definition offered by Chalmers Johnson: "a sweeping, fundamental change in the political organization, social structure, economic property control, and the predominant myth of social order, thus representing a major change in the continuity of development."[2] When such an event includes armed conflict, we may refer to it as "revolutionary warfare," which may or may not include guerrilla warfare. John Baylis defines guerrilla warfare as "a particular kind of military operation, or paramilitary operation, performed by irregular, predominantly indigenous forces which can, but need not necessarily be used to achieve revolutionary ends."[3]

As the nominal leader of the military forces of the Viet Nam Doc Lap Dong Minh Hoi (Vietnam Independence League), or Viet Minh, Vo Nguyên Giap has gained a particular mystique among Western strategists. It was as if he cast and fused a magic bullet capable of penetrating the armour of modern Western power. His strategy has been veiled in mystery, seemingly steeped in Eastern mysticism beyond the grasp of Western understanding. Arising from his mystique was a crisis in Western strategic thought that infected a broad spectrum of contemporary thinkers. In 1963, Hannah Arendt predicted grandly that revolutionary war would replace interstate war altogether as a result of the nuclear stalemate.[4] Numerous interstate wars have come and gone, and theorists continue to grapple with this problem.

However, the real "problem" for Western thinkers lies not in Viet Minh strategy but in the narrow Western perceptions of the nature of strategy itself. The roots of this problem can be traced back to the sentiments in the era prior to the great European wars of this century. In his 1901 book *Small Wars: Their Principles and Practice* C.E. Callwell proclaimed that "small wars" represented all wars, save those in which regular European armies engaged one another.[5] The essential difference lay not in the scale of the conflict but in whether such war was "civilized," with the combatants obeying the conventions of "civilized" peoples, or "uncivilized," with combatants ignorant of them.

This essay examines the First Indo-Chinese War and attempts to identify the factors that determined who would be victorious. The aim here will not only be to understand "why the French lost" but also, by using lessons from history, to reveal some of the wider implications for Western strategic thought about revolutionary wars.

ORIGINS OF THE WAR

In June 1940, Vo Nguyên Giap travelled to China and met Ho Chi Minh for the first time. Ho sent Giap to train with Mao Zedong's forces briefly before news of the German invasion of France caused Ho to order his thirty followers back to the French colony of Vietnam. At first they were only a nuisance to the Vichy French colonial troops, but by 1945 the Viet Minh had become a military force of 100,000 troops, which backed their position as the most potent indigenous political power.[6] In August of that year, with the general surrender of the Japanese and the disarming of their occupation forces in Vietnam, a power vacuum was created in Hanoi, and Ho moved quickly to fill it.

Ho's provisional government would be short-lived, however. In early 1947, French troops arrived back in force, to revive the colonial claim. Negotiations for the return of power to the French dragged on in both Hanoi and Paris through the summer and fall of 1946, to no consequence. Frustration turned into violence on the streets of Hanoi in December and continued for eight years. The First Indo-Chinese War had commenced.

Giap's forces in 1946 consisted of three general categories of troops. Two were incorporated into a command structure consisting of five "Interzones," each made up of several provinces. Four zones were located in the north and one in the south, reflecting the relative strength of the Viet Minh in these two areas. The Main Forces, which had begun as the Propaganda and Liberation Units two years previously, became the regular troops. Organized at this point into nothing more than battalion formations, their total number during this period was approximately fifty thousand. Regional troops were semi-regulars recruited from the specific provinces or districts in which they fought. These forces were also organized into battalion strength but were generally less effective than the main force units. Their tasks were confined to reconnaissance in advance of Main Force units or local defence.

Not included into the Interzone command structure were the "Popular Forces," or guerrilla forces, raised from individual villages or hamlets. These were subdivided into two groups. The "Dan Quan" included members of both genders and all age groups and did not engage in any combat duty, but it provided the backbone of the Viet Minh logistics network which, as we see below, proved vital. The "Dan Quan du Kich," in contrast, was restricted to males between eighteen and forty-five years of age. In addition to harassing French outposts, their duties included preparation of the battlefield in advance of Main Force units, setting mines and booby traps, as well as minor engineering work. All recruits would first join such a unit. When needed, the soldier would be "promoted" to Regional Forces and then to the Main Forces. Thus the Main Forces would receive a well-trained soldier, often with combat experience.

THE ORIGINS OF VIET MINH STRATEGY

Yet these forces were still militarily weaker than the French regular forces, and it took a special strategy to exploit the strengths of the Viet Minh and the weaknesses of the French. The sources of Viet Minh strategy do not reveal themselves easily in the murky writings of the leader most associated with its military arm. The reader might assume that Giap's strategic theory had been drawn directly from the Marxist-Leninist tradition. Many clues, however, both in his writings and elsewhere, point to more banal origins.

One influential source of Viet Minh strategy is Vietnam's own history. Subject to Chinese occupation for over a thousand years, the Vietnamese finally and violently shed China's imperial yoke in AD 939. In 1278, Vietnamese forces under Marshal Tran Hung Dao were one of the few peoples to defeat the invading Mongols on the field of battle. In fact, Dao was an early advocate of protracted resistance – a doctrine embraced by the Viet Minh seven centuries later.[7] After this success, Vietnam flourished and began conquering the societies that lay to the south, including the powerful Hindu kingdom of Champa (1470–71), until its armies came to the shores of the Gulf of Siam. In the seventeenth and eighteenth centuries tensions between the north and south of the country flared into protracted civil conflict, which prompted development of an extensive police apparatus.[8]

The most significant contribution to Viet Minh strategy, however, may be attributed to Mao's People's Army, which was close to a decade more advanced in its own guerrilla struggle. Giap's only formal military education was taken at Mao's "Kangta" school of guerrilla warfare, in Yenan.[9] Prominent on the school's reading list was Mao's treatise *Guerrilla Warfare*, written shortly after his famous "Long March" fetched the fledgling communist movement from the jaws of the Nationalist army and delivered it to the safety of the caves of Yenan province.

Despite Giap's fame, the most influential personalities in the development of Viet Minh strategic theory were Ho Chi Minh and the man who converted Giap to communism, Truong Chinh. He is lauded by Bernard Fall as the only relevant (as well as the most plainly understandable) Vietnamese communist ideologist, and Giap's most important writing merely borrows from him.[10] Truong was a staunch Maoist (his name is actually a pseudonym meaning "Long March" in Vietnamese), and his ideas amplified Mao's theories of revolutionary war.

The first and most important lesson imported by Truong and Ho was that no action in the revolutionary environment is exclusively military. Rather than abiding by Clausewitz's famous dictum that war is politics by other means, Mao states plainly that "politics is war without bloodshed."[11] All actions, whether armed or not, have political relevance, which takes primacy over its military significance. Military action, in other words, is merely another form of political expression. Second, the Maoist conception of strategy itself is very different from that of the West. Mao's political/strategic theory is intended to provide a blueprint for future actions in only the most general of terms,[12] because he believed that specific strategies could be made only by the commander in the field, in accordance with the circumstances that he encounters. Maoist theory therefore is not a deterministic formula for commanders to apply in future conflicts; it is a means by which a commander may conceptualize his options, given the current strategic environment.

Truong's strategic theory, which would become known as the theory of the "Strategic Offensive," provided a more specific formulation of three stages of revolutionary conflict than initially described by Mao. These stages were defined by the modes of conflict employed by the insurgent forces. One of these modes, "positional warfare," wherein a force contrives to take and hold vital ground, rests at the heart of traditional Western strategic thought. Mao identified it as indispensable also to a revolutionary force in defeating a determined enemy.[13]

Truong emphasized as well two other modes of combat that are usually ignored in traditional Western manuals on strategy. "Mobile" warfare and "guerrilla" warfare played to the weaknesses of more powerful but entrenched opposition. While unable to sustain a focused offensive, insurgent forces would sow disorder and confusion among an enemy; such "mobile" tactics employed quick but coordinated attacks along a wide front, followed by a withdrawal before the opponent could launch a counter-offensive. Tailored to less organized insurgent forces was "guerrilla" warfare, which achieved the same effect over a more protracted period. For Truong, this method involved small units used over a wide area to make harassing attacks against the enemy's weak points.[14]

The first stage of the "strategic offensive" was referred to by Truong as the "stage of contention," which was similar to Mao's "protracted" war. During this phase the enemy forces are militarily stronger than the revolutionary forces because the enemy still controls most major population centres and the lines of communications between them. The strategy is to maintain the defensive, but the tactics employed are to attack constantly, from the safety of well-hidden sanctuaries, using guerrilla warfare. Next comes the "stage of equilibrium." At this point the enemy has lost the offensive initiative and the opposing forces are its equal in strength. Mobile warfare becomes the dominant tactic, though both guerrilla warfare and positional warfare are used to a limited degree. The aim of this stage is to begin to destroy the enemy piecemeal while wearing down its will to resist. The final stage is the "general counter-offensive," launched when the balance of forces has tipped in favour of the revolutionary force, causing the enemy's forces to withdraw into the vital population centres. While mobile warfare remains the dominant tactic, positional warfare will be ultimately used to dislodge the enemy from the areas in which it remains.

ANIMATING THE STRATEGY

With this strategic blueprint in hand, Giap set about to animate it. Though they were the ultimate victor, the Viet Minh had few victories on the battlefield. Sustaining a protracted effort, with many setbacks, over such extended lines of communications presented the most difficult challenge of all. Giap recognized this in his "100 Page Plan" of early 1950, and, with the arrival of Mao's communists on the Chinese border in late 1949 Giap could acquire the materiel he needed to match the firepower of the French.[15] The organization he built to move huge amounts of materiel from the Chinese border to the battlefield should shatter any stereotype of the Viet Minh as merely a backward guerrilla force. Though it still relied on primitive means of transport, the organization was as advanced as any Western army, since coordination of huge numbers of porters required the most advanced staff work. George Tanham's study of the Viet Minh supply system estimated that a minimum of forty thousand porters per division was required; this number would increase should the division be required to employ heavy equipment. Coordinating this system demanded accurate staff tables and route planning to bring the necessary material to the front-line soldier. Such tables calculated, for example, that the porters could move 25 kilometres per day (20 at night), carrying 25 kilograms of rice or 15 to twenty kilograms of arms over level ground (the porters often consumed as much as 90 per cent of the rice they were carrying by the time they reached their destination).[16] Similar figures were worked out for oxen, bicycles, and a multitude of other simple methods of transport.

Rather than limiting mobility, the primitive infrastructure, combined with advanced staff capabilities, lent the Viet Minh forces a peculiar kind of mobility that offered both advantages and disadvantages over the French forces. The European battlefields of the Second World War emphasized manoeuvre warfare, in which the crucial element was speed, enhanced by mechanization. The Viet Minh did not acquire significant amounts of mechanized transport until 1953, when the Chinese managed to supply them with as many as one thousand vehicles. Even then, the vehicles were used mostly to transport supplies from the Chinese border to the main supply depots in northern Vietnam.[17] Otherwise, troops and supplies travelled exclusively by muscle power. The use of porters and dismounted soldiers meant that the Viet Minh were much less restricted than the French in the terrain they could traverse. Their potential lines of advance were more numerous and, as a result, less easy to identify and to interdict. Additionally, Giap assigned porter units and, whenever possible, combat units to specific areas, thereby allowing them to become intimately familiar with the terrain. Porters, for example, often trod the same small section of a supply route back and forth, over and over again.[18] This would allow porters, and soldiers, to learn the most efficient and safe track to follow and to blend more easily into the local population. All of this created great difficulty for an enemy attempting to challenge the movement of the Viet Minh forces, especially from the air or vehicles. This logistics system allowed the Viet Minh to manoeuvre and to strike at widely separated points without warning.

These advantages came at the cost of greater viscosity in their movement. Fewer weapons and equipment could be carried by muscle power than by motorized transport, and less quickly. The Viet Minh were, however, capable of rapid movement. During Giap's invasion of Laos during the 1952–53 campaign season, his forces advanced at an average of sixteen kilometres (measured in a straight line) per day, implying a ground march of as much as an astonishing thirty-two kilometres per day along the winding mountainous tracks of the border region.[19] This is a respectable rate of advance for even a mechanized force over such terrain; however, the striking power of Giap's units was limited. After 1949, for example, the reorganized Main Force regiments each contained a support company of 120-mm mortars, but though the companies had a strength of two hundred troops, each company could operate and supply only two mortars.[20]

The movement of sufficient forces into position for any sustained engagement therefore required considerable time and effort. The result was that the Viet Minh had little ability to exploit success or enemy weakness quickly. The most marked example was the lack of action that followed Giap's successes in his first offensive campaign along the Chinese border in the 1949–50 campaign season. Though the Viet Minh had cleared the French from all of their border posts along the Chinese border by November 1950, and with at least four months remaining in the dry season, it was January before Giap could muster another offensive fifty kilometres south into Tonkin towards Hanoi itself. Two precious dry months were lost because Giap required one month per division to move the necessary supplies into place.[21] On a wider scale, this meant that the Viet Minh lacked the mobility and firepower to challenge a significant French force directly and win. Until the Viet Minh could overcome this imbalance, the best result that they could achieve would be a prolonged stalemate.

By 1950 Giap had expanded and reorganized his forces, most notably forming the Main Force units into five operational divisions, thereby converting his fighting force into a modern, conventional army. While Giap retained the ability to conduct guerrilla operations through his People's Army units and some independent regiments of his Main Force, it was clear that conventional operations to seize and hold ground were becoming a major focus of Viet Minh strategy.

Giap's reorganization included the integration of three or four battalions into regiment-size units. Each regiment contained a headquarters, a small communications unit, and a support company of heavy mortars. Regiments were combined into divisions of twelve thousand troops, which also included a signals company and an engineer battalion. Also formed during this lull was a modern staff system based on the French model.[22]

While the size and organization of the Viet Minh force matched that of most Western armies, weapons did not. Most had been captured from the French or the Japanese or dropped by the Americans during the war. The result was a force that was only lightly armed and with a wide mix of incompatible weapons. Ingenious factories were fashioned deep in the Viet Bac region to supply ammunition for these weapons, as well as grenades and even heavy mortars. This was merely a stop-gap measure; despite their numbers, the Viet Minh remained outgunned by the French.

THE SHIFTING BALANCE

The arrival of the Chinese communists on the Vietnamese border in late 1949 addressed the material limitations of the Viet Minh, as heavy weapons soon began to flow to them.[23] In addition, the Chinese provided training for the Viet Minh commanders in the conventional tactics that their force would soon undertake in earnest. The tide had begun to turn definitively against the French, and they would not undertake a successful offensive operation from this point on. The initiative had passed to Giap, allowing him to build his forces towards the general counter-offensive.

By the start of the 1952–53 campaign, Giap had created two more divisions, including a "heavy" division, consisting of one engineering and two artillery regiments. This division incorporated some of the equipment now being infiltrated into Vietnam by the Chinese. Giap's Main Force units alone had between 110,000 and 125,000 troops, compared with France's combined expeditionary forces of 90,000.

The results of this campaign season reflect the Viet Minh advantage well. In December 1952, Giap attacked the French garrison at Na San, south of the Black River. Though the assault failed, resulting in seven thousand casualties, Na San remained surrounded by Giap's forces for the whole of the next year.[24] The French finally conceded that the garrison had to be evacuated. They did so by a clever ruse, convincing the Viet Minh through false radio messages that the many aircraft arriving at the garrison's airfield were bringing reinforcements. The aircraft were in fact arriving empty, enabling them to evacuate the entire garrison of twelve thousand without provoking a Viet Minh attack. The surprising ease of the withdrawal gave the French commander, Henri Navarre, the false hope that the French could establish, defend, and withdraw from a fortified air head. This was to be the method he would use to defend Laos. He would establish his key air head at Dien Bien Phu in Vietnam, near the Laotian border.

In October 1953, Giap launched his invasion of Laos itself, sending three divisions over the border. To counter the attack, Navarre launched an assault that succeeded in retaking Dien Bien Phu on 20 November. Leaks from the French government to the media made it clear that the French were prepared to make a stand at Dien Bien Phu in order to maintain an airlink to Laos. In response, Giap decided to make the remote garrison the site of the decisive battle of the war. He moved three divisions towards the garrison, and by the end of January he had between forty and fifty thousand troops surrounding the garrison of ten thousand.

The Viet Minh preparations for the battle were remarkable. Whole stretches of road were camouflaged with branches set between the tops of trees, creating a tunnel invisible to the French air forces. New roads and bridges were built and rebuilt after French air attacks. Surrounding the garrison itself, the

Viet Minh dug their artillery into covered bunkers overlooking the valley in which the garrison sat. Chinese supplied radar-controlled anti-aircraft guns that were set around Dien Bien Phu and along the Viet Minh resupply routes, forcing the French to fly at greater altitudes and thereby reducing their effectiveness in both aerial resupply for the garrison and interdiction of Viet Minh supplies. The Chinese also supplied Katyusha rocket batteries, lending great firepower to the Viet Minh. When the Viet Minh were in place, their positions were less than two thousand metres from the outer French trenches and less than four thousand metres from, and in direct sight of, the only French supply line, the airstrip.

Giap began his assault on 13 March, and the fighting that followed over the next seven weeks resembled tactics "from the First World War." This included trenching towards the French positions and sometimes tunnelling underneath them to set charges. By 7 May the Viet Minh had suffered twice as many casualties as the total original strength of the French garrison at Dien Bien Phu. Despite this, the garrison finally did fall, and, with it, the French will to fight to hold its possessions in Indo-China. [25]

One of the keys to Giap's victory was the sustenance provided by the rural population. Where the Western forces poured material resources into the conflict, the Viet Minh fed in human beings. In the end, the latter proved decisive. As Ho Chi Minh boasted to French representatives in 1946, as both sides braced for war, "You can kill ten of my men for every one of yours, but even at those odds, you shall lose and I shall win." The losses that Giap suffered at Dien Bien Phu were not unusual for his forces. In January 1951, at Vinh Yen in the Red River Delta, Giap lost an astounding fifteen thousand casualties, three-quarters of his entire attacking force, and still failed to oust the French. [26]

Yet to be able to absorb such losses continually, the Viet Minh needed something to give them an edge over their enemy. Their greatest practical advantage was derived not from an inherently superior strategy, or from great generalship, but from political roots that pushed deep into Vietnamese society. These roots sustained the Viet Minh forces for several years when they were at a distinct disadvantage in firepower relative to the French and then allowed them quickly to transform themselves into a sophisticated field force, capable of outgunning the French in positional warfare.

Though Giap's Viet Minh forces emerged as a ragtag and ill-armed force, they gained natural advantages over the French by virtue of their political power. Through this control the Viet Minh established a system that efficiently supplied their forces with food and new recruits. O'Niell estimated that, though the Viet Minh had a fighting force of 300,000 in 1954, this number was misleading to Western observers, for the Viet Minh had over one million porters in their service. [27] The kind of mobility that the Viet Minh relied on depended on masses of human labour in non-combat roles. It was the ability of the Viet Minh to recruit the necessary numbers of people, despite the casualties suffered in fighting formations, that held the key to their victory. Their most significant achievement in this war was creation of a force, in less than five years, sufficient to defeat the French. The capability to achieve this feat sprang from the very foundation of politics in Vietnam at the time.

THE POLITICAL WAR

The Viet Minh's advantage in recruiting may seem obvious, given that they were an indigenous group. However, the French had their own allies among the civilian population as well; minority groups in Vietnam often actively supported the French. The 1947 operation in which two battalions of T'ai tribesmen, led by French officers, cleared the Viet Minh out of the Fan Si Pan mountain region between the Red and Black rivers provides an isolated example of the effective use of that indigenous support. This area remained largely free of Viet Minh infiltration for several years.[28] The French also received the active support of Vietnam's Catholic minority, the Muong people living on the south bank of the Black River, and the Montegnard peoples of the central highlands. Despite Vietnam's long history of conquest, these peoples had successfully resisted Vietnamese incursions for centuries. They had survived and prospered through trade with foreigners, including Europeans, and had everything to lose with the passing of the French colonial regime. Yet the French lost even these regions, which had been defended successfully by the locals alone for centuries.[29]

To this day, analysts of this conflict disagree about the exact nature of the factors that led to Viet Minh hegemony in North Vietnam in 1954. Perhaps the victory cuts too closely to the roots of Western perceptions of the nature of war and strategy in the industrialized world. The victory seems to turn against a century of feverish advances in weapons technology, which appeared to have thoroughly subjugated strategy to the position of little more than a response to technology.

John McAllister and Paul Mus argue that the political defeat of the French occurred even before the first shots were exchanged with Viet Minh guerrillas in the jungle of the Viet Bac region. The failure of the French to influence Vietnamese society stemmed from the fact that they had never, even at the height of their colonial power, managed to penetrate it. The thick wall of bamboo and thorny plants that surrounded the typical Vietnamese village provides a rich analogy for its traditional isolation from central authority. Historically, the villages of this subsistence agrarian society were tied together by a central government, the court of the emperor, which was more a coordinator of the nation's affairs than a true national authority in the modern Western sense. The Vietnamese people paid taxes, selected their sons for military service, and even developed what little national infrastructure there was collectively, through the village council of notables. Power was overwhelmingly vested in these councils, spread across the countryside. The trading class that built and populated the small cities was primarily Chinese or made up of those controlled by the Chinese, and then by the French. In this way the Vietnamese isolated themselves from foreign dominance, even when their lands were "occupied."

Though discontent had long been sown by the time of the Japanese occupation, it was the events of the occupation and its aftermath that sealed the fate of French colonialism. The power of the French had been easily swept aside by the Japanese. Even the Allies in the Pacific after the defeat of Japan failed to include French forces in the acceptance of the surrender of Japanese forces and occupation, mandating the north to China and the south to Britain. Facing a political challenge from the Viet Minh on their return, the French turned to the authority of the pliant emperor, Bao Dai. This action merely represented another nail in the coffin of French colonialism. The villages had lost faith in their emperor under the Japanese occupation, during which Boa Dai had become a Japanese proxy.

Mus paints this event in terms of a traditional Chinese political concept, which had been imported by Vietnamese culture – the "Mandate of Heaven." He explains that the Vietnamese people perceived that the imperial government had lost its "virtue" – it could no longer sustain itself; and the time had come for it to pay for its past abuses. Political history shows that the Vietnamese have been remarkably quick to reject the moral authority of a fading regime in favour of a new one. While the French sought to anchor their renewed colonialism in the legitimacy of the emperor, they committed a fatal error in failing to recognize the Vietnamese notion of legitimacy.

Even though the Viet Minh had been in power for a short time, their creation – the Democratic Republic of Vietnam, established in 1945 – profoundly changed Vietnamese society. The traditional village council of notables, which the emperor and the French had failed to subvert completely, were finally swept away, often violently. In their place the Viet Minh created councils dominated by worker and peasant unions that supported the party. This demonstrated the moral power of the Viet Minh. To the vast majority of the peasantry the Viet Minh represented a force that could establish itself in power and displace the declining influence of the emperor. The people were investing their faith in the "virtue" of the Viet Minh. [30]

CONCLUSION: THE VICTORY AND VIET MINH STRATEGY

The predominant Western paradigm concerning the First Indo-Chinese War betrays a misunderstanding of Viet Minh strategy and attaches undue importance to their fighting doctrine in defeating the French. The conduct of Viet

Minh campaigns was in many ways flawed, and tremendously costly. Though this fighting doctrine is critical to any explanation of the course of the conflict, the cost of this struggle was borne not by the revolutionary soldiers alone, but by a significant portion of the civilian population. Ultimately, Viet Minh fighting doctrine relied as much on the political strength of the movement as the political level did on the movement's military strength.

The image of the victorious Viet Minh forces as a ragtag band of guerrillas is the first myth that may be usefully discarded. A critical element in Viet Minh strategy was the organization of an immense logistical structure that could overcome the difficult terrain. The Viet Minh also depended on willing allies, especially China. But the Viet Minh, by 1953, with Chinese assistance, while not divorced from guerrilla tactics, had become a force which, by dint of its superior firepower, could take and hold ground against the French. Until Giap could transform his forces into a powerful conventional force capable of employing positional tactics, he could hope only to deprive his adversary of the strategic initiative. Victory could not, and did not, come until the Viet Minh could match the French on the battlefield.

France, in contrast, could not match the political and material support mustered by the Viet Minh. Apart from some American assistance, France fought alone. And with u.s. support amounting to less than u.s.$1 billion of the u.s. $12 billion spent by France on the war, France did not have the resources to prosecute the war effectively. By 1953, the Viet Minh were a larger, better-equipped, and better-supplied conventional force than their French adversaries.[31]

Where the French forces suffered a disadvantage, the Viet Minh enjoyed an advantage, for they did not lack willing allies. The Chinese, in particular, may be credited with building the Viet Minh forces into a modern, well-equipped, and quite conventional fighting force.

A second great myth that may usefully be dismissed is that which portrays Giap as the great strategist. As discussed above, the greatest influence on Viet Minh strategy was Mao. Giap's strength was as a pragmatic practitioner of Mao's strategic theory, which evolved with changes in fortune. Yet despite its shortcomings, the strategy followed by Giap prevailed.

Of course, for every winning strategy there is a losing strategy, which, in some ways, inevitably becomes its corollary. While the aim here is not to provide a detailed account of French strategy, it is worthwhile accounting for that corollary, as it provides an understanding of the strengths of the winning strategy. In this case, a key reason for the French failure was that the French treated the insurgency in Indo-China as primarily a military problem. In so doing they ignored the political context of the war. Specifically, they failed to search for and address the underlying causes of the unrest, of which the Viet Minh were ultimately able to take advantage. Perhaps the most blatant example of this insensitivity was their support of Bao Dai, who had also been a puppet of the Japanese on the Vietnamese throne.[32] While the French provided for the political, economic, and military needs of the urban and trading classes, they displaced the traditional political structures of the much greater source of manpower and material – the huge rural class. Viet Minh political forces filled this vacuum within the village power structures, and so their forces could roam unmolested in the sustaining sea of the populace.

Yet the casualties suffered by both sides do not reflect the French failure. The Viet Minh suffered casualties dramatically higher than the French in almost every engagement, regardless of outcome. However, rather than reflecting the relative success of the French, these casualties represent the price paid by the supporters of the Viet Minh. This fact provides another clue to the real success of the Viet Minh and the corresponding failure of the French.

The Viet Minh prevailed, despite their huge losses, because of their political influence over the thousands of villages throughout the countryside. Through the exertion of moral influence on village councils, or often through outright coercion, they made good their losses in personnel. The villages sustained the struggle through its years of materiel insufficiency and propelled it to victory when the Viet Minh leadership was able to acquire adequate firepower. Mus, alone among prominent Western authors, seems to have perceived the decisive power of the village councils. He reminds us that, though Vietnam achieved its territorial advances militarily, it held them over the last two millennia against all foes through the political power of the village. Only in those areas where the traditional village failed to flourish was its military power challenged.[33]

Giap's success is further evidence of the primacy of politics over strategy within the Viet Minh. It also reflects the duality contained within Maoist doctrine, for Giap was not solely a military figure. During the Paris peace talks of 1946, attended by Ho and Pham, Giap was acting leader of the entire Viet Minh organization. His stature near the top of the political leadership, and the strong role of the party in decision making and indoctrination within the military forces, point to a great interdependence between the two realms. Revising Clausewitz's famous dictum, Mao stated that "politics is war, without bloodshed." The great strength of Viet Minh strategy rested in the ability of its leadership to cause one to serve the other, establishing the interdependence reflected in the dual structure of the Viet Minh movement.

In the final analysis, it must be considered merely incidental that the leadership of this revolutionary movement was communist. Ultimately, the Viet Minh, like its mentor, Mao, rode on widespread political dissatisfaction. Through the support of foreign communist movements and prudent leadership, the Viet Minh managed to focus this expression and mould it to their vision. Giap's brilliance was in his plying of the waters between politics and war that Mao so perceptively identified. He intimately understood the connection between politics and war that Clausewitz had enunciated for a

Western audience at the beginning of the age of modern warfare. The self-absorption of the West in its European wars has narrowed the Western paradigm of strategy to a point where its definitions of this concept may no longer be adequate to understand conflict in the modern world. Giap's experience, shorn of its near-mythological aspects, is a clear example of an alternative paradigm of strategy which bears examination by students and practitioners of war.

NOTES

1 Baylis, "Revolutionary Warfare," 209.
2 Chalmers Johnson, cited in ibid., 211.
3 Ibid., 212.
4 Ibid., 209.
5 Excerpted in Freedman, ed., *War*, 315.
6 Davidson, *Vietnam at War*, 41.
7 Fall, *Street without Joy*, 111.
8 McAllister and Mus, *The Vietnamese and Their Revolution*, 34.
9 O'Ballance, *The Indo-China War 1945–1954*, 40.
10 Fall's comments are contained in the introduction to Truong, *Primer for Revolt*, viii.
11 Baylis et al., *Contemporary Strategy*, 212.
12 Shy and Collier, "Revolutionary War," 839–43.
13 O'Ballance, *The Indo-China War 1945–1954*, 16. A detailed definition of this term is contained in Truong, *Primer for Revolt*, 115.
14 Truong, *Primer for Revolt*, 116.
15 Davidson, *Vietnam at War*, 75.
16 Tanham, *Communist Revolutionary Warfare*, 70.
17 Ibid.
18 O'Neill, *General Giap*, 72.
19 Davidson, *Vietnam at War*, 155.
20 Tanham, *Communist Revolutionary Warfare*, 42.
21 Davidson, *Vietnam at War*, 91.
22 Ibid., 58.
23 Ibid., 75.
24 Ibid., 147.
25 Ibid., 256.
26 Karnow, *Vietnam*, 17, 108–27.
27 Davidson, *Vietnam at War*, 72.
28 Ibid., 50.
29 McAllister and Mus, *The Vietnamese and Their Revolution*, 33–4.
30 Ibid., 69, 128.

31 Ibid., 281.
32 A more detailed account of French insensitivity to Vietnamese nationalism is contained in O'Ballance, *The Indo-China War 1945–1954*, 252.
33 McAllister and Mus, *The Vietnamese and Their Revolution*, 44.

Vo Nguyên Giap: A Strategy for Protracted Revolutionary War

LCOL PAUL F. WYNNYK

They are not supposed to pulverize the core, but to nibble at the shell and around the edges.[1]

Clausewitz

Clausewitz's views on "popular uprisings" were based, to a large degree, on an analysis of the French experience during the Peninsular War, and he wrote that an uprising is "[l]ike smoldering embers, it consumes the basic foundations of the enemy forces ... [A] general conflagration closes in on the enemy, driving him out of the country before he is faced with total destruction."[2]

Clausewitz examined "popular uprisings" from a purely military perspective, and in this regard it is useful to discuss the political connotations of both revolutionary and guerrilla war. "Revolutionary war" is commonly used to describe war conducted in order to gain political power; therefore it does not occur between nation states because at least one of the belligerents is indigenous to the nation in which it fights. As well, revolutionaries, by definition, have clear aims and goals and are generally willing to pursue these goals over long periods of time. Finally, revolutionary war is not absolute, and the distinction between revolutionary war and war between nation states can easily become blurred by foreign involvement of a material or military nature.[3]

Guerrilla warfare, in contrast, is but one of several means of waging revolutionary war, which can "range from nonviolent political mobilization of people, legal political action, strikes, agitation, and terrorism, to large-scale battles and conventional military operations."[4] It is also possible for guerrillas to have no political or revolutionary aims, though the potential of guerrilla warfare has been widely recognized by astute twentieth-century revolutionaries.

Giap was a revolutionary who mastered the entire spectrum of revolutionary conflict, through a detailed study of history. An adept propagandist and guerrilla leader, he was also a competent military strategist who employed conventional forces to defeat two major powers. His strategy was based on theories of revolutionary warfare enunciated by Mao Zedong, himself "a peasant who learned from history" (see the essay by B.R. Struthers above). This essay focuses on Giap's involvement in "The Ten Thousand Day War,"[5] the reasons for his success, and the relevance of Giap to the modern strategist.

VO NGUYÊN GIAP

No study of the modern Vietnamese revolutionary movement can be undertaken without examining the roots of its ubiquitous military leader, Vo Nguyên Giap. Born in 1912 in Quang Binh, one of the poorest provinces of central Vietnam, Giap grew up in poverty. In 1924 he began studies at the *Lycée national* in Hué, which was noted for its mix of traditional and progressive education. The school was a natural choice for those Vietnamese who aspired to positions of authority, and its alumni included many nationalists, including Ho Chi Minh, his future patron and the political leader of the Vietnamese revolutionary movement. In 1926, Giap joined the *Tan Viet Cach Menh Dang* – the Revolutionary Party for a Great Vietnam. After leading student demonstrations to protest the plight of rice and rubber farmers during the Depression, Giap was sentenced, in 1930, to three years in jail. He served three months, was released for good behaviour, and "[w]ith the single-minded concentration and energy that were to become his hallmarks, he threw himself into his academic work."[6]

After completing his studies at the *Lycée national*, Giap moved to Hanoi, the site of French Indochina's only university. There he studied law, passed his *licence en droit* in 1937, and began postgraduate studies in 1938. It was at this time that his political activities began to occupy the bulk of his time, and Giap wrote for several pro-communist Vietnamese and French publications. While the communist movement was not the only nationalist movement in Vietnam, it was the strongest, and many nationalists gravitated to it for this reason. Giap, now preoccupied with his political activities, withdrew from his studies. Though he failed to write the exam for a certificate in administrative law his "progress to the University of Hanoi and his record at the University have established his intellectual reputation as of an order comparable to those of the leaders of nations much more powerful than Vietnam."[7]

Politics was at the centre of Giap's life. However, he took the time for occasional personal diversions, and he wed the daughter of his professor and landlord in 1938. While this was unquestionably an astute move, Giap's ardour was genuine. A few years later, his wife and her sister were captured by the French and tried for conspiracy against the security of France. Giap was never to see his wife or sister-in-law again. His wife died in prison in

1943, while her sister was guillotined. Giap escaped to south China, where he spent over a year with the Red Chinese in Yenan. The influence of the Chinese Communists on Giap was significant, and it was in China that he met Ho Chi Minh. "Ho immediately took a liking to the young firebrand and entrusted him with a most difficult mission: the organization of a Communist military force inside Vietnam."[8]

THE FIRST INDO-CHINESE WAR

In October 1944, Ho ordered Giap to form an "Armed Propaganda Brigade for the Liberation of Vietnam." On Christmas Eve of the same year, elements of this organization crossed from China into Vietnam and massacred the garrison of two French border posts at Phy Khat and Na Ngan. When Japanese occupation forces overthrew the Vichy French on 9 March 1945, they had few troops to control the countryside. The Viet Minh filled the void and assiduously avoided contact with the Japanese, and there was only one recorded Viet Minh attack on a Japanese outpost.

On V-J Day – 15 August 1945 – Ho Chi Minh and Giap entered Hanoi with thousands of Viet Minh. On 2 September, Ho Chi Minh proclaimed the independence of the Democratic Republic of Vietnam. France was initially reluctant to recognize this independence, but it did so on 6 March 1946, under the proviso that Vietnam would remain in both the Indo-Chinese Federation and the French Union. Unsure of Viet Minh intentions, the French began rapidly to increase their military presence, particularly in the south, where the Viet Minh were not well established.

During this period, Giap began what would become a life-long duality in the role of soldier and politician. In addition to retaining his duties as commander-in-chief of the People's Army, Giap was appointed minister of defence. For four months from June 1946, Giap was also the de facto president and minister of the interior, while Ho Chi Minh and key ministers were in Paris for negotiations. Giap was not a mere caretaker, and "[i]n a series of swift stabs, he destroyed the back-country strongholds of the nationalist parties; executed hundreds of Vietnamese nationalists and even such old comrades in arms as the Trotskyite leader Ta-Thu-Thau, a personal friend of Ho Chi Minh."[9]

The Paris negotiations proved fruitless, however, and savage fighting broke out in Hanoi in late 1946 and early 1947. The French drove the Viet Minh into the countryside and by the end of March 1947 controlled all the major delta and coastal towns in Tonkin and Annam. Giap and Ho escaped to a jungle base approximately 130 kilometres north of Hanoi, and from this location they directed a country-wide guerrilla campaign. Isolated French garrisons were savagely attacked, usually at night, and the Viet Minh dispersed when French reinforcements arrived. "In view of the serious economic and military weaknesses of France after World War II, the French Army in 1947 was in an extremely unfavourable position to attempt the defeat of the Viet Minh."[10]

Giap continued to direct the guerrilla war from his jungle base until late 1950, when he mounted a major assault against French defences in northern Tonkin. Operating from isolated locations within Vietnam and from China, the operation was a resounding success. The French were eventually forced to abandon most of northern Indochina and consolidate around the Red River valley in Tonkin. The defeat came as a severe blow to the French High Command, which, "in ignorance of the true strength of the Viet Minh and keenly conscious of the dishonour of retreating before lesser breeds, had chosen a plan involving its troops in a high degree of risk."[11]

The French dispatched their leading soldier, General De Lattre de Tassigny, to re-establish French supremacy in Indochina. Giap, inspired by the successful guerrilla campaign, "was flattered by the appointment of the prestigious de Lattre as his chief opponent and was anxious to test him."[12] In reality, it was Giap who was to be severely tested. By the end of 1950, de Lattre had reoccupied most of the areas taken by the Viet Minh and rebuilt French morale. Giap's forces were now equipped with heavy weapons from China, and, buoyed by the victory of the Chinese Communists in their homeland, Giap launched several premature assaults against the French in the Hanoi and Haiphong regions. By mid-July 1951, the Viet Minh had suffered 20,000 casualties, had lost the initiative, and were forced to withdraw to jungle bases to reconstitute and to rethink their strategy. Though victorious, the French wished to prevent a recurrence of a similar offensive and established a series of watch-towers and fortifications around the Red River Delta known as the "de Lattre Line."

The next three years were characterized by continued guerrilla warfare and French over-confidence. Giap had learned from the costly assaults in the Red River Delta and would not attack in strength again unless it was on his terms. Instead, he relied on a campaign of infiltration and terrorism. The de Lattre line "was about as effective as a sieve, ... [and] the 'rotting away' (*pourissement*) of the delta" began in earnest.[13] De Lattre was relieved because of ill-health, and both the Viet Minh and the French intensified their activities, but it was not until the siege of Dien Bien Phu that Giap was to engage the French in a major battle.

Dien Bien Phu is a small crossroads town, 350 kilometres northwest of Hanoi, leading to Laos. It was there that General Henri-Eugène Navarre, the new French commander, attempted to manoeuvre the Viet Minh into a set-piece battle. Navarre hoped to establish a firm base from which he could move out and destroy the Viet Minh, with the aim of reaching negotiations favourable to the French. The idea was not unsound, for though the French had to rely entirely on air support, the Viet Minh had no apparent way of moving up vehicles, equipment, and heavy weapons. The French eventually put six battalions of infantry, one regiment of artillery, and a company of engineers into Dien Bien Phu.

Unbeknown to the French, Giap had made the following appreciation of the French position: "Dien Bien Phu was a very strongly fortified entrenched camp. But on the other hand, it was set up in a mountainous region, on ground which was advantageous to us, and decidedly disadvantageous to the enemy. The only means of supplying Dien Bien Phu was by air ... We could overcome all difficulties in solving the necessary tactical problems; we had, in addition, an immense rear, and the problem of supplying the front with food and ammunition, though very difficult, was not insoluble. It was on the basis of this analysis of the enemy's and our own strong and weak points that we solved the question as to whether we should attack Dien Bien Phu or not. *We decided to wipe out at all costs the whole enemy force at Dien Bien Phu.*"[14]

The siege of Dien Bien Phu lasted from 20 November 1953 until 7 May 1954. French intelligence had badly miscalculated Giap's ability to mobilize civilians to move heavy guns and supplies forward. Over a period of six months, Giap's forces moved over two hundred pieces of artillery and their stocks of ammunition through several hundred kilometres of jungles. The Viet Minh captured the Dien Bien Phu airfield on 27 March 1954, sealing the fate of the French garrison. Of the original 15,000-man garrison, the surviving 10,000 surrendered to the Viet Minh on 7 May 1954. "When the smoke cleared, the French had suffered their greatest colonial defeat since Montcalm had died at Quebec."[15]

The débâcle spelled the end of a century of French involvement in Indochina. Following the defeat of the Dien Bien Phu garrison, talks in Geneva partitioned Vietnam into a North and a South. A cease-fire went into effect on 1 August 1954, but, lest the French think that the Viet Minh had lost their will to fight, Giap conducted intense guerrilla warfare until well after this date. Both Ho Chi Minh and Giap were pleased with their new legitimacy, but neither believed that the agreement was anything more than a pause. The United States, which hitherto had provided only material aid to the French, now began making substantial contributions of military equipment, instruction, and economic aid to South Vietnam.

INTERNAL STRUGGLES AND THE SECOND INDO-CHINESE WAR

In accordance with the agreement reached in Geneva, all Viet Minh military forces were to be concentrated in North Vietnam. While Giap complied by removing all Main Force (regular) units from South Vietnam, he had no intention of withdrawing or disbanding local cadres. Instead, these guerrilla elements were given instructions to go underground and await further orders. In this way, Giap maintained the critical infrastructure required to conduct guerrilla warfare in the second phase of his struggle.

Ho Chi Minh's government, in which Giap remained a cabinet member, began a series of land reforms aimed at eliminating landlords and transferring political power to the peasant class. The purge associated with the reforms was ruthless, and many supporters of the revolution were executed simply because they owned land. By 1957, 100,000 people had been put to death, but few peasants had possession of their own land because of the administrative incompetence of the government. The country was on the verge of economic ruin, and many undoubtedly longed for a return to the colonial administration. Robert J. O'Neill, Giap's Australian biographer, made the following observation: "The mere fact that Giap remained a member of the inner cabinet which carried this policy into effect underlines the fundamental ruthlessness which he showed with regard to the lives of his troops between 1951 and 1954, and leads one to wonder whether, if Giap had had to operate within the restrictions which his opponents had to observe regarding human suffering, he would have been a successful general at all." [16]

None the less, the regime prospered and, with Chinese backing, sponsored continuous insurrection in South Vietnam. The guerrilla cells that Giap had ordered to remain dormant at the time of partition became active once again and were known as the Viet Cong. Despite increasing amounts of American aid, Viet Cong's support grew in the face of the abuses and widespread corruption of the South Vietnamese government, led by Ngo Dinh Diem. The instability of the government culminated in a series of back-to-back coups d'état in late 1963 and 1964. Faced with the prospect of total collapse of the South Vietnamese government, the United States became more deeply involved.

Despite the popular myth that he personally commanded the 1968 siege of Khe Sanh in the hope of achieving another Dien Bien Phu, Giap in fact directed the entire war effort from Hanoi. His methods were not significantly different from those employed against the French, and he continued to preach the merits of dispersion and patience to his field commanders. It was during the late 1960s that Giap fully enunciated his theory of the three-stage revolutionary war. The first stage was considered the strategic defence, and action was taken only on the political and propaganda fronts; Giap waged war in this manner where there were large concentrations of American troops and little Viet Cong support. The second stage consisted of mobile guerrilla operations, and hit-and-run tactics were employed in areas with significant Viet Cong activity but no North Vietnamese units. The third stage involved cooperation between Viet Cong guerrillas and North Vietnamese regulars, and this cooperation posed a major problem to American forces assigned to the border region of the demilitarized zone. [17]

The turning point of the Second Indo-Chinese War, and perhaps Giap's greatest strategic success, was the Tet Offensive of 1968. Concentrating on meeting real and anticipated Communist advances in the countryside, American and South Vietnamese forces did not maintain large garrisons in major population centres. Giap saw an opportunity, and he launched a wave of attacks throughout the main cities and towns of South Vietnam. The offensive was a clear-cut tactical defeat for North Vietnam, but, ironically, a major strategic victory. Until this point, the Americans believed that they were winning the war in Vietnam, but Tet altered this perception by serving as a major catalyst for the anti-war effort in the United States. The u.s. secretary of defence, Clark Clifford, headed an inquiry into the Tet Offensive, and, as a result of what he learned, " 'the great hawk became the great dove' … [He] wanted to get out of Vietnam and 'to get out right away.' " [18]

From the time of the announcement of the American troop withdrawal in 1969 to its completion in 1973, Giap continued his pursuit of the three-phase revolutionary war. Soviet and Chinese aid continued to abet the North Vietnamese effort, and it was soon apparent that the inherently corrupt South Vietnamese government could not survive indefinitely. Yet during this period, Giap continued to advocate a strategy of patience, advising his field commanders not to expect the fall of Saigon until the late 1970s. However, his cautious approach gave way to boldness as it rapidly became apparent that the Americans would not recommence bombing to halt the North Vietnamese advance. Hué and Da Nang fell to Giap's forces, and on 30 April 1975 the North Vietnamese flag was raised over Saigon. This effectively meant the end of South Vietnam, for the remaining South Vietnamese forces located south of Saigon gave up without a struggle. Vietnamese Communists "had against all odds endured and fought the century's longest war," [19] and Giap had presided over the entire struggle.

SUCCESSES AND FAILURES

How was it that Giap was to lead the military resources of a so-called Third World nation in the defeat of two major world powers? The answer is multifaceted and a topic of ongoing analysis. Many of the ideas espoused by the Viet Minh were not original; both Giap and Ho Chi Minh borrowed heavily from the writings of Mao Zedong. Yet what sets the Vietnam experience apart from other modern revolutionary wars is the dramatic success of the Vietnamese Communists. Mao may have given Giap many of his ideas, but there can be no doubt that Giap was an excellent student.

In May 1938, Mao stated that "the War of Resistance will be a protracted war." [20] Giap understood the theory of protracted war well and from the outset made it clear to his subordinates that the struggle would be long and difficult. For this reason, Giap was seldom in a hurry to engage the enemy until conditions were favourable to the Viet Minh, even if this meant delays of several months or years. This leisurely approach to operations stood in marked contrast to that of the French and Americans, who were under constant political pressure to achieve decisive tactical- and operational-level results. The French and Americans, for the most part, had success at these levels but ignored the welfare of the Vietnamese people as a whole in the pursuit of tangible victories. "In a short war, military acts which erode the basis of political support – such as failure to administer those civilians caught in the theatre of war – may be tolerable in terms of the overall result; in a protracted war, the ultimate strength is the political will of the entire nation, and any loss of political strength represents an equal or greater loss of military strength."[21]

Another factor that contributed to victory was the ability of the Vietnamese people to endure sacrifice well beyond the level that their enemies would tolerate. During the period of significant American involvement, from 1965 to 1973, Giap's forces suffered an estimated 2.5 million combat fatalities – over ten times as many as those incurred by American forces. Both France and the United States had significant gaps between their strategic aims in Vietnam and the degree of sacrifice that their respective nations were willing to tolerate in achieving those aims. Conversely, the Viet Minh laboured under no such illusion, and Giap once remarked: "[E]very minute, hundreds of thousands of people die all over the world. The life or death of a hundred, a thousand, or of tens of thousands of human beings, even if they are our own compatriots, represents really very little."[22] Giap's remarks contrast sharply with Western concepts of limited liability and underscore the extremist views for which he was renowned.

Ironically, Giap was a master at winning public support despite his beliefs concerning the value of human life. Much of this support was derived from the emphasis that he placed on the "human element," based on Mao Zedong's thoughts concerning the supremacy of man over weapons. Mao said that "the basis for guerrilla discipline must be the individual conscience."[23] In the late 1950s, Giap collated a number of essays he had written on revolutionary war with the intention of publishing an insurrection manual for underdeveloped countries. The resultant work, *People's War People's Army*, was first published in Vietnamese in 1960. Mao's influence regarding the importance of the individual was evident in the following passage: "In contacts with the people, [you should] ... follow these three recommendations: 1) to respect the people; 2) to help the people; 3) to defend the people ... in order to win their confidence and affection and achieve a perfect understanding between the people and the army."[24]

This grassroots understanding of human motivation and will was a significant weapon in Giap's struggle against technologically superior foes. It also enabled the Viet Minh to mobilize virtually the entire population in some areas, which contributed to the failure of French and American intelligence to predict major engagements such as Dien Bien Phu in 1954 and the Tet Offensive of 1968. Logistics was, more often than not, the decisive factor in Giap's planning. Faced by difficult terrain, a shortage of supplies, and a constant threat, Giap had to enlist a vast force of porters; one million were needed to sustain an army of 300,000. Individuals who engaged in such work were regarded as genuine heros, and, in extolling them, Ho Chi Minh stated that "a pick stroke in the road has the value of a bullet shot at the enemy."[25]

The idea of political supremacy over military affairs, even at the tactical level, was embraced at an early stage by both Giap and Ho Chi Minh. In October 1944, Ho ordered Giap to establish an "Armed Propaganda Brigade for the Liberation of Vietnam." Ho elaborated by stating that the brigade was to concentrate "more on political action than on military force, because it is an instrument of political propaganda."[26] Giap put this order into practice by forbidding action to be taken against the French if there was a chance of collateral damage to Vietnamese or their property. Political officers were assigned at the company level and were granted sufficient power to overrule the military commander should the situation warrant. Below company level, political supervision was carried out by all soldiers, though political officers were occasionally assigned to individual squads to check party loyalty.

The basic building block of the Viet Minh organization was the three-man cell, and the daily routine included a period for political discussion and self-recrimination. "No man knew when one of his cell colleagues would report him to a political officer for lack of political ardour ... [W]ith these command techniques, Giap obviously had no problems of disobedience, not only with regard to a specific order but also to general tactical and strategic notions."[27] This concept of political supervision seems to contradict Giap's ideas on human motivation enunciated in *People's War People's Army*, where he stated that his army was motivated by "mutual affection of brothers-in-arms, love at the same time pure and sublime, tested and forged in the battle, in the struggle for the defence of the Fatherland and the people."[28]

Throughout the Vietnamese conflict, Giap strove to maintain a simple and inherently flexible organization within the military. This simplicity was maintained throughout a three-tier structure that excluded civilians mobilized for porter duties: "Experience in carrying out the people's war over the past 25 years in our country has proved that the three categories of troops – (1) main force units, (2) regional forces, and (3) guerrilla and self-defence militia forces – are the most appropriate organizational form to mobilize all people to fight the enemy."[29]

All units within this organization, regardless of their position within the three-tier structure, were based on the three-by-three principle adopted from the Chinese Communists. All units and formations, from platoons to armies, consisted of three identical sub-units, whose primary role was combat or combat support. Beginning at the platoon or company level, a fourth sub-unit was included to provide administrative and logistic support.[30] Though the three-by-three principle was not inviolate, it did ensure that Giap consistently maintained a three-to-one ratio of combat to support troops. Even when one considers the employment of Vietnamese porters by the Viet Minh, this ratio stands in sharp contrast to the administratively heavy organizations required to maintain French and American combat troops in Indochina.

Of course, besides the indigenous effort, the success of the Vietnamese revolutionary movement can be attributed, at least indirectly, to the material and moral support of the Communist bloc. The Kremlin was careful to avoid direct assistance to the Viet Minh because of the potential of direct conflict with the United States. None the less, the Soviet Union was relatively generous in financial assistance, providing Hanoi with annual subsidies of over $1 billion during the late 1960s. China's support, by virtue of its contiguous border with Vietnam, was somewhat more tangible and included provision of vehicles, equipment, and supplies. In addition to logistical support, the Chinese contributed training areas and secure bases for the Viet Minh. Giap remained conscious of the fact that successful guerrilla warfare required space for manoeuvre and deceit – space that was often unavailable in Vietnam. However, these geographical limitations were "compensated for by the existence of an inviolable foreign base, which provid[ed] equipment and diplomatic support."[31]

From a Western point of view, one of Giap's least-understood successes was his ability to instill and maintain excellent morale within his army, despite tremendous losses. In this regard, Giap is credited with creating a professional army "surpassing any other in its 'human' capabilities."[32] While the ability of the Vietnamese to endure, coupled with such cultural factors as religion and unquestioned respect for superiors, undoubtedly sustained morale, Giap implored his subordinates to instill morale at the unit and sub-unit levels. Lieutenant-Colonel William Henderson, a retired U.S. army officer who served as a company commander in Vietnam, discussed Giap's uncanny ability to maintain morale in Why the Vietcong Fought. Henderson concluded that the values, attitudes, and behaviour of both Viet Cong and North Vietnamese soldiers were "shaped by three strong forces: party organization and ideology; unit and sub-unit leaders; and a primary group of soldiers with strong and homogeneous values."[33]

Giap's generalship was not infallible, and a number of rather serious errors were made, particularly in the early phases of the conflict against the French. During the ill-fated assaults in the Red River Delta during 1950, Giap was responsible for the decimation of some of his best regiments. In hindsight, it is almost certain that these units could have been used to better advantage had they remained in the jungle and waited for the French to come to them. In this regard, Giap failed to understand the French school of *offensive à l'outrance*, of which General de Lattre was an outspoken advocate. The rather crude strategy of the Viet Minh in 1950 may be blamed on their entire leadership, for the decision to launch a major offensive was a collective one. Nevertheless, Giap possessed "insufficient thought about wider matters of strategy, a common enough fault amongst senior military commanders, but one which might have been avoided had Giap received some formal tuition in the history of strategic thought before he rose to the height of Viet Minh Commander in Chief."[34]

There is debate, even today, over Giap's conduct of the Tet Offensive. Despite the strategic success of the battle, North Vietnamese Regulars and Viet Cong were decimated, and it is unlikely that any general, even Giap, would have considered losses of this magnitude as an acceptable factor in his plan. Giap's conduct of the early phases of the First Indo-Chinese War and the Tet Offensive seem to be in direct contrast with the advice of Friedrich Engels, who stated that it is "our duty to protect the scarcely formed core of our proletarian Party, not to sacrifice it uselessly."[35] Giap's failure to heed this advice is probably a reflection of his personal priorities, in which he placed nationalism above communism. Though a founding member of the Vietnamese Communist party and a life-long student of history, Giap seldom referred to Engels or Marx. Like Ho Chi Minh, Giap was not a vocal supporter of the theory of worldwide communism and espoused only those aspects of communism that furthered Vietnamese independence and unity.

CONCLUSION

What relevance does Giap's successful conduct of a protracted revolutionary war have to the modern strategist? If nothing else, Giap's leadership provides a useful example of the execution of the three classical phases of revolutionary war "from the strategic defensive through guerrilla warfare to the counter-offensive."[36] Though this theory is attributed to Mao Zedong, Giap's adherence to these classical phases is perhaps the best example of Mao's theory being put into practice. It was the failure of both the French and American governments to understand this theory that contributed to their defeats, "in large part because ... [they] never grasped the kind of war being fought nor the particular Vietnamese conditions that gave the war its revolutionary character."[37]

For most of the conflict, Giap simultaneously undertook the duties of senior politician and top soldier. This melding of two of the most important positions in a country at war provided a unity of military command and political direction that could simply not be matched by Giap's adversaries. "The separation of political power and military force is an essential feature of a liberal system of government, but when such a government sends its soldiers against a man like Giap, it finds that they commence their task with a handicap which few survive for long."[38] In summary, civil–military relations were harmonious in North Vietnam.

Giap's willingness to accept consistent tactical defeat in the pursuit of strategic victory is also worthy of note. With the exception of Dien Bien Phu, both the French and Americans were almost always tactically victorious, largely because of pressure from their respective governments to achieve quick and decisive results. Giap, in contrast, was under no such pressure and took tactical defeat in stride, provided that it contributed to the overall strategic aim of creating one Vietnam. Yet Giap's victory was, in many ways, hollow – he won the war but in the long run has lost the peace. Millions of Vietnamese died during the Indo-Chinese wars to satisfy the war aims of North Vietnam, and the post-1975 American embargo, coupled with the sudden and complete termination of Soviet aid in the late 1980s, has brought Vietnam to the brink of economic collapse. In many ways, the plight of the agrarian peasant, whom Giap staunchly defended from the 1930s on, has not improved. In evaluating Giap's record, John Shy and Thomas W. Collier claimed that "revolutionary warfare, waged against any but the most feeble regime, is hardly a magic prescription for military and political victory."[39]

Perhaps a few words are in order here about some aspects of the cultural gap between Vietnam and its Western adversaries. While cultural differences affected the strategies employed by the combatants in the Indo-Chinese wars, the root of the conflict – the desire for self-determination – was as dear to the Vietnamese as it was to the French and Americans. In the eyes of the Americans, and to a lesser degree the French, the spectre of communism seems to have overshadowed the fact that the Vietnamese struggle was really nothing more than an independence movement. Communism was merely the quickest means to arrive at this independence.

The Americans, in particular, had only to examine their own independence movement to understand what was happening in Vietnam. Ho Chi Minh's Proclamation of Independence of 1946 quoted several passages, word for word, from the U.S. Declaration of Independence.[40] Viewed in this light, it is not unreasonable to suggest that Giap was a Vietnamese George Washington. Though the outcome of the war might not have been different, American decision makers would have been better prepared had they looked beyond the cultural and ideological differences and recognized some of the common threads in the two nations' experience. A better appreciation of the situation in Vietnam, framed against an understanding of the American Revolution of some two hundred years earlier, would have led to the conclusion that cultural and ideological differences played a smaller part than at first might seem apparent in this protracted war of independence.

Finally, to put Giap's successes and failures into context, a brief examination of the concept of limited war is in order. Neither the French nor the

Americans approached the Vietnamese problem as a full-scale war, which contrasted sharply with the perceptions and the official policies of the leaders in Hanoi. Though the Americans advocated a worldwide policy of flexible response, whereby the necessary means – ranging from diplomatic effort to full-scale conventional war – would be used to deal with international security issues, the American government clearly wanted to limit the conflict. This was a major strategic error, for it "showed that keeping a war limited to the extent one desires depends on the willingness of the opponent to accept the limitations."[41] If American strategists had studied Giap's Viet Cong insurrection manual, *People's War, People's Army*, they would have realized that Giap placed no limits on his pursuit of a unified and independent Vietnam.

Could the French and Americans have been successful against Giap had they altered their strategies? With the luxury of hindsight, it is safe to say that a French and/or American victory might have been possible, but the Indo-Chinese wars would have had to have been conducted in an entirely different manner. First, the population of Vietnam, in particular South Vietnam, was extremely vulnerable to insurgency. As a result, only massive intervention, and ultimately the establishment of a French or American protectorate, would have countered this vulnerability. Second, neither the French nor the Americans were trained, equipped, or organized to fight against an insurgency. Though the Americans had spectacular success with the employment of special forces during the early phases of American involvement, these troops made up less than 10 per cent of the total force. Perhaps a stronger "hearts and minds" campaign, reinforced by more special forces, might have altered the outcome of the conflict. Third, and perhaps most crucially, popular support within both France and the United States was not strong enough to justify a war of the scale and duration required to defeat Giap. Had either country had the will to carry on with the war in the face of mounting casualties, Giap might have been threatened. Given that neither France nor the United States could have, for a variety of reasons, significantly altered their conduct of the Indo-Chinese wars, the best course of action might well have been non-involvement.[42]

NOTES

1 Clausewitz, *On War*, ed. Howard and Paret, 480–1.
2 Ibid., 480.
3 Shy and Collier, "Revolutionary War," 817.
4 Ibid.
5 Maclear, *The Ten Thousand Day War*, ix.
6 Fall, "Introduction," to Giap, *People's War, People's Army*, xxx.

7   O'Neill, *General Giap*, 202.

8   Fall, "Introduction," to Giap, *People's War, People's Army*, xxxiii.

9   Ibid., xxxvi.

10 O'Neill, *General Giap*, 50.

11 Ibid., 78.

12 Sully, *Age of the Guerrilla*, 150.

13 Buttinger, *Vietnam*, 743.

14 Giap, *People's War, People's Army*, 166–9.

15 Fall, *Street without Joy*, 30.

16 O'Neill, *General Giap*, 167.

17 Ibid., 194.

18 Maclear, *The Ten Thousand Day War*, 218.

19 Ibid., 349.

20 Mao Tse-tung, "On Protracted War," 53.

21 O'Neill, *General Giap*, 63.

22 Fall, "Introduction" to Giap, *People's War, People's Army*, xxxvii.

23 George, *The Chinese Communist Army in Action*, 25.

24 Giap, *People's War, People's Army*, 56.

25 Sully, *Age of the Guerrilla*, 144.

26 Giang, *Les grandes dates*, 46.

27 O'Neill, *General Giap*, 66.

28 Giap, *People's War, People's Army*, 58.

29 Giap, "The Party's Military Line," 6.

30 Henderson, *Why the Vietcong Fought*, 34.

31 Paret and Shy, *Guerrillas in the 1960's*, 29.

32 Henderson, *Why the Vietcong Fought*, 119.

33 Ibid., 119–20.

34 O'Neill, *General Giap*, 85.

35 Marx and Engels, *Selected Correspondence*, 522–3.

36 Ibid., 62.

37 Shy and Collier, "Revolutionary War," 856.

38 O'Neill, *General Giap*, 204.

39 Shy and Collier, "Revolutionary War," 860.

40 Carver, "Conventional Warfare in the Nuclear Age," 787.

41 Osgood, *Limited War Revisited*, 37–48.

42 Buttinger, *The Smaller Dragon*, 299.

Brown-Water Navies and Counterinsurgency Operations

LCDR HAROLD J. HENDERSON

Riverine warfare and counterinsurgency operations may seem to be subjects of a bygone era in "the new world order." It is difficult to imagine a setting today in which the two might be brought together again and demand the attention of a superpower such as the United States; however that is what occurred in Vietnam, over twenty-five years ago. Even then only limited attention was paid to these types of operations during the Vietnam War, fought as they were by a relatively small number of personnel, operating relatively small units. Only a handful of articles and service documents were ever published about these operations at that time, and virtually nothing has been written about riverine warfare and counterinsurgency operations since. In fact, the most recent publication that deals with the subject, *Vietnam: The Naval Story*, edited by Frank Uhlig, Jr, is only a collection of material that appeared over twenty-five years earlier in the U.S. Naval Institute's *Proceedings* and *Naval Review*.

Today the u.s. Navy's war cry is "From the Sea," and, indeed, there is new attention being given to littoral warfare by most modern blue-water navies. Still, this does not encompass riverine warfare or counterinsurgency operations. However, if there is a need to go beyond littoral warfare, the lessons to be gleaned from the American experience in Vietnam are available from history and need not be relearned at a heavy price in lives and money. For there might be less than the one hundred years that separated the American Civil War and Vietnam, before either the United States or UN forces could be required to intervene in another war requiring similar operations.

A MAHANIAN NAVY

When the United States committed its forces to combat in Vietnam in August 1964 it was just coming to grips with the concept of flexible response and its armed forces were only beginning to devolve from a preponderant reliance on nuclear weapons. They had forgotten the lessons of the Korean War and failed to learn the lessons from the French in Vietnam. [1] This failure led to the confused and ineffective employment of u.s. forces in Vietnam. Examples included the 3rd Marine Amphibious Force being deployed statically, as army units, and hence losing the advantage of their mobility; the army adapting the marines' vertical envelopment tactics, necessitating creation of their own rotary-wing air force; and air force and naval aviation concentrating the bulk of their bombing effort on cutting the Communist supply lines, a tactic proven ineffective in Korea. [2] Other targets that air attacks were directed against were "by and large meaningless and stupidly selected," including suspected truck parks, ferry landings, and others with absolutely no military value. [3]

The u.s. Navy (usn), built on Mahanian principles, was also unprepared for unconventional warfare. It had been developed to counter the Soviet Union and command the seas. Its fleets were comprised of aircraft carriers, with nuclear-armed Vigilante bombers embarked, escorted by nuclear-armed cruisers and destroyers, and supported around the world with overseas bases. It was ill-prepared, materially and doctrinally, for a limited war against a nation that offered no challenge to its dominance of the major sea routes and, indeed, could muster only a very insignificant coastal naval force. [4] Unfortunately for the usn, it was not allowed to exercise its command of the seas fully because the u.s. government chose until 1972 not to blockade the coast of North Vietnam and, in particular, close Haiphong Harbour, through which over 85 per cent of the North's military imports arrived. [5] In Vietnam, the usn was required to control the coastal and inland water lines of communications instead of the major sea lines of communication for which it had prepared. Thus the usn, a blue-water navy, had to resort to the type of brown-water operations that it had abandoned at the turn of the century, largely as a result of Mahan's advocacy of an ocean-going fleet. In fact, it was obliged to fight the war in Vietnam following principles best enunciated by Sir Julian Corbett at the beginning of the twentieth century. [6]

Though restrictions imposed on the usn prevented it from blockading North Vietnam until late in the war, one of its first actions was to implement a "defensive" blockade of South Vietnam. This began as a blockade off the coast of South Vietnam to prevent Communist insurgency and resupply but was afterward extended to that country's frontiers with Cambodia and Laos on the rivers and canals of South Vietnam. In concert with the riverine patrols came revitalization of combined operations of the type that Corbett described in his naval histories and considered an essential element of naval operations in his strategic principles. Indeed, the u.s. Mobile Riverine Force (MRF), with the modern addition of airborne assault, epitomized these combined operations.

Perhaps because the force was comprised of only relatively minor small craft, the u.s. commander-in-chief Pacific, Admiral U.S.G. Sharp, did not even mention the riverine operations in his 1968 report on the air and naval campaigns against North Vietnam.[7] This may have reflected the USN's institutional focus on major combatants and the blue-water navy, but, the riverine forces provided the strength and mobility required to impede significantly the flow of enemy supplies and insurgents into South Vietnam. It accomplished this through intensive "policing" operations of Vietnam's principal transportation routes – the inland waterways. Additionally, the MRF markedly reduced the control and influence of the insurgent Viet Cong (VC) in the Mekong Delta through its highly successful strikes on VC forces operating there. In this way the brown-water navy helped achieve the objectives of counterinsurgency operations and pacification in a limited war that was not intended to destroy North Vietnam.[8]

GROWING U.S. INVOLVEMENT IN VIETNAM

The United States first became involved in Vietnam when its concern about Communist expansionism overrode its distaste for French colonialism. Initially this entailed providing military material to France in its war against Ho Chi Minh's rebels from 1946 to 1954.[9] Following the defeat of the French at Dien Bien Phu in May 1954, an agreement for a cessation of hostilities was reached at Geneva in July 1954. As part of the agreement Vietnam was divided into two parts at the 17th parallel, and the belligerents were required to withdraw their forces, the French to the South and the Viet Minh to the North. When the Viet Minh withdrew, however, about five thousand of their troops remained to form a nucleus for future operations, complemented by about three thousand members of the Communist political apparatus.[10]

For two years following the cessation of hostilities the French and u.s. military worked together to forge a South Vietnamese military. Finally, in April 1956, the French Naval Forces Far East was disestablished and the u.s. Military Assistance Advisory Group (MAAG) assumed full responsibility for advising the South Vietnamese forces.[11]

Late in 1959 there was a marked increase noted in the number of Communist insurgents from North Vietnam. The United States reacted by transferring additional equipment to South Vietnam, predominantly in the form of patrol craft. In 1961, when it was apparent that the flow of Communists to the south was continuing unimpeded, President John F. Kennedy announced an expansion of the Military Assistance Program for Vietnam. [12] In December 1961, USN forces began to play a limited role, assisting the Vietnamese Navy (VNN) with its coastal patrol in the vicinity of the 17th parallel. This activity was confined to radar-equipped USN ocean minesweepers vectoring VNN units to intercept radar contacts. In February 1962, similar operations were commenced, with destroyer escorts participating, in the Gulf of Thailand. [13]

Meanwhile, in 1960, the National Liberation Front (NLF) was established in South Vietnam. It was a Communist-dominated organization – in effect, the political wing of the VC guerrilla forces. The NLF was central in organizing mass associations in rural areas to support the Communist movement and producing anti-government propaganda. [14]

The situation in South Vietnam continued to deteriorate with increasing political unrest, and in November 1963 the president was deposed by a generals' coup and killed. This caused additional chaos and three years of turmoil in the senior leadership. [15] The North Vietnamese, seeing an opportunity to gain further ground, decided shortly afterward to step up military aid to the VC. The guerrillas' actions had been circumscribed by their wide variety of weapons and limited supplies of required ammunitions. In 1964, Hanoi began to provide shipments of standardized, single-calibre arms and ammunition and more modern supporting weapons. [16] This committed Hanoi to significantly increased infiltration, and the easiest and cheapest means of transporting this material was by the sea.

When it was realized that infiltration was increasing along the coast, the Vietnamese Junk Force, comprised of civilian irregulars operating sail-powered junks, was increased in size and motorized in the hope of increasing its effectiveness. However, in January 1964 the USN conducted a study of the situation with a team of eight officers headed by a Captain Bucklew, USN. The team's report was critical of the effectiveness of the existing coastal patrol and recommended further augmentation of VNN forces with USN personnel and equipment. It also concluded that U.S. forces might have to deploy to the Mekong Delta rivers to stop the Communist infiltration. [17]

The Bucklew Report provided the impetus for a rapid change in the posture of USN forces in Vietnam. Among the changes were the MAAG being absorbed by the U.S. Military Assistance Command Vietnam (MACV), and the Navy Section MAAG becoming the Naval Advisor Group, MACV. Major construction was also begun on ports to support U.S. military sea lift and naval operations, and an order was placed for thirty-four river patrol craft (RPC). [18] In August 1964, North Vietnamese torpedo boats attacked the U.S. destroyer *Maddox*, while it was on patrol in the Gulf of Tonkin, resulting in commitment of U.S. fighting forces to the Vietnam conflict.

THE BROWN-WATER NAVY

The "Vung Ro Incident" in February 1965 led to creation of the forefather of the brown-water navy. Vung Ro is a bay in the central coastal area of South Vietnam, almost half-way between the demilitarized zone (DMZ) and Saigon (see Map 1). On 16 February 1965 a U.S. army medical helicopter returning from a mission spotted a camouflaged vessel lying in the bay and reported it. Subsequent investigation revealed that it was about 45 metres long and displacing approximately one hundred tons. Air strikes were called in, and the vessel was sunk. Arrangements were then made for South Vietnamese forces to inspect the wreck and the beach area for any related activity. The investigating forces did not at first show up, as they had been ordered, and then failed to complete their task when they encountered opposition ashore. It was only with U.S. prodding and assistance that the beach was secured several days later and a large cache of automatic weapons and ammunition was discovered.[19]

This incident provided the final proof for the USN of the ineffectiveness of the VNN's coastal patrols and the South Vietnamese military's lack of organization and resolve to prosecute insurgents. Subsequently, early in March 1965, the USN joined the VNN in its coastal patrols to interdict infiltrators in Operation Market Time. Patrols were established to stem two types of traffic – the coastal trade, comprised mostly of junks transiting north and south along the coast, and the often-larger vessels approaching the coast further from seaward to avoid interception by the inshore patrol forces.

The patrol of coastal waters was enhanced by reorganization of the Vietnamese Junk Fleet, and augmentation by USN and U.S. Coast Guard patrol craft. Patrols further offshore were conducted by larger units, including destroyers, landing ships (tank), and ocean minesweepers supported by USN maritime patrol aircraft and helicopters. Through a succession of changes, the operational command of these forces was transferred from the commander-in-chief Pacific to the commander of the MACV, and operational control from the commander of U.S. Task Force (TF) 71 to the chief of the Naval Advisory Group (CNAG). Finally, the forces of the Coastal Surveillance Force were designated TF 115.[20]

The number of interceptions made by TF 115 forces made it difficult to assess the effectiveness of the operation. It was believed that the lack of a significant increase in interceptions was indicative of the coastal insurgency operations' having been either stopped altogether or rerouted. In September 1965, a meeting was held in Saigon to discuss the progress of Market Time operations and the way ahead; it concluded with two major recommendations: augmentation of the coastal patrol forces and creation of an extensive river patrol. The U.S. brown-water navy was born.[21]

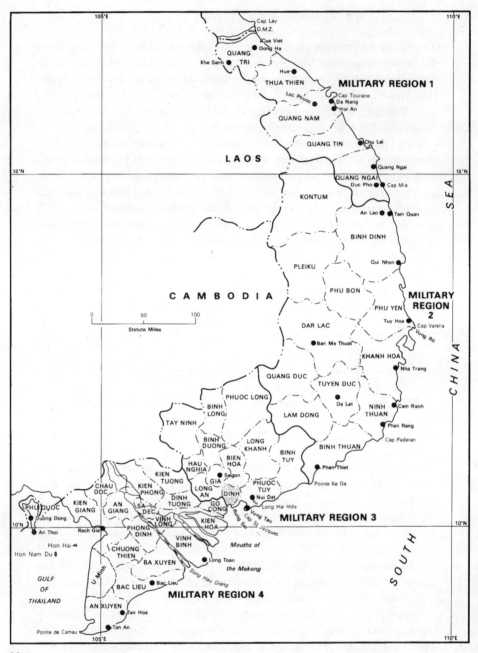

Map 1
Military regions, South Vietnam.
Source: Fairfax, *Navy in Vietnam*, 4.

The first river patrols were instituted during the fall of 1965, from the Saigon Navy Yard, using four landing craft personnel (large), or LCPLs, to control VC cross-channel traffic in the Rung Sat Special Zone.[22] Commencing in December 1965, with establishment of another task force, TF 116, USN Riverine Forces steadily grew over the next four years, until they were turned over to the Vietnamese in 1970. In January 1967, the River Assault Force (later designated the Mobile Riverine Force), TF 117, was established, followed in February 1968 by Task Force Clearwater and finally by Sea Lords (Southeast Asia Lake, Ocean, River, and Delta Strategy), TF 194, in late 1968. Each task force had its own area of operations and specific missions, which are considered in further detail below.

OPERATION GAME WARDEN

The River Patrol Force, TF 116, was established under the operational control of CNAG and operated in the III and IV Corps Tactical Zones (CTZs)[23] and the Rung Sat Special Zone (RSSZ) (see maps 2 and 3). The mission of TF 116 was "to assist the Government of South Vietnam in denying the enemy use of the major rivers of the Delta and the Rung Sat Special Zone."[24] The RSSZ, known also as the "Forest of Assassins," was situated on the sea approaches to Saigon and had provided a safe haven to pirates and criminals for years. Now it provided cover to Communist insurgents and VC operations against shipping destined for Saigon.

The original concept of operations for Game Warden was to establish two forces of river patrol boats (PBRs) in the vicinity of the Delta and Rung Sat river mouths. Each force was to be equipped with ten PBRs and a team of two Huey UH-1B helicopter gunships – the pair designated a light helo fire team (LHFT) – and be supported by a landing ship (tank). Early into Game Warden it was discovered, however, that the PBRs' operations were too often restricted by offshore sea and weather conditions. The concept was subsequently abandoned, and seven support sites ashore were selected and developed instead.[25]

TF 116 was originally made up of 120 PBRs, twenty LCPLs, a landing ship dock, and eight UH-1B Huey helicopters, nicknamed "Seawolves."[26] The helicopter forces were expanded to twenty-two aircraft in September 1967 and designated helicopter attack (light) squadron three (HA(L)-3).[27] In February 1967 a force level of 250 PBRs was authorized.

TF 116 was first organized in two task groups (TGs), with TG 116.1 operating as the Delta River Patrol Group and TG 116.2 as the Rung Sat Patrol Group. The first PBRs that arrived "in country" commenced patrols in the RSSZ in April 1966, with operations expanding to the Delta area the next month.[28] The PBRs were distributed between the two operational areas, with eighty operating in the Delta as part of TG 116.1 and forty in TG 116.2 in the

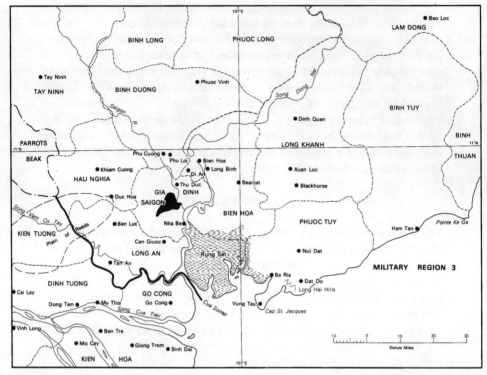

Map 2
III Corps Combat Tactical Zone.
Source: Fairfax, *Navy in Vietnam*, 8.

Map 3
IV Corps Combat Tactical Zone.
Source: Fairfax, *Navy in Vietnam*, 15.

Rung Sat. TG 116.2 also included a mine counter-measures (MCM) unit, in view of its additional responsibility for protection against the mining of shipping routes to Saigon.[29]

By 1968, TF 116 had grown considerably and was comprised of four task groups, situated on the Bassac, Co Chien, and My Tho and in the Rung Sat. The first three were in fact the original TG 116.1 divided into three groups because of expanding operations. Each task group was assigned approximately the same number of craft, except that the Rung Sat had no landing ship (tank) assigned to it for support; however, it did retain its minesweepers.[30] In June 1968 a new task group was formed, the Upper Delta Patrol Group, charged with conducting counterinsurgency operations near the Cambodian border.[31] The Game Warden helicopter forces were also augmented by sixteen OV-10 Bronco aircraft. These lightly armed, fixed-wing reconnaissance aircraft, especially designed for counterinsurgency, were assigned to TF 116 in April 1969.

The riverine forces were born of the same basic necessities as conventional blue-water naval forces – to secure the use of the waters (in this case, inland waters) for the friendly forces and deny their use to the enemy. As such, the riverine forces comprised a wide range of water craft employed in greatly diversified activities. These activities included minesweeping, escort of materiel and personnel, combined operations with amphibious assault forces for area sweeps, fire support for friendly land forces, counterinsurgency, interdiction of Communist supplies, and pacification of areas wrested from the VC. The workhorses of the riverine forces were the PBRs, which were employed for patrol, transport, and fire support, working in close cooperation with LFHTs.

Though U.S. forces had conducted riverine operations previously in their history,[32] the lessons from those campaigns had been lost over time. When the decision was made in 1965 to operate riverine forces in Vietnam, the USN started essentially from scratch, modifying existing equipment and acquiring new equipment. It also had to relearn the doctrine and tactics for such operations.

As already mentioned, PBRs were the principal patrol craft on the inland waters. Their shallow draft and speed made them highly mobile, and their fire power, for a small craft (ten metres long), was substantial.[33] Their operations were based on two-boat patrols, with tactics to be determined as dictated by the local situation. In other words, the tactics were improvised and developed through trial and error.[34]

Patrols were typically of twelve hours' duration, with half of the patrols conducted at night. The PBRs would normally transit to and from their patrol areas at high speed and then patrol with a combination of slow speed and drifting. The drifting tactic was developed to overcome the PBR's noisy engines, thereby enhancing their stealth and ability to surprise enemy forces.[35] Much of their time on patrol was boring for the personnel, particularly during their early operations, when they were not so aggressive in hunting out enemy forces. Their duties consisted of continually checking river banks and Vietnamese river craft, which were primarily sampans. In a single month Game Warden PBRs detected 200,000 water craft, conducted cursory inspections of half of these, and did close inspections of as many as 50,000.[36]

The waterways were important in VC communications, and when personnel and materiel were not actually transported on the waterways they typically moved on footpaths alongside of them. PBRs were often engaged in serious fire-fights when they surprised VC forces travelling along, or crossing, a river. They were also the subjects of VC ambushes. To enhance their "survivability," as well as to expand the area of their patrol coverage, they developed a tactic of "lead" and "cover" boats. The lead would normally precede its team mate by 400–600 metres. Otherwise, however, PBRs on patrol remained in separate patrol areas and relied on other forms of support if they were engaged.[37] This additional support could be provided by artillery, depending on where the engagement occurred, but was most often furnished by Seawolves and later, commencing in 1969, Bronco aircraft.

The Seawolves, operating in pairs as LFHTs, were employed in direct support of PBR operations and armed patrol of the river delta areas. Priority was always given to supporting PBRs in contact with enemy. The helicopters were available around the clock, with 80 per cent of their time spent standing to, ready to be airborne at three minutes' notice. They were normally co-located with the PBRs, either ashore or on their floating bases, and able to reach the PBRs within fifteen minutes of receiving a call for assistance.[38]

While airborne, the aircraft would normally operate well above tree-top level to enhance their visual search and to avoid the increased hazards of small-arms fire at low altitude. Their tactics were similar to those employed by army helicopter gunships, but modified to meet the special requirements of close coordination of fire-power, communications, and movement between the helicopter and PBR. When patrolling, the lead aircraft would normally fly about thirty metres higher than his wingman, thereby enabling the latter to fire beneath the lead aircraft in case of trouble. When engaging targets, the LHFTs would set up a circular pattern, with each helicopter alternately engaging the enemy while the other provided cover.[39]

In April 1969, the first OV-10 Bronco armed reconnaissance aircraft joined the PBR support forces in Operation Game Warden. While these aircraft had greater speed, endurance, and heavier armament than the Seawolves, they were unable to operate from the PBR bases or to provide the same accuracy of fire against small, evading targets as the helicopters. Additional air support was provided by a range of aircraft, right up to B-52 bombing strikes against VC base areas from which operations were conducted against PBRs.[40]

PBRs were also involved in combined operations, ranging from major assaults to insertion of small forces of Vietnamese Regional Forces (RF) or Popular Forces (PF). The former involved cooperation with amphibious units of the Army's Mobile Riverine Force, TF 117, or Marines along with airborne assault to envelop and sweep enemy-held areas along rivers or in the RSSZ. In such operations the PBRs provided cover and advance patrol of the waterways, ahead of the assault forces being landed. Once sweep operations were under way, the PBRs would provide a blockade of the river to prevent enemy escape. Two such major assaults were undertaken in the RSSZ, one in 1966 and the other in 1969.[41]

Operations with Vietnamese PF or RF forces were normally organized by the PBR task groups themselves to clear areas in which they were being repeatedly harassed by VC forces. The task group would send representatives to a South Vietnamese village and solicit the assistance of the PF or RF outpost chief to employ some of his forces to conduct a sweep of the area where the PBRs were coming under attack. The operation would be conducted in a manner similar to the large-scale assaults, but with much smaller forces. One or two PBR patrols would transport the Vietnamese forces for insertion, and then other PBRs and a LHFT would support the sweep operation.[42]

Finally, in addition to trying to destroy enemy units in South Vietnam, the American and South Vietnamese forces sought to overcome their influence on the people and secure their support for the government, through pacification operations. As a means of overcoming the influence of VC insurgents, the riverine forces were extensively involved in psychological operations (psyops) in the river regions around which the majority of the population lived. Psyops were confined largely to propaganda aimed at countering the VCs' propaganda and trying to induce them to turn themselves in. A program called "Open Arms," run by the South Vietnamese government, offered amnesty, on-the-job training, and resettlement.[43]

In addition to psyops, the PBRs were involved both directly and indirectly with civic action programs aimed at pacifying the population. These programs included rebuilding structures destroyed by the VC, digging wells, and providing medical treatment to the sick and injured.[44] A typical operation would involve the PBRs transporting a team of USN and VNN hospital corpsmen to a hamlet for a combined MEDCAP (Medical Civil Action Program) with a team of local musical entertainers, U.S. cartoon movies, and candy for the children.[45]

THE MOBILE RIVERINE FORCE

The precursor of the Mobile Riverine Force – the Mekong Delta Mobile Afloat Force – was established during the summer and fall of 1966 to conduct search and destroy missions along the rivers. At that time it was considered that 75 per cent of the rural population in the Delta and perhaps two-thirds of its substantial rice crop (80 per cent of the nation's harvest) were controlled by the VC, thereby providing a valuable source of both tax revenue and food to the vc. The MRF was very similar in composition and operations to the French navy's riverine force created in 1946, which was designated *divisions navales d'assaut* and came to be called "*Dinassauts.*"[46] During the First Indo-Chinese War (1945–54), the *Dinassauts* operated in both the Red River and Mekong River deltas.[47] Following the departure of the French navy, the VNN operated its own Riverine Assault Group, inheriting its units and doctrine from the French.[48] However, this group was of limited effectiveness,[49] which led the U.S. army to form its own riverine force to counter insurgency in the Mekong Delta.[50]

The plan for the MRF evolved to consist eventually of a floating base with accommodations for a full army brigade and all the necessary navy support elements. It was to be comprised of four self-propelled barracks ships, two landing-craft repair ships, two landing ships (tank), and two squadrons of thirty-four converted mechanized landing craft (LCM-6) and sixteen assault support patrol boats (ASPBS). The LCM-6s were eventually converted to armored troop carriers, command and control boats, monitors, and one refueller.[51]

TF 117 was officially activated on 28 February 1967 under the operational control of CNAG, now designated Commander Naval Forces Vietnam (ComNavForV), in his capacity as an operational commander.[52] By June 1967, the MRF was up to full strength for its converted LCMs, and, with the U.S. 9th Infantry Division embarked, it also had its own artillery, provided by barge-mounted 105-mm howitzers towed along with the base or employed in advance of operations.[53] The first phase of a typical TF 117 operation entailed selection of an objective – a known vc unit or stronghold in the Delta – and the transit of the assault forces to the landing area by land, air, and river, embarked in the armoured troop carriers. The river assault force proceeded much as a standard naval convoy, conducting an opposed transit prepared for attack by mines, enemy water craft, or ambush by land forces. As such the armoured troop carriers were preceded by some of the assault support patrol boats (ASPBs), dragging chain sweeps to cut wires to shore-commanded mines, while other ASPBs provided additional protection ahead, on the flanks, and astern. The protection of the ASPBs was further augmented by the monitors, and the force was given cover by tactical air and armed helicopters.[54] Additionally, to help conceal its impending operations, the MRF often transited to its objective area under cover of darkness.

An assault would be conducted from the waterway and the air to envelop the enemy position in all dimensions. As the troops disembarked, the monitors and ASPBs would station themselves to provide fire support to the land forces and covering fire for the armoured troop carriers. Other ASPBs would station themselves along the river as a blocking force to close the water avenues of escape to the enemy forces.[55] The land operations, covered by the fire-power of the ASPBs, monitors, artillery, and air support, would continue typically for two to four days, following which the land forces would be re-embarked by the river assault force boats or helicopters. The extraction would be given the same type of cover as the initial assault, and, as a further precaution against ambush, the MRF units would take an alternative route to their base. [56]

The MRF's initial operations were conducted in the RSSZ, with major sweeps conducted to regain control of the waterways adjacent to the shipping routes to Saigon. They were then expanded further into the Delta, and occasionally undertaken with the added support of Game Warden PBRs and assistance from South Vietnamese marines and river assault groups. [57] The mobility and strength of the MRF proved critical to the salvation of several of the Delta's cities during the 1968 Tet Offensive. During that time, it went from one battle to another without relief and was credited by General Westmoreland as having "saved the Delta." [58]

TASK FORCE CLEARWATER

Task Force Clearwater had its origins in the struggle to support the Third Marine Amphibious Force (III MAF) situated in the I Corps CTZ, south of the DMZ. It was one of the most hotly contested areas in Vietnam and the key supply route for transport of material to Hué and Dong Ha in the Perfume and Cua Viet rivers regions. Unfortunately for the American forces, the two rivers were narrow and easily interdicted by enemy mines, rocket grenades, and automatic weapons. Consequently, early in 1967, the commander of the III MAF requested thirty to forty PBRs or ASPBs to ensure safe transit of supplies. [59] The request for support was approved, and TF Clearwater was activated on 24 February 1968 and placed under operational control of the general commanding III MAF. It was divided into two groups, the Hue River Security Group and the Dong Ha River Security Group. Because of a paucity of assets, only one group could be formed at a time. The Hué River Group was the first to become operational, with a mobile base (MB) established initially at Tan My. It comprised ten PBRs and five LCM-6s, which had been converted locally to minesweepers. In March, one of the river assault divisions of TF 117, less its ASPBs, was attached to the Cua Viet Security Group. [60]

Until the Tet Offensive, the Clearwater PBRs had been conducting the same type of operations as in Game Warden; but afterward the commander of TF Clearwater had to divert all his assets to convoying logistics craft up the rivers. As part of this changed role, he requested more fast patrol craft to replace the slower TF 117 craft. This request resulted in ten additional PBRs being provided from the Rung Sat. These were divided between the two Clearwater groups, and the attached TF 117 unit, less six ATCs retained as minesweepers, was returned to the Delta. [61]

By June 1968, the battle for Hué was over and the Perfume River had been pacified. Consequently, in September 1968, the mission statement for Clearwater forces was changed to facilitate operations similar to Game Warden.

These included psyops, visit and search, cordon and search, amphibious insertions, and resource and population control work.[62] In mid-1969, each of the two security groups comprised a patrol unit (PBRs) and an MCM unit. New equipment was also being developed; the Hué River group tested patrol air-cushion vehicles (PACVs), while the Cua Viet group had a specially equipped LCPL surveillance unit.

SEA LORDS

First because of Operation Market Time, and then increasingly because of Operation Game Warden, the Communists shifted their supply lines inland through neutral Cambodia and Laos.[63] In addition, intelligence had repeatedly indicated that the bulk of enemy war materiel entering the III and IV Corps areas was entering Cambodia from the sea.[64] Consequently, in late 1968 and early 1969, Game Warden operations were largely redirected, with the combined efforts of task forces 115, 116, and 117 being assigned to Operation Sea Lords. This operation was intended to complement the Market Time blockade of the coast with an inland naval patrol from the Gulf of Thailand to an area northeast of the "Parrots Beak," a large area of Cambodia extending eastward and closest to Saigon.[65]

Sea Lords operations were conducted between November 1968 and January 1969 and were comprised of four essentially separate operations, as indicated in the table on p. 164. In Operation Search Turn, heavy craft of the MRF and ground troops secured the area around the Gia Long Xuyen and Ca San Canals in the upper Mekong Delta, and then permanent naval patrols were established as a barrier on these waterways.[66] Next, Operation Foul Deck, later renamed Tran Hung Dao, placed naval patrols on the Rach Gian Thanh and Vinh Te Canal at the Cambodian border.[67] Operation Giant Slingshot was centred on the Vam Co rivers, which straddled the "Parrots Beak," and was characterized by frequent heavy clashes between river patrol boats and the enemy.[68] The forces for this operation included Game Warden PBRs, two VNN river assault interdiction divisions, a division of ASPBs from TF 117, and a multitude of aircraft, including Sea Wolves, Cobras, and OV-10 Broncos. Other units, including artillery, also supported the operation.[69] To the west, a Canal Campaign was conducted by Swifts (PCFs) of TF 115 operating up the canals of the upper Mekong Delta from the Gulf of Siam. Finally, in the centre, Operation Barrier Reef, comprised of PBRs and boats of TF 117, was established as the final link in the chain of barriers on 2 January 1969.[70] This concentrated barrier deployment was believed to be very successful, based on the sharp rise in fire-fights with the enemy, seizure of large arms caches, and the back-up of enemy war materiel in the north. The barrier operation might have been even more effective had the army been prepared to augment the river patrols with river bank patrols; however, it did not commit the forces required to conduct these patrols.[71]

Table
Sea Lords Operations

Operations	Fire-fights	Munitions caches uncovered	Other caches uncovered	Confirmed enemy killed	Enemy captured
Search Turn (began 2 Nov. 1968)	200	14 (11.0 tons)	1 (1 ton)	219	27
Tran Hung Dao (began 16 Nov. 1968)	276	3 (11.4 tons)	0	470	26
Giant Slingshot (began 6 Dec. 1968)	1,044	244 (137 tons)	22 (384.9 tons)	1,910	232
Barrier Reef (began 2 Jan. 1969)	77	1 (0.4 tons)	0	189	46

Sources: Fulton, *Vietnam Studies*, 172.

CONCLUSION

The USN was forced to resort to brown-water operations in South Vietnam when U.S. government constraints prevented American forces from taking more effective action to prevent the supply of enemy forces. Such action could have included the complete blockade of the North Vietnamese coast, preventing the flow of arms and other war supplies into North Vietnam for shipment to forces in the South. It might also have involved unrestricted bombing of the North's industrial and population centres, denying the North the means of producing war supplies and the human resources required to pack them on their backs through the jungles. Such bombing might have also had a more significant effect on the North's will to fight than propaganda leaflets. Instead, war supplies for Communist forces in the South continued to be produced in the North and shipped to the South by various means.

One of the most efficient means to get provisions from the North into South Vietnam was by water transport. "Some French naval officers have gone so far as to estimate that 90 percent of the communications system of Indochina is by water, whether by the China Sea, the rivers, and their confluences, or by canal."[72] Hence the USN was forced initially to conduct interdiction operations off the coast of South Vietnam. As Operation Market Time began to tell on the enemy's coastal supply lines, their supply lines moved inshore and into the inland waterways. As Operation Game Warden put the squeeze on these supply lines, the enemy increasingly used the routes from "neutral" Cambodia and Laos, whence the supplies required for the Tet Offensive were believed to have entered South Vietnam. This was the major impetus for Sea Lords, commencing in late 1968, which significantly blocked the lines of communications emanating from Cambodia.

In the final analysis, it is difficult to assess the effectiveness of the riverine operations in the Delta, as they never entirely secured the area. To make such an assessment, it would be necessary to have access to the appropriate North Vietnamese war records. However, it is certain that the riverine forces made life for the VC much more difficult and probably prevented another offensive in the Delta as significant as that of Tet. Riverine forces proved again the importance of strength and mobility and demonstrated the significance of the type of combined operations that Corbett had advocated over a half-century earlier.

Today, as we approach the turn of another century and a new millennium, the lessons learned in Vietnam fade further and further into the past, and the likelihood of a similar war involving the United States or another Western nation as a belligerent appears to diminish. However, this does not rule out the possibility of there being such a war. Perhaps the next time some country might be required to conduct riverine operations, it will be to assist in peace-keeping operations or in the growing war against narcotics. Elements of the USN and other Western navies are already employed in the Caribbean on counter-narcotics operations. If there is ever the united desire and will, those operations might move to the rivers of Southeast Asia again to interdict and destroy the narcotics that originate in that corner of the world. Whatever the circumstances, the experience and lessons of the brown-water navy in Vietnam offer a sound foundation for future riverine operations.

NOTES

1 Thayer, "Patterns of the French and American Experience in Vietnam," 36; and Coletta, *The American Naval Heritage*, 521.

2 Reynolds, *Command of the Sea*, 578–579.

3 Lehman, *Command of the Seas*, 64.

4 Reynolds, *Command of the Sea,* 577.

5 Uhlig, *Vietnam: The Naval Story*, 3.

6 Schurman, *Commentary on War Course.*

7 Sharp, "Report on Air and Naval Campaigns against North Vietnam."

8 Baylis, "Revolutionary Warfare," 147.

9 Coletta, *The American Naval Heritage*, 521.

10 Hooper et al., *The United States Navy and the Vietnam Conflict*, 304.

11 Ibid., 336–7.

12 Schreadley, "The Naval War in Vietnam," 184.

13 Ibid., 185.

14 Westmoreland, "Report on Operations in South Vietnam," 203.

15 Schreadley, "The Naval War in Vietnam," 186.

16 Ibid., 186.

17 Ibid.

18 Ibid.
19 Ibid., 187–8.
20 Ibid., 188–9.
21 Ibid., 191.
22 Wells, "The Riverine Force in Action," 414–15.
23 The CTZs were redesignated military regions (MRs) on 1 August 1970. Fairfax, *Navy in Vietnam*, 5.
24 Schreadley, "The Naval War in Vietnam," 192.
25 Swarztrauber, "River Patrol Relearned," 125.
26 Schreadley, "The Naval War in Vietnam," 192.
27 Swarztrauber, "River Patrol Relearned," 139.
28 Schreadley, "The Naval War in Vietnam," 192.
29 Swarztrauber, "River Patrol Relearned," 125.
30 Ibid.,128.
31 Ibid., 129.
32 Among earlier USN experiences with riverine warfare were the American Revolution; the War of 1812; the War with Mexico, 1846–48; and the American Civil War. See Fulton, *Vietnam Studies: Riverine Operations*, 3–8.
33 See Swarztrauber, "River Patrol Relearned," 133–4; and Mumford, "Jackstay: New Dimensions in Amphibious Warfare," 85.
34 Swarztrauber, "River Patrol Relearned," 125.
35 Ibid., 137.
36 Ibid., 135.
37 Ibid., 137.
38 Ibid., 140.
39 Ibid.
40 Ibid., 156.
41 Ibid., 125; and Schreadley, "The Naval War in Vietnam," 204.
42 Swarztrauber, "River Patrol Relearned," 155.
43 Ibid., 137.
44 Ibid.
45 Ibid., 155.
46 Fulton, *Vietnam Studies*, 10.
47 Ibid., 17.
48 Swarztrauber, "River Patrol Relearned," 155.
49 Fulton, *Vietnam Studies*, 24.
50 Ibid., 26.
51 Schreadley, "The Naval War in Vietnam," 194.
52 Ibid., 194.
53 Ibid., 195.
54 Fulton, *Vietnam Studies*, 35–6.
55 Dodd, "The Mobile Riverine Force," 86.
56 Fulton, *Vietnam Studies*, 37.

57 Schreadley, "The Naval War in Vietnam," 194.
58 Ibid., 197.
59 Swarztrauber, "River Patrol Relearned," 130.
60 Ibid., 131.
61 Ibid.
62 Ibid., 132.
63 Coletta, *The American Naval Heritage*, 528; and Swarztrauber, "River Patrol Relearned," 152.
64 Schreadley,"The Naval War in Vietnam," 199.
65 Ibid.
66 Fulton, *Vietnam Studies*, 181.
67 Schreadley, "The Naval War in Vietnam," 199.
68 Fulton, *Vietnam Studies*, 182.
69 Swarztrauber, "River Patrol Relearned," 153.
70 Schreadley, "The Naval War in Vietnam," 199.
71 Ibid.
72 Searle,"The Case for Inshore Warfare," 3.

Eliminating the Shadows: Applying Counterinsurgency Doctrine to Peacekeeping

MAJOR RICHARD ROY

Canada has a long and proud history of peacekeeping, having participated in practically every United Nations (UN) mission since the first one in 1948. Today, an average of four thousand Canadian soldiers serve on UN missions annually, and Canada continues to see peacekeeping as a method of contributing to international stability. As a result of this experience, Canada is acknowledged as one of the world's leaders in developing peacekeeping doctrine. However, since the end of the Cold War in 1989, there have been major changes in the nature of peacekeeping operations. Prior to the end of the Cold War, traditional peacekeeping missions involved interposing lightly armed forces between international belligerents. An agreed-on cease-fire and belligerents' command and control of their forces were required before the mission was put into place, and, over the last forty-five years, functional doctrine has evolved for this type of intervention.

However, new trends have emerged since 1989, as the number of new missions has increased tremendously, and many UN efforts are being established in countries still in the midst of civil wars. A wider variety of tasks are being demanded of military forces in these intrastate conflicts, and peacekeeping has become more difficult, as the warring parties do not necessarily want peace, nor are there clear front lines. The advent of these so-called second-generation missions[1] has led to the call for sweeping reforms in the UN's management of these operations. The reforms demanded include a more unified approach to command and control, more detailed and comprehensive planning, and the development of an appropriate doctrine. The efforts to develop doctrine centre on the requirement for unity of effort at all levels, control of the population, and the rebuilding of the social, economic, and political structures of the assisted countries.

As even a cursory review of the writings on counterinsurgency shows its obvious links with second-generation peacekeeping, the aim of this essay is to outline some aspects of its doctrine that may be applicable to peacekeeping. The first part outlines the roots of counterinsurgency doctrine and its current status. A short discussion of trends in peacekeeping follows. Next comes an examination of the aspects of counterinsurgency doctrine that could be useful in peacekeeping. The last part discusses the educational aspects of merging the two doctrines. An opportunity now exists to integrate the most relevant elements of both by applying the lessons of history to this task.

Terminology is still in flux; I use the following definitions in this essay: "Doctrine" comprises the fundamental principles by which military forces guide their actions. Doctrine serves as a model for commanders at all levels, but, it need not be a rigid, limiting set of rules; it should be selectively and flexibly applied to each UN mission. I use "peacekeeping" in this essay in its broadest sense, including peacekeeping, peace enforcement, and peace building.[2]

THE ROOTS OF COUNTERINSURGENCY

Robert Aspery's *War in the Shadows* shows that guerrilla warfare has been one of the constants in the history of warfare. Alexander the Great, Julius Caesar, and Napoleon all had to contend with it, and it will probably remain a significant part of modern conflicts. Counterinsurgency theorists, however, are virtually unknown before the twentieth century,[3] and the theories that have emerged are intimately linked to the forms of revolutionary guerrilla warfare they were designed to counter. The development of counterinsurgency doctrine in this century can be broadly divided into three phases: 1900–45, 1945–88, and post–Cold War.

The doctrinal roots of counterinsurgency were established during the first phase, 1900–45, as Western countries encountered guerrilla activity as they expanded their colonial empires. Suppression of insurgencies was a common response to guerrilla activity, but suppression as a doctrine succeeded in this period only because of the colonizers' technological superiority and their willingness to use extremes of force.[4] The colonizers were also aided by the fact that most guerrilla movements did not have cogent nationalist tendencies, strong organizations, or mass appeal. The best theoretical and practical works from this period include the writings of a small cadre of French marshals, led by H. Lyautey and J.-S. Gallieni; C.E. Callwell's *Small Wars*; and the U.S. Marine Corps's *Small Wars Manual*.

In the second phase, 1945–88, the rise of well-organized, ideologically driven insurgencies led to a more comprehensive response. Mao's agrarian insurgency model was widely imitated in the post-1945 world.[5] Insurgents scored perhaps their greatest successes in Vietnam (twice), in Algeria, and in Afghanistan, which proved that Western democracies were not the only victims of insurgencies. Despite the perception of overwhelming success by insurgents after the Second World War, there were some successful counter-insurgency campaigns during this period. In Greece, Malaya, and the Philippines, varying degrees of success were achieved against guerrillas, and each campaign was influenced by certain situation-specific conditions.

However, the interpretation of lessons from these campaigns and their integration into subsequent counterinsurgency doctrine were often unsuccessful. The French model, developed after withdrawal from Vietnam, where France fought an enemy that owed a great debt to the Communist Chinese theory of revolutionary warfare, was ultimately a failure.[6] The initial impetus for the American model was provided by President John F. Kennedy, who perceived a global communist threat from insurgencies,[7] but it did not alter the conventional force paradigm of the U.S. military establishment in this period. Both the French and the U.S. models fostered extremist attitudes that hampered their moral utility. In addition, they lacked a combined political-military strategy and demonstrated over-reliance on technology and fire-power, which often adversely affected the prosecution of the campaign. The inadequacy of these models was clearly demonstrated by the failure of U.S. policy in Vietnam, yet the U.S. model still remains commonly practised in the post–Cold War era.[8]

Insurgencies changed with the demise of the bi-polar world brought on by the end of the Cold War, but counterinsurgency doctrine, renamed "limited warfare," retains its previous simple requirements for success. The change was prompted by the collapse of the Soviet Union and its proxies and the improved counterinsurgency capabilities of Third World regimes.[9] Though no classical insurgencies have yet emerged, historical experience suggests that they will continue to occur, even though some argue that insurgencies may now be reactive, secessionist, or perhaps commercially or spiritually driven.[10] Whatever the case, to be successful, new counterinsurgency doctrine will have to respond to the specific nature of the new insurgencies, and, while conventional military forces will usually wish to exploit their technological edge, they must understand that technology is neither a panacea nor a substitute for effective doctrine.[11]

Though there seem to have been relatively few successful examples of counterinsurgency doctrine, its foundation is quite simple – it must be based on establishing the legitimacy of the government in the eyes of the local populace and acceptance of its capacity to coerce where necessary.[12] The four guiding principles of successful counterinsurgency are unity of effort, maximum use of intelligence, minimum use of violence, and development of responsive government.[13] Unity of effort requires coordinated action and centralized control at all levels and an overall strategic plan and the political will to implement it. The British experience in Malaya is a good example.[14] Accurate intelligence, the basis for all effective action, ensures that the targeted opposition is quickly and selectively dealt with. All sources of intelligence should be exploited, but the local population remains the best source. A threatened government must carefully examine all courses of action to respond to insurgent violence, and a guiding principle should be the minimum and selective use of force to maintain order. To maintain popular support, the government must ensure that it acts within the law, because torture and excessive or indiscriminate violence will only drive more people to support the insurgents.[15] In addition, positive measures are required to ensure that a government is responsive to the people's demands, thereby enhancing its legitimacy. To be truly effective, responses must address the root causes of the insurgency and not be seen as merely a tactical ploy. The government's ability to mobilize personnel and resources and to motivate citizens to support it will often be reflected in its ability to respond effectively to the people's key demands.

PEACEKEEPING TRENDS

Prior to 1989, UN peacekeeping doctrine had some coherence. Troops were interposed between warring parties only when there were acceptable temporary cease-fire agreements in place. The troops were lightly armed, had limited rules of engagement, and observed strict neutrality. The warring parties were expected to keep tight command and control over their armed personnel.[16] Traditional peacekeeping regulated interstate conflict, and UN troops were deployed, usually in a linear fashion, between international belligerents, frequently on national boundaries. The aim of these missions was essentially maintenance of a cease-fire by passive means so that negotiations could be carried out.[17]

Though initially reluctant, Canada participated in most of these traditional UN missions.[18] During the 1980s an average of 1,643 Canadian military personnel were deployed annually on UN peacekeeping missions, and the Canadian government never planned to commit more than two thousand to them.[19] The majority of UN taskings were observer missions, with combat arms units being deployed in only two instances.[20] Prior to 1988 only one in five authorized peace missions was related to intrastate conflict; since then, 62 per cent have dealt with intrastate conflict, and the proportion has increased since 1992.[21]

Responding to intrastate conflict has made UN missions multidimensional. The UN now seeks to rebuild the social, political, and economic structures of a country that has been shattered by conflict. New tasks include humanitarian assistance, monitoring no-fly zones, preventive deployments, protecting safe areas, and hunting down war criminals.[22] Intrastate UN missions are now more common than traditional peacekeeping.[23] However, a gap exists between traditional UN doctrine and the requirements of its new missions. For instance, there are often unclear boundaries between the belligerent and irregular forces, and these forces frequently operate outside the control of a central authority. Additionally, and perhaps most important, intervention has occurred when the warring parties are not committed to peace or have used the peace negotiation process only as a means of gaining tactical advantage.

According to Stephen Steadman, the UN has become involved in these missions because of humanitarian concerns, good intentions, and the assumption of reasonableness and rational thought on the part of the belligerents.[24] Despite these altruistic goals, there is a clear lack of understanding on how to conduct these interventions successfully at a practical level.[25] The absence of a coherent strategy for peacemaking and peacebuilding and the temporary nature of the new missions may marginalize the benefits of new interventions and may increase the risks confronted by soldiers deployed on UN missions.

The immediate similarities between the conditions generating the requirement for new peacekeeping doctrine and the conditions that generated new counterinsurgency doctrine are apparent. There a number of limitations, however, in the direct transfer of the concepts of counterinsurgency to peacekeeping. The most evident is the lack of an enemy in peacekeeping missions and the protracted nature of counterinsurgency warfare. The neutrality implicit in traditional peacekeeping demands that there be no recognized enemy; impartiality has been the key to avoiding conflict. In second-generation peacekeeping, with no clear front lines and irregular forces often still operating in areas under UN jurisdiction, UN troops are at greater risk than with traditional peacekeeping. However, even with calls for more muscular peacekeeping, it is still essential to use only the minimum force to achieve the aims of the mission and to avoid provoking the warring factions into targeting UN forces as "the enemy."

For counterinsurgency to be effective, it must be protracted if necessary. For political reasons, second-generation UN missions are being planned for short duration,[26] but this does not account for the normally protracted nature of most civil wars, in which there are no "quick-fix" solutions. If short duration remains a UN objective, the application of some counterinsurgency techniques may still be useful in the short term, but they run the risk of having little lasting value.

As peacekeeping becomes more complex, a clear doctrine is required to resolve philosophical and operational problems.[27] Canada's latest peacekeeping doctrine publication is based more on traditional peacekeeping missions than on the realities of second-generation peacekeeping, and it contains no historical studies of counterinsurgency among its main references.[28] But the fact that Canada does not have a cultural heritage of counterinsurgency could be advantageous in its development of a doctrine for second-generation UN operations, as Canadians can study counterinsurgency with less emotional attachment to military actions in their recent past, perhaps allowing for the integration of the best elements of counterinsurgency theory into peacekeeping doctrine.

PRINCIPLES OF COUNTERINSURGENCY IN A PEACEKEEPING CONTEXT

Caution is required in determining which aspects of counterinsurgency doctrine can be transferred to peacekeeping because of the muddled, historical realities of some counterinsurgency campaigns. Frequently, lessons from these campaigns are both poorly interpreted and haphazardly integrated into subsequent doctrine models. For instance, the French model nurtured extremist views and procedures in Algeria. Similarly, the U.S. failure in Vietnam is partially attributable to inability of the U.S. military establishment to accept and integrate counterinsurgency doctrine into its operations.[29] Efforts in Guatemala and El Salvador demonstrate the strategic failure that can occur when the sound doctrine is subverted for repressive ends. Nevertheless, the fundamentals of counterinsurgency have relevance to second-generation peacekeeping.

There is currently considerable debate concerning the requirement to have unity of effort during UN missions. The Canadian Department of National Defence (DND) publication *Peacekeeping Operations* contains a chapter dealing with aspects of coordination with the wide variety of agencies in a mission area. Coordination is required with diplomats, other UN agencies, the International Red Cross, other government agencies, non-governmental organizations (NGOs), and the media. The activities of the NGOs in peacekeeping illustrate the need for unity of effort, as most NGOs have a different motivation and different goals from military forces.[30] Their desire to alleviate immediate human suffering may inadvertently prolong the conflicts, as the articles they deliver, primarily food and medicines, if captured by irregular forces, sustain their operations. Currently, coordination is voluntary, and this does not permit the detailed, directed integration of plans necessary to improve local conditions consistently over the long term. Lofty ideals must be meshed with practical realities, and NGOs' activities, along with those of other agencies operating within a sector, need to be centrally coordinated for the overall, long-term benefit of the area.

In peacekeeping missions, as in war, accurate and timely intelligence is needed to carry out operations effectively. At all levels of the mission detailed knowledge of current operational conditions is required to allow effective responses to be planned more easily and to maximize the potential to defuse crises before they escalate. In addition, intelligence is critical to negotiating in peacekeeping situations. The methods of intelligence collection normally used in peacekeeping are overt. Sources include air reconnaissance; contacts with the local population and civilian officials; professional and social contacts with military forces, liaison officers, the media, and host nations; and reports from belligerent governments.[31]

As in counterinsurgency, however, human intelligence should receive the primary emphasis. To develop a comprehensive local picture, given a limited tour length and lack of knowledge of both geographic factors and of the local irregulars, great emphasis should be placed on developing local contacts. Other sources can supplement but not replace this valuable source of information. A common technique for intelligence collection in this manner is through highly visible patrolling, which can be used to gain information dominance in the area.[32] Limiting the use of patrols at night, similar to practices used by U.S. forces in Vietnam, sacrifices information control of the countryside to irregular forces.[33]

The use of minimum force in both counterinsurgency and in peacekeeping operations is critical to success, because the best solutions are facilitated not imposed. The rules of engagement for UN forces are usually developed early in mandate planning. There are no conditions that call inevitably for the use of force; therefore the rules of engagement should allow for a graduated transition from peaceful responses to armed intervention, if necessary. The use of unnecessary force could undermine the credibility, viability, and acceptability of the mission. Having rules of engagement based on minimum force does not imply that there is not a requirement to employ or possess fire-power, as some degree of credible coercion must be available. What is critical is controlled and precise application of that fire-power to designated targets. The Americans' use of indiscriminate fire-power in Vietnam critically affected the population's acceptance of their intervention in that conflict.[34] In both counterinsurgency and in peacekeeping, a large part of the battle is for the support of the population, and the ability to apply strictly controlled, retaliatory fire-power will help in discouraging irregular forces and maintaining support among the local population. The defeat of insurgents can best be accomplished through neutralization of their organization and support among the population through the strictly controlled and limited application of fire-power.

Second-generation peacekeeping also includes attempting to rebuild the assisted country. Existing governments may require assistance in establishing their legitimacy by convincing the population that participation in existing structures is more worthwhile than supporting the insurgent movement, and the government must therefore react to the population's legitimate complaints and needs. Where no recognizable administration exists, there may be a need to establish a temporary, UN-sponsored government.[35] Military forces deployed on such missions must be capable of assisting in this situation.

This response can take two forms: either a military administrative system or military participation and support to a civilian structure. If civilian organizations cannot be safely established in certain areas, the administration/ government of the contested territory could be delegated to the military. The *Section administrative spécial* organized by the French in Algeria is an example of this technique.[36] Current Canadian doctrine is not developed to undertake a task of this scope; therefore military participation in an imposed UN government structure seems more probable. This participation could include security functions, carrying out civic construction, and conducting educational programs and perhaps mine clearance. Civic reconstruction would be a deliberate act of policy, not an act of charity or compassion.

The activities of the public affairs cell are described in some detail in DND's *Peacekeeping Operations*; however, they are geared mainly towards preparing news releases for home consumption.[37] Little emphasis seems to be placed on informing the local population of the goals of the UN mission, even though psychological operations can, in some cases, replace the requirements for fire-power and combat operations in peacekeeping.[38] Greater efforts, perhaps closer to true psychological operations and propaganda, are required if the public information cell is to mobilize local support effectively.

TRAINING AND EDUCATIONAL REQUIREMENTS

Despite the importance of UN operations over the past fifty years, the Canadian Armed Forces have spent very little time on training for peacekeeping;[39] however, the counterinsurgent nature of second-generation peacekeeping demands a revision to current training. The usual explanation offered by government and military authorities for this lack of specific training is that a competent combat-capable soldier will adequately fulfil the duties required for UN operations. The United States followed a similar philosophy for its operations in Vietnam and had limited success.[40]

New military education programs should be developed to acquaint personnel with the social aspects of modern peacekeeping and to temper the bravado engendered by training for conventional war by the sympathy, tolerance, and compassion required in peacekeeping.[41] Most significantly perhaps, the yardsticks of success will have to change.[42] The skilful manipulation of violence can no longer be regarded as the primary indicator of success. Goals for UN operations must be viewed from the long-term perspective. Soldiers must recognize that, though many tasks spawn short-term frustrations, their accumulated efforts may contribute to a successful resolution of the conflict.

Education and training, therefore, particularly pre-deployment training, must be reformed to inform soldiers better about the nature of the conflict they are being deployed to monitor. Junior leaders need to be the preliminary target of such revised education, because if current trends continue, most of them will spend a significant amount of their career on peacekeeping missions in civil wars. Understanding the parameters of counterinsurgency will improve their capabilities to deal with circumstances in theatre. For example, viewing missions as protracted "counterinsurgency" efforts may temper both the individual's and the unit's frustrations when little seems to be accomplished after a six-month tour.

CONCLUSION

There is every indication that Canada and other nations that wish to support UN missions will continue to support the use of force internationally. The metamorphosis of peacekeeping into its second-generation structure needs to be clearly recognized in these circumstances. The doctrine and training that were suitable prior to 1989 are no longer applicable. Continued participation has increased the risk to which Canadian soldiers are exposed; however, the development of an appropriate doctrine will modify this risk somewhat.

Traditionally, Western armed forces have accorded little attention to counterinsurgency doctrine. The obvious parallels between it and the new peacekeeping call for a detailed effort by Canadian and other interested armed forces to study and to apply appropriate aspects to peacekeeping. An improved doctrine and better education of troops assigned to UN duties would prepare them more adequately for the types of conflict they will see in the future. A better perspective on the nature of the struggles they monitor and on the value of their effort may measurably improve their morale. Through the effective application of selected principles of counterinsurgency, Canada, and other like-minded nations, can ensure that they retain credible peacekeeping forces well into the future.

NOTES

1 Roper et al., *Keeping the Peace*, 4. Second-generation peacekeeping includes the active process of building peace – national reconstruction, transition to democratic government, and humanitarian assistance.
2 Canada, Department of National Defence (DND), *Peacekeeping Operations*. For detailed definitions of these terms see Annex A of that document.
3 Beckett, *The Roots of Counter-Insurgency*, 8.
4 Ibid., 11.
5 Metz, *Counterinsurgency*, 6.
6 Paret, *French Revolutionary Warfare*, 4.
7 Metz, *Counterinsurgency*, 6.
8 Cable, *Conflict of Myths*, 279–85.

9 Metz, "Insurgencies after the Cold War," 63.

10 See Metz, *Counterinsurgency* and "Insurgencies after the Cold War."

11 Stephens, "The Transformation of 'Low Intensity' Conflict," 141–61. Stephens advances the argument that technology will solve all the problems with insurgencies, particularly from an air-power perspective. This "war winning technology from the air" argument has historically been proven to lack credibility but is mirrored in the Canadian government, *Towards a Rapid Reaction Capability for the United Nations*.

12 Cable, "Reinventing the Round Wheel," 229.

13 United States Government, *Military Operations in Low Intensity Conflicts*, 2–9.

14 For details on this campaign see Clutterbuck, *Conflict and Violence in Singapore and Malaysia*.

15 Paret, *French Revolutionary Warfare*, 69–76. Paret outlines the adverse effects that torture had both on the Algerians and on the French forces carrying out these acts.

16 Steadman, "UN Intervention in Civil Wars," 41.

17 Roper, "A Wider Range of Tasks," 4.

18 Jockel, *Canada and International Peacekeeping*, 11. Canadian governments in the early postwar period saw peacekeeping as a drain on scarce defence resources.

19 Ibid., 2.

20 Ibid., Appendix. Infantry battalions were used only for UNEF I and in Cyprus.

21 Canadian Government, *Towards a Rapid Reaction Capability*, 3.

22 Daniel and Hayes, eds., *Beyond Traditional Peacekeeping*, xvi.

23 Canadian Government, *Towards a Rapid Reaction Capability*, 3.

24 Steadman, "UN Intervention in Civil Wars," 50.

25 Bergstrand, "What Do You Do When There's No Peace to Keep?" 6.

26 Roper, "A Wider Range of Tasks," 4.

27 Canadian Government, *Towards a Rapid Reaction Capability*, 34.

28 DND, *Peacekeeping Operations*, ii.

29 Cable, *Conflict of Myths*, 279–85.

30 DND, *Peacekeeping Operations*, 3–6–2.

31 Ibid., 7–6–2.

32 Ibid., 11–4–6; and United States Marine Corps, *Small Wars Manual*, 6–12. Information dominance occurs when the counter-insurgency forces know in extraordinary detail about all the activity in their sector. Guerrillas would then not be able to function effectively, as all their movements would either be observed or be reported by the local populace. The marines used permanent roving patrols to dominate an area.

33 DND, *Peacekeeping Operations*, 11–4–9. It is recommended that operations be restricted at night for safety reasons. While this practice minimizes losses, it allows irregular forces to dominate the night. Static observation posts will not give the surveillance coverage necessary to offset the irregulars' freedom of movement.

34 Blaufarb, *The Counterinsurgency Era*, 81.
35 Roper, "A Wider Range of Tasks," 11. There was no recognizable government in Somalia nor an effective government in Bosnia.
36 Paret, *French Revolutionary Warfare*, 46–52.
37 DND, *Peacekeeping Operations*, chap. 10.
38 Blaufarb, *The Counterinsurgency Era*, 47. Psychological operations can replace fire-power in counterinsurgency. There is a similar application in peacekeeping.
39 Jockel, *Canada and International Peacekeeping*, 56.
40 Cable, "Reinventing the Round Wheel," 252.
41 Galvin, "Uncomfortable Wars," 14; and United States Marine Corps, *Small Wars Manual*, 1–17.
42 Galvin, "Uncomfortable Wars," 16.

PART III

Conflict in the Twenty-First Century

Computers and Strategy:
It's the Thought That Counts

MERVYN BERRIDGE-SILLS

The computer is a valuable tool, but nothing more, for the armoury of the future. A thoughtful commander will recognize the limits of that tool and of the role of the computer. Information operations and information warfare seek to employ the computer and its information management and communications capabilities as a new weapon, or even as a new form of warfare. However, the effect of the computer on strategic thinking, and the impact of the adaptation of human thought processes to computer capabilities and methods, have not been thoroughly analysed. If, on examination, we discover distortions and biases in historical examples, or if we find weaknesses in our practices, then we have received fair warning. It then becomes our responsibility to compensate for these concerns in our evolving use of the tool.

This essay examines the part being played in warfare today by the computer. First, I attempt both to determine the computer's current influence on strategy and to raise some concerns about its integration into past and current decision-making processes. I do so by discussing the operational use of computers by the military, especially as a substitute for experience. Second, I consider the extent to which the use of computers in simulation is a potential source of faulty strategic assumptions, basing my analysis on historical examples of how assumptions have been formulated in past conflicts. Next, I examine the role of computers in war gaming as a significant factor in the evolution of strategy and look at differing opinions concerning the validity of war games held by civilian strategic planners of nuclear war. Finally, I consider the application of computers to nuclear war.

I hope that this integration of multiple, but related trends will reveal the danger posed by unrecognized assumptions and uncontested evaluations in a computerized environment. In this essay, I focus on the American use of military computers, as the U.S. military is the most enthusiastic and experienced user of advanced technology and operates in an unusually open society. There is no comparable literature for so wide a use of computers available for the military of any other country.

The computer is the product of a new, quantitative way of thinking. It is the current embodiment of a scientific approach that started to flourish during the First World War. Before 1914, even the artillery had more faith in instinct than in measurement, and "the idea that field artillery could shoot accurately at targets that the gun layers could not see appeared pretty farfetched."[1] However, during the Great War, new technology was quickly assimilated by gunners, and they became increasingly reliant on technical solutions to tactical problems. Their experience made plain the need for new approaches to the problems of warfare. At first, advances in engineering, particularly in the internal combustion engine, were the foci of attention. These improvements created an accelerated and extended form of war, resulting in the interwar development of radar, sonar, gun predictors for automated gun laying, and loaders for automated gun loading.

These developments evolved further during the Second World War, particularly in electronics. As the new tools were introduced, new applications of the underlying principles became obvious to the scientists working on the problems. Among these scientists were Alan Turing in Britain, working on the Bombe (a device that simulated, at very high speed, multiple possible rotor settings of the German Enigma encryption unit[2]), and John von Neumann in the United States, working on both the electronic numerical integrator and computer (ENIAC) in the Ballistics Research Laboratory at the Aberdeen Proving Grounds in Maryland and the atomic bomb research facilities at Los Alamos.[3] These men and their colleagues laid the theoretical and practical foundations of computing science and started the military's interest in it, which would continue after the war. For example, the (U.S.) Office of Naval Research alone is estimated to have funded 40 per cent of all basic research in the United States in 1948, and military funding of the research and development of the transistor in Bell Labs constituted 25 per cent of the total outlay.[4] It is evident from these figures that the military played a significant and often underappreciated part in the development of the modern computer industry.

The changes that the computer has produced in society are evidence of its potential. Dr Vannevar Bush, writing in 1949, did not even use the word "computer," but in talking of electronics he said: "These circuits could now be constructed to perform intricate computations or sequences of reactions. They could be combined with mechanical masses of gears and levers ... The important point was that such combinations could do things a man could not do, they could go where a man could not be sent, they did not become confused in the stress of battle, and as techniques improved they became reliable and relatively inexpensive when produced on production lines." [5] This statement underestimates the flexibility that we recognize today in the computer. It can function as record-keeper, paymaster, and stores clerk. The computer "crunches numbers"; its first uses were for ballistic calculations for the artillery, for which it was developed, and later for nuclear physics. It permits simulated training for aircrew, tank gunners, and infantrymen that would otherwise be constrained by expense. It makes and breaks encrypted communications and increasingly operates communications networks. It permits weapons to become almost autonomous, with fully autonomous weapons under experimental evaluation at the moment. What Bush foresaw has now become pivotal in Western warfare. Those "circuits" he referred to have also taken on the responsibility for much of the command and control infrastructure and are emerging as the critical factor in target selection and designation at both the strategic and the tactical levels.

The advent of new technologies and capabilities, with unappreciated vulnerabilities, has raised concerns before. For example, Barbara Tuchman's assessment of the new technology in use during the execution of the Schlieffen Plan in August 1914 concluded: "Nothing caused the Germans more trouble, when they were operating in hostile territory, than communications. Belgians cut telephone and telegraph wires; the powerful Eiffel Tower wireless station jammed the air waves ... [German army headquarters'] single receiving station became so clogged that messages took from eight to twelve hours to get through. This was one of the 'frictions' the German General Staff, misled by the ease of communications in war games, had not planned for." [6]

The technology of today has its historical roots in the organization of effort. Human beings are organizing animals. The aim of war has been to weld the largest available and feasible quantity of soldiers into a force subject to the will of a single commander. Where mass, speed, and will have been combined more effectively on one side than on another, victory has tended to go to that side. The most significant factor is the will of the commander, imposed on subordinates through discipline, training, organization, morale, leadership, command, and control. In pursuit of the ability to wield armed forces as the personal weapon of the commander, effort over the centuries has concentrated on three areas: delegation of subsidiary duties through a hierarchical organization;[7] simplification of tasks to rigid standards through drill and practice, in an attempt to make people as reliable as machines;[8] and an attempt to replace people with machines wherever possible, for reasons of predictability, reliability, and cost savings.

The value of mechanization can be followed through the evolution of firearms. The process began with the muzzle-loading arquebus, which required a loading drill of fifty-six movements.[9] In 1590, the maximum rate of fire was considered to be ten rounds per hour.[10] This was followed by the two to three rounds per minute (rpm) for the Brown Bess fired "by the book" in 1717;[11] then by the 1,200 rpm of the MG42 in 1942[12] and the 6,000 rpm of the M61A1, "Vulcan," 20-mm cannon in current use.[13]

For it to be effective on the battlefield, the Brown Bess used the men of a battalion, acting in unison, firing and reloading by ranks under the direction of officers, who were in effect wielding an inaccurate multi-barrelled weapon. The MG42 is classified as a crew-served weapon, since effective use requires separate loader, spotter, and operator. The Vulcan or its shipborne cousin, the Phalanx, requires an external power source for its ammunition feed and computer-driven target tracking. Four battalions of 750 men each in the firing line at Waterloo had the same fire-power as a single Vulcan has today, with incomparably less accuracy, range, or weapons effect. The Vulcan's concentration of fire-power has been achieved by mechanical ingenuity and an integration of systems extending far behind the firing line.

This integration enables systems designers, engineers, logisticians, armourers, and commanders to put a weapon on the battlefield without having (or being able) to venture there themselves. It also permits a concentration of fire that minimizes interference with the will of the commander. The requirement to manoeuvre four battalions of infantry, through the intermediary commands of brigade, battalion, and company commanders, made generals into drillmasters, whereas a single weapon, with power-driven machinery substituting for the sustained efforts of three thousand men, translates wills into action far more responsively. It also permits training resources to be concentrated on key individuals, to bring those individuals to the highest pitch of efficiency, and to discard those who cannot reach it. The skill of those individuals, however, is still required to bring that firepower to bear, but the scope for that skill is being steadily reduced by capabilities introduced into weapons by the programming of computers.

Combat arms have been the most conspicuous beneficiaries of the form of mechanization introduced by computers in warfare. This has been true across all services, as the following excerpts show. In land warfare, tanks are usually equipped with a fire-control system incorporating a laser rangefinder, laser sight, and electronic fire-control computer, and guns can routinely hit "a moving [target] at 2,000 m[etres] with the first shot."[14]

The impact of the new technology on aerial bombardment produced an even more dramatic impact: precision-guided munitions are able to hit almost any target that can be detected and have been credited with "at last making air doctrine effective."[15] At sea, the problems of gunnery are shared with the army, and the use of missiles with the air force, but a singular contribution is made with naval mines, which are now capable of using active acoustic signals to identify targets "and then take whatever action has been programmed into its data processor."[16]

These are all extensions of technologies that already existed. Artillery predictors had been integrated with both radar and with 3.7-inch anti-aircraft guns in the 1930s;[17] the German radio-controlled Henschel Hs 293 rocket-powered glide bomb, for attacking shipping from safe distances, was successfully tested in 1940;[18] and mines employed a variety of mechanisms, such as acoustics, pressure, and magnetism, to "recognize" a target.[19]

Computers were also intended to be crucial in the one area where active warfare has not yet been conducted – in space. For example, in the (U.S.) Strategic Defense Initiative, one of its most complex features, battle management, "would be the responsibility of an elaborate network of computers."[20] These advances in weaponry, taken together, have changed warfare. And even though technologically advanced nations appear to have an overwhelming battlefield advantage, these technologies can be stolen and replicated, or, more simply, they can be bought. Argentina, for example, might have had even greater difficulties in the Malvinas/Falklands dispute without French aviation and missile technology.

An unrecognized and vulnerable aspect of military computers is the extent to which they are used in the administrative infrastructure of armies. Computers assist in running the modern military in the same way that they do so in the modern corporation. Any modern force is as little able to switch back from computerization to paper record-keeping as a major bank could handle its current volume of transactions without computers. It would be a bold analyst who claimed that the inner workings of an integrated, computerized system were reproducible, or even comprehensible, in a non-computerized environment. At either extreme, traditional military skills, from range estimation to mental record-keeping, will be displaced or devalued.

Computers were also crucial in the rise of the intelligence community during the Cold War. They collected information, through passive monitoring and active reconnaissance; they collated it, functioning as switching centres and accumulating databases; and they interpreted it, calling on those databases and harnessing their speed and accuracy to carry out functions such as cryptographic analysis. Finally, they disseminated the results, through the communications networks that they controlled.

Such applications of the computer are operational – that is, tactical or organizational, rather than strategic. Their effective use may transform force structure, mobilization, logistics, and striking power. They may yet reveal an Achilles' heel, when used in combat against a peer force that chooses to target them. None the less, they can be accommodated as changes in a profession that has faced continuous technological change since the mid-nineteenth century. When the tool can change the way in which we consider the methods of conducting war, it can have a direct impact on strategy, in that it changes the way we think.

Three particular and interlinked aspects of computerized warfare stand out because they have the potential to change strategic thinking: simulation, operational analysis, and war gaming. Simulation has the potential to replace practical experience – the traditional baseline for strategic thinking – with a pyramid of simulated experiences.

Many of the new weapons and weapons platforms are used primarily or solely through computer instrumentation, which can be used to simulate the devices, without expending or risking weapons or weapons platforms, putting near-real experience of a range of situations at the disposal of future operators. Aircraft simulators, for example, permit situations to be created and enacted that offer near-experience at low cost and no risk. Simulation can range from a tank or aircraft to an aircraft carrier and can in turn be fed into a battlefront simulator or a global simulation.

Single-device simulation, however complex, is a necessity, given the cost of operation and the intricacy of the new tools. "Virtual reality" devices are making simulators seem almost as real as operation of the actual equipment would be.[21] The simulator for a new device may simulate the design characteristics of the perfect device, however, rather than of reality. In real life, a device may have been improperly assembled, or a weapon may never have been used in combat, and therefore may not perform according to specifications. The reality of battle damage, or wear and tear, also presents difficulties in predictive simulation.

It is in simulation not of devices but of systems with their multiple assumptions about inputs that we enter a dangerous realm. Just as inputs about components can be misleading if the simulation is constructed on assumptions that are not matched in reality, so inputs concerning the behaviour and interaction of multiple systems can be misleading if based on faulty assumptions. The danger lies in dependence on the simulation as a substitute for practical experience. There are two basic rules of data processing: keep it simple, stupid (KISS), which is meant to deter analysts and programmers from developing algorithms that contain too many points of potential failure; and garbage in, garbage out (GIGO), which reminds them that the computer processes data uncritically and that judgement must be exercised about the validity of all data.

Napoleon said: "Nothing is gained in war except by calculation."[22] Certain assumptions can be made based on experience or innate characteristics, such as fuel and ration requirements, the range of vehicles, ships, and airplanes, and the effects of encounters between mismatched forces. These can all be considered tactical equations. The operational use of assumptions based on the extrapolation of chains of logic to secondary and tertiary implications, and further, is relatively new, but it has dominated military thinking in the last fifty years. Operational analysis constitutes the second strand of the interaction of computers and strategists.

The explicit use of assumptions and analysis can be traced back most directly to the operational analysts of the Second World War. An example is that of RAF Coastal Command's depth-charge settings for anti-submarine warfare. Traditionally, depth charges had been set at thirty metres, the probable depth achieved by a diving U-boat after detection. But J.E. Williams pointed out that a U-boat, given sufficient warning to reach such a depth, would not have continued on its original heading. Since the lethal radius of a depth charge was only six metres, it was unlikely to connect with a U-boat that had reached thirty metres and would certainly not damage a U-boat either caught on the surface or immediately after diving. Since the location of a surprised U-boat could be fixed more accurately, he recommended a depth setting of eight metres. Once this was adopted, the kill rate rose two and a half times.[23]

The British operational analysts had their counterparts in the United States. The massive American materiel contribution to the Allied war effort threatened to overwhelm U.S. armed forces with the work needed to control and direct the flow of men, equipment, and munitions. The United States Army Air Forces (USAAF) responded by raising a corps of staff officers to function as professional managers, under the name of Statistical Control. They applied the mathematics of mass production to the allocation, flow, and use of equipment and extended the efficiencies employed by industry into the military community.

At the end of the war in Europe, one striking example serves to show what could be accomplished by such methods: "The Army Air Force had begun to redeploy heavy bomb groups of B-17s and B-24s from Europe to the Pacific to crush Japan. But Stat Control's beancounters disagreed with the plan, arguing that the US should use the newer B-29 bombers instead. Stat Control proved that B-29s could drop 28,000 tons of bombs per month in only 15,000 combat hours. It would have taken the B-17 and B-24 groups more than 90,000 hours to accomplish the same goal. The study found that by using B-29s, 70 per cent of combat crews killed, missing and wounded could be saved along with a quarter of a billion gallons of gasoline a year."[24]

One of the "beancounters" in the USAAF was twenty-nine–year-old Lieutenant-Colonel Robert S. McNamara. He took back to civilian life a respect for the statistical analysis of problems that was ideally suited to the Ford Corporation, which he joined immediately after the war and in which he rose to be president. His management expertise led to his selection in 1961 as secretary of defence in John F. Kennedy's administration.

As secretary of defence, he centralized control of defence spending and based decisions on spending on a quantified basis, equivalent to the practices at Ford. However, "In government agencies, there was no broadly accepted numerical measure of benefit, no return on investment, no profit."

This "made cost-benefit analysis less useful and harder to apply in non-profit organizations. Even so, McNamara insisted that every project meet the test of rational analysis."[25] The emphasis on quantification at the time of the Vietnam War affected military thinking. General William Westmoreland, commander of U.S. forces in Vietnam (known as Military Assistance Command, Vietnam, or MACV), would be identified as the author of a new approach to warfare, treating it "as a production system that can be rationally managed and warfare as a kind of activity that can be scientifically determined by constructing computer models."[26]

One particular measure of effectiveness – the body count – came in for a great deal of criticism from U.S. civilians. The civilian community saw in it an unpleasantly graphic accounting of war, whereas the military saw the potential for an objective measure of effectiveness in what was, for the enemy, primarily a ground war, fought by the Americans in what they considered an artificial theatre limited by arbitrary borders made by diplomats. The potential for distortion in this apparently objective unit of measure was not well understood at the time, and troops and officers were rewarded on the basis of counted bodies.[27] There was little requirement for proof of enemy affiliation of the bodies, and there were assumptions made about the count itself: "Not only was the body count accepted as accurate, but it was further *multiplied by 1.5, meaning a 50 per cent increase!* In this way an entire apparatus of lies was constructed. Numbers became the basis for more numbers."[28]

By the fall of 1967, war managers were living with multiple, systematic falsification.[29] It started in the field, where enemy dead would be estimated after a fire-fight, and bystanders would be counted as enemies. It would be subject to inflation as it climbed the command chain. Finally, false figures would be fed into unproven models of enemy capability. The purely quantitative approach to conventional war was shown to be vulnerable to GIGO by the Tet Offensive: "MACV analysts and officers tended to produce estimates that supported existing policy and the preferences of senior administration officials ... Because shared beliefs were so pervasive, it is impossible to determine whether MACV analysts and officers produced intelligence to please themselves or senior administration officials. They tended to produce intelligence that confirmed beliefs about the decline of the communist military, thereby pleasing everybody except a few pessimists at the [Central Intelligence Agency]."[30]

MACV was estimating North Vietnamese losses, and the strength of the remaining forces, to create a case for victory through attrition. "The end comes into view" and "the enemy's hopes are bankrupt" were two phrases used by Westmoreland, testifying before Congress on 21 November 1967.[31] On 31 January 1968, the North Vietnamese army and the Viet Cong mounted a joint assault throughout South Vietnam, but particularly at Hué and in Saigon. The offensive was beaten off, with Hué being taken back after three weeks of particularly bitter fighting, but American confidence had been shaken. The Tet Offensive is generally accepted as an American victory, but one that lost the war. The military, which had already forfeited the confidence of a significant part of the American nation, now lost credibility with the political leadership.

Clark M. Clifford, who took office as secretary of defence on 1 March 1968, immediately after the Tet Offensive, chaired a task force to determine how the military's request for a further 200,000 men (to the 525,000 already in Vietnam) should be met: "We [the Department of Defense] were not instructed to assess the need for substantial increases in men and materiel; we were to devise the means by which they could be provided. [32] ... When I asked for a presentation of the military plan for attaining victory in Vietnam, I was told that there was no plan for victory in the historic American sense ... 'Given these circumstances, how can we win?' We would, I was told, continue to evidence our superiority over the enemy; we would continue to attack in the belief that he would reach the stage where he would find it inadvisable to go on with the war. [33] ... I was convinced that the military course that we were pursuing was not only endless, but hopeless." [34]

This American experience in Vietnam should not be seen as invalidating quantitative assessments of military performance. It does suggest, however, that quantification be put in the larger strategic context and be subject to critical scrutiny. Clifford had been unable to find a militarily achievable objective, let alone a plan to achieve it. The assumptions, based on dubious input, concerning the effect on the enemy of the policy of attrition had been brought into disrepute by enemy behaviour, which failed to match the quantitative model. The Americans can be considered to be the first nation to lose a war by invalid modelling of the enemy in the computer model of the war. The crippling of the North Vietnamese military during Tet was politically offset by the u.s. domestic loss of political confidence in the military and its ability to anticipate the enemy.

Parallelling the rise of operational analysis, however, was a surge in war gaming, which is the third link between computers and strategists. The modern military war game can be traced back to the *Kriegsspiel* introduced in the Prussian army in the early nineteenth century. [35] The necessity of calculating troop deployments and encounters in a quantitative method has been of increasing interest to the military staffs of the world ever since. This interest has had a corresponding effect on the complexity of the calculation of significant factors. As the value of operational quantitative analysis came to be recognized, so too was the ability of the computer to manipulate numbers and symbols: "In 1958 ... the Naval War College retired its wargaming room ... In its place came the Navy Electronic Warfare System [NEWS] ... NEWS computers were supposed to determine whether the target was hit ... The navigational computers would then slow down the ship that was hit and eliminate damaged weapons from its armament repertoire."[36]

The line between war games and reality can easily become blurred, because the game has real value when used to model reality. Examples are the British army's modelling a German invasion of Belgium in 1905 and solving mobilization and logistical problems in time for 1914;[37] and the Germans' fighting the Americans in the Huertgen Forest, in 1944, straight from the games board on which they had been preparing an anticipatory model of the engagement for planning purposes.[38] War games do not always turn out as desired, however. Sometimes the game is changed in the expectation that reality will alter to keep pace, and then one is playing with sympathetic magic, which has not been accepted in mainstream Western society for several centuries. An example is the Japanese navy, modelling the tactics of both sides when planning the assault on Midway Island and refusing to take aircraft carriers off the board after their (gamed) destruction by air attack from Midway. This gamed event anticipated the real attack by American carrier-borne aircraft at the Battle of Midway.[39] At the transparent level of "fudging the results," the u.s. navy was avoiding taking carriers off the game board, or out of the exercise, as late as 1981.[40]

A significant convergence between quantitative analysis and simulation (which would lead to an involvement in war gaming) had been taking place at the RAND corporation. RAND had been formed at the end of the Second World War, at the request of the u.s. air force (USAF), to conduct scientific research into questions of military significance. It was a multidisciplinary organization, with groups of academics in mathematics, physics, economics, social sciences, and other disciplines. The USAF was its major client and the custodian of America's strategic nuclear capability, in the form of Strategic Air Command. This situation inevitably drew RAND into the area of nuclear strategy. RAND's multidisciplinary approach was initially an advantage, combining the strengths of the historical approach with the analytical support furnished by the quantification of the factors and their presentation in scenarios. However, this advantage lasted only as long as the two main schools were mutually supportive.

The USAF was comfortable with statistical analysis, and less so with abstract logic. The effect within RAND was to polarize two schools of strategic thought in increasing opposition and, ultimately, mutual rejection, with disparaging references being made to "the essay tradition" from the statisticians, and to "an astonishing lack of political sense" from the historians.[41] In essence, the Jominians of mathematics, headed by Albert Wohlstetter, a RAND analyst preoccupied with quantitative analysis, took precedence over the Clausewitzians, under the philosopher-strategist Bernard Brodie. This split would have a profound effect on war gaming and would draw together quantitative analysis, simulation, and war gaming in a deterministic mindset.

In current war gaming, the numbers are already in the computer, subject to preprogrammed minor changes[42] to adjust circumstances, but not premises. The numbers are to be responded to and are not to be questioned. This situation is in contrast to the more humanist approach, where moves, their rationale, and their outcomes are discussed in a seminar atmosphere. The acceptance of the numbers is, in large part, the result of the complexity to which the games have evolved. Modern computerized war games can require megabytes of input data and take a team of data-preparation analysts months to create. The mass of data makes the war game more akin to a simulation. Simulations are subject to error based on both KISS, because of their complexity, and to GIGO, because of the probability that errors will occur in data preparation or entry. Some war gamers have commented that "what we are dealing with when we use the word data is really non-data; it is mainly the output of other models, most of which have not been validated."[43] Further, "If it comes out with a right answer, no matter how it got the answer, that's the right answer, and so it's used."[44]

As models get more complex, they rely more on databases of data of uncertain origin or vintage. As their inputs rely more on other games, they get more removed from reality. Any simulation of behaviour in a model should be open to question, and if no answers are forthcoming, or if the answers cannot stand up to scrutiny, then the game involved is not merely useless, but potentially dangerously misleading. One of the most striking examples of this phenomenon at the operational and strategic levels has been in the planning for nuclear war.

Since 1945, the superpowers have prepared for a nuclear war that could be waged only in models. The only experience available is based on two relatively primitive bombs, of 12,500 TNT-equivalent tons yield, or 12.5 kilotons (KT), and 22 KT,[45] exploded over Hiroshima and Nagasaki, and a number of tests conducted under relatively unrealistic conditions. There is no clear evidence that the two bombs used in war achieved anything other than the destruction of their targets. The U.S. *Strategic Bombing Survey* concluded that the Japanese would have surrendered before an invasion had been launched without the use of atomic weapons,[46] and there has been little agreement, then or since, over the utility, necessity, or morality of such weapons or their successors. At the height of the nuclear arms race, however, it was estimated that there were available the equivalent of over 600,000 Hiroshimas in yield. This was possible with weapons such as the Soviet SS-9, with an estimated 18 megaton (MT) warhead, and the SS-18, with eight multiple independently targetable re-entry vehicle (MIRV) warheads, estimated at 2 MT each.[47] Given the incredible destructive power represented by these numbers, we can assume that the models have not yet captured all that we need to know about such weapons.

The command and control of nuclear forces have also been tightly coupled to computers, and there have been numerous misread warnings over the years of the dangers latent in the coupling of the new technologies. On 5 November

1960, the u.s. ballistic missile early-warning system (BMEWS) detected a 99.9 percent certainty of a massive Soviet missile attack, which turned out to be the rising moon.[48] On 3 June 1980, a failing integrated circuit chip – in a communications multiplexer – modified test traffic to indicate enemy missile launches, causing a threat-assessment conference among North American Air Defense Command (NORAD), the National Military Command Center (NMCC), and Strategic Air Command (SAC), all of which had received misleading (but, fortunately, different) messages.[49] Reassuringly, neither of these incidents escalated further, which provokes another consideration: "The response system, once the credibility of a warning is thought to have been established, is apparently so complex as to provide considerable safeguards against an accidental war; it is hard to imagine that the system would actually work. Of course, this means that it provides little defense against an actual attack."[50]

This point is particularly apt, since the United States tries to centralize control of the strategic weapons in the hands of its president, which has been the case since 1948, when Budget Director James Webb wrote to President Harry Truman: "The idea of turning over custody of atomic bombs to those competing, jealous, insubordinate services, fighting for position with each other, is a terrible prospect."[51]

Weapons that would be launched, should it be necessary, are pre-targeted, because targeting is a complex business based on launch site, vehicle type, load, flight time, and time on target. The targeting information carried in the "football" that accompanies the American president everywhere was (in 1985) apparently seventy-five pages of closely typed text. Only President Jimmy Carter ever attempted to achieve any familiarity with the script, the process, or the options; and the options are very limited, being, it would seem, inaction or a massive counter-launch, given the potential for the strategic decapitation of the United States if the president delayed his decision.[52]

It is appropriate to close a crucial circle among computers, strategy, nuclear weaponry, and war gaming. I hope that I have shown that computers are just a tool, which that can be used, with reservations, to direct operations and that the conduct of strategy, to be effective, should be based on experience. Our direct experience of nuclear weaponry is not as small as we sometimes think. A lack of information, as in radio silence on the opposing side, can be as informative as positive data. Our experience, since 1945, is that we, the human race, have resisted the use of nuclear weaponry through crises and wars, despite perceived advantages and disadvantages on each side and a bewildering variety of available weapons, doctrines, and strategies.

Always, however, just out of vision, have lurked the war games. Herman Kahn and Bernard Brodie both worked for the RAND Corporation as nuclear strategists; they have both expressed cautions about reliance on gaming. Kahn was concerned about analytical extrapolation: "Starting with such models enables one to define language, form concepts, and discuss and emphasize some elementary principles more clearly than by choosing examples from the real world. Trouble can ensue if the lesson learned from such models is blindly applied to more complicated and real problems."[53] Brodie was worried about the translation of rational models into the less rational domain of human behaviour: "Devices like war gaming are of no use in determining what deters what ... The main trouble with simulations, including war games, in this respect is that one simply cannot reproduce in the game room the kinds of emotion, especially of fear and anxiety, that would certainly be at work in any cabinet room during a major crisis that might involve use of nuclear weapons ... There are of course other shortcomings as well, which makes some of the more experienced practitioners of war gaming dubious of its value as anything other than an educational tool for the players themselves, and certainly not a reliable way of deriving final answers to strategic problems."[54]

In January 1981, RAND and Science Applications Incorporated (SAI) competed for a contract that became the RAND Strategy Assessment Center (RSAC) after RAND's victory: "On one side [RAND] were robots capable (with a little fiddling) of mindlessly going to nuclear war, and on the other side [SAI] were human beings who usually could not. On one side was a world encapsulated in a computer, and on the other side was a world drawn from human history and the personal experiences of the players."[55]

The "robots capable ... of mindlessly going to war" had been found to be necessary because of human reluctance to cross the nuclear threshhold.[56] Therefore a number of IVAN and SAM players were created, with artificial personalities, demonstrating character traits taken to be typical of Russian and American decision-makers, to permit enactment of more controlled scenarios.[57] This takes us a step further than seems wise. The warning systems are computer-controlled, as is the targeting. The time span available will probably inhibit any flexibility in weapon use. Human beings cannot even be trusted to act out the roles assigned to them in a game and must be replaced by computers; otherwise, the computer models are invalidated. It is at this point that it is possible to invoke Murphy's law, which states that anything that can go wrong will.

If we are willing to accept that Clausewitz still represents an influence on military thinking, then we must reconsider his statement: "Combat is conducted with physical weapons, and although the intellect does play a part, material factors will dominate. But when one comes to the effect of the engagement, where material successes turn into motives for further action, the intellect alone is decisive. In brief, tactics will present far fewer difficulties to the theorist than will strategy."[58]

Modern practice, starting with the operational analysts of the Second World War, has been to calculate the material factors on an ever-increasing scale. Little attention has been paid to "the effect of the engagement" as a motive for further action, because the theorists have extended their theories into doctrines for weapons use on a large scale. They have confused large-scale tactics with strategy, substituting numbers for motives, and quantification has become the indicator of victory. The use of overwhelming force is not to be discounted as an argument, as has been recognized in such sayings as "God is with the big battalions" and "Quantity has a quality of its own." Reliance on superior numbers or fire-power can, however, result in the sort of hubris that led to the failure of the Schlieffen Plan, which failed in flexibility of execution. It can lead to immediate results, as on the First Day on the Somme, when the tactical plan overestimated effects of artillery fire and underestimated the effects of defensive machine-gun fire. Similarly, hubris preceded the Tet Offensive, with the United States miscalculating the balance of military and political values. Unreflective acceptance of numbers or routine acceptance of a programmed interpretation of them could be fatal for the commander who is responsible for turning material success into "motives for further action."

A check of any current issue of *International Defense Review* will demonstrate the extent to which computers are now critical to weaponry. They have not been tested on a battlefield, where they face an enemy equally well-equipped and indoctrinated in their use and deployment, and the associated countermeasures. History suggests that the test will come, though not necessarily in the immediate future. When it does, people may be forced to improvise replacements for key components of the fighting and command infrastructure, but this improvisation may well have to be performed by a generation that cannot imagine functioning without computer support.

We are facing an era where costs and custom dictate that the majority of war experience that anyone has accumulated, from the private soldier to the commander, has been gained through computer simulations. These simulations will have represented best guesses about performance, capability, and conditions. It is unknown how well they will simulate the friction of war. We often rely uncritically on the answers produced by the black box; we seldom check the sources of the data; we do not examine the internal processes of the box itself. The wise commanders of the future will understand the limitations of the model and avoid dependence on it.

The temptation to extend the use of computers further, to integrate steps from one system to another, must be resisted. One of the great dangers in planning operations is to see the enemy as the mirror image of oneself. If both sides rely on their computers for decision making, then conflict tends towards mutual escalation. If either side goes outside the computer model, then there is the possibility of introducing the unprogrammed. Humans must be left "in the loop," at points between discrete system components, where judgment can be exercised and control implemented. The commanders able to deduce "motives for further action" will likely be the true strategists and the ones who are able to influence the course of events in the manner they wish.

NOTES

1 Morgan, *Peace and War*, 28.
2 R.V. Jones, *Most Secret War*, 99; West, *The SIGINT Secrets*, 214; and Edwards, "A History of Computers and Weapons Systems," 46–7.
3 Edwards, "A History," 48–51.
4 Ibid., 52. For a more critical view of the military involvement in electronics research and development, see Kaldor, *The Baroque Arsenal*, 67–72.
5 Bush, *Modern Arms and Free Men*, 16.
6 Tuchman, *The Guns of August*, 214.
7 General Staff, War Office, *Field Service Pocket Book, 1916*, 56–7.
8 "Obviously, I had been shaped with some care. To an extent I would scarcely have thought possible, I had given myself up to those who with undeniable craftsmanship had created a soldier out of my common civilian clay ... I did more or less what I was designed to do. And I refrained from doing what was not in the operating manual that covered my particular mechanism." Bendiner, *The Fall of Fortresses*, 12. Bendiner was a USAAF navigator.
9 Preston, Wise, and Werner, *Men in Arms*, 104.
10 Delbruck, *The Dawn of Modern Warfare*, 40.
11 Rogers, *Weapons of the British Soldier*, 93.
12 Fitzsimons, ed., *Weapons and Warfare*, Vol. 17, 1,863.
13 Ibid., Vol. 24, 2,582.
14 Ibid., Vol. 6, 592.
15 Dugan, "The Air War," 28.
16 G.K. Hartmann and Truver, *Weapons That Wait*, 94.
17 Fitzsimons, ed., *Weapons and Warfare*, Vol. 2, 128.
18 Ibid., Vol. 13, 1,358.
19 G.K. Hartmann and Truver, *Weapons That Wait*, chaps. 3 and 4, 86–120.
20 Hassig, *Understanding Computers*, 112.
21 "Under the Skies," 84–5.
22 Fuller, *The Conduct of War*, 47.
23 Blackett, *Studies of War*, 215.
24 Byrne, *The Whiz Kids*, 51.
25 Ibid., 399.
26 Gibson, *The Perfect War*, 156.
27 Ibid., particularly 114–17.
28 Ibid., 158.
29 Ibid., 162.
30 Wirtz, *The Tet Offensive*, 275.
31 Sheehan, *A Bright Shining Lie*, 698–9.
32 Clifford, "A Viet Nam Reappraisal," 441.
33 Ibid., 443.
34 Ibid., 445.
35 Goerlitz, *The German General Staff*, 59.

36 Allen, *War Games*, 129–30.
37 Ibid., 115.
38 Ibid., 123.
39 Ibid., 122.
40 Ibid., 277–80.
41 Herken, *Counsels of War*, 74–101.
42 Allen, *War Games*, 307.
43 Jack A. Stockfisch at the Leesburg Workshop on Theater Level Gaming, 1977, cited in Allen, *War Games*, 289. Stockfisch is identified by Allen as being an "economist and sober critic of modelling," but his succinct views reflect the tone of other respondents from higher positions in the formal community of military modelling.
44 Robert Schneider, from the Office of the Secretary of Defense's Planning Analysis and Evaluation Group, also at Leesburg, 1977, cited in Allen, *War Games*, 289–90.
45 Rhodes, *The Making of the Atomic Bomb*, chap. 19.
46 Herken, *Counsels of War*, 25.
47 Joseph and Gladstone, "The Strategic and Theater Nuclear Balance," 85. Different numbers are available: the ss-9 has been estimated at up to 25 MT, Kaplan, *The Wizards of Armageddon*, 351; and the ss-18 has been assigned ten MIRV warheads, Dunnigan, *How to Make War*, 440.
48 Boring, "Computer System Reliability and Nuclear War," 126.
49 Ibid., 104–5.
50 Perrow, *Normal Accidents*, 291.
51 Cited in Ford, *The Button*, 115.
52 This is a summary of a number of concerns that can be found in Ford, *The Button*, 14–16, 84–92.
53 Kahn, *Thinking about the Unthinkable*, 134.
54 Brodie, *War and Politics*, 412.
55 Allen, *War Games*, 318.
56 Ibid., 44–8.
57 Ibid., 321–7.
58 Clausewitz, *On War*, trans. and ed. Howard and Paret, 2nd ed., 162.

Stealth Technology: A Revolution in Air Warfare?

LCOL RONALD BLANK

History is replete with situations in which the continuous cycle of weapons development has brought about striking new technical advances in warfare, appearing to render everything that came before obsolete. The crossbow, the musket, the machine-gun, and the submarine all had an enormous effect on their respective epochs. The proponents of one of the latest advances in aerospace technology, aided by dramatic film footage, have made similar claims for "stealth aircraft." Could anyone who witnessed the staggering display of the Allied coalition air forces in January 1991 on television ever forget one of the most amazing video pictures ever shown? The image of the Iraqi air force headquarters in Baghdad being destroyed by a single bomb that flew down the ventilation shaft and exploded inside will remain etched in the minds of those who saw it. What type of aircraft could penetrate the highly sophisticated Iraqi air defence system and, untouched by the defences, drop its ordnance with such telling effect?

With the appearance of the "stealth" F-117 fighter-bomber, the nature of air warfare entered a new era. The seeming invisibility of this aircraft, combined with its lethal precision-guided munitions (PGMs), has raised many doubts about the capability of air defence systems to detect and to warn of the approach of this class of aircraft, let alone intercept it before it reaches its target.

This essay surveys technical advances in stealthy, or low- and very-low observable (LO/VLO) aircraft – a technology that is going somewhere unknown but is simultaneously exciting and sobering. It briefly examines the history of air vehicles using such technologies, shows how some aircraft were developed and employed, and then suggests what technical and operational initiatives might meet the challenge of this rapidly evolving threat to aero-space defence. It concludes with an assessment of the long-term future of stealth technology in air warfare, based on its relevance to some of the traditional principles of war.

HISTORICAL SURVEY

Low observable aircraft have been designed for many more years than is commonly recognized. In the First World War, both the United Kingdom and Germany were working on separate and similar attempts to build an aircraft invisible to the human eye. Scientists experimented with "a transparent bi-plane with a fuselage coated with cellophane foil rather than the opaque cloth then in use. But, cellophane was not built for this task: when wet, it could not stick to the fuselage, and reflections of the sun's rays from the smooth surface were visible at long range."[1] While technically sophisticated surveillance systems were not yet in place, airborne and ground observers were in plentiful supply, and this attempt at invisibility did not yield tactically useful results.

In the Second World War, radar and radar counter-measures affected the outcome of the air war over Europe. A common myth is that radar was a "secret" weapon that was crucial to the outcome of the Battle of Britain. In fact, Germany's radar (but not its air defence system) was superior in many ways to British radar. The story of radar in the war is a complex one, involving electronic countermeasures (ECM) and electronic counter-countermeasures (ECCM) by both the Allies and the Axis. Measures and counters employed included window (chaff), countered by doppler radar and frequency hopping; airborne-intercept radar, countered by passive radar detectors; and jamming of fighter-control frequencies, countered by data-link transmissions to fighters.[2] The lesson of the air war over Europe is that any technological advance, no matter how revolutionary it might seem at the time, will be quickly countered by an opponent with the scientific and industrial base to do so. Technology can confer a tactical advantage, but for only a brief period of time.

Following the development and operational deployment of radar technologies by both the Allies and the Axis, American and British engineers were working on separate projects to reduce the radar reflectivity of aircraft. The United States was developing radar-absorbing material (RAM) called MX-410, which was painted onto the surface of test aircraft.[3] However, this substance was found to be too heavy and was not considered very satisfactory. Probably the most successful example of stealthy techniques in the Second World War was the British De Havilland Mosquito aircraft. Though built almost entirely of wood, primarily to reduce the use of scarce strategic metals, the aircraft doubled as both an unarmed Pathfinder and a long-range fighter-bomber. Using low-level penetration tactics, the Mosquito's low-radar reflectivity, resulting from its largely wooden construction, made it very difficult for German radar to detect.[4]

Another approach to reducing aircraft radar cross-section (RCS) was the "flying wing" concept. In 1940, the Northrop Company produced a test model of a "flying wing" bomber called N-1M.[5] After the war, Northrop's experience led to the development of the massive, four-engined YB-35 "flying wing" and the follow-up YB-49, six–jet-engined bomber. Both aircrafts' designs made head-on visual cuing difficult and offered a small RCS. The U.S. government ordered some YB-49s, but cancelled the order after one crashed. Instead, the more conventional, but not very stealthy B-58 and B-52 were put into service. In Britain, the "flying wing" design could be seen in the Vulcan bomber, which served as the United Kingdom's main nuclear-strike bomber for three decades. When first deployed, it was operated at altitudes above 15,000 metres, where the fighters of the day could not reach it. As fighter performance at high altitudes improved, however, the RAF found the Vulcan extremely manoeuvrable at lower altitudes. And the Vulcan's attack tactics were changed to exploit its ability to fly at low level and manoeuvre away from enemy fighters, rather than its being given a particularly stealthy design, because, except when head on, it was quite visible to radar from most aspect angles.

As the aircraft design community's knowledge of the influence of different shapes and components on RCS increased, the United States was able to exploit this expertise in the development of the U-2 and the LO SR-71 reconnaissance aircraft, the first aircraft to incorporate many stealthy techniques on a large scale. RAM material covered sharp edges, chines, and elevons; the wing and body were blended to reduce RCS; radar-absorbent plastic honeycomb, specially designed to cope with high temperatures, accounted for 20 per cent of the wing areas; and the entire aircraft was painted with a black "iron ball" ferrite paint that absorbed radar energy. Iron ball paint works on the premise of a "mutability envelope" that the pilot can manipulate by adjusting controls in the cockpit.[6] The control changes can vary the polarity of the coating, literally making the aircraft suddenly invisible to radars.[7] Further development continued in the 1970s as massive computing power allowed a quantitative assessment of the radar-defeating qualities of different parts of an aircraft, depending on their design and their composition. It was now possible to design an aircraft with a balanced RCS and to reduce the return from different surfaces of the aircraft.[8] Under the project "Have Blue," an experimental stealth aircraft (XST) was built and flown by the Lockheed Aircraft Company at its secret plant, known affectionately by its staff as the "Skunk Works."

Lockheed had many highly skilled engineers and mathematicians who were charged with designing new aircraft for the U.S. government. Denys Overholster, a mathematician and radar specialist, had discovered a scientific paper by a Russian named Ufimtsev, who in the 1950s had been employed on similar research efforts for the Soviet Union. Surprisingly, he had been permitted to publish his findings, which offered a new method to reduce radar reflectivity through changing an aircraft's shape. This would be the key to the RCS puzzle. Lockheed convinced the U.S. air force (USAF) to spend $20 million from a secret appropriations fund, and, adding $10 million of its own money, it went to work on the design and production of two experimental XST aircraft. This work revolutionized theories on aircraft observability.[9]

U.S. President Jimmy Carter subsequently authorized development of a production stealth fighter in 1978. Codenamed project "Senior Trend," this venture resulted in the F-117. Fifty-nine aircraft were delivered to the USAF, and, despite three highly publicized crashes of either XST or F-117 aircraft, a picture of the F-117 was not made available to the public until 1988, when the first grainy photo was released.[10] The fighter was used during the U.S. military action in Panama and had been proposed for a part in the raid on Libya in 1986, but the Libyan mission was vetoed by the Joint Chiefs of Staff because of the risk of the loss of such advanced technology.[11] Now that the aircraft and its effectiveness are well known, the F-117 fleet's home base has been changed from the secret facility in Tonopah, Nevada, to Holloman Air Force Base (AFB), New Mexico, where approximately forty-five aircraft are stationed. Temporary detachments have been sent to bases in Alaska, Japan, and the United Kingdom. One author has reported that an F-117 was flown within thirty kilometres of a Soviet-manned air defence radar without being detected.[12] If this is true, then the utility of any strategic defence system can be questioned. What is the point in building an expensive air defence system if it can be penetrated so easily?

TECHNOLOGY DESCRIPTION

Understanding the technology behind the latest LO/VLO aircraft designs is important if one is to grasp its strengths and weaknesses. In attempting to reduce aircraft visibility, aerospace engineers concentrate on three areas when designing an LO/VLO aircraft: the visual spectrum (flying-wing bombers such as the B-2), the thermal or heat spectrum (the SR-71, flying in extremely cold temperatures in the stratosphere), and the radar spectrum (the F-117).

The F-117 has a unique profile. The structure has been cut into many diamond shapes, and all edges are rounded. This design and manufacturing technique is called "faceting," and it deflects radar energy outward in many directions away from the radar receiver, permitting the aircraft to be nearly invisible. The entire airframe is covered with Fibaloy, a product from Dow Chemical that "is produced by embedding glass fibres in plastic ... [R]eportedly [it] is strong enough for use as external aircraft skin and for some internal structural members, without metal reinforcement."[13] To reduce

RCS further, only 10 per cent of the structure is made of metal, iron ball is applied to the surface, and all access panels and doors are specially shaped. Reinforced carbon fibre is used extensively because of its ability to dissipate radar energy and to reduce the infrared (IR) signature of the fighter.[14] PGMs are carried internally to reduce RCS and drag. The aircraft has no onboard radar to betray its presence, using only IR acquisition to identify and track targets. To keep its own IR signature low, the F-117 uses non-afterburning GE 404 engines. Since, with these engines, it cannot go supersonic, the aural signature is significantly reduced; it was further decreased by absorbers and shields. The GE 404 also has greatly decreased emissions of carbon particles and water vapour, whose presence could aid sensor systems in detecting the aircraft. Finally, to keep it from being visually spotted in the sky, fuel additives are provided to avoid creating exhaust contrails.[15]

Of all the means of detecting aircraft such as the F-117, radar remains potentially the most effective, and RCS thresholds are affected by several factors. Radar reflectivity is relative not only to the target size but also to its shape. Flat metal surfaces perpendicular to the radar transmitter are the most easily detected by radar. Engineers have known for many years how the radar detectibility of aircraft varied with the shape of the aircraft and the angle at which the radar beam struck the aircraft's surface. Exact RCSs have been meticulously calculated, by comparing the strength of the return from the target with that of a reflective sphere with a one–square-metre cross-section. Thus, the term RCS is always related in "X" square metres.[16] The table on p. 202 illustrates the relative RCS measurements for several types of aircraft and cruise missiles.

The RCS of the F-117 from the head-on aspect would make it appear on a radar scope to be the size of a small bird or a cloud of insects – i.e., almost invisible.[17] This presents special challenges to air defence planners.

LO and VLO aircraft have been on the market for many years. "The SR-71 and the B-1B are considered first-generation stealth. The F-117 is second generation; the advanced cruise missile is third; the B-2, fourth; and the F-22, fifth generation."[18] But whatever their technical production lineage, aircraft roles can significantly affect RCS. Though the F-22 is a more modern development, its RCS is greater than the older design of the B-2. While being highly reliant on stealthy materials to optimize invisibility, the F-22 is still an air superiority fighter that must have agility, speed, and fairly large air-to-air weapons, such as the AIM-7 Sparrow and AIM-9 Sidewinder missiles. Consequently, afterburning engines, the tail, and the missiles all add to its RCS. This is in direct contrast to the B-2 bomber, designed from the outset for the lowest possible RCS, to maximize overall system invisibility on its solo bombing runs against high-value targets.

Given nearly fifty years of demonstrated stealth capability, there have been strenuous efforts by engineers working in the counter-stealth arena.

Table
Selected air vehicles and their radar cross section

Air vehicle	Radar cross–section (m^2)
B-52	1,000
B-1B	10
B-2	0.000001
F-22	0.5
F-117	0.01
Air Launched Cruise Missile (ALCM)	0.25
Advanced Cruise Missile (ACM)	0.001

Source: Marsh, ed., *Stealth and Future Military Aircraft*, 40.

Engineers and operational planners have contemplated several issues. Can a detection system be designed that will provide 360-degree coverage at all altitudes? Can the system be defeated by electronic counter-measures? Will it detect all sizes of aircraft and missiles, no matter what their RCS may be?

To answer these questions, and to find out how effective the LO/VLO aircraft designs were before committing themselves to their development, scientists and air defence experts have carried out a variety of tests. "Since the early 1970s, the [US] Air Force and Department of Defense have worked assiduously to identify weaknesses in the stealth approach that could be exploited by a potential opponent. This has included undertaking an extensive, independent counter-stealth team effort supported by highly qualified engineers and scientists investigating all means for countering stealth technologies. The goal has been to find the 'Achilles heel' which would negate the value of these technologies."[19]

More than forty Soviet and Western systems have been tested against the stealth aircraft. These include acoustic systems (using microphone arrays to listen for overflying aircraft), bi-static radar systems (the receiver and transmitter are in different locations, thus nullifying the impact of faceted aircraft), infrared detection schemes,[20] corona discharge detection, interaction with cosmic rays, magnetic disturbance detection, hybrid bi-static space radar, high frequency (HF) surface wave radar, very high frequency (VHF) radar, detection of aircraft emissions, radiometric detection, air vehicle aerodynamic wake detection, and ultra-wideband (impulse) radar.[21] If a totally effective counter-stealth technology has been discovered, no one is yet saying so publicly.

Despite these efforts, stealth aircraft, such as the F-117, have been described as "essentially undetectable by any airborne radar except the AWACS radar platform, which was effective only at a very short range. Most ground-based missile-tracking radars would not detect it until it was inside the minimum range of the missile systems."[22] Ground-based early warning radars have an equally difficult time detecting these aircraft. The Iraqi air force was unable to shoot down any F-117s during the Persian Gulf operation even though Iraq was believed to have had one of the best air defence systems in the world, even better than the systems deployed in the former Warsaw Pact region.[23]

In the short period leading up to the forty-seven–day Persian Gulf War, the U.S.-led coalition deployed more than two thousand modern fighters, bombers, and transports into the operational theatre. The after-action analysis states that the coalition flew a total of 109,876 combat sorties. Of this number, the USAF flew 59.3 per cent, the U.S. navy 16 per cent, the Allies a combined 15.7 per cent, and the U.S. Marine Corps 9 per cent. The F-117 Nighthawk fleet was small in numbers compared to other aircraft types, comprising only 2.5 per cent of the total deployed force. The Nighthawks flew less than 2 per cent of the total, or approximately 1,300 sorties. According to the Pentagon's after-action studies, however, the F-117s destroyed 43 per cent of the total Iraqi strategic targets put out of action, with nary a scratch being suffered by them.[24]

Throughout history there have always been methods devised to counter new weapons. As we have seen, during the Second World War, German and Allied scientists played "cat and mouse," trying to defeat the other side's latest technological edge. A counter to a new milestone in mankind's ability to kill has always seemed just around the corner, and this decade is no different.

COUNTER-STEALTH TECHNICAL INITIATIVES

Two active radar emitters appear to hold promise in counter-stealth capabilities. The first is the over-the-horizon (backscatter), or OTH-B, radars fielded in the United States and Australia in the last ten years. This radar operates in the very low HF band, and U.S. tests in 1988 apparently determined that the radar could detect targets at the one-half wavelength of the radar's 28-MHZ frequency, or as small as 5.3 metres in size. The OTH-B's program director claimed that this would enable it to detect "vehicles of interest such as cruise missiles."[25] Another active detection technology under investigation is space-based radar (SBR). Though many potential types and configurations of an SBR network are being studied, it is the bi-static concept, where transmitters are placed on four or five satellites in a geosynchronous orbit, and receivers are located on airborne platforms such as AWACS or large transport aircraft modified as command and control platforms, that holds the most promise for detection of LO/VLO aircraft and missiles.[26]

The advent of stealth technology has temporarily given some air forces an almost undetectable approach to their targets. Defensive surveillance and engagement forces are apparently ineffective against this threat, as evidenced in the Persian Gulf. If historical precedents can serve as a guide, eventually a robust air defence command and control network will be developed that will permit it to see all known threats. Just how "leak-proof" such a system might be is obviously a product of the effectiveness of the technical arrangements of the defence.

One of the most encouraging and affordable sensor technologies for the defence is ground-based bi-static radar, where the receiver and transmitter are in separate locations. This type of sensor apparently possess good low-level and LO/VLO detection, tracking, and RCS measuring capabilities. Future bi-static radar systems may use dedicated, cooperative and non-cooperative transmitters.[27] Cooperative transmitters include military and civilian radars, and the term "non-cooperative" is used to denote TV and radio stations that may be broadcasting and whose signals may be of use to the defensive system. With the capability to use transmissions from non-military sources, the military defence system can focus on providing large numbers of bi-static receivers. These receivers have several advantages: they are passive (use transmitters of opportunity); they can be unattended; they can be mobile (making them harder to detect); and they can be linked together or "internet-ted" (enabling them to cover a larger area than only one receiver could monitor). These characteristics make it more difficult for the attacker to know where the defensive receivers are and when they are operational.

Such bi-static receivers give an approximate, though useful indication of the RCS of targets as they pass by, and this approximation can permit skilled surveillance operators or artificial intelligence–based computers to make judgments concerning the nature of the detected object. For example, even if the system can provide only a rough measurement of RCS, these data can allow operations personnel to "discriminate" between airborne objects: if an object has a moderately large RCS (1.0 to 5.0 square metres, ± 0.5 square metres), the operator could assume that it may be a LO target, but not a VLO cruise missile or stealth fighter-bomber. The same logic could be applied if the bi-static system measures a very small RCS (0.1 to 0.001 square metres). Though the operator could not say precisely what it is, it can confirm what it is not – an airliner or non-stealthy bomber. As these systems become more accurate, they will come closer to providing a true, non-cooperative identification system.

Even with a worst-case capability for a bi-static system to measure RCS, one can still postulate the ability to discriminate between (as opposed to identify) classes of detected airborne objects. This could lead to a capability to classify objects passively, as shown by the Table on p. 205.

Table
Categories of target that might be classified by passive systems

Size	Class of target
Big	Bombers, transports, airliners
Medium	Business jets, light aircraft, fighters
Small	Cruise missiles, LO/VLO aircraft

Investigations have identified two principal disadvantages with the systems: targets must be in line-of-sight of both the transmitter and the receiver, and ground clutter affects the radar return. Nevertheless, bi-static systems can detect and measure the shadow created by an aircraft as it moves between the transmitter and receiver, and, though the LO/VLO target may not reflect radar energy to the receiver, the resultant "hole" or lack of reflected energy might be useful to the detection and tracking of these aircraft. [28] By detecting such "shadows," a defensive system may be able to detect and track all classes of targets, including those that are "totally absorbing." [29]

Even more advanced "active" detection systems may soon be able to detect stealth aircraft. It has been reported that the USAF's laboratory in Rome, NY, is currently conducting demonstrations into a state-of-the-art passive sensor system capable of ground-based or airborne surveillance. "The system utilizes sources of illumination and provides a detection and tracking capability commensurate with traditional monostatic systems of equivalent power. Additionally, this system can provide an emitter identification capability to establish an illuminator source file and to find and classify various electronic emissions. This system has been field tested against a variety of airborne and ground-based targets and has been shown to be an accurate and reliable system." [30] It is expected to be a mature technology in the year 2000.

A PROPOSED DEFENSIVE OPERATIONAL CONCEPT

A surveillance system capable of detecting all classes of targets would be best served, theoretically, by a mixture of receiver types. The system could include standard monostatic radar to track non-stealthy targets and many inexpensive bi-static receivers throughout the area of responsibility, using cooperative and non-cooperative transmitters. The data from the bi-static receivers would require continuous monitoring to ensure that "normal," status-quo readings are known. This would permit the air defence system to recognize suspicious situations when the picture being received was not "normal." To deal with large amounts of data, minicomputers could be used to monitor the picture received by the bi-statics, and the computers would be programmed to relay an alarm when unusual readings were detected. Once alerted by the computers of an abnormal situation, operations personnel could scramble fighters to investigate. The operations personnel would be either at an operations centre, with the data being forwarded to them, or in mobile, widely dispersed mini-operations facilities linked to a control centre. Since the detection capability of the bi-static receivers is limited by line-of-sight, many of them would be needed to provide adequate coverage for a given area. Based on the relatively low cost of using whatever cooperative and non-cooperative transmitters exist near the areas of interest, this type of air defence system would probably be only slightly more expensive to operate than the one that the North American Aerospace Defence Command operates today.

For a new system to be reliable and effective, the RCS of aircraft and missiles of interest would have to be known, to ensure that valid targets were not missed through an error in the design and operation of the bi-static receivers. Even so, no system would be foolproof, "because attacking stealth aircraft may have been designed to counter a particular defensive system."[31] However, the more diverse the defensive system, the more difficult it would be to deceive.

CONTINUING TECHNICAL DEVELOPMENTS

It has been suggested by some analysts that warfare is undergoing a military-technical revolution, and that this is the third one in history.[32] Other analysts have chosen to label this phenomenon a unique revolution in military affairs.[33] The first revolution, for many observers, was the invention of gunpowder; the second has been described as the cumulative impact in the late nineteenth and early twentieth centuries of the products of the industrial revolution, the railway, machine-gun, aircraft, and submarine. Phillip Meilinger has claimed that the current technology leap is so staggering that it could be called the first revolution, as previous leaps were so minor in comparison as to be labelled insignificant.[34]

While, for some, the impact of nuclear weapons would overshadow all other technologies, it is just as reasonable to suggest that aerospace power technologies, especially their impressive advances in such areas as LO/VLO and PGMs, would stand out. The world's aerospace defence networks must first adapt their operational procedures to recognize that nearly invisible aircraft and missiles do exist and then develop the necessary technical solutions. There are efforts already under way in defence research establishments and industry designed to produce an effective counter to the LO/VLO aircraft. A serving USAF officer, Ronald C. Durbin, has suggested: "A single breakthrough in any of a dozen (or more) scientific disciplines has the potential to negate their edge ... [and], ... robbed of their stealth, they become sub-optimal platforms."[35]

A war is rarely won or lost on a single initiative. Just as defensive technologies are being developed, research and development (R&D) in fighter and bomber aircraft have continued since the Persian Gulf War. There were two recent attempts by aerospace companies to design a stealthy replacement for the U.S. Navy's (USN's) venerable A-6 Intruder bomber. However, both the A-12 and A/F-X fighter-bomber development projects were cancelled before they got beyond the early design stage because of the exorbitant cost and drawn-out schedules. Lockheed's Advanced Development Company has proposed to the USN that the F-117 aircraft be modified for carrier operation. An afterburning version of its F404 engine to aid in carrier takeoffs and landings, GPS receivers, an advanced infrared acquisition and designation unit, and new, unspecified signature reduction work would be added to the aircraft for approximately $2.7 billion. The USN has not yet agreed to the proposal, though some officials believe that the high cost will make funding unobtainable.[36]

Another U.S. aircraft development that has incorporated stealth technology is the updated McDonnell F/A-18 E/F. Operated in less-modern versions by Canada, Australia, Spain, Finland, Malaysia, Kuwait, and Switzerland, the latest version of the USN's main fighter-bomber has just rolled off the production line and will be operational by 1998. The company developed five different proposals for the aircraft to satisfy modern requirements for tomorrow's air battle before the USN selected the one it wanted, and all featured "special technology," a reference to stealth techniques.[37] This includes redesigned engine intakes, heavily modified to reduce RCS, and leading-edge flaps built with a deep-section, radar-absorbent structure using multiple layers of graded, absorbent honeycomb to maximize counter-radar effectiveness.[38] Meanwhile, the USAF's new air superiority fighter, the Lockheed/Boeing F-22, is now in advanced development and was to begin flight testing in 1997. While, according to some analysts, the competing Northrop F-23 lost to the F-22 in the air force competition because it sacrificed manoeuvrability for total stealth capability, the less stealthy, but more agile F-22 is now turning out heavier than originally wanted – an indication of the significant weight premium for a stealthy design. The new takeoff weight is classified, but it is known that it is much higher than the design goal. This could force a change in future air force design theories to recognize the inherent advantages of incorporating the concepts of both stealth and agility in aircraft and, using appropriate tradeoff analysis, to adjust the optimum balance between technologies.[39]

Elsewhere, other high-profile development projects are incorporating the latest techniques in LO/VLO technology into next-generation fighters. The British/German/Italian Eurofighter 2000, the Swedish JAS 39 Gripen, and the French Rafale are all being developed with significant reliance on stealth techniques developed by those nations' R&D communities. Meanwhile, Russia is developing a stealthy derivative of the SU-27 air defence fighter called the SU-35. Anyone reviewing a picture of the aircraft would recognize many similarities between the F/A-18 E/F, Eurofighter, Rafale, and the SU-35. It was recently revealed that Russia has also been designing a stealthy, forward-swept–wing, vectored-thrust aircraft called the SU-32.[40] Undoubtedly, there are other, still-unobserved models being developed there that will incorporate even more reverse-engineering of the F-117 and F-22 to close the technological gap further.

IMPACT ON AEROSPACE POWER

It has been suggested that stealth technology is perhaps the most revolutionary advance in military technology since radar and the atomic bomb.[41] The commander of the Iraqi air defence forces in the Gulf War undoubtedly agreed that "revolutionary" was not too far-fetched a description for the lessons taught by the F-117 in that war.

Aerospace power is well recognized as a fundamental component of national security. It is distinguished by its inherent characteristics of flexibility, perspective, speed, range, responsiveness, concentration, fire-power, and shock effect. In modern warfare, aerospace operations have made a major contribution to combat power,[42] and, while aerospace power is not necessarily the most important component in all situations, because of limitations of impermanence, payload, and vulnerability, it has become pervasive in virtually all aspects of warfare. Success in war therefore depends on a nation's understanding of aerospace power and on its credibly translating its inherent advantages into technological applications that can be supported with suitable doctrine, training, and employment to guarantee national security.

In a relatively short period, aerospace power has rapidly developed to its current position in modern warfare through extensive technological achievements. However, authors such as David MacIsaac caution us that whenever commanders have sought out strategic advantages that depend on advanced technology, that technology has often had less influence on the battlefield than expected.[43] However, the application of technology in such areas as stealth and PGMs has significantly changed air warfare. The examples of the U-2, TR-1, SR-71, F-117, B-2, cruise missiles, and air vehicles now under development are vivid testimony to the vast technological edge conferred by LO/VLO techniques. Because of the strong desire to reduce collateral, non-combatant casualties in any modern conflict, a stealthy, PGM-equipped fighter-bomber or cruise missile may be the best weapons in a commander's arsenal to strike high-priority targets in heavily defended areas. No longer can heads of government, commanders-in-chief, and other key staff ever feel secure in their homes, workplaces, or heavily protected command bunkers hundreds or thousands of miles behind the battle area. Forces employing stealthy aircraft and missiles can threaten command and control elements that once were considered safe.

However, Phillip Meilinger believes that this capability could be creating another set of problems for commanders. He states that there is historical evidence available to suggest that politicians now expect PGMs and stealth technology to provide them deadly accuracy with little or no collateral damage, thus bringing the concept of "surgical strike" to its ultimate level of achievement. The opportunity to strike only the designated target, without damaging others, could become so crucial to political leaders that they may insist on this performance standard on all occasions. With the ability of the media to provide near-instantaneous, unfiltered bomb-damage assessment for the world via satellite TV, Meilinger believes that this media coverage could increase the value of aerospace power and its precise impact technologies, in contrast to the less precise area weapons used by maritime, and especially by land, forces.[44]

In the lexicon of western military forces, it is generally accepted that there are nine principles of war,[45] and stealth technology is particularly relevant in three of them. "Surprise" is achieved when the enemy has been struck at a time or place or in a manner for which it is unprepared. "Economy of force" is achieved when mass has been created by the fullest use of available forces on the enemy's vital point(s). Finally, the principle of "offensive action" has been adhered to when the initiative has been seized, retained, and fully exploited.

The F-117 and modern cruise missiles are extremely capable platforms that have pushed these principles of war – surprise, economy of force, and the offensive – to their most potent achievements to date. The first coalition air component commander, General Michael Dugan, just after the Gulf War, concluded: "[T]he efficiency of the F-117 gives it an effective striking power far out of proportion to the numbers of aircraft involved ... 4,500 B-17 bombers in World War II would have had to drop 9,000 bombs to have the same probability of hitting the Iraqi Air Force Headquarters as would a single F-117 ... [T]he F-105 in Vietnam would have taken 95 missions with two 2,000-pound bombs apiece to achive the same probability of kill as one F-117."[46]

The implications of the foregoing example are far-reaching and will undoubtedly continue to shape the principles of war for many years. For instance, the highly important considerations of valid target selection, management of overall logistical resources (personnel, weapons, and aircraft), and the commander-in-chief's strategic options contained in the campaign plan are all affected by this new technology. Even when hostilities are not contemplated or imminent, these resources may yield future cost efficiencies in peacetime. Military establishments and governments everywhere are coming to realize the enormous cost benefits derived from purchasing a few stealthy, PGM-equipped fighter-bombers, instead of many conventional, but less "survivable" and less operationally effective aircraft.

In Canada, for example, the air force has started down this road by placing an order for laser designation/infrared target acquisition pods, laser-guided bombs, and infrared-guided Maverick air-to-ground missiles for its CF-18 fleet to provide an initial PGM capability. It is expected that any eventual replacement for Canada's CF-18 fleet will incorporate the latest developments in stealthy technologies. The impact of stealth on traditional principles of war will probably be significant and enduring. The influence of these technologies are simply too pervasive not to noticeably affect most aspects of contingency planning, operational deployments, and combat operations well into the next century. Despite their far-reaching effects on many aspects of war, historical experience suggests that counters to stealth technology will be developed sooner rather than later.

CONCLUSION

The "pendulum of technology and tactics," which started in motion at least 2,500 years ago, is never at rest. It swings between offence and defence over time, and right now, in air warfare, technology favours offensive forces, which are clearly ahead of defensive systems. However, in the past, the continuous cycle of weapons development and countermeasures on the battlefield has meant that the advantage held by one type of warfare or technology has often been fleeting, as was demonstrated by the Allied bomber offensive in the Second World War. Those in the air defence community can also take heart from the Second World War bomber example, because it showed that defences against non-nuclear attacks need not be "leak-proof" to inflict serious reverses on attacking aircraft. The Royal Air Force's Bomber Command found that loss rates, to all causes, of 7 per cent or more over several months seriously impaired the fighting efficiency of its force.[47] In addition, despite all the Allied technical advances and German reverses, by July 1944 the German air defence organization had largely overcome Bomber Command's tactical countermeasures and was in a position to inflict prohibitive casualties on the attacking force. The capture of important elements of the German air defence system after D-Day by advancing Allied troops was one of the main reasons why that system finally collapsed.[48]

Given the small numbers of stealth aircraft that are operational, because of their high cost, the same advantages are likely to accrue to the air defence forces in the future. Both sides of the aerospace development battleground, offensive and defensive, will continue to seek an edge over their opponents, and stealth and counter-stealth technologies will continue to play a prominent role. Historical evidence and the newest technical developments in aviation also suggest that stealth technology will spread widely and that effective countermeasures, though they will be developed, will lag significantly behind the spread of stealth technology.[49]

NOTES

1 Shel, "Stealth Aircraft Come of Age," 23–37.
2 Greenhous et al., *The Crucible of War*, is one of the best accounts of the complexity of this battle. See especially 689–727 and 123, 167, 543, 587–8, 589–90, 734, 822.
3 Barker, *The RAF at War*, 133.
4 Shel, "Stealth Aircraft Comes of Age," 32.
5 Richardson, *Stealth*, 66.
6 Ibid., 49, 98–9.
7 During an air defence exercise near Florida in 1979, the author was controlling two F-106 interceptors attempting to intercept and simulate destruction of a USAF Special Forces CC-130. The target aircraft was covered with iron ball paint, and when the pilot changed the polarity of the material, the aircraft disappeared from the radar scopes both on the ground and on the airborne radar of the F-106s. The intercept was unsuccessful, as a visual sighting of the aircraft could not be made and the target's position was never discovered.
8 Brown, *Fundamentals of Stealth Design*, 1.
9 Rich, *Skunk Works*, 1.
10 Richardson, *Stealth*, 69–70.
11 Sweetman, "Wobbly Goblin," 30.
12 J. Jones, *Stealth Technology*, 80.
13 Ibid., 45.
14 Ibid., 77.
15 Rich, *Skunk Works*, Extract, 5.
16 Sweetman, *Lockheed F-117A*, 9.
17 Ibid., 49.
18 Ibid., 23.
19 "The USAF Case for the B-2," 3.
20 The concept has already been put into practice by Thorn EMI Electronics. The company has fielded the air defence and alerting device (ADAD), which is being accepted by the British army, as reported in *Asian Defence Journal* 7 (1991): "ADAD is the first of a new generation of aircraft detection and targeting systems. The system uses a rotating mirror which scans a 360 degree azimuth field of view for a IR detector assembly, detecting aircraft targets from their thermal signatures … [D]etection range of the system is classified but is thought to be at least 20 km."

21 "The USAF Case for the B-2," 5.

22 Sweetman, *Lockheed F117-A*, 23.

23 "Stealth, What Is It Really?" 25.

24 Cohen and Keaney, *Gulf War Air Power Survey Summary Report* and *White Paper: Air Force Performance in Desert Storm*. Similar statistics are also available from the *Gulf War Debriefing Book*.

25 Hayward, *The Air Defence Initiative*, 8.

26 Ibid., 11.

27 Skolnik, *Radar Handbook*, 25.4, 25.8.

28 Ibid., 25.17.

29 Ibid., 25.18.

30 Rome Laboratory, *Advanced Technology Data Sheet*, 1. Advanced technology data sheets for this important air force laboratory are available on the Internet for ready reference.

31 Richardson, *Stealth*, 175.

32 Colonel John A. Warden, III, to Paul Wolfowitz, letter, subject: Comments on Study by Colonel Andy Krepinevich quoted in Meilinger, "Ten Propositions Regarding Airpower," 17–18. This essay is a fascinating analysis of the historical impact of the principles of war in the past seventy-five years.

33 Fairbairn et al., "Historical Analogies and the Ultimate Paradox," abstract, on the internet at www.cdsar.af.mil/cc.html.

34 Meilinger, "Ten Propositions Regarding Airpower," 18.

35 Durbin, *CADRE Air Chronicles*, Current Issues, 1, on the internet at www.cdsar.af.mil/ci/roles/bomber.html.

36 Boatman, "Reheated F-117A on Offer to US Navy," 5.

37 Braybrook, "Design Analysis: F/A-18 E/F," 12.

38 Sweetman, "The Future of Airborne Stealth," 35.

39 Ibid.

40 "Radical Sukhoi Design to Fly This Year, Says Russia," 3.

41 "Stealth, What Is It Really?" 24.

42 Funnell, "Foreword," to Funnell, *Royal Australian Air Force Air Power Manual*, 1.

43 MacIsaac, "Voices from the Central Blue," 646–7.

44 Meilinger, "Ten Propositions Regarding Airpower," 14.

45 *Air Force Manual 1–1*, Vol. I, 1–1.

46 Dugan, "First Lessons of Victory," 213.

47 Webster and Frankland, *The Strategic Air Offensive against Germany*, Vol. III, 108.

48 Greenhous et al., *The Crucible of War*, 822.

49 O'Connell, *Of Arms and Men*, 6–12.

Beyond the Line: Strategy in Support of Space Control

CAPT JUSTIN SCHMIDT-CLEVER

"The oldest military maxim concerns the advantages of holding and using the high ground" and the advantages that it confers for both observation and the employment of forces.[1] The introduction of military air power at the beginning of the twentieth century changed, for most observers, the military concept of what constituted the high ground, and it is possible to discern a similar situation emerging as military forces begin to exploit more fully the technologies of the space age.

Carl von Clausewitz remarked: "[E]very age [has] its own kind of war, its own limiting conditions, and it own peculiar preconceptions. Each period [holds] to its own theory of war."[2] The developing strategies that will influence the employment of military force in outer space will not be the unexpected divinations of science. As was the case with other revolutionary technologies, strategic thought regarding the integration of new technology will appear as evolutions of existing strategic thought.[3]

Military strategy in outer space, as on earth, is governed by the relationship of strategic goals to available means. Though the technical basis for space operations may vary from those employed in the air or at sea, the formulation of policies in which military forces are used to achieve national goals in space is subject to limitations similar to those imposed by other environments. In this regard, the current American fascination with outer space revisits some strategists' fixation with the doctrine of strategic bombing during the interwar period.[4] The aim of this essay is to examine strategies designed to control the space near earth and to consider how they are similar to military strategies from the past and how they may differ in the unique environment of outer space.

"A distinct threshold is crossed when atmospheric forces and powered flight yield to hard vacuum and a state of weightlessness." Furthermore, beyond this line "the absence of gravity and a molecular environment provides a distinctly different" operational medium than earth's atmosphere,[5] enabling satellites and their support systems that operate in space to detect military build-ups and to monitor dispositions of military forces around the globe.[6] Controlling the flow of information from outer space is critical to maintaining efficient and modern command, control, and communications systems. However, it is these systems and resources that are the prime target of an adversary seeking to disrupt, paralyse, or mislead an opponent.

In discerning the fundamental importance of these systems and their potential vulnerability, the United States has sought to protect its military advantage through the development of new strategic and operational policies designed to secure the "high ground." In the case of space systems, these policies have been consolidated into the concept of space control, which seeks to develop and to protect space applications that are of direct military value. This involves the operational and strategic policies oriented towards protecting friendly space systems and to negating the effectiveness of an enemy's space systems. However, the ultimate arbiter of success in a space control campaign is determined more by the relative degree to which combatants prosecute these two interrelated goals.

In October 1961, U.S. President John F. Kennedy declared: "Control of space will be decided in the next decade, and the nation which controls space can control the earth."[7] Recently, the U.S. Air Force (USAF) chief of staff, General Ronald Fogleman, echoed Kennedy's sentiments in an address to the cadets of the U.S. Air Force Academy. In discussing space operations as a fourth dimension[8] of war, Fogleman broached not only the future of air and space power in the next century, but also what he and others believe to be the future of the USAF and American national security. His comments reflect those of other senior USAF leaders who have stressed that space operations are an "important redirection" for the USAF,[9] because the international situation has changed dramatically since 1961.

Kennedy's remarks were made to a United States still alarmed by the unexpected orbit of one man-made satellite, the Russian *Sputnik* in 1957, whereas Fogleman spoke in a world orbited by over three thousand satellites, two-thirds of which are designated for reconnaissance or military surveillance.[10] In addition, Fogleman emphasized that assets in space were "force multipliers because they allow our nation to remain engaged, despite having fewer ships, fewer brigades, and fewer fighter wings forward deployed."[11]

He also indicated that the U.S. satellites could directly influence events on earth. In this respect, the advent of satellite technology parallels the introduction of reconnaissance aircraft at the beginning of the century, except that

American satellites are constantly on station, forcing "adversaries to restructure, to hide."[12] This capability is sometimes referred to as "virtual presence."[13] The introduction of reconnaissance satellites, like the advent of aerial reconnaissance during the First World War, reduced an opponent's freedom of action. And, as with aircraft in the First World War, many nations possess space systems that are capable of observing tactical operations.[14]

The information provided by space-based platforms, ranging from the data derived from satellites for weather forecasting and communications to sophisticated surveillance, military reconnaissance, and missile warning data, has become essential to most military operations. The most dramatic example of this trend can be seen in global positioning systems (GPS) satellite technology. These satellite-based navigation aids have revolutionized navigation and have been incorporated in various forms into military hardware, from supply trucks to precision-guided munitions.[15] GPSs are now omnipresent in items throughout the American arsenal, and the demand for GPS services has spread to the civilian sector and to foreign markets. Yet the roots of all this extend back over thirty years.

American activity in outer space began as a response to Soviet accomplishments, and from its inception in 1957 the American space program sought to catch up with and to compete with the Soviet Union's space program. Though the National Aeronautics and Space Act of 1958 prescribed that "it is the policy of the United States that activities in space should be devoted to peaceful purposes for the benefit of all mankind,"[16] the first operational American satellite systems were committed to military purposes. The first of these, an ancestor of the current Defence Support Program, was the Missile Defence Alarm System (known as MIDAS), which was operational by the early 1960s. Later that decade, the USAF was providing reliable meterological data to support military operations through the Defence Meteorological Satellite Program.[17] American space activity is regulated in accordance with the dictates of U.S. international and national policies and throughout its evolution has also been subject to a growing body of bilateral and multilateral agreements. In 1963, the United States entered into the first of nine agreements designed to regulate various aspects of space activity,[18] through its ratification of the Limited Test Ban Treaty, which, among its other provisions, banned nuclear explosions in outer space. This was followed in 1967 by the Outer Space Treaty, of which article IV strengthened the prohibitions of the earlier treaty with a restriction against placing nuclear weapons, or other weapons of mass destruction, into orbit around earth, deploying them on celestial bodies, or stationing them in any manner in open space.

Later, the United States subscribed to the International Telecommunications Convention, which seeks to manage the electromagnetic spectrum to minimize radio-frequency interference among communications satellites.

Though military communications facilities are specifically exempted, the convention still has major implications for military–civilian joint ventures and for military agencies that lease time on commercial satellites.

In 1971 the United States and the Soviet Union signed the Hot-Line Modernization Agreement, which established direct, two-way satellite communications. They later signed the Accident Measures Agreement of 1971 and the Prevention of Nuclear War Agreement in 1973. The latter pledged the signatories to respect each others' surveillance and missile warning systems, prohibiting direct interference with both terrestrial and space-based components of systems employed in those roles.[19]

The Anti-Ballistic Missile Treaty of 1972 sought to enhance the Outer Space Treaty's prohibition on basing weapons in space. Whereas the latter sought only to exclude deployment of nuclear weapons or other weapons of mass destruction, the former now pledged both nations to refrain from deploying space-based weapons as part of any anti-ballistic missile defence system.[20] In addition, the first interim agreement on the Limitation of Strategic Offensive Arms (SALT I), also concluded in 1972, reinforced earlier efforts to protect missile warning systems, including their space-based components. Later a series of other international arrangements was concluded through the United Nations (UN).

In 1975, the UN sponsored the Convention on Registration of Objects Launched into Outer Space (to which the United States subscribed), which bound signatories to provide the secretary-general with information on all space launches, including "the general function of the space object." However, to date no space object has been formally registered for military purposes.[21] Finally, the Treaty on the Limitation of Strategic Offensive Arms (SALT II), 1979, further enhanced the provisions of the Outer Space Treaty by banning development and deployment of systems "for placing into orbit nuclear weapons or any other kind of weapons of mass destruction, including fractional orbit missiles."[22]

Though during the past four decades this collection of international treaties and policies has served American interests in using outer space, the situation in the 1990s has become increasingly complex, and the current regime of voluntary cooperation and compliance may not be sufficient to protect national interests and to address American national security concerns. This growing complexity is the result of the interaction of a number of factors. First, the collapse of the Soviet Union and the proliferation of space technology mean that outer space is no longer principally the domain of only a few advanced nations. Thus the existing system of regulations, developed in a bipolar world, is becoming more difficult to maintain as more nations obtain access to space.

Second, advances in ballistic missile technology and the proliferation of weapons of mass destruction have left the United States and its interests, including the use of space, less secure. Moreover, there is a growing reliance on space technology and space systems by the United States to counter these perceived threats. The terms of the Ballistic Missile Defence Act of 1992 reflect this and provide a legal framework for the development and eventual deployment of systems to protect the United States and its vital interests from such threats as ballistic missile attack or "rogue launch" by third parties.[23]

Third, space has begun to develop as a commercial frontier, as space-based communications and navigation technologies are increasingly harnessed in the civil sector.[24] The growing economic potential of space technology and space applications is reflected in both the proliferation of dual-use space platforms for civil–military purposes and the growing number of joint military–commercial ventures.[25] As indicated above in Fogleman's remarks, American reliance on space will only increase with the continued drawdown of conventional forces. Operations such as Desert Shield/Storm and Vigilant Warrior revealed both effective use of space technology and its incorporation into combat units,[26] as well as growing reliance on space technology to maintain U.S. military superiority in the face of continued force reductions and redeployments.[27] Logically, this situation will lead not only to the continued use of space for force support and enhancement activities, but also eventually to the employment of weapons systems, based both in space and on earth. Extending this reasoning, it seems apparent that as space capabilities become available to more nations, those governments will probably also seek to employ their space assets for military purposes.[28] Therefore, it is possible that "space surveillance and control will become as important as airspace or sea-lane surveillance and control."[29]

The American government has subscribed to the existing international regime regarding the employment of military forces in space, based on an interpretation of article III of the Outer Space Treaty, which states that "international law, including the Charter of the United Nations, applies to the use of Outer Space." Though the UN Charter specifically prohibits the employment of force or the threatened use of force between nations as a means of solving disputes, article 51 recognizes the right of self-defence. The situation involving outer space is therefore viewed as analogous in certain respects to the high seas and international airspace, in that, under international law, it is permissible to conduct defensive military activities such as surveillance and patrolling.[30]

Codification of this interpretation was clearly demonstrated in (U.S.) National Security Directive 30, which in part stated that "the United States will conduct those activities in space that are necessary to national defence. Such activities contribute to security objectives by (1) deterring, or if necessary, defending against enemy attack; (2) assuring that enemy forces cannot prevent our use of space; (3) negating if necessary, hostile space systems;

and (4) enhancing operations of United States and allied nations."[31] Referred to as "Freedom of Space,"[32] in direct allusion to the doctrine of freedom of the seas enunciated by Hugo Grotius in the seventeenth century,[33] this government directive seeks to establish a legislative framework for the development of a strategy to support the continued use of space for the pursuit of American national interests and security objectives, in line with the provisions of the UN Charter and the Outer Space Treaty.

As Grotius put forth a doctrine to preserve the world's oceans as a common frontier for all nations, "freedom of space" seeks to protect the concepts embedded at the heart of the Outer Space Treaty. These concepts include the preservation of outer space as the common heritage of all humankind, by extending the legal doctrine of *Res Commuis*[34] into space and thereby creating a "global commons" in outer space. Freedom of the seas has been a basic tenet of U.S. security policy for nearly two centuries. Furthermore, in defence of its own interests and in support of guaranteed, unimpeded access to the world's oceans, the United States has fought wars and engaged in numerous smaller military actions. Central to the American concept of freedom of the seas is a belief that seafaring nations must possess not only the resolve, but also the capability to enforce, if necessary, their own access to the world's oceans and to aid others to the same end.[35]

With regard to the peaceful use of outer space, military action to guarantee access is inconsistent with the basic legal principles of the Outer Space Treaty and related agreements and instruments, including the UN Charter. However, the concept of a "global commons" is threatened by the growing importance and duality of military and non-military space technology and the increasing significance of outer space to U.S. economic and military power. Technological advances and the growing number of nations and nongovernmental organizations may begin to threaten or dilute American dominance in outer space, which is based on technological superiority and the fact that U.S. satellites are already on station. These on-site resources solidify American claims to certain orbital positions – a figurative occupation of the "high ground." In assessing the threat to American dominance, certain elements within the United States, not least the USAF, have concluded that for the United States to remain a superpower into the twenty-first century, the nation must recognize that "the amount of material we can place in space will be far more important than any nuclear or conventional force measure."[36]

The logical conclusion of this reasoning can be seen in the pronouncements of senior USAF officials, who stress advanced technologies and improved orbital lift capability, designed to reduce the cost of placing objects in orbit. Regardless of American motivation, neither of these goals is inconsistent with the spirit of the Outer Space Treaty. However, the shift to a multi-polar world and the proliferation of space technologies, as well as the emergence of competing interests in space, mean that American interests can no longer be adequately guaranteed solely by a regulatory framework of bilateral or multilateral agreements. The majority of these agreements had at their heart the need to avoid war on earth and to prevent the deployment of weapons of mass destruction into outer space. Though it would appear that these efforts had proved successful during the Cold War era, when space activity was simply an adjunct of superpower confrontation on earth, they do not seem well suited to the expanding dimensions of space activity and the evolving place of outer space in assuring American national security.

Thus the United States, in order to protect its national interests, must formulate a new framework, including new international agreements. However, technological advances and proliferation, coupled with an increase of space-capable nations demanding input, will make attempts to conclude future international agreements more lengthy and drawn out and, perhaps in the long run, less satisfactory for American interests. Therefore the United States will also need to stimulate the continued evolution of space polices, such as "freedom of space" and, with it, policies for the employment of armed force to protect its own interests, possibly in conjunction with other space-faring nations, but unilaterally, if need be. The conclusion of this policy will be the formal establishment of a space control doctrine and military space forces to implement it.

The terms of National Security Directive 30 charge the United States to develop an operational doctrine to establish "freedom of space" and the military capability of deterring or, if necessary, defending itself against enemy attack. Moreover, it seeks to ensure that enemy forces cannot prevent American access to the benefits of outer space. Finally, it recognizes that the ability to defend oneself against hostile space systems is integral to the accomplishment of any policy[37] of moving beyond space-supported defence to space-oriented defence, as was envisioned in the Strategic Defence Initiative of the late 1980s and in the Ballistic Missile Defence Act of 1992.

However, at present, it is the less spectacular uses of space technology that are changing the nature of warfare on earth.[38] Consequently, to protect its current military advantage, the United States believes that it must control outer space and, if necessary, deny its use to others. This can in part be accomplished under the current regime of the "peaceful exploration of Space."[39] However, to secure its future and implement an effective space control doctrine, the United States must take action to control a number of strategic choke points in space.[40]

The high ground of outer space, far from being empty, has a unique topography. These topographical features are composed of low earth orbits, polar orbits, equatorial and geosynchronous orbits, and various Lagrange points[41] in space.[42] As well, certain geographical locations provide particular advantages for the establishment of tracking and control centres. Furthermore, given the limitations of astrodynamics, specific geographical locations on earth offer optimum orbital insertion pathways between the surface and orbit. Control measures that provide for freedom of action are central to effective space control. Dominance of this high ground can, in part, be achieved by occupation of the choke points with space systems, by weapons systems designed to provide route protection along orbital insertion pathways, and by production of a new generation of hardened satellites designed to be more survivable.

In seeking to manage control of space to support national military objectives, a nation may use any one, or a combination, of the following methods and tactics: electronic warfare, weapons designed or targeted to damage or destroy ground installations, and weapons designed or targeted to damage or destroy space-based systems. These systems include the entire catalogue of conventional and nuclear weapons, as well as the exploitation of some emerging technologies. The selection of tactics and weapons will depend not only on the technological capabilities of the nations involved, but also their policy objectives. In the case of the United States, the main aim of space control is to protect the use of space by friendly forces and, if possible, deny that use to an enemy. Thus any actions taken to negate an adversary's use of space must not interfere with the exploitation of space by friendly forces.

Driven by the need to protect its own or allied space assets, a space-faring nation would be unlikely to engage in large-scale operations to shoot down hostile satellites, given the existing state of anti-satellite weapons. Destruction of objects at orbital velocities with conventional kinetic weapons would create a large amount of space debris. This orbiting debris, unlike shrapnel on earth, which falls to the ground in seconds, would remain in orbit until it either struck another object or fell into the atmosphere. The relative stability of orbital debris fields was noted by the Canadian Defence Telecommunications Research Establishment in the 1960s and served as the inspiration for its project "Westford," which sought to seed earth orbit with copper needles 1.75 cm long to serve as a natural orbiting reflector for earth-based radio transmitters. However, radio astronomers and satellite users swiftly registered their opposition to the possible employment of such a system, maintaining that at a minimum it would be a nuisance and, at the extreme, a deadly threat.[43] The effects of even the limited employment of anti-satellite weapons was inadvertently demonstrated by the Soviet Union during trials of its conventional anti-satellite weapons program in the 1970s. Twenty years later, the debris from these trials still accounts for 9 per cent of space objects currently tracked by the United States. More American satellites could be destroyed in the collateral damage resulting from even a limited anti-satellite campaign than from a direct attack.[44]

Though it would seem that anti-satellite weapons may prove highly effective, there are other limiting factors. Given the current state of technology, any of the following existing weapons systems might be employed in an anti-satellite role: anti-ballistic missile systems, co-orbital anti-satellite systems, such as Kinetic Kill Vehicles,[45] and intercontinental and submarine-launched ballistic missiles.[46] Though each weapon system is capable of achieving hard kills, all are limited in their ranges.

The current Russian anti-ballistic missile system, based on a *Gorgon* exo-atmospheric missile, is fused with a nuclear warhead; however, since it is apparently able to destroy satellites at an altitude of only two hundred kilometres, this would place just a few u.s. reconnaissance satellites at risk. Moreover, this system's utility is limited by the possible collateral effects of detonating a nuclear warhead directly over one's own territory and by the fact that, like coastal artillery, earth-based weapons systems must wait for a target to enter their arc of fire before they can engage them. [47]

The Russian co-orbital anti-satellite interceptors are able to reach satellites in polar orbits up to altitudes of two thousand kilometres. Though they could possibly reach some American weather, reconnaissance, navigation, and civilian remote sensing platforms, these represent only 17 per cent of u.s. satellites. Furthermore, it is estimated that at present Russia possesses only twelve such interceptors.

Finally, the flight paths of modern intercontinental and submarine-launched ballistic missiles reach an apogee of fourteen hundred kilometres. It is therefore possible that such missiles could be fused to detonate in proximity to an orbiting satellite. Though technically feasible, their application for this task poses certain problems. First, these missiles would prove rather unresponsive in such a role because their access to the target is based on their ground location. Further, the more complex nature of targeting an in-flight intercept based only on the observed data of the target satellite's orbital parameters would limit the missiles' effectiveness. Second, it would prove difficult to minimize collateral damage and down-range effects from such a detonation. As a consequence, these missiles may prove equally dangerous to an attacker's own space assets as to an adversary's.[48] The majority of current satellite systems orbit earth at altitudes ranging from eight thousand kilometres to geosynchronous orbits of thirty-six thousand kilometres, all currently well outside the range of conventional anti-satellite weapons.

The explosion of a nuclear device, however, would present a serious threat to all satellites and their ground infrastructure within range of the detonation. The effects of the detonation would include the saturation of the area with high levels of radiation, an electromagnetic pulse, thermal radiation, ground shock, and blast overpressure. The outcome for ground- and space-based systems would vary with the altitude of the nuclear blast. Nuclear weapons detonated near earth's surface would affect primarily ground installations and satellites within the line-of-sight of the explosion.

Generation of an electromagnetic pulse – the result of the interaction between gamma radiation and gaseous molecules present in the atmosphere and earth's natural magnetic field – represents the greatest potential danger to the various components of space systems. An electromagnetic pulse is analogous to an electromagnetic shock wave[49] and is capable of inducing damaging voltage surges in all forms of electronic components. It would result in the burnout of all unprotected electronic systems, civil or military, partly because of a skin charge and internal arcing. As spacecraft are constructed largely of non-conductive dielectric materials, their surfaces will collect an electrostatic charge until it is eventually released by arcing – analogous to the spark produced by a spark plug. These static discharges can damage computer logic and control systems, electrical control systems, and potentially entire satellites.[50] Furthermore, an electromagnetic pulse travels almost instantaneously and saturates an extremely large area. It is estimated that a nuclear airburst at an altitude of 300 kilometres would produce an electromagnetic pulse effect over an area the size of Australia.[51] Thus no other weapon poses such a widespread and pervasive danger, striking large areas virtually instantaneously. Though the effects of nuclear detonations are potentially devastating to earth- and space-based systems, their immediate use in a space or terrestrial confrontation is currently a limited threat. However, emerging technologies may be able to generate substantial electromagnetic pulses using conventional fused warheads.[52]

At the other extreme from the massive, uncontrolled levels of emission resulting from nuclear detonations lies the measured use of the electromagnetic spectrum. Known variously as electronic combat or electronic warfare, it is broadly defined as military action undertaken to determine, exploit, reduce, or prevent hostile use and/or to protect and retain friendly use of the electromagnetic spectrum.[53] Its principle offensive application is the jamming of an adversary's systems. Space systems can be jammed by directing electromagnetic energy against the satellite or ground-based systems and can be orchestrated to disrupt the function of satellite control systems. Conventional satellite systems are susceptible to electromagnetic disruption, and a signal of only one-tenth the strength of the legitimate signal can render a data link unusable. However, before any type of electronic warfare against space systems is undertaken, an adversary "must carefully analyse the cost benefit associated with such an operation."[54] Ultimately, jamming is a power play won by the side willing to invest the greater signal strength, and thereby be able to capture and to control the electromagnetic spectrum. Any nation capable of fielding a sophisticated satellite system is therefore probably well equipped to fight a successful campaign for control of the electromagnetic spectrum.

In addition, conventional weapons and electronic warfare weapons systems based on emerging technologies may in the future be capable of employment as anti-satellite weapons. The United States and Russia have both conducted research into and developed high-powered, ground-based lasers that can damage or destroy satellites even at the highest geosynchronous orbits. The United States operates a deuterium fluoride laser at the White Sands Proving Ground, and the Russians have a similar facility at the Tyuratam Test Centre.[55] In theory both systems are capable of disabling or destroying satellites, but, as with other ground-based systems, they are capable of engaging targets only within a limited arc of fire. In addition to high-powered laser weapons, Russia has conducted experiments to develop high-power, radio-frequency weapons.[56] Though growth in these technologies may offer a profitable area of exploitation in the future, they are currently only experimental.

Any campaign waged for space control with anti-satellite weapons would ultimately be attritional, and, given the current state of satellite and anti-satellite technology, such a strategy would render near-earth space unusable to potential adversaries and, more important, to oneself. Pursuit of such methods would rapidly negate a nation's strategic goals. Following such a policy would prove counterproductive to maintaining space control and would be akin to nuclear mutually assured destruction in relation to the exploitation of outer space. Anti-satellite technology may eventually transform the capacity to enforce space control, but its chief utility is as leverage in diplomatic exchanges designed to enhance and expand legislated space control. Furthermore, though the ability to convert an existing weapons system to an anti-satellite role allows a sizeable portion of the world's nations potentially to threaten space systems, the political and physical fallout from these weapons means that they most probably would be employed only in desperation, and primarily by powers that do not possess the technological base for effective anti-satellite operations.

Since the main aim of a space control doctrine is to maintain the flow of space-derived information and services to friendly forces, the perfection and development of the systems that produce that information should receive the greatest share of effort. Given the probably unsatisfactory outcome of an attritional anti-satellite campaign, the United States should concentrate on continuing to develop satellite technologies, and the associated disciplines of orbital lift and communications. The road to success in seeking space control lies, for the present, in the realm of defensive measures. Thus the technical developments required for fielding space control forces must be directed towards enhancing the ability of space systems to perform their basic missions. Satellite hardening, proliferation of platforms allowing for larger numbers of satellites in a number of orbital planes, using higher orbits, integrating stealth technology into future platforms, and increasing the manoeuvrability of satellites to allow them to evade threats will be the preferred tactics.

Therefore, under current conditions, military space programs should remain oriented primarily towards these technologies instead of towards development of space weapons systems. Advances in electronic warfare dedicated to electronic countermeasures and electronic support measures hold promise as systems that support the primary mission of friendly satellites and can also be employed offensively against hostile space systems. Furthermore, it is exactly these technologies and systems that the civil sector will produce, and that can be effectively harnessed by the military, that will be of value not only to military consumers but also to domestic and foreign markets.

U.S. national policies that encourage this "beans over bullets" route may help not only to ensure continuing American technical superiority, but also to enhance U.S. military competitiveness, along with the economic, scientific, and technical facets of national security. Coincidentally, this type of strategy is fairly consistent with the current international regime governing the development of outer space. Thus pursuing it would fit well into existing American diplomatic and political strategies. As the Italian air power theorist Giulio Douhet remarked when he contemplated conflict in the "third dimension": "[V]ictory smiles upon those who anticipate the changes in the character of war, not those who wait to adapt themselves after changes occur." [57]

The world has moved beyond the spectre of weapons of mass destruction in outer space. However, the changing strategic role of outer space, and the related competition for space resources, may increase the probability of conflict. Ironically, conflict will probably start not as a result of some attempt to dominate earth with an orbital weapons system but instead from a desire to preserve the "freedom of space" for peaceful and profitable uses against unwarranted intrusion or exploitation.

Though a distinct line is crossed when atmospheric forces yield to a hard vacuum and a state of weightlessness, military strategy in outer space is not beyond the line that governs the relationship of strategic goals to available means. The USAF has gone to great lengths to publicize the unique nature of space operations, as was the case in the interwar period, with the doctrine of strategic bombing. However, even though the technical basis of space operations may differ from those of the air or the sea, the formulation of policies in which military forces are used to achieve national goals are subject to the same limitations imposed on other environments.

NOTES

1 *Spacecast 2020*, Vol. I, 1.

2 Clausewitz, *On War*, trans. and ed. Howard and Paret (1976), 593.

3 Layton, "Waging Tomorrow's Wars," 1.

4 See MacIsaac, "Voices from the Central Blue," 629–35, for a discussion of this issue.

5 Myers and Tockston, "Real Tenets of Military Space Doctrine," 59.

6 Layton, "Waging Tomorrow's Wars," 19.

7 Quoted in Worden and Jackson, "Space, Power and Strategy," 43.

8 Fogleman, "Air and Space Power in the 21st Century."

9 Carns, "Closing Remarks."

10 Hammond, "The Militarization of Space," 235.

11 Fogleman, "Air and Space Power."

12 Ibid.

13 Linhard, "The Power of Information," 24.

14 *Air Force Doctrine Directive 4*, 17.

15 Gourley, "GPS," 19–20.

16 United States Department of the Air Force, *Legal Principles*.

17 Moorman, "Space," 15.

18 Gray, *American Military Space Policy*, 78.

19 Ibid.

20 Anti-Ballistic Missile Treaty, 1972, article V, para. 1, cited in Goldman, "Transition of Confusion," 165.

21 Bundy et al., "The President's Choice," 266.

22 Ibid.

23 March 1992 Briefing Package for Ambassador Henry F. Cooper, Director of the Strategic Defence Initiative Organization, *Strategic Defence Initiative: Global Protection against Limited Strikes (GPALS)*. U.S. Government Printing Office.

24 Gourley, "GPS," 19–20.

25 Windall, "Cooperation."

26 Moorman, "Space," 20.

27 Ibid., 18.

28 Ibid., 22.

29 *Spacecast 2020*, Vol. I, 28.

30 United States Department of the Air Force, *Legal Principles*.

31 Coumatos and Poulos, "U.S. Must Guarantee," 60.

32 Ibid.

33 Hugo Grotius, a Dutch jurist, introduced his freedom of the seas doctrine in 1608. He developed it to provide justification and protection to Dutch mercantile interests, in the face of a fifteenth-century papal bull that provided legal and ecclesiastical sanction for the division of the world's resources and oceans between the Catholic kingdoms of Portugal and Spain. Coumatos and Poulos, "U.S. Must Guarantee," 60–1.

34 "Things Common to All." It refers to these things used and enjoyed by everyone – even in single parts – but can never be exclusively acquired as a whole, such as light and air.

35 Coumatos and Poulos, "U.S. Must Guarantee," 60.

36 Windall, "Cooperation."

37 Coumatos and Poulos, "U.S. Must Guarantee," 60.

38 Jablonsky, *The Owl of Minerva*, 62.

39 Worden and Jackson, "Space, Power and Strategy," 50.

40 Ibid.

41 These are a number of points in space where the interplay of gravitational forces in the earth-moon system allows for objects placed there to remain stable relative to the system.

42 Worden and Jackson, "Space, Power and Strategy," 46.

43 Jelly, *Canada*, 30.

44 Power, "Space Control," 30.

45 Self-guided missiles of limited range that close with their target and destroy it through the direct transfer of kinetic energy through collision.

46 Forestier, "Into the Fourth Dimension," 9–9.

47 Neil Johnston, in ibid., 7–8.

48 Ibid., 9–9.

49 Kopp, "A Doctrine," 2.

50 Forestier, "Into the Fourth Dimension," 9–19.

51 Ibid., 9–14.

52 Kopp, "A Doctrine," 3.

53 Forestier, "Into the Fourth Dimension," 9–2.

54 Ibid., 3–5.

55 Ibid., 9–10.

56 Ibid.

57 Douhet, *The Command of the Air*, 118.

Conventional Arms Control and Intelligence: A Symbiotic Relationship

CAPT EDWARD C. DENBEIGH

The past ten years have seen a fundamental shift in a paradigm that we had come to know in a familiar, albeit at times uneasy, way. With the Cold War ended, the Warsaw Pact disbanded, and the Soviet Union disintegrated, a realignment of power is currently under way, and its outcome is unclear. Significant advances have been made in a number of areas, including de-mocratization and conflict resolution.[1] At the same time, there has been a rise in local conflict, as ethnic groups (those emancipated as well as those that are not) assert themselves in a world where one superpower and its satellites have disappeared.

The power vacuum left by the disintegration of the USSR and the late 1980's trend of growing economic exhaustion of most Western states are two major factors that fuelled the sudden rise in nationalism worldwide. With the East–West confrontation eliminated, all things seemed possible. But in the search for the promised land, competing interests between the newly emerging states have given rise to widespread regional conflicts on a scale not seen since the close of the Second World War. As well, old-line, tradi-tional collective security organizations have been attempting to cope with the challenges.[2] In many ways, the Cold War was comforting, at least in the sense that opposing camps were relatively clearly defined.

The progress towards a safer world, most evident in the dramatically reduced threat of global war, is balanced by this persistence of conflict within and between states.[3] Despite great strides in arms control, conventional arms proliferate. This is a paradox that continues to plague humanity.

The great effort invested during the twentieth century towards realistic arms control agreements is, in keeping with the theme of this book, a good example of how people learn from history. The first, tentative efforts embodied in the Hague Conferences gave way to ever more serious attempts, no doubt spurred on by the hopeless nightmare and carnage of the First World War and the spectre of global annihilation following the advent of the nuclear age. But, as we have learned from historical experience, ongoing arms control efforts will enjoy success only if supported by effective intelligence. Intelligence is a valuable commodity throughout the entire process, from simple contemplation of negotiation to ongoing verification once an agreement is reached.

Thomas J. Hirschfeld has noted that intelligence and arms control are totally different functions; however, one will assist the other. Arms control seeks reductions and limitations in force among adversaries. Successful completion of this seemingly unnatural act requires enormous amounts of information to be evaluated and a steady stream of carefully considered judgments about the opponent.[4] Ongoing verification operations can, in turn, aid the intelligence community in confirming or denying an assessment derived through other means. When conducted in harmony, the two functions are complementary and can offer dividends in confidence-building between two or more potential antagonists.

The aim of this essay, therefore, is to examine the state of arms-control verification efforts and the symbiotic relationship that exists between those endeavours and the intelligence community. In an effort to narrow the scope, and because of the range and complexity of the many treaties, agreements, and ongoing negotiations, I look only at conventional arms control.

A HISTORICAL PERSPECTIVE

The goal of eliminating war, or at least mitigating its effects, goes far back in history. The second Ecumenical Lateran Council outlawed the use of the crossbow among Christians in 1139. Robert L. O'Connell has observed that the edict, as perhaps humanity's first overt attempt at arms control, is deserving of more attention than it usually receives. In particular, the effort to enforce weapons parity and what amounted to the technological status quo was prophetic of arms control in the future. O'Connell notes that there was also an element of situational ethics present that would tend to be found in future efforts at arms control, since the church in no way discouraged the use of the crossbow against Islamic opponents.[5]

In modern times, disarmament came into focus with the multinational Hague Conferences of 1899 and 1907. These and subsequent efforts – the Washington Conference (1921–22) and the Geneva Conference (1932) – met with only modest success. The announced purpose of the Hague Conferences was to promote disarmament. Though no agreement was reached on arms limitation per se, the conferences codified the rules of war as they affected noncombatants and neutral shipping.[6] Unfortunately, with absolutely no establishment of some means for monitoring or enforcing compliance, this "edifice of legalism" was quickly reduced to a shambles by the desperation of the combat in the First World War.[7] The single important result was creation of the Permanent Court of Arbitration, or Hague Tribunal. It was largely superseded in 1921 by the Permanent Court of International Justice, which was in turn replaced in 1945 by the International Court of Justice.[8]

The Washington Conference (1921–22) was the first of several attempts at naval disarmament made after the First World War. The gathering has usually been viewed as something of an anomaly, an idealistic exercise that set up several useful guidelines for naval strength but at the same time set the pattern for a style of public diplomacy that would come to symbolize the "feckless pacifism" of the interwar era.[9] The key political settlement of the conference was the Four Power Treaty, signed on 13 December 1921, in which the United States, Britain, Japan, and France pledged to consult one another if any of their island possessions in the Pacific were threatened. The same powers, plus Italy, signed the Five Power Naval Armaments Treaty in February 1922, lauded as the most successful disarmament pact in history. It provided for a ten-year hiatus in building warships of more than 10,000 tons and established a ratio among the signatories regarding the number of these ships they could have. The London Naval Conference of 1930 extended the Washington agreement to cruisers and destroyers, but the Japanese abrogated the treaties in 1934.[10]

The World Disarmament Conference of 1932–37 was the final interwar effort to achieve armaments limitation. Disarmament had been a major objective of the League of Nations since its establishment after the First World War, but the reluctance of certain powers, most notably France, to disarm without adequate security guarantees had blocked agreement. From 1926 onward, the League sponsored meetings of a preparatory commission to lay the groundwork for a disarmament conference. The United States and the USSR, though not then League members, took part in these talks. The World Disarmament Conference opened in Geneva in February 1932 with sixty nations represented. Since delegates could not agree on either the budgetary limitations proposed for air, land, and naval forces or the categories of weapons to be restricted, the conference made no appreciable headway. Various plans were suggested, including one by u.s. President Herbert Hoover, which proposed a one-third reduction in the defence components of armed forces, but to no avail. In turn, France continued to be insistent on security and Germany on its right to equality with the other powers. After adjourning in March 1933, the representatives met again in October; Germany withdrew, however, from both the conference and the League. This move destroyed any chances for success, and though the conference continued to meet sporadically until April 1937, it reached no agreement.[11] The final death knell for the effort rang with Germany's invasion of Poland, in September 1939.

In retrospect, arms control initiatives in the interwar period can be viewed as being something more than a sedative for war-weary publics. The efforts dealt with weapon specification and control with unprecedented seriousness and achieved broad support among the populations of all state participants. However, as noted by O'Connell, it is still possible for countries to move in two opposite directions at once, and in the case of Germany, Italy, and Japan, history was not on the side of the angels.[12]

More recently, significant progress has been made since 1975 in the elimination, reduction, and control of various categories of conventional weapons. Appropriately enough, the two principal agreements were reached (for the most part) between the two opposing sides of the post-1945 East and West blocs.

Several years of negotiations on conventional arms control and disarmament in Vienna concluded in November 1990 with formal agreement on the Treaty on Conventional Armed Forces in Europe (CFE Treaty) and the Vienna Document. Developed under the umbrella of the Conference on Security and Co-operation in Europe (CSCE), the twenty-two states of the NATO alliance and the members of the crumbling Warsaw Pact Treaty Organization signed the treaty in Paris on 19 November 1990. Signatories must adhere to ceilings placed on treaty-limited equipment, specifically tanks, armoured combat vehicles, artillery, combat aircraft, and attack helicopters. Additionally, they are required to exchange data annually on treaty-limited equipment, organization, force structure, and military establishments. Signatories have the right to participate in on-site intrusive inspections as part of the verification process and are obliged to receive inspections based on formulae derived from total numbers of objects of verification and inspection-sharing quotas.[13]

For example, if a signatory state declares that it possesses one hundred objects of verification (units subject to inspection), then it is liable to a passive quota total of ten to twenty on-site inspections under section II of the treaty's Protocol on Inspections. The total will vary depending on what point has been reached in implementation of the treaty. As of 15 March 1996, the proportion of total objects of verification will be 15 per cent for perpetuity. As well, the two signatory blocs maintain a formula to divide their share of inspections among their members based on the number of inspections to which each state is liable. This quota system, however, is purely voluntary. For example, since Canada now declares only one object of verification, theoretically it would not be eligible to conduct any inspections. By gentleman's agreement, states within NATO with many inspections under the quota allot a certain number to smaller states such as Canada and Luxembourg. As a treaty signatory, Canada has the right to conduct an inspection wherever and whenever it feels the need, as long as the party being inspected has not exhausted its quota. However, to prevent the system from becoming clogged with conflicting inspections, the NATO bloc instituted the inspection-sharing quota; the former East bloc maintains a similar system.

The treaty received wide coverage in the press and was acknowledged by both academic and non-governmental groups working for arms control, such as the Stockholm International Peace Research Institute, as the first conventional arms control treaty to limit, and in some cases require the destruction or conversion of, military equipment. But, within days of the initial exchange of data, it was readily evident that the USSR was interpreting the treaty so as to preserve military equipment and organizations – namely, naval and strategic rocket force units possessing treaty-limited equipment – from the constraints intended by the agreement. Fortunately, by June 1991, bilateral negotiations between the United States and the USSR broke the deadlock, ensuring that all Soviet equipment covered by the treaty was indeed accounted for within treaty constraints.[14]

In separate negotiations in Vienna on Confidence and Security Building Measures (CSBMs), the members of the CSCE agreed on a new package of CSBMs at the same time as the CFE Treaty was signed. The Vienna Document 1990 (since superseded by the Vienna Document 1994), perhaps because it was part of an evolutionary process, received little of the fanfare given the treaty. Unlike the treaty, which is legally binding on the signatories, the document depends on its moral force for compliance and builds on the Stockholm Concluding Document (1986) and its predecessor, the Helsinki Final Act (1975). It supersedes and incorporates many of the features found in its predecessors.[15] Other efforts such as the Open Skies Treaty and the United Nations Arms Registry have reinforced the tendency towards openness and transparency in military matters.

THE TWO DISCIPLINES

Arms control, a term popularized in the early 1960s, refers to the voluntary, negotiated limitation or reduction of weapons and their means of delivery, between and among countries. It is distinct from disarmament, which seeks to eliminate, also by international agreement, the means by which countries wage war.

Arms control aims to reduce the likelihood of war, to limit the extent of damage should war occur, and to reduce expenditures on military forces. Despite several decades of more-or-less constant effort, most observers would agree that arms control has compiled a mixed record. It is, for example, with respect only to reduction of the likelihood of war that proponents of arms control can claim any real success.[16]

In the post-1945 era, nuclear arms control aroused almost as much opposition as support in the United States, as critics focused on two alleged defects of the process. The liberal critique asserted that arms control did little more than legitimize military competition, particularly between the United States and the Soviet Union. Conservatives, in contrast, sometimes objected to arms control on the grounds that the countries with which the United States negotiated on the limitation of military forces, especially the Soviet Union, could not be trusted to comply with the terms of agreements. [17]

Keith Krause and David Mutimer have observed that, since the advent of the nuclear age, the agenda of arms control has been divided between "weapons of mass destruction" and "conventional weapons." The former usually includes nuclear, biological, and chemical weapons as well as their related technologies. The latter has seemingly included everything else. In what can only be described as a cruel paradox, almost all international non-proliferation efforts (both multilateral and bilateral) since the end of the Second World War have been directed towards weapons of mass destruction. Yet, in the same period, almost all of the more than 40 million war-related deaths have been from conventional weapons. Krause and Mutimer assert that, when one adds to this the dramatic increase in the sophistication and destructiveness of so-called conventional weapons, it is difficult to explain the continued divergence in treatment between the two traditional camps. [18]

In contrast to arms control, an intelligence operation is the process by which governments, military groups, businesses, and other organizations systematically collect and evaluate information for the purpose of discovering the capabilities and intentions of their rivals. With such information, or intelligence, an organization can both protect itself from its adversaries and exploit their weaknesses. [19]

Strategic or national intelligence is processed information about foreign nations that is collected by governmental intelligence agencies. Strategic intelligence commonly encompasses national security, political, economic, and social trends in the target nation. Military intelligence is produced by specially trained military or civilian analysts and usually includes the strengths, weapons technology, and estimated military capabilities of actual or potential enemies. [20] It is this latter type of intelligence that provides the key to the development and maintenance of any successful arms control regime.

THE INTELLIGENCE KEYS TO THE KINGDOM

Sergey Koulik and Richard Kokoski have observed that arms-control verification may involve either highly intrusive on-site inspection procedures, deemed necessary because of the multilateral nature of the agreements, or non-intrusive, technological, means of verification (both national and multinational). These latter means are, at present, primarily the domain of the United States and Russia. None the less, the technological capabilities of several other states (such as France) are advanced, and those of others are quickly gaining ground. In addition, some of the intelligence acquired by the nations with access to sophisticated technical means may be passed to other nations through multinational or bilateral agreement, thereby providing further reassurance of compliance. Another important capability, infrequently discussed in connection with arms control verification, is the ability of even small nations to intercept inexpensively the communications traffic of other countries.[21] In addition to the traditionally covert methods available to verify a treaty or agreement, there are new opportunities for acquiring vast amounts and various types of information as a result of the opening up of much of central and eastern Europe. For example, in 1990, the Central Intelligence Agency (CIA) set up a task force to explore the ways and means of exploiting the "deluge of open-source information" now available with the fall of the Iron Curtain.[22]

When considering the methods available for treaty monitoring, it is important to bear in mind the adequacy of verification. What could and should be considered a militarily significant violation? For example, it has been argued in some military and policy circles that, in the monitoring and verification of individual states' data releases, distributed yearly in accordance with the CFE Treaty, a violation of 10 per cent is politically significant, while 20 per cent is thought to be militarily significant. The detection of the former could spark the exchange of diplomatic notes, while the latter could lead to increased military alert or even limited mobilization in a specific geographical area. Therefore signatories should have their own, independent means of verifying treaty compliance.

National technical means (NTMs) of collecting intelligence are those methods that can be brought to bear without the cooperation of the country being monitored. They run the gamut from satellites in a wide variety of earth orbits to sophisticated eavesdropping efforts. The two broadest categories of NTM are imagery intelligence (IMINT) and signals intelligence (SIGINT). IMINT refers to images captured by satellites, aircraft, and so on, while SIGINT involves the interception of all types of electromagnetic signals, including all forms of communications, radar emissions, and so on.[23] NTMs may be characterized as the foundation of a verification regime, even though most signatories (as in the case of the CFE Treaty) do not enjoy access to most of the information NTMs provide. This in no way casts doubt on the value of the necessary and wide-ranging cooperative monitoring allowed for by the treaty. Inspections conducted on the ground or from most aircraft do, however, require active cooperation. Though the political climate in Europe would not lead one to anticipate any serious problems in this regard, NTMs are basically unaffected by the potentially mercurial nature of a region's political atmosphere.[24] As noted by Koulik and Kokoski, satellites, when exploited to the fullest, can profoundly affect verification of arms control treaties.

NTMs have not always enjoyed pre-eminent popularity in all arms control cases. William C. Potter noted that the development during the 1960s of improved NTMs for monitoring potential opponents is usually credited with making progress in arms control feasible. He maintains that the Americans' confidence in their ability to monitor the Soviet Union's weapons systems, for example, was a critical factor in the u.s. decision, vis-à-vis the first Strategic Arms Limitation Treaty (SALT I), to abandon its long-standing demand for on-site inspection. NTMs also provided the primary means by which the verification requirements for SALT II were met. However, reliance on NTMs came under increasing assault by critics of SALT, who maintained that verification should be designed to meet the needs of arms control, not the other way around. They argued that cooperative measures, particularly intrusive, on-site inspection, should be the preferred means to verify treaty compliance.[25] As it turned out, this argument was acted on when the terms were agreed to regarding the CFE Treaty and Vienna Document(s). As noted above, both provide for extensive on-site verification, supplemented by NTMs.

A MUTUALLY BENEFICIAL ARRANGEMENT

The relationship between arms control and intelligence can be simultaneously obvious and obscure. Intelligence makes arms control possible, but the relations between the intelligence function and the arms control process are neither simple nor always straightforward.[26] Greater policy objectives may supersede one or the other (and sometimes both). For example, the intelligence community may detect a possible violation of treaty limits and seek to confirm its suspicions by requesting an intrusive, on-site inspection under either section VII or VIII of the CFE Treaty. This may be prevented if that community's government feels that a greater policy objective (which may be far removed from arms control and security – i.e., bilateral trade) would be impeded or harmed by exposing the anomaly.

Thomas J. Hirschfeld maintains that arms control agreements have three stages: contemplating some trade-off, negotiation, and living with the consequences. Intelligence has a different task at each stage. During contemplation, it estimates how many of each "item or potential item of account" the potential adversary has (for example, how many aircraft of specific capability). That information allows the designers of an agreement to identify what items they wish to reduce or limit. Intelligence also identifies how the opponent might use these items and how well the weapons systems might perform under various circumstances and conditions. This assessment gives the negotiator an abstract sense of their potential trading value.[27]

The negotiation phase presents additional tasks for the intelligence community. These include more detailed attention to those elements of the adversary force that would be reduced or limited, as well as those elements that could be used to circumvent agreement terms if the treaty were in force. Attention shifts to analysis of what the adversary's reaction might be to some actual, current proposal and to speculation about what counter-proposals the adversary might make. This is at once both a short- and a long-range process. The negotiating delegation asks the intelligence community for information, issue by issue, about the adversary's likely positions at impending negotiating sessions and for indications of longer-term major shifts in the adversary's stance. At this stage, the intelligence community itself needs some protection. While providing assessments to the negotiators, it tries to ensure that the level of detail or form of words used by the negotiators does not reveal sources or methods used to gather the information. [28]

Hirschfeld sees the third, or maintenance stage as perhaps the most difficult. The question of how detailed inspections need to be to maintain the agreement has never been satisfactorily resolved by the participants. That dilemma hides the more fundamental political dispute of whether arms control itself is beneficial. Hirschfeld notes how, historically, arms control proponents such as former u.s. president Jimmy Carter have argued that the risk of clandestine violations is much less damaging to security than the absence of the benefits to be derived from some particular agreement and that the risks of detection (and the ensuing embarrassment) outweigh the potential security gains from violation. [29]

Conversely, sceptics about arms control object to the very notion of a negotiated agreement with a committed adversary. Doubting that any agreement would alter ambitions, they fear such arrangements can only hurt defence programs. Since they see few incentives for compliance, they believe that such agreements require very stringent verification standards. They argue, for example, that because the Russians, they believe, will take any opportunity to gain an advantage, the West needs to insist on intrusive monitoring, an active policy of violation exposure, and the potential for implementation of sanctions on evidence of violations. [30] This logic ignores, of course, the possibility for the United States to skirt agreements.

Clearly, intelligence communities can be caught in the middle of conflicting aims and goals. Therefore, Hirschfeld maintains, they must be careful to maintain both the appearance and the practice of objectivity. They should accordingly try to narrow their task to monitoring the opponent, which then confines intelligence judgments to what the Russians, for example, are doing and how their forces are changing. Such a stance leaves judgments about, for instance, whether such changes are significant in the overall balance, what the net effects on Western security are, or whether a particular type of Russian behaviour is or is not an actual, partial, or pro forma violation of some provision to others who set policy and conduct ensuing operations. Intelligence professionals are normally neither elected officials nor operations staff and therefore do not carry the burden of accountability in the same manner that an elected official does. Yet the answers to such questions as those described above depend critically, if not entirely, on an intelligence contribution.[31]

SYMBIOSIS

James McIntosh contends that each participating state, by employing the intelligence cycle on a regular basis within the framework of agreements such as the CFE Treaty and the Vienna Document, should come to feel increasingly confident of the intentions and behaviour of its neighbours if it is constantly advised of their military activities and deployments. This confidence in turn would contribute to the natural growth of an arms control–based security regime encompassing all of Europe and, potentially, North America.[32]

The arms control process depends on detailed agreements that specify what is permitted, qualitatively and quantitatively, in developing, maintaining, and deploying certain kinds of weapons systems. William E. Burrows has argued that, since the benefits of successful cheating are considerable (being able to hide assets may carry the day in some future military adventure), agreements must stipulate that their provisions be verifiable by NTMs. It can be argued further that were it not for these devices, there would be no arms control, because it is the technology that allows each side to satisfy itself that the various provisions are, for the most part, not being contravened.[33]

Before the acquisition of NTMs, most agreements were virtually unverifiable beyond limited inspection/observation opportunities. Indeed, agreements such as those regarding non-combatants and neutrals covered in the Hague Conventions largely fell apart once the battle was joined in the First World War. However, as noted by Burrows, the concept of cheating, particularly where treaty language is vague, is "often very much in the eye of the beholder" and tends to reflect his or her political inclination. Policy makers who are convinced that Russia is some malevolent force waiting to rise again view intelligence in one way, while those who regard the Kremlin somewhat more benignly often interpret it in an entirely different light.[34]

Burrows notes the obvious contradiction in the frequent assertions by the U.S. Reagan administration that the USSR was consistently cheating on strategic arms control agreements while it simultaneously claimed that those agreements were not adequately verifiable. Without precise NTMs for monitoring purposes, could the United States be certain that treaties were being honoured?[35] Intelligence gathered solely to support certain government policies (directed intelligence) is both dishonest and dangerous; but, as discussed above, greater policy objectives may carry the day, and selective use of the available facts is a time-honoured tradition in diplomacy.

CONCLUSION

O'Connell maintained that arms control, in order to succeed, must be a cooperative effort among signatory groups. This may sound naïve and far easier to advocate in the abstract than to achieve in reality. Yet unilateral national strategy, which is the only other workable approach, has produced only dangerous and unsatisfactory results, mainly because it is inherently adversarial. The East–West arms race stood as testimony to just such an approach. Both governments and militaries have wisely taken a lesson from the failures of the past. Arms control offers a feasible remedy, but only if both sides believe that it is in their mutual interest to partake, and do so in exactly that spirit. [36]

Intelligence could live without arms control, but the reverse is not true. Without the means to monitor and detect possible violations, any treaty is an empty shell. While it would be nice to think that all signatories are fully committed to the success of any agreement, broader national policy objectives may temper adherence.

This is not to say that arms control verification does not provide valuable data to the intelligence mosaic. The intelligence process is highly synergistic and uses a wide variety of sources and means (often playing off each other) to gather raw information for processing into finished intelligence. Arms control verification is a special type of open-source intelligence gathering, wherein the collector conducts the operation with the full knowledge, and tacit agreement, of the target. Beyond the obvious import of quantitative verification and compliance, analysis is a more abstract but still important aspect of intelligence involvement and gives an analyst a more "hands-on" perspective. Intrusive, on-site inspections provide a window on such intangibles as morale, leadership, training, and, in the broadest sense, intentions and capabilities. At the same time, the arms control process is served by the assistance of, and possible direction by, intelligence in order to verify or dispel suspicions.

In the final analysis, both arms control and defence intelligence are concerned with military security. As such, they have a symbiotic and synergistic relationship. The involvement of intelligence should be viewed as a positive factor. By its nature, intelligence is benign; what policy and operations authorities choose to do with it may be less so. It is axiomatic that good intelligence can reduce the likelihood of threat misconception or, conversely, can discover potential problems that can be resolved diplomatically, not militarily. When conjoined, the two stabilize and sustain any nation's national policy objectives aimed at the elimination, reduction, and control of various categories of weapons.

NOTES

1 Canada, Department of National Defence (DND), *1994 Defence White Paper*, 3.
2 Ibid., 3.
3 Ibid.
4 Hirschfeld, *Intelligence and Arms Control*, 14.
5 O'Connell, *Of Arms and Men*, 95–6.
6 "Hague Conferences," in *Grolier Electronic Encyclopedia*, 1992 ed. (hereafter *Grolier*.)
7 O'Connell, *Of Arms and Men*, 238–9.
8 "Hague Conferences."
9 O'Connell, *Of Arms and Men*, 271.
10 "Washington Conference," in *Grolier*.
11 "Geneva Conference," in ibid.
12 O'Connell, *Of Arms and Men*, 275.
13 DeClerq, *The Stockholm Concluding Document and Exercise Observations*, 1.
14 Ibid., 1–2.
15 Ibid., 2.
16 "Arms Control," in *Grolier*.
17 Ibid.
18 Krause and Mutimer, "The Proliferation of Conventional Weapons," 39.
19 "Intelligence and Counter-intelligence," in *Encyclopedia Britannica: Macropaedia*, Vol IX, 15th ed.
20 Ibid.
21 Koulik and Kokoski, *Verification of the CFE Treaty*, 31.
22 "CIA Role in the 90's: Is Foreign Business the Enemy?" *International Herald Tribune*, 14 Nov. 1990, 3.
23 Koulik and Kokoski, *Verification*, 32–3; and Ondreka, "Imaging Technologies," 80–96.
24 Ondreka, "Imaging Technologies," 33.
25 Potter, *Verification and Arms Control*, 1.
26 Hirschfeld, *Intelligence and Arms Control*, 9.
27 Ibid., 14.
28 Ibid., 15–16.
29 Ibid., 16.
30 Ibid.
31 Ibid., 16–17.
32 MacIntosh, "International Verification Organizations," 113.
33 Burrows, *Deep Black*, viii–ix.
34 Ibid., ix.
35 Ibid.
36 O'Connell, *Of Arms and Men*, 308.

The Statistical Study of War: The Relationship between Democracy and War

LCDR GUY R. PHILLIPS

The study of war can take many forms. Often, such study is undertaken by historians seeking to determine the "truth" of what happened in a particular conflict. But such documentation of historical "facts" should also be coupled with an analysis to find the causes of and link between events. Political scientists and international relations scholars also study war, with their major purpose being to determine the causes of the various forms of state-level conflict; however, their data sets may be quite limited. A new area of study examined in this essay marries the two disciplines of history and political science. The first stage in this process is the compilation of historical data about inter- and intrastate conflict. Next, these databases of war are analysed by the political scientists to categorize and quantify the elements and factors involved in war. The final step is the statistical analysis of those data. The resulting studies provide quantifiable historical experience to guide decision-makers.

One lively area of statistical research, particularly in the United States, concerns the apparent absence of wars between democracies. Though the absence of wars had been noted previously, it was Michael Doyle's 1983 essay "Kant, Liberal Legacies, and Foreign Affairs" that first propounded the relationship as a theory.[1] By 1988 the theory had reached a level of acceptance such that Jack Levy was to claim that the state of peace between democracies was "the closest thing to a law in the study of international relations."[2] The role of democracy in reducing conflict is now regularly being espoused by u.s. officials as part of its post–Cold War strategy: "Democracy is rooted in compromise, not conquest. It rewards tolerance, not hatred. Democracies rarely wage war on one another. They make reliable partners in trade, in diplomacy, and in the stewardship of our global environment. And democracies, with the rule of law and respect for political, religious, and cultural minorities, are more responsive to their own people and to the protection of human rights."[3]

In order to study this possible relationship as a strategic concept, this essay first briefly addresses some of the theories of and bases for the study of the causes of war. It then considers the compilation of data about war and democracy. It next critically assesses the theory that democratic governments are less likely to wage war on each other. To provide a contrast to this theory, I discuss at some length the recent study by Edward Mansfield and Jack Snyder regarding the propensity for emerging democracies to go to war,[4] along with their evidence about the frequency of wars undertaken by stable regimes. I look also at some of the reasons for these tendencies to go to war. The essay concludes with an assessment of how democratic states may protect themselves, given these historical and statistical findings.

THEORIES ABOUT THE CAUSES OF WAR

There are several theories about the causes of war. Kenneth Waltz, in his classic work *Man, State and War*,[5] identifies three basic causes: human behaviour, internal politics, and international politics. While the focus of this essay is on one aspect of internal politics, an understanding of the other approaches is relevant to the relationship between democracy and war.

Several theorists have looked for a relationship between being *homo sapiens* and humans' tendency to fight among themselves. Scholars such as Raymond Aron have attempted to show that an animal's aggressive response to fear, pain, or the infringement of its space is similar to the human's reaction to its own insecurity, greed, envy, selfishness, or stupidity.[6] Some of the latter factors may be recognized in the actions of elites in states changing regimes – a possible cause of war addressed below. This approach also compares such animalistic behaviour to that of the state, using geopolitical considerations to evaluate competition between states, similar to Darwin's notions of survival of the fittest.[7] This approach also looks at war as being a function of human imperfection.

The political realist school exemplified by Hans Morgethau takes some of the "bad" human attributes and equates them to the self-defence actions of nation-states trying to survive within an anarchical world order. In this way of examining the world, the regime of sovereign states is seen as a "violent, hostile environment," and states must always be ready to kill or be killed and to intimidate others from attacking. The opposite school – the political idealists – claim that the natural state of international affairs is peace, not war.[8] This group sees the common interests of humanity and of states as the basis for a pacific relationship, so that national interest is best served by promoting the universal goals of peace and prosperity.[9] Many of the proposed solutions for dealing with this world of sovereign states come in some form of collective arrangement. The more common form is based on bilateral or multilateral alliances for collective self-defence. Recently, however, the pacific settlement of disputes through an institutional mechanism or the giving up of some sovereignty is the means used to keep the peace among states.

The more moderate political idealists believe that, while war is endemic to human nature, domestic institutions can control it. For example, Sir Norman Angell, author of *The Great Illusion* (1911), believed that war would become more improbable because increasing economic ties between nations would make it uneconomical.[10] Immanuel Kant believed that liberal, democratic, or republican institutions of state are the ideal.[11] For him, the key elements were the freedoms of the legal equality of subjects, representative government, and separation of powers, coupled with the "cosmopolitan law" aspects of international commerce and free trade and the pacific union of states through treaties.[12] This school, embodied in Woodrow Wilson's speeches about the First World War and the League of Nations[13] and the more recent writings of Michael Doyle,[14] argues that republican or democratic nations, by their nature, do not fight each other. Readily evident in this notion is a moralistic element from the first human-cause theory – that some states are inherently bad. Alternatively, the Marxist-Leninist perspective sees war as the result of the struggle between capitalism and communism: "Once Socialism triumphs, the state will whither away, and with it the phenomenon of war."[15]

THE QUANTITATIVE ANALYSIS OF WAR

Before considering the possible correlation between democracy and war, one must first define the concepts and establish the bases for their quantification. This section accordingly looks at the definitions of war and democracy used in some of the studies that have quantified these social phenomena.

War can be defined in many ways. Quincy Wright's *A Study of War* analyses the definitions applied by different academic disciplines. Wright considers war in the broadest sense as "a *violent contact* of *distinct* but *similar* entities."[16] According to him, international scholars and diplomats, by contrast, tend to follow Grotius's definition of war as "the condition of those contending by force." One must discount from this definition such things as duels and violence between juridically unequal entities. In this approach, thresholds are hard to define, and there is a grey area of international events such as "intervention, aggressions, reprisals, defensive expeditions, sanctions, armed neutralities, insurrections, rebellions, mob violence, piracy, and banditry." To this list could be added terrorism. For those studying war from the military perspective, however, force must be taken to be armed force by armies, navies, and air forces and excludes moral, legal, and economic force. Clausewitz defined war as "an act of violence intended to compel our opponents to fulfill our will." Sociologists add the requirements that it involve actual conflict and that it be a socially recognized form or custom.[17] Wright proposes a synoptic definition: "War is seen to be a state of law and a form of conflict involving a high degree of legal equality, of hostility, and of violence in the relations of organized human groups, or, more simply, the legal condition which equally permits two or more hostile groups to carry on a conflict by armed force."[18]

Statistical research concerning definitions of war provide an interesting contrast to descriptive definitions. The quantitative analysis of the causes of war started in the 1930s with the work of Quincy Wright and Lewis Richardson. In 1963, Melvin Small, a history professor, and David Singer, a political scientist, initiated the Correlates of War research project to identify the variables associated with the onset of the international wars since the Congress of Vienna of 1816. They wanted to discover "the trends and fluctuations in the frequency, magnitude, severity, and intensity of war ... [and to conduct a] systematic search for the most potent independent and intervening variables."[19] They first published their data and findings in 1972;[20] in 1982 the data were updated in *Resort to Arms*. While the principal difference between the first and second data sets was the addition of civil wars, the newer work also included nine wars that took place between 1965 and 1980 and refined some of the data about the earlier wars.[21]

The Correlates of War project now includes data about 118 international wars and 106 civil wars. Small and Singer quantify these two classes of war by duration (measured in months), severity (battle-connected deaths), magnitude ("nation months"), and intensity (fatality ratios by population and duration). They also analyse these data by developing indices of the annual amounts of war, regression lines to compare the amount of war between successive periods, and regression analysis for cycles and periodicity. They further examine war at the national level by developing the total, average, and normalized war experience of nations and the national rankings in victories, defeats, and battle deaths.

Other scholars are now producing their own data sets and analysis. For instance, the political scientist Jack Levy has considered the trends of great power wars from 1495 to 1975 and has concluded that, while their frequency has decreased, they have been "more serious in terms of severity, intensity, magnitude, and concentration."[22] In Canada, Kalevi Holsti's analysis of 177 wars identifies conflict-causing issues and considers how these issues and the attitudes of the policy-makers towards the use of force have changed over the years.[23] The pinnacle of statistical and quantitative analysis of war remains in the United States, however, with works by researchers such as Bruce Russett[24] and Rudolph Rummel.[25]

This area of quantitative research is not restricted to the most extreme form of interstate violence. Political scientists Charles S. Goochman and Zeev Maoz have examined the stages leading up to war and have categorized fourteen types of military acts (only one of which they define as "war"), which they divide into three categories: the threat of force, the display of force, and the use of force.[26] The threats are to use force, to blockade, to occupy territory, and to declare war. Display of force comprises alert, mobilization, and show of force. Use of force can involve blockade, occupation of territory, other uses of military force (such as having regular armed forces fire on the armed forces, population, or territory of another state or enter its territory), seizure of material or personnel, a clash (military hostilities between regular armed forces lasting at least twenty-four hours), declaration of war, and, ultimately, war itself.[27]

Mansfield and Snyder claim that the study of the war databases shows that democracies fight wars about as frequently as do other classes of states.[28] By using restrictive definitions, however, they support the conclusion that democratic states do not fight other democracies.[29] Therefore the definitions used and the bases for quantifying the concepts involved will be crucial to acceptance or rejection of the hypothesis.

Mansfield and Snyder expanded the Correlates of War database to include wars against non-state actors, as in colonial wars.[30] To be classed as a participant in an interstate war each state was required to have contributed at least one thousand troops or to have suffered at least one hundred casualties; for a war against a non-state actor, there had to be at least one thousand casualties per year for the state and its allies.[31] While the reliance on one thousand as the figure to qualify as a war may seem arbitrary (along with the starting date of the data set), Holsti believes that "the addition of several wars from lowering the number to 750," for instance, "would probably not alter most findings."[32]

THE DEFINITION, CLASSIFICATION, AND QUANTIFICATION OF DEMOCRACY

As a dictionary definition, democracy is simply "government by all the people, direct or representative."[33] Any serious study of the subject, however, will uncover various dimensions of this word – for example, a set of values, such as notions of a common good, popular sovereignty, political equality, and majoritarianism, or an accepted set of societal procedures for reflecting "the will of the people as a whole rather than that of an individual or of a small élite."[34] Minimal definitions of democracy require at least periodic elections between candidates who compete for the votes of a substantial portion of the adult population. Candidates must be able to "compete for public attention, be free to disseminate their political platform, have media access, and not feel threatened."[35] To be effective, this process must take place within the context of a broad range of civil liberties (the freedoms of the press, of association, and of speech) and the rule of law, in the sense that the elected do not have unlimited powers over the electors.[36] Finally, the outcome of the elections must determine who makes state policy, particularly foreign and military policy.[37]

The primary database used to correlate war and democratic states is the Polity II study by Ted Robert Gurr.[38] His methodology was to create indices of democracy and autocracy from o to 10 based on the following five variables: the competitiveness of political participation; the strength of the rules regulating participation in politics; the competitiveness of the process for selecting the chief executive; the openness of executive recruitment; and the strength of the constraints on the chief executive's power.[39] By comparison, Bruce Russett combined these indices to develop a composite index from −100 for the extreme state of autocracy to +100 for the highest form of democracy.[40] The median area of this latter scale requires, however, another expression – "anocracy" – to reflect state characteristics in which democratic and autocratic features are mixed, or in which very little power is given to public authorities.[41] In using Gurr's and Russett's research, Mansfield and Snyder consider that states can be either in one of three stable regime categories (autocracy, anocracy, and democracy) or moving from one regime to either autocracy or democracy (autocratizing and democratizing).

These measurements contain a strong bias towards such U.S. structural and procedural concepts as the separation of legislative and executive powers. One could readily argue that the selection of the executive from within the elected body, as is done in the British parliamentary tradition, is far more democratic than the selection of a cabinet from the private sector. Once the U.S. Senate has consented to the nomination of a cabinet official, there is no further accountability to the electorate, not even for the removal of that individual. One may also question the extent to which the United States is democratically effective, given the low percentage of its citizenship that votes, because of lack of voter registration or lack of interest.[42]

THE STATISTICAL THEORIES

Russett describes the relationship between democratic states and war as a complex phenomenon: "(a) Democracies rarely fight each other (an empirical statement) because (b) they have other means of resolving conflicts between them and therefore do not need to fight each other (a prudent statement), and (c) they perceive that democracies should not fight each other (a normative statement about principles of right behavior), which reinforces the empirical statement."[43] Russett is prepared to state only that democracies rarely fight one another, not that they never do so or have never done so. For many years states had to be in proximity in order to fight one another in a war, and the number of democratic states was not high enough for there to be any significance in their lack of conflict. In this latter respect, Russett notes that only twelve to fifteen democracies existed by the end of the nineteenth century. [44]

Russett also provides a short list of possible exceptions to the general rule, with starting dates: United States versus Britain (War of 1812); Roman Republic (Papal States) versus France (1849); the u.s. Civil War (1861); Ecuador versus Colombia (1863); the Franco-Prussian War (1870); the Boer War (1899); the Spanish American War (1898); the Second Philippine War (1899); the First World War (Imperial Germany versus the Western democracies) (1914), the Second World War (Finland versus the western democracies) (1941), Lebanon versus Israel (1948) and (1967). However, each of these conflicts failed to meet at least one of the criteria and therefore was excluded. In the majority of cases, the states were considered not to have been sufficiently democratic. The remainder were outside the time frame: the War of 1812; did not involve sovereign states: u.s. Civil War, Second Philippine War, and Boer War; or did not reach a significant level of casualties to warrant being called a war: World War II (Finland versus the Western democracies) and Lebanon (1967). [45]

There are two possible explanations for the relationship between democracy and war. The first is that the absence of war is based on the *internal* institutional constraints of democracy (a Kantian notion). The first such institutional constraint is the restraining effect of public opinion – those who must pay the price can exact retribution by not re-electing the democratic leadership. The second constraint is foreign policy being made in the open. The third constraint is the constraint of checks and balances of the state domestic structure (a crucial structural feature of the u.s. constitution). The particular elements of the checks and balances (the method of executive selection, institutionalized political competition, and the pluralism of decision making in foreign policy (either individual or institutional)) are very similar to the way democracy was quantified in Gurr's Polity II study.

The second possible basis for the absence of wars is the shared values of democratic states. The cultures, perceptions, and practices of such states result in pacific attitudes towards politics and dispute resolution, and these values are ascribed to the state's international behaviour or its perceptions of the other democratic states. Also, democratic states learn this behaviour from experience and wish to expand their positive interaction. This then creates a community of interests.

There has, however, been some criticisms of the theory. First, there may be other reasons for there being no war among democracies. David Spiro proposes that random theory can account for the lack of war – correlation does not equal causation. As noted above, the statistics in this area are affected by the small number of democracies over the past two centuries and the limited occasions for them to fight one another (the proximity requirement). John A. English has called the proposition that democracies tend not to fight each other "a dangerous presumption." He argues that the reason that democracies rarely fought in the past was that they "were few and far between and tended naturally to be allies." He suggests that as their numbers increase democracies "may begin to act like India and Pakistan."[46]

Second, the factors propounded by the realist school or the balance-of-power theorists may be preventing the warring.

Third, the analysis is very selective in its definitions of democracy and war. Perhaps the issue should be not whether there are enough casualties but whether the state acts in a non-forcible manner – in other words, not employing any of the threats listed by Goochman and Maoz. If one focuses on the normative aspects of democracy – i.e., assumes that democracies are good – one may exclude too much of democratic states' behaviour in a crisis that involves the threat of force. Covert operations, overseas stationing or "training" deployments, and the more overt gunboat diplomacy do not produce the casualty thresholds set by the statistical analysts.

Fourth, some see problems in the nature of the analysis. One commentator, David Spiro, wonders why, if the reason for the democratic peace is the *normative* or *behavioural* aspects of democracies, researchers use the *institutional* measures of democracy. Is it too hard to quantify the norms of democratic thought? Some question the measures of democracy. Spiro asks why the researchers arbitrarily pick a cutoff mark for the qualification of a state's being democratic. As an example, he notes that Maoz and Doyle disagree on two-thirds of their individual lists of democratic states; according to Maoz's cutoff mark on Gurr's Polity II democracy scale, France was not a democracy after 1981, El Salvador is, and Belgium does not qualify until 1956![47]

Christopher Layne criticizes the theory on the basis that the realist school's theories provide the reason for there being no war between democratic states – international politics, great power security, economic competition, the rise and fall of great powers, and the formation and dissolution of alliances in an anarchic, self-help system provide all the rationale one needs to explain the phenomenon.[48] In an anarchical system without a central rule-making and -enforcing body, self-help is used in defining a state's interests and the employment of the means to secure them. Democracy theorists posit that this international system can be changed, whereas the realists say that states can change internally but the international system will not.[49]

Having considered some aspects of the theory that democracies do not wage war against each other, we now examine whether the pursuit of the democratization of states is a worthwhile endeavour. Mansfield and Snyder's method for determining the relationship between regime change and war is based on the statistical independence of democratization or autocratization and the state's subsequent involvement in war. They calculated the expected frequency of democratization and war, democratization and no war, autocratization and war, autocratization and no war, no regime change and war, and no regime change and no war, assuming that the probability of war is the same, whether the regime changes or not. They compared expected with observed frequencies and calculated a Pearson chi-square (x^2). The chi-square indicates the extent of the difference between the two frequencies: the greater the value, the lower the probability that regime change and war are statistically independent.[50]

Mansfield and Snyder's measurement of changing regimes is based on three of the components of democracy: the openness of executive recruitment; executive constraints; and the competitiveness of political participation.[51] The regimes were studied for change occurring in periods of one, five, and ten years and their involvement in war over the same three time-frames.[52] Their databases support two hypotheses. The first is that democracies do not fight other democracies. The second is that the change of government from one form to another, very often that of moving towards democracy, increases the chances that a state will go to war. Mansfield and Snyder comment: "States like contemporary Russia that make the biggest leap in democratization ... from total autocracy to extensive mass democracy ... are about twice as likely to fight wars in the decade after democratization as are states that remain autocracies. However, reversing the process of democratization, once it has begun, will not reduce this risk."[53] They concluded that democratizing states were about two-thirds more likely to go to war. A state that had not changed in the previous decade had a one-in-six chance of fighting a war, whereas a state that was undergoing democratization had a one-in-four chance of being in a war within the next decade.[54] The relationship was greatest for the ten-year periods and weakest for the one-year periods.

The strength of the relationship between democratization and war fluctuates, depending on which measurement of democratization is used. The effects of democratization are strongest when just the openness of executive recruitment is measured. In these instances, states democratizing are twice as likely to engage in war as those not experiencing any change. Where only the competitiveness of political participation is used, the tendency for a democratizing regime to go to war is about 75 per cent higher than that of a stable state. Mansfield and Snyder also found that the length of time following the change was also statistically significant in three instances of the eight categories for the one-year periods, four of eight for five years, and six of eight for ten years.[55] The results were also significant when the three democratization type changes (anocratization from autocracy, democratization from anocracy, and democratization from autocracy) were measured. The greatest risk of war occurred in those states shifting from autocracy to democracy.[56]

As with democratization, a shift towards autocracy also increases the likelihood of war. Mansfield and Snyder found when comparing autocratizing states with ones that did not experience any change that in sixteen out of the twenty-four tests there was an increased risk of war. Within a ten-year period, states shifting from democracy to autocracy were especially likely to fight in all types of war, states moving to autocracy from anocracy were more likely to fight interstate wars, and yet states that shifted to anocracy from democracy were not likely to fight at all. Mansfield and Snyder's conclusions are that the biggest leaps in democratization will increase the possibility of interstate war and the biggest changes in autocratization will lead to wars against non-state actors.[57]

REASONS FOR DEMOCRATIZATION TO CAUSE WAR

Several reasons have been advanced why incipient or partial democratization will cause such states to go to war. One is the rise of nationalism, as exhibited by the breakup of the former Yugoslavia, and Armenia and Azerbaijan.[58] The major factor, however, would appear to be the linkage of nationalism and "domestic political competition" after the breakup of an autocratic regime: "Elite groups left over from the ruling circles of the old regime, many of whom have a particular interest in war and empire, vie for power and survival with each other and with new élites representing rising democratic forces. Both old and new élites use all the resources they can muster to mobilize mass allies, often through nationalistic appeals, to defend their threatened positions and to stake out new ones."[59] Thus war can result from strategies promoting a strong sense of nationalism or seeking to enhance the nation's prestige that become unmanageable with the political coalitions of the time.

Public opinion may not be the driving factor behind the moves towards war; in fact, it often is against war at the outset. Rather, "élites exploit their power in the imperfect institutions of partial democracies to create *faits accomplis*, control political agendas, and shape the content of information media in ways that promote belligerent pressure-group lobbies or upwellings of militancy in the populace as a whole." Mansfield and Snyder describe this as the "aftershock of failed democratization." Along with the effectiveness of the elite groups' propaganda, the incentive for weak leaders to engage in prestige-enhancing foreign-affairs strategies in an effort to heighten their authority is another cause of war. Institutional weaknesses in the states in transition are another possible cause. While stable democracies do not fight one another and, in fact, fight about as frequently as other states, when they do fight "they seem to be more prudent: they usually win their wars; they are quicker to abandon strategic over-commitments; and they do not fight gratuitous 'preventive' wars."[60]

According to Mansfield and Snyder, democracies do not fight each other because of "the self-interest of the average voter who bears the costs of war, the norms of bargaining and conflict resolution inherent in democracy, the moderating impact of constitutional checks and balances, and the free marketplace of ideas." The barriers to developing such democratic traditions in emerging democracies are the weakness of the new institutions and the resistance of the social groups that would be losers in the process. Emerging democracies lack the necessary institutions of strong political parties, independent courts, a free press, and free elections that might influence the foreign policy process.[61] The institutional skills required for a stable and fully functional democracy and faith in its processes are not acquired merely by the declaration of a freely elected leader. Mansfield and Snyder describe the problems for such states as follows: "[A]lmost none of the major institutions of representative government work in a reliable way: constitutional courts take sides on transparently political grounds; elections are postponed or announced on short notice; and political parties are transitory élite cliques, not stable organizations for mobilizing a mass coalition."[62] In each case of the failure of democratic process, the press lacked independence because of bribery or censorship and could not effectively contribute to a full and fair public debate.[63]

Mansfield and Snyder claim that the extent to which the ruling elites in an emerging democracy will hold back that process depends on the "mobility of their assets and skills." The authors claim that those most interested in slowing democratization are "those with a parochial interest in war, military preparation, empire, and protectionism."[64] The link between these interests and the state is significant: "[W]ar made the state and the state made war."[65] Such militaristic attitudes, however, are not the exclusive domain of the outgoing ruling elites.

Mansfield and Snyder note four reasons for the political impasse that breeds short-range thinking and "reckless" policy making in the democratizing process. First, the widening of the political spectrum in emerging democracies makes formation of stable coalitions difficult.[66] Second, the threatened but still powerful interest groups take inflexible and short-sighted positions over their interests.[67] Third, the threatened elites tend "to mobilize allies ... but only on their terms."[68] This mobilization takes place in a competitive setting among the elite group, which attempt to garner mass support in order to counter other mass threats. The elites' resources allow them to influence the direction of participation, but it still is difficult for a single group to control the outcome, which leads to ungovernability and impasse. Ideology is absolutely critical to this process, with nationalism being the one most commonly propounded. The mobilization of mass opinion to match that of the elite interest groups prevents the masses' influence having a moderating or compromising effect. Fourth, weakening of the central authority prevents the democratic institutions from integrating the competing views and interests. The reasons for the weakness of the new authority are weak parties, a lack of mass loyalty, rigged and intermittent elections, and distrust of institutions. [69]

The competition between the elites will also result in apparently contradictory coalitions ("squaring the circle or integrating opposites") where the resultant policy attempts to integrate antithetical elements. This leads to over-commitment and the provocation of many enemies at once, while the elites claim that the interstate conflicts are the result of the other states being hostile. Such beleaguered states often resort to risky strategies in an effort to shore up their prestige, but these will lead to apparent "slights" to the state's reputation, thereby giving a justification for going to war. [70]

CONCLUSION

Mansfield and Snyder believe that, even though there is an increased risk of war from a state undergoing democratization, resorting back to the old form of rule will not decrease the risk. The efforts of the international community must be not just a strategy for promoting democracy and managing the risks but rather one of assisting democratic institutions and, in some cases, providing a "golden parachute" (including not ending up in jail) for the threatened elites.[71] Part of the answer is creation of a "free, competitive, yet responsible marketplace of ideas," since pluralistic debates can be skewed towards the rich and powerful elites' interests.

Thus the way to promote such aids to the democratizing states will be training and the cross-fertilization of ideas and operating methods for the various democratic institutions, whether political, governmental, or private. There must be support for the various components of democracy, especially recognition of the rule of law and the importance of human rights. Such lessons are not quickly integrated into a society or culture. Additionally, old animosities and rivalries last for many years, sometimes generations.

These comments may be applicable to the democratizing states, but what can be done to protect the democracies from those states that resort to war? Collective defence may not always provide the necessary protection. One suggestion[72] is that deterrence theories need to be examined to determine how dictators such as Saddam Hussein can be discouraged from engaging in conflict. Part of the answer is that those major forces in the international world, whether the major powers or the United Nations, must not send mixed signals. While there is no lack of norms for states and rulers to follow, the enforcement of those norms has often been lacking. Perhaps the International Criminal Tribunal for the former Yugoslavia and Rwanda may provide part of the answer on how to deal with elites that transgress the accepted bounds of behaviour.

Having examined the relationship between democracy and war, one can see in this area of study that this "American" approach contains both normative attractions (that democracy is good) and the fascination with scientific and technical methods. Whether one is prepared to accept the hypotheses discussed above depends on one's views of statistical analysis and one's acceptance or not of the "American" approach. Even though the analysis can be criticized in its method and for its bias towards American political culture, the research and findings should not be dismissed out of hand. If there is any validity to them, they deserve further development, critical scrutiny, and analysis to determine how the findings might be incorporated into plans and action by the democratic states.

NOTES

1 Spiro, "The Insignificance of the Liberal Peace," 50.

2 Ibid.

3 U.S. President Clinton's 1993 address to the United Nations, as cited in McCaffrey, "Human Rights and the Commander," 10.

4 Mansfield and Snyder, "Democratization and the Danger of War," 5–38.

5 Waltz, *Man, State and War.*

6 Karsh, "The Causes of War," 65.

7 Ibid., 65.

8 Ibid., 66.

9 Ibid., 67.

10 See Waltz, *Man, State and War,* 17, 74, 224.

11 Karsh, "The Causes of War," 66.

12 Russett, *Grasping the Democratic Peace,* 4.

13 "We have no quarrel with the German people ... It was not upon their impulse that their government acted in entering this war. It was not with their previous knowledge or approval. It was a war determined upon as wars used to be determined upon in the old unhappy days when peoples were nowhere consulted by their rulers and wars were provoked and waged in the interests of dynasties or of little groups of ambitious men who were accustomed to use their fellow men as pawns and tools. Self-governed nations do not fill their neighbor states with spies or set the course of intrigue to bring about some critical posture of affairs which will give them the opportunity to strike and make conquest ... Cunningly contrived plans of deception or aggression, carried it may be from generation to generation, can be worked out and kept from the light only within the privacy of courts or behind carefully guarded confidences of a narrow and privileged class." Woodrow Wilson's war message to the U.S. Congress, 2 April 1917, as cited in Russett, *Grasping the Democratic Peace,* 3. See also Waltz, *Man, State and War,* 83–4, 110, 118, 125, 144.

14 Doyle, "Liberal States and War," 105–7.
15 Ibid.
16 Wright, "A Study of War," 69.
17 Ibid., 69.
18 Ibid.
19 Small and Singer, *Resort to Arms*, 4.
20 Singer and Small, *The Wages of War*.
21 Small and Singer, *Resort to Arms*, 14–16.
22 Singer and Small, "Introductory Notes" to Jack Levy, "Historical Trends in Great Power War," reprinted in part in Small and Singer, *International War*, 38–43.
23 Holsti, *Peace and War*.
24 Russett, *Peace, War and Numbers*.
25 Rummel, *Understanding Conflict and War, Vol. IV, War, Power, Peace*; and *Vol. V, The Just Peace*. Rummel is also noted for his work on the extreme cases of non-democratic intrastate violence, which he terms "democide"; see Rummel, *Death by Government*.
26 Goochman and Maoz, "Militarized Interstate Disputes."
27 Goochman and Maoz's analysis shows that the "major powers are again the prime participants either as initiators or targets of disputatious behavior"; Small and Singer, "Notes from the Editors," in Singer and Small, *International War*, 45.
28 Mansfield and Snyder, "Democratization and the Danger of War," 8.
29 Ibid.
30 Ibid., 11.
31 Ibid., 11, n 20.
32 Holsti, *Peace and War*, 10.
33 *The Oxford Dictionary of Current English* (1984), 193.
34 Van Loon and Whittington, *The Canadian Political System*, 77–8.
35 Babcock, "Getting to Democracy," 2.
36 Ibid.
37 Mansfield and Snyder, "Democratization and the Danger of War," 8. Thus, the War of 1812 is excluded from the data because Britain's suffrage was too low; Germany in 1914 is excluded because, though the Reichstag was elected by a universal suffrage with a 90 per cent turnout, cabinet officials were nominated by the Kaiser.
38 Gurr, *Polity II*.
39 Mansfield and Snyder, "Democratization and the Danger of War," 9.
40 See Russett, *Peace, War and Numbers*, 76. Russett and Maoz define their regime index (REG) as the measure of power concentration (PCON), which is based on the difference between their democracy and autocracy indices, which is expressed as: PCON(DEM-AUT), ibid.
41 Mansfield and Snyder, "Democratization and the Danger of War," 9.
42 Dye and Ziegler, *The Irony of Democracy*, 216–21.
43 Russett, *Peace, War and Numbers*, 4.

44 Ibid., 20.

45 Ibid., 16–18.

46 Spiro uses as an example the fact that there are many weekly lottery winners but members of his family have never won. The conclusion that there is a family trait causing the lack of winning would be patently wrong. Spiro, "The Insignificance of the Liberal Peace," 51. English, *Marching through Chaos*, 44.

47 Spiro, "The Insignificance of the Liberal Peace," 56.

48 Layne, "Kant or Cant,"5–49.

49 Ibid., 10–12.

50 Mansfield and Snyder, "Democratization and the Danger of War," 12.

51 Ibid., 9–12, nn 12, 14, and 16.

52 Ibid., 11.

53 Ibid., 6.

54 Ibid., 12–13.

55 Ibid., 14–15.

56 For instance, a change from anocracy to democracy increased the chance of any type of war from approximately 15 per cent to 100 per cent, and interstate war from approximately 35 per cent to 115 per cent, compared to states that remained anocratic. The figures for a shift from autocracy to democracy were approximately 30 per cent to 105 per cent and 50 per cent to 135 per cent for all wars and interstate wars, respectively, when compared against the states remaining autocratic. A change from autocracy to anocracy resulted in about a 70 per cent increase. Ibid., 17.

57 Ibid., 18.

58 Ibid., 6.

59 Ibid., 7.

60 Ibid., 20–1.

61 Ibid., 22.

62 Ibid., 23.

63 Ibid.

64 Ibid., 24–5.

65 Tilly, "Reflections," as cited in ibid., 25.

66 Ibid., 26–7. As examples, Mansfield and Snyder cite the inability of Britain's Whigs and Tories to form a stable coalition during the period before the Crimean War, the divisions within the left and right groups in Wilhelmine Germany, and the final days of the former Yugoslavia.

67 Ibid., 27–8. The examples cited for this factor are the agricultural protection of Prussian landowners; the organizational autonomy of the Japanese military in an autarchic empire, and the Serbian military and party elites' advocating a Serbian nationalistic state.

68 Ibid., 28. Some examples of the special abilities are "monopolies of information" (the German navy's "expertise" in making strategic assessments); "propaganda assets" (the Japanese army's "public relations blitz justifying the invasion of

Manchuria"); "patronage" (Lord Palmerston's dispensation of British foreign service positions for the sons of cooperative journalists); and "wealth" (the Krupps' funding of nationalist and militarist leagues in Germany).

69 Ibid., 28–30.
70 Ibid., 32–3.
71 Ibid., 36.
72 The ideas expressed here were part of a presentation made by John Norton Moore to the Canadian Council on International Law, Annual Conference, held in Ottawa, on 20 October 1995. See also Moore, "Government Structures," 36–41.

The Media and the Conduct of War

LCOL J.R.D. GERVAIS

Military power and a free press are both essential elements of a free society. As parts of a complex social system, they influence each other not in accordance with any "master plan" but rather as their diverse and sometimes contradictory actions influence the perceptions of the individuals who combine to make up "the military" and "the media."[1]

The underlying problem is that the military and the media hate each other because neither soldiers nor reporters understand the nature of war. The soldiers understand fighting. The journalists understand communications. Neither group knows that the political impact of combat depends on the communication of fighting. The military–media relationship is symbiotic. Media need to see the action. We [the military] need for them to see it, because battle is meaningless until it is credibly communicated to the world.[2]

The press is the watchdog over institutions of power, be they military, political, economic or social. Its job is to inform the people about the doings of their institutions.[3]

Over the years, in many nations, the relationship between the military establishment and the media could be described as contentious; a relationship filled with deeply rooted suspicions and prejudices, discoveries of improper conduct, and periods of strained communication and half-hearted cooperation. Through the nineteenth and twentieth centuries the military and the media have frequently been at odds over many topics of importance: freedom of information, censorship, fiscal responsibility, and so forth. Like it or not, however, the media have changed the face of modern warfare. Revolutionary technological advances in the last two decades provide an instantaneous capability to broadcast live, graphic war images and reports from virtually anywhere in the world to millions of viewers around the globe. That tremendous capability, along with the high degree of battlefield access and the sheer numbers of reporters certain to be present in all future military operations, underscores the magnitude of the media impact facing military planners and commanders today.

Prudent military planning demands that commanders do more than simply support the media. Commanders need to understand how the media presence on the battlefield evolved, how the media affect their operations, and how to exploit their presence. Conversely, the media have a role to play in democratic societies, and journalists must seek to accomplish their tasks with due regard for national security. A solid, working knowledge of military forces, their culture, and their methods would go far to bridging the gap, real or perceived, between journalists and the armed forces that fight in the conflicts on which they report.

This essay seeks to explain how the relationship between the military and the press has evolved over time, especially in combat. By examining the development of military–media relations from the past to the Gulf War, we can get a view of the probable future of this relationship in democratic nations and how armed forces can cope with the problems that are endemic to it.

WAR REPORTING: A HISTORICAL PERSPECTIVE

More than twenty-five hundred years ago, Sun-tzu, in emphasizing the crucial role of intelligence and deception in the outcome of the battle, wrote of the need for the commander to maintain total "control" over all information. [4] That task was relatively straightforward into the early nineteenth century, as the media had no way to disseminate information quickly enough to affect the outcome of battle. The battles of the English Civil War of the 1640s, for example, were reported for the rudimentary news journals of the time by correspondents who, to gather information, had to share a vantage point with those civilians who were unwillingly caught up in the battle areas. Correspondents did not need exceptional privileges of access and movement to be where the action was. [5]

Also, the limitations of time and space in communications rendered the concept of military censorship moot. During the American War for Independence, for example, newspapers had no organized means of covering battles or war-related events but relied almost completely on the random arrival of private letters and of official and semi-official messages. Editors clipped copy from other newspapers – both foreign and domestic – that used similar methods of reporting. [6] Most war reports were prepared at second hand, inaccurate, and quite tardy. Similar conditions prevailed during the War of 1812, with coverage of campaigns and incidents being almost as haphazard. [7]

According to Frank Mott, it was the American War with Mexico (1846–48) that received more news coverage than any previous war in any part of the world.[8] Through the use of writer-soldiers, writers enlisted as correspondents, and soldier-writers, printers, and reporters who had joined to fight, along with a combination of telegraph, railway, and pony express, the public got a taste of the drama; war became big news and newspaper circulation soared. The press, however, was invariably pro-military, partly because the reporters themselves were combatants or were at least involved in the action, but mainly because the war itself was successful and popular. This was a time of early U.S. imperialism, the notion of "Manifest Destiny" was widely accepted, and the U.S. public was on the side of its government.

In 1857, *The Times* of London sent William Howard Russell to the Crimea to report on French and British operations. Russell was an accomplished journalist and has been called "the first and greatest war correspondent."[9] His work marked the beginning of a new era in war coverage – that of civilian reporters being organized to report a war accurately to the civilian population. Up to this time, correspondents had romanticized battles and military heroes, catering to popular taste. Russell, in contrast, dug into instances of military incompetence and questioned the need for the taxpayer to fund the venture at all. He wrote about the horrors of the army's medical system, the foolish charge of the Light Brigade, and the ravages of disease on the troops. His reporting dramatically increased the circulation of *The Times* and caused other papers to rush out correspondents of their own. Soon these reporters were laying before the British taxpayer dramatic portrayals of serious problems and were questioning the ability of senior commanders. They aroused the anger of the British public by criticizing the organization of the British army, particularly as it concerned lack of food, clothing, and medical care for the soldiers. This in no small way helped bring about a swing in public opinion, a parliamentary vote of no confidence, and the fall of the government of Lord Aberdeen, despite the allies' ultimate victory.

The British establishment accused Russell of ruining Britain's worldwide public image and betraying sensitive military information to the enemy.[10] It seems "that before the war ended the army realised that it had made a mistake in tolerating Russell and his colleagues, but by then it was too late. The war correspondent had arrived."[11] Two important lessons about the media became clear during this conflict. First, the press could dramatically affect public opinion and therefore the government (especially in a democracy), to the point of unseating it. Second, war copy sells well, particularly if it is sensational or controversial. Nations in conflict would thereafter attempt either to enlist the cooperation of the press or to restrain it.

The American Civil War (1861–65) was arguably the greatest single event in American history, and for some it was therefore vital that it be "properly reported by correspondents of ability and integrity." Phillip Knightly explains that the opportunities for good reporting were clearly present. Soaring newspaper circulations, resulting from the tremendous demand for news of the war, generated huge profits, which were used in part to send more correspondents into the fray; some five hundred for the North alone. [12]

The technology of the day could not carry photographs to the newspaper page, but the telegraph was available for large-scale use for the first time – some 50,000 miles of line in the eastern United States alone. Americans were able to read about events the day after they occurred. But journalists were so quick to take advantage of this ability to get the news out quickly, and editors were so unreasonably demanding of their correspondents, that ethics were largely sacrificed. Referring to the fact that the deeds of the war correspondents of the Civil War have been overly romanticized, Knightly remarked: "The legend conveniently overlooks the fact that the majority of the Northern correspondents were ignorant, dishonest, and unethical; that the dispatches they wrote were frequently inaccurate, often invented, partisan, and inflammatory."[13] The people's "right" to know became the people's "want" to know. The market was for entertainment, and the end justified the means.

President Abraham Lincoln, in an attempt to control the transmission and dissemination of strategically important information, gave the military control of all telegraph lines and made censorship of the press a function of the War Department. Censorship was imposed by both North and South as official policy, with marginal results at best; not only was there no prior experience on which to draw, but also the press had become so aggressive, independent, and prosperous that it resisted any form of restriction. [14] The rules for censorship had to be written as the war carried on, making the learning process difficult and open to much criticism and bad faith. Recognizing the power of the press, Secretary of War Edwin Stanton began to issue his own dispatches through the Associated Press to combat the rumours and alarmist reports made by some correspondents. These daily war bulletins began the practice developed in later wars for government officials to describe briefly the operational situation and administration policy. [15]

War correspondents generally were mediocre at their task but war correspondence nevertheless developed into a special branch of journalism. [16] Media–military relations in the Civil War set the tone for much of what was to follow in the next century and a half, particularly in the areas of control and use of communication and the application of rules of censorship. [17]

Knightly described the period between the American Civil War and the First World War as the "Golden Age" for war correspondents: "[T]he military establishment was slow to realize the power of this newly awakened section of public opinion and allowed correspondents to write virtually what they liked."[18] The uninhibited press coverage of the Spanish–American War of 1898 was a case in point. In a shameful effort to increase "market share," competing newspapers supported the imperialist interests of u.s. foreign policy and "fought the war as determinedly as they had fostered it." [19] They presented a thrilling adventure story that increased newspaper circulation and rallied public support. Loren Thompson suggested that the rise of yellow journalism in papers such as the *New York World* and *New York Journal* and their ridiculously antagonistic coverage of the Cuban rebellion was, in fact, blatant agitation for u.s. intervention. He concluded that "the war was unquestionably avoidable and occurred largely to satisfy the promotional goals of competing New York newspapers."[20] Frederick Chiaventone suggested that whether or not the decision to fight was influenced by the press is immaterial. The media thought that they not only could, but should, intervene in the formulation and execution of foreign policy. [21]

By the end of the nineteenth century, however, governments were beginning to become more sophisticated in their handling of the press in wartime. The British military eliminated most of its problems with the press during the Boer War by commissioning reporters as officers in the army and subjecting them to field regulations.[22] The young Winston Churchill, for example, a correspondent with the *Morning Post*, was enrolled as a nominal member of the South African Light Horse Regiment. After some confusion, the British army also centralized its censorship effort and, for the first time, clearly defined the categories of information of most value to the enemy. [23]

Access to the battlefield took on new meaning with the outbreak of the First World War in 1914. The horrific static warfare on the Western Front caused a strict delineation of military and civilian space as civilians were withdrawn from the battle zones, leaving depopulated areas under military control. Trench warfare, coupled with the absence of civilian populations, allowed for easier control and manipulation of the press. "The mobile journalist able to venture at pleasure into war zones was supplanted by the château journalist who became virtually an appendage of the general staff."[24] The British and the French initially excluded newsmen from the battlefield. German officials, in contrast, recognized an opportunity to influence world public opinion and allowed reporters from neutral countries to visit their armies under escort and even singled out prominent correspondents for special treatment. The British and French gradually relented when they realized that the suppression of independent news from the front damaged civilian morale.

News had become a strategic commodity in the First World War, a means of shoring up civilian morale and influencing neutrals. But, in order to keep public support during extremely trying times, governments could hardly allow the whole truth to be published.[25] The new concept of "total war" required policies of censorship, and for the Allies this meant attempting to paint a picture of the moral right of their cause. Chiaventone explained that, in the context of the time, many on the Allied side felt that the war was indeed "a struggle for the survival of the Western democracies" and therefore required that certain sacrifices be made.[26] There followed a deliberate Allied campaign of propaganda and censorship aimed at vilifying the enemy and encouraging public support for a crusade for democracy. The media became a weapon of war and were made to view the conflict as honourable and just. And even if relations with military authorities were turbulent at times, on the whole the media cooperated by accepting the military's rules and by concentrating on human interest and morale-building stories.[27]

American correspondents, in particular, enjoyed special treatment by the Allies prior to the U.S. entry into the war.[28] And after its entry, in April 1917, the U.S. government was keenly interested in controlling the press. U.S. officials created the Committee on Public Information (CPI) to coordinate government propaganda and to act as governmental liaison with the newspapers. Propaganda and censorship efforts were taken from the direct control of the U.S. military, and the CPI released its own highly respected news sheet, under the theory that if enough worthwhile material were provided to the newspapers, there would be little need for stringent censorship. This proved an extremely effective practice, backed up as it was with legislation that empowered the government to ensure that no violations of security would go unpunished and with stringent rules for accreditation.[29]

Mott has suggested that despite the censorship imposed on the American correspondents by both the U.S. and European authorities, Americans were better informed as to the progress of the war than people in any other nation.[30] Be that as it may, from the journalistic point of view, according to Clem Lloyd, press controls of the First World War "set extreme standards for restrictive censorship, military mendacity and manipulation of journalists and news coverage" that would last until the invasion of Grenada in the early 1980s.[31]

The Second World War is often touted as the high point in the history of military–press relations. It was the first war covered "live," using radio. Access and mobility for journalists had improved considerably since 1918, though some military zones, such as the Russian front, were difficult to penetrate. After the Normandy invasion, correspondents were relatively free to move behind, and sometimes ahead of, the Allied forces.[32] This was possible because the dissemination of information was controlled at the source through censorship. Correspondents were not allowed in theatre without being accredited, and one of the conditions for accreditation was to agree to submit all copy to military censorship.[33] Journalist Drew Middleton believed that censorship enabled correspondents to be better informed about the war, and he has been quoted as saying: "As long as all copy was submitted to censors before transmission, people in the field, from the generals on down felt free to discuss top secret material with reporters."[34]

Throughout the war, American and British correspondents cooperated with the military. Whether this was attributable to the overall strength of military–press relations at the time or to censorship is difficult to establish. Nevertheless, on the whole, correspondents went along with the official scheme for reporting the war because they believed that it was in their nation's interests to do so. The reporters knew that the public supported the Allies and opposed Hitler before they put pen to paper. Any other position would receive no audience. John Steinbeck later reflected: "We were all part of the war effort. We went along with it, and not only that, we abetted it. Gradually, it became part of us so that the truth about anything was automatically secret and that to trifle with it was to interfere with the war effort ... Yes, we wrote only a part of the war but at that time we believed, fervently believed, that it was the best thing to do."[35]

The military also considered war correspondents part of the war effort. General Dwight Eisenhower told a group of newsmen in 1944: "I have always considered you as quasi-staff officers, correspondents accredited to my headquarters."[36] So it was that the Allied system for controlling correspondents was accepted as being an operational requirement and grew to the point where it was as important in the planning for D-Day as any other support element.

The magnitude of the media coverage and the large numbers of journalists in the war produced the concept of media pools. It became common in all areas of the theatre to pool pictures, but the pooling of news reports was usually limited to large-scale operations where the number of correspondents had to be limited for their own safety. The radio was first pooled in the Normandy invasions and had a dramatic effect on the listeners. Technology allowed radio coverage to increase throughout the war to the point where direct reports could be received from any point in the European theatre. The intimate relationship that had developed between the military and the media maximized the potential of radio technology to the benefit of the Allied cause and the maintenance of the military's good public image.[37]

In retrospect, newsmen have looked back critically at their role in the Second World War and have generally not liked what they have seen. There is a feeling that they should have done things differently: less obvious identification with the Allied cause, less incorporation into the military machine, and more objective reporting. Knightly agreed but asks what, if anything, could have been done to change the course of events.[38] He suggested that Charles Lynch, a Canadian who had been accredited to the British army for Reuters, said it all thirty years later: "It's humiliating to look back at what we wrote during the war. It was crap ... We were a propaganda arm of our governments. At the start the censors enforced that, but by the end we were our own censors. We were cheerleaders. I suppose there wasn't an alternative at the time. It was total war. But, for God's sake, let's not glorify our role. It wasn't good journalism. It wasn't journalism at all." [39]

The Korean War began on 25 June 1950 when North Korea invaded South Korea. The West came to the rescue, led by the United States, under the umbrella of the United Nations, but it was an unpopular and undeclared war, plagued by issues that had military and political underpinnings. It was to be the beginning of the ebb of military–press relations.

The handling of the press in Korea differed significantly from that of earlier conflicts. At first General Douglas MacArthur, as the UN commander in Korea, dismissed the concept of field press censorship and relied on self-censorship. However, the guidelines for voluntary censorship were vague and proved unsatisfactory to both the military and the press. There were many security breaches during this period of self-censorship (25 June to 21 December 1950) and a lack of organized press coverage on the part of military planners as a whole. Moreover, the early reporting was quite critical by the standards of the Second World War. Correspondent Marguerite Higgins wrote: "So long as our government requires the backing of an aroused and informed public opinion ... it is necessary to tell the hard bruising truth ... It is best to tell graphically the moments of desperation and horror endured by an unprepared army, so that the American public will demand that it does not happen again." [40]

By July 1950, the voluntary code of censorship, which had been initially aimed at preserving military secrecy, was expanded to include "criticism of Command decisions or of the conduct of Allied soldiers on the battle-field." [41] Following Chinese Communist entry into the war in November 1950 and the second fall of Seoul, outspoken criticism of the military leadership by front-line correspondents increased tension between the military and the press to crisis proportions. On 18 December 1950, the U.S. secretary of defence, General George C. Marshall, in a meeting in the Pentagon with several top media representatives, concluded that "the security of information from the combat area is the responsibility of the military." [42] On 21 December, MacArthur ended voluntary censorship and imposed full military censorship. This turn of events was not welcomed by most correspondents, who, though frustrated by the confusion of voluntary censorship, were under pressure to prove their patriotism and "get on side." [43] They did, however, and went along with the military's view of how the war should be reported for the remainder of the conflict. [44]

But even if press methods in the field during the Korean War became reminiscent of the team reporting of the Second World War, there was still one important element missing: popular support back home. Unlike in the world wars, there was no censorship on the U.S. home front. Opinions about the war were many and varied and did not necessarily rely on the reports coming from Korea. News analysis was often critical and probably contributed to the unpopularity of the war.[45] The traditional adversarial relationship between the press and the military, resolved up to this point through censorship, would soon become confrontational, as the u.s. public began to question the government's motives in fighting limited wars without a clear objective of victory.

The war in Vietnam, for many, was the low point in military–press relations in the United States. The legacy of distrust it produced between the military and the press was in clear contrast to the Second World War experience.[46] From the media's point of view, there were, to be sure, instances of irresponsibility of which they cannot be proud. Yet, despite the total absence of censorship, the simple accreditation process,[47] and the freedom of access, an accurate picture of the war was not getting across, or when it was, it was not a pretty one. However, by and large, the media felt that their duty to inform the people had been carried out and that the final outcome of the war had, in a sense, vindicated their efforts.[48]

But not all of the u.s. coverage was negative. In fact, postwar studies and analyses have shown that the preponderance of coverage was either favourable or neutral.[49] Nevertheless, it was undeniable "that press reports were still often more accurate than the public statements of the administration in portraying the situation in Vietnam."[50] Most of those who fought in Vietnam had the impression that the reporting was mostly unfavourable, and many in the military felt that the press was a major factor in the u.s. withdrawal from Vietnam.[51]

From the u.s. military's point of view, the coverage of the Tet Offensive was especially misleading and negative. Peter Braestrup, in his important work *Big Story*, concluded: "[T]he performance by the major American television and print news organizations during February and March 1968 constitutes an extreme case. Rarely has contemporary crisis-journalism turned out, in retrospect, to have veered so widely from reality."[52] He blamed this unsatisfactory performance on the fact that the special circumstances surrounding the Tet Offensive had a rare and overwhelming impact on the "special susceptibilities and limitations" of American journalism. Consequently, the initial, unsubstantiated reports of defeat were not corrected as the situation became clearer. Therefore, what was in effect a u.s. military victory would remain, in the minds of the American public, a major setback – the turning point for public support for the war.

Trust in the media was made more difficult with the arrival in Vietnam of many young and inexperienced reporters who knew little about the military or the Vietnamese. Their reports were often inaccurate or negatively biased, and some were simply trying to make a name for themselves.[53] The military allowed itself to be drawn into the politics of the war and eventually found it-self "selling" it to the public. President Lyndon Johnson's strategy of limited war led to considerable criticism at home – it was not the American way of war – and the military increasingly blamed the press for the credibility prob-lems it experienced, accusing television news in particular of "turning the American public against the war."[54] Hammond concluded that the military inadequately assessed the nature of television coverage, because what alien-ated the American public in both the Korean and Vietnam wars was not news coverage but casualties. Statistical analysis shows some support for this view, as public support dropped by 15 percentage points whenever total U.S. casualties increased by a factor of ten.[55] Lloyd argued that the blind concentration on the impact of television is a gross over-simplification in that it ignores the effect of the print media on the war's popularity even before TV reached its maximum impact.[56]

Regardless of the outcome of this debate, the fact remains that a strong antipathy emerged between the press and the military in the United States as a result of the Vietnam War. The media became the enemy in the eyes of the military, and a generation of American officers grew up with the credo of, "duty, honour, country, and hate the media."[57] More serious, however, both institutions began the post-Vietnam era with completely opposite views on their roles in war. The media were convinced that they had met their obliga-tion vis-à-vis the public's right to know the facts; the military was equally convinced that the media had done a great disservice to the country through irresponsible conduct, and it vowed never to let that happen again. The U.S. military had determined "that it was essential in future limited conflicts to deny media access and mobility, and to limit and carefully control access to official information."[58]

As a result of this view, a total news blackout was applied to the U.S. inva-sion of Grenada in 1983. Journalists who sought access to the area were turned back, and several who reached the island on their own were detained on a U.S. command ship until the initial phases of the intervention were over. In these circumstances, the only coverage supplied to the world media was by U.S. army public relations officers. The outcry from the press was predict-able, and the American public was left to make an informed evaluation and to judge the merits of the operation in the absence of independent, first-hand battlefield reports. The joint task force commander, Vice-Admiral Joseph Metcalf III, argued that, though the public was probably not well served in the reporting of the operation, the press spent more time discussing its free-doms than reporting the story.[59]

Regardless, the secretary of defence was forced to convene a commission in 1984 to review the episode and to recommend a workable procedure for such situations in the future. The panel did not include media representatives among its members, despite attempts to do so, because the media generally felt that it was "inappropriate from a conflict-of-interest standpoint for working reporters and editorial personnel to sit on a government-sponsored panel to make recommendations concerning future military–media relations." Despite the media boycott, the "Sidle Panel," chaired by Major-General Winant Sidle, made eight recommendations, the most notable of which was to use media pools.[60] Many feel that the panel restored the impetus to improve military–media cooperation and to provide a framework for the media and the military to cultivate a mutually beneficial relationship.

The Pentagon press pool, recommended by the Sidle Panel, was first put into effect during the U.S. invasion of Panama in December 1989, but the results were less than satisfactory. The military did not adequately plan for timely media access to the battlefield; therefore the national media pool was unable to cover military actions until the second day of the operation. "Pool journalists arrived in Panama hours after the fighting at the key points of Rio Hato and Patillo had ceased, and they were kept well away from continuing fighting at the Commandancia."[61] According to pool procedures, reporters had to be escorted at all times. Official policy prevented public affairs officers and reporters from entering combat situations because the military does not typically send personnel into combat zones without operational reasons. This was seen as being in direct conflict with the need for adequate combat coverage. The result was that there were no independent eyewitness accounts of these battles.

Initial planning for the operation had included media coverage. Unfortunately, media planning was halted, apparently due to the actions of an office outside the Public Affairs chain of command. On 17 December 1989, President George Bush made the decision to execute the operation, and Secretary of Defense Richard Cheney stated that the media pool would be deployed to cover it. Planning for the media resumed three days before the operation, but it was too late to be properly integrated into the operational plan. Pool members and then media executives accused the administration of using the pool to manipulate coverage of the operation. The pool reporters were not given free access and were allowed the use only of communications equipment that proved to be generally unreliable. Also, planning did not allow for follow-on support to expanded media coverage by a larger number of journalists.[62]

Combelles argues that Panama was not a job for which the pool was suited. Unlike Grenada, Panama "was neither especially remote nor without a wide range of reporters already in place." The confusion of the situation made aggressive reporting rather difficult. Other reporters in Panama from the beginning of the invasion also failed to obtain any combat footage and could not get access to U.S. military forces unless they had made arrangements for an escort.[63]

Once again the media outcry that followed the operation resulted in a call from the assistant secretary of defence, Public Affairs, for a report on the Panama press pool. In March 1990, that report was prepared by Fred Hoffman, a retired assistant secretary. His report had seventeen recommendations, none of which was properly followed up by either the press or the military.[64] It should not have come as a surprise, therefore, that the military–press controversy raised its head again at the first opportunity – the Gulf War.

Iraq invaded Kuwait on 2 August 1990, but Western and Arab leaders consulted for a week before the United States announced that it would deploy troops in Saudi Arabia. Initially, the host nation, Saudi Arabia, was reluctant to allow the Western media to enter its country. On 10 August, the Saudi Arabian government agreed to accept the Department of Defence News Media Pool, and by 13 August the initial pool members and their military escort officers had arrived in Dhahran. After a week of preparation, they had laid the groundwork for the many journalists who would follow (by December the number had reached 800, and it would grow to 1,600 at the height of the war). The Joint Information bureau was set up to coordinate a system for accreditation and media assistance in cooperation with the Saudi Arabian Ministry of Information. The bureau functioned as news media coordinator and release agency. It processed hundreds of inquiries for routine media visits, responded to human-interest and issue-oriented stories, produced military press releases, and was also responsible for escorting the media into the field.[65]

However, the press could not be expected to police itself, and neither could the huge number of reporters be allowed to join the troops. Therefore a pool concept was developed by both the military and the press that would place a group of approximately 130 journalists in pools with units in the field, despite the strain it would cause on communications and logistics. The news media organized themselves into four pools – print, radio, TV, and picture – and coordinated the registration and assignment of reporters to serve in the combat pools set up by the military. Escorts played the essential role of liaison between the reporters and the troops and were responsible for balancing the needs of operational security with the public's need to know. This, of course, has been the historical dilemma and was the reason why the press policy of the Persian Gulf War was created.

This press policy was quite explicit and covered such items as transportation, messing, billeting, accreditation, and restrictions on releasable information. There was no field press censorship. Nevertheless, accusations of censorship were made by the media in general as a result of the pool system and the strict requirement for escorts. Complaints included the restrictively tight control of the pools, the isolation from negative news, and news management designed to provide a sanitized version of the war.[66] Lloyd explained that the arrangements made by other nations for their journalists were also "swamped by the media management policies ordained by the United States."[67] For the American journalists, he remarked, the traditional press freedoms guaranteed by the u.s. constitution's First Amendment were given short shrift, despite challenges in the u.s. Federal Court. The court supported the military. Even though, technologically, the media outdistanced the military's public affairs establishment, this did little good without direct access to the battlefield. The military was in control – the battlefield extended deep into enemy territory, and access to friendly territory was difficult outside of the pool system.[68]

u.s. Secretary of Defense Cheney spoke of two overarching principles in the development of u.s. press policy in the Gulf. First, military needs would come before journalistic rights. Second, perhaps to avoid falling into the "credibility gap" left as the legacy of Vietnam, President Bush did all the right things, according to Braestrup: "He called up the reserves, secured the assent of Congress and the support of the United Nations, defined the objective, fixed a decisive strategy, and was prepared to use maximum force."[69] Bush had the backing of the American people, and he let the military do its job. The lessons of the Vietnam experience were applied.

WHERE TO GO FROM HERE?

Technology is making the influence of the media an increasingly significant part of conflict in today's world. Technological advances will free the media from the grasp of the military and make it a greater threat to operational security than ever before. The potential already exists for the media to circumvent the military's access controls through satellite-based global telephone systems that will allow transmission of a reporter's copy from anywhere in the world. Consequently, the military may not be able to constrain the media effectively in the future. Also, the number of reporters on the battlefield has steadily grown and, with it, the responsibility for the operational commander to develop sound support plans that will cater to the media's needs while balancing the allocation of limited resources with the number of journalists in the field. It is all the more important, therefore, that there be constructive discussions between the military and the media, within national and in international forums, to facilitate the development of effective and workable guidelines for media coverage in times of war.

There is a basic need for a better understanding of the respective roles and responsibilities of the military and the press in democratic states. The military seems to recognize the potential of the media to convey messages, deceive the enemy, and gather information useful to the prosecution of war (the impact of cnn throughout "Desert Storm" is a case in point). The importance of keeping the public informed has grown, and the military of democratic nations must accept the fact that an informed population matters in terms of morale and support to sustain the effort. Thus the media must be allowed to report good news and bad news alike. An operation may not always go the way "our" military has planned, and so, given the instantaneous nature of the media, public support could shift radically in a short period, as with the U.S. effort in Somalia. Though the media may not always have a legal or constitutional right of access to military operations, the military has much to gain from working and improving relations with the press.

Preparing both sides to deal with each other will likely be the single most difficult task to be undertaken in resolving the military–press dilemma because the cultural divisions between the two cannot, and indeed should not, be eliminated. The military will likely be able to achieve significant results in this area, being an institution whose effectiveness and ultimate success rest largely on the thorough training of its members in all aspects of military planning and the execution of operations. Training on military–media relations is already available in most senior staff colleges and defence colleges of Western nations' armed forces. The media, however, have much work to do if they are to correct their problem of lack of expertise on the military. In fact, why should the media be motivated to do so other than on an as-required basis? Even more fundamentally, the media must come to grips with the internal challenges of their industry if they are to present a concerted front on issues related to coverage of conflicts.[70] Here again the question is whether, from the media's point of view, a concerted front is at all necessary. Stephen Aubin pessimistically stated that in the area of self-criticism and self-reform, the track record of the media is not good, and so, the difficult history of military–media relations may repeat itself.[71]

The secret of successful military–media relations is cooperation. The military and the press rarely recognize the fact that they fundamentally need each other. The need for the press to cooperate with the military is obvious: noncooperation may seriously impair its access to military operations.[72] Less obvious is the need for the military to cooperate with the media. The public has the right to know what the military is doing, except when operational security or troop safety dictates otherwise. The media have the responsibility of providing this information objectively to the public. As the Sidle Panel concluded: "The optimum solution to ensure proper coverage of military operations is to have the military – represented by competent, professional public affairs personnel and commanders who understand media problems – working with the media – represented by competent, professional reporters and editors who understand military problems – in a nonantagonistic atmosphere. The panel urges both institutions to adopt this philosophy and make it work."[73]

These conclusions remain valid today, if not more so, as the instances of limited conflict and the ubiquity of the media increase. But such a utopian situation is unachievable. The task of the military is to defend the democratic values of the state from external and, under special circumstances, internal threats. Military forces abide by a code of conduct and answer to the elected government. Most of the media are motivated substantially by profit and are not self-regulated as a profession. Strict rules of cooperation and coordination of effort would not be in the interest of journalistic freedom or the often careerist, opportunistic, and even purely sensationalistic ambitions of some individual journalists. This divergence in aims cannot be reconciled. At best, the military and the media can attempt to minimize their differences on a conflict-by-conflict basis and critique the results after the fact. In the case of military–press relations, history is bound to repeat itself.

NOTES

1 Eccles, *Military Power in a Free Society*, 150.
2 Noyes, "Like It or Not," 33.
3 Trainor, "The Military and the Media," 4.
4 Sun-tzu, *The Art of War*, 136–40.
5 Lloyd, "The Case for the Media," 46.
6 Frank Luther Mott, cited in Cochran, "Press Coverage," 17.
7 Ibid., 196.
8 Ibid., 248.
9 Knightly, *The First Casualty*, 4.
10 Joseph J. Mathews, cited in Hammond, *Public Affairs*, 3.
11 Knightly, *The First Casualty*, 17.
12 Ibid., 20.
13 Ibid.
14 Hammond, *Public Affairs*, 4.
15 Knightly, *The First Casualty*, 27.
16 Ibid., 39.
17 Edwin Emery and Michael Emery, cited in Cochran, "Press Coverage," 26.
18 Knightly, *The First Casualty*, 42.
19 Edwin Emery and Michael Emery, cited in Cochran, "Press Coverage," 28.
20 Loren B. Thompson, cited in Aubin, "The Media's Impact," 56.
21 Chiaventone, "Ethics and Responsibility," 69.
22 Hammond, *Public Affairs*, 4.
23 See Thomas Pakenham's insightful history, *The Boer War*.
24 Lloyd, "The Case for the Media," 47.
25 A fact that generated the myth, in Germany, that its armies were defeated not in the field but from behind – i.e., by Communists and Jews. The Nazis would thrive on this legend.
26 Chiaventone, "Ethics and Responsibility," 70.
27 Hammond, *Public Affairs*, 4–5.

28 Knightly, *The First Casualty*, 121–3, supports the idea that U.S. entry into the war
     was largely a result of a major propaganda effort carried out by the British gov-
     ernment through the American correspondents attached to the British army.
29 Cochran, "Press Coverage," 34.
30 Frank Luther Mott, cited in ibid.
31 Lloyd, "The Case for the Media," 48.
32 Ibid.
33 Knightly, *The First Casualty*, 275.
34 Ibid., 316.
35 Ibid., 276.
36 Ibid., 315.
37 The Second World War witnessed a growing emphasis on public relations within
     the military that eventually led to elevation of public information programs to
     separate staff status. The success of this effort owes much to the close ties
     between the military and the press.
38 Knightly, *The First Casualty*, 330.
39 Ibid., 333.
40 Ibid., 337.
41 Mott, *American Journalism*, 853.
42 Ibid., 854.
43 Knightly, *The First Casualty*, 345–6.
44 Ibid., 355–6.
45 Cochran, "Press Coverage," 46–7.
46 Halloran, "Soldiers and Scribblers," 151. General Eisenhower wrote in *Crusade
     in Europe*: "The commander in the field must never forget that it is his duty to
     cooperate with the heads of his government in the task of maintaining a civilian
     morale that will be equal to every purpose." The principal agency to accomplish
     that task, he said, was the press: "I found that correspondents habitually
     responded to candour, frankness, and understanding."
47 A free lance journalist could obtain a Military Assistance Command, Vietnam
     (MACV) card by producing two letters from any news agencies or newspapers
     prepared to buy his materials. Knightly, *The First Casualty*, 403.
48 Ibid., 423.
49 See, for example, Samisch, "Comparison."
50 Hammond, *Public Affairs*, 388.
51 Sidle, "A Battle behind the Scenes," 55.
52 Braestrup, *Big Story*, 508.
53 Ibid., 54.
54 Hammond, *Public Affairs*, 387.
55 Ibid.
56 Lloyd, "The Case for the Media," 50.
57 Trainor, "The Military and the Media," 2.
58 Lloyd, "The Case for the Media," 51.

59 Vice-Admiral J. Metcalf III, "The Press and Grenada."
60 A U.S. Department of Defense national media pool, consisting of a small media contingent (ten journalists representing wire services, TV and radio networks, newspapers, and photo agencies), manned on a rotational basis and available for immediate, worldwide deployment for the initial coverage of military operations, was established in 1985 in Washington, DC.
61 Lloyd, "The Case for the Media," 52.
62 Combelles, "Operation *Just Cause*," 79–81.
63 Ibid., 79–83.
64 Hoffman, "Review of the Panama Pool Deployment."
65 Cochran, "Press Coverage," 73–4.
66 Sidle, "A Battle behind the Scenes," 61.
67 Lloyd, "The Case for the Media," 53.
68 Aubin, "The Media's Impact," 58.
69 Braestrup, "Foreword."
70 Bain, *Gotcha!,* exposes the myths and ills of the media in Canada by providing concrete examples of "instances in which they have served the public badly by yielding to political bias, ingrained negativity and intellectual laziness."
71 Aubin, "The Media's Impact," 60.
72 Lloyd, "The Case for the Media," 57–8, relates an incident in the Gulf War where French TV crews managed to evade their escorts and enter restricted areas. This, coupled with a previous situation where the French journalists boycotted their army and refused to report its activities, led to the imposition of severe restrictions on access by the Defence Ministry. U.S. media controls were also an affront to many journalists, American or others, but the threat of deportation or loss of accreditation was an effective deterrent to even the most persistent, independent journalist.
73 Sidle, "A Battle behind the Scenes," 63.

Bibliography

Addington, Larry H. *The Blitzkrieg Era and the German General Staff, 1865–1941.* New Brunswick, NJ: Rutgers University Press, 1971.

Air Command and Staff Program. *Aerospace Doctrine Manual (ACSP 1-Draft).* Toronto: Canadian Forces Command and Staff College, 5 June 1993.

Air Force Doctrine Directive 4, Air Force Operational Doctrine: Space Operations. Washington, DC: Department of the Air Force, 1995.

Air Force Manual 1–1, Vol. I, Basic Aerospace Doctrine of the United States Air Force. Washington, DC: Department of the Air Force, March 1992.

Akenson, Donald Harmon. *God's Peoples.* Montreal: McGill-Queen's University Press, 1991.

Alexandrov, Victor. *The Tukhachevsky Affair.* Englewood Cliffs, NJ: Prentice Hall, 1964.

Allen, Thomas B. *War Games.* New York: Berkley Publishing Corporation, 1989.

Anderson, M. *Insurgent Organization and Operations: A Case Study of the Viet Cong in the Delta, 1964–1966.* Santa Monica, Calif.: Rand, 1967.

Antal, John. "Maneuver versus Attrition." *Military Review,* 12 (Oct. 1992), 21–33.

Asprey, Robert B. *War in the Shadows: The Guerrilla in History. 1975.* New York: William Morrow and Co., 1994.

Aubin, Stephen. "The Media's Impact on the Battlefield." *Strategic Review,* 20 (winter 1992), 55–61.

Babcock, Glenys A. "Getting to Democracy." *Behind the Headlines,* 53 no. 1 (autumn 1995), 1–17.

Bain, George. *Gotcha! How the Media Distort the News.* Toronto: Key Porter Books, Limited, 1994.

Barker, Ralph. *The RAF at War.* Chicago, Ill.: Time Life Books, 1981.

Bassford, Christopher. *Clausewitz in English: The Reception of Clausewitz in Britain and America 1815–1945*. New York: Oxford University Press, 1994.

Baylis, John. "Revolutionary Warfare." In John Baylis et al. eds., *Contemporary Strategy*, Vol. I, New York: Holmes and Meiers Publishers Inc, 1975.

Beckett, Ian F.W., ed. *The Roots of Counter-Insurgency: Armies and Guerilla Warfare, 1900–1945*. New York: Blanford Press, 1988.

Bellamy, Christopher. "Antecedents of the Modern Soviet Operational Manoeuvre Group." *Journal of the Royal United Services Institute*, 129 no. 3 (Sept. 1984), 50–8.

– *The Evolution of Modern Land Warfare*. London: Routledge, 1990.

Bellin, David, and Chapman, Gary, eds. *Computers in Battle*. Orlando, Fla.: Harcourt, Brace, Jovanovich, 1987.

Bendiner, Elmer. *The Fall of Fortresses*. New York: G.P. Putnam's Sons, 1980.

Bergstrand, B.M. "What Do You Do When There's No Peace to Keep?: A Low Intensity Conflict Model for Peacekeeping in the New World Order." In *The War Studies Papers*, Vol. I, J.P. Culligan et al., eds., *Studies in Peacekeeping*, Kingston, Ont.: Royal Military College of Canada, 1993.

Beringer, Richard, Hattaway, Hennan, Jones, Archer, and Stills, William. *Why the South Lost the Civil War*. Athens, Ga.: University of Georgia Press, 1986.

Berton, Pierre. *Vimy*. Toronto: McClelland & Stewart, 1987.

Bidwell, Shelford. *Gunners at War*. London: Arms and Armour Press, 1970.

Bidwell, Shelford, and Graham, Dominick. *Firepower: British Army Weapons and Theories of War, 1904–45*. London: Allen & Unwin, 1982.

Blackett, P.M.S. *Studies of War*. Edinburgh, Oliver and Boyd, 1962.

Blaufarb, Douglas S. *The Counterinsurgency Era: U.S. Doctrine and Performance 1950 to the Present*. New York: Free Press, 1977.

Boatman, J. "Reheated F-117A on Offer to U.S. Navy." *Jane's Defence Weekly*, 21 (5 March 1994).

Boring, Alan. "Computer System Reliability and Nuclear War." In David Bellin and Gary Chapman, eds., *Computers in Battle*, Orlando, Fla: Harcourt, Brace, Jovanovich, 1987.

Braestrup, Peter. *Big Story*. New York: Anchor Books, 1978.

– "Foreword" to *Hotel Warriors: Covering the Gulf War*. (Washington, DC: Woodrow Wilson Center Press, 1991).

Brander, Michael. *The Tenth Royal Hussars*. London: Cassells, 1969.

Braybrook, R. "Design Analysis: F/A-18 E/F." *Air Pictorial*, 48 no. 1 (Jan. 1996), 11–15.

Brodie, Bernard. *Strategy in the Missile Age*. Princeton, NJ: Princeton University Press, 1959.

– *War and Politics*. New York: MacMillan Publishing, 1973.

Brown, Alan. *Fundamentals of Stealth Design*. Calabasas, Calif.: Lockheed Corporation, 1995.

Bucholz, Arden. *Moltke, Schlieffen, and Prussian War Planning*. New York: Berg Publishers, 1991.

Bundy, McGeorge, Keenan, George F., McNamara, Robert S., and Smith, Gerard. "The President's Choice: Star Wars or Arms Control." *Foreign Affairs*, 67 (fall 1988), 265–78.

Burns, E.L.M. *General Mud*. Toronto: Clarke & Irwin, 1970.

Burrows, William E. *Deep Black: Space Espionage and National Security*. New York: Random House, 1986.

Bush, Vannevar. *Modern Arms and Free Men*. New York: Simon and Schuster, 1949.

Butson, Thomas. *The Tsar's Lieutenant, The Soviet Marshal*. New York: Praeger, 1984.

Buttinger, Joseph. *The Smaller Dragon*. New York, Frederick A. Praeger Publishers, 1958.

– *Vietnam: A Dragon Embattled*, Vol. I. New York: Frederick A. Praeger Publishers, 1967.

Byrne, J.A. *The Whiz Kids*. New York: Currency Doubleday, 1993.

Cable, Larry E. *Conflict of Myths: The Development of American Counterinsurgency Doctrine and the Vietnam War*. New York: New York University Press, 1986.

– "Reinventing the Round Wheel: Insurgency, Counter-Insurgency, and Peacekeeping Post Cold War." *Small Wars and Insurgencies* (autumn 1993), 228–62.

Carns, Michael P.C. "Closing Remarks." Delivered 10 November 1994. On internet at *The Knowledge Warrior News Center*, http: //www.acsc.au.af.mil/News.htm.

Canada, Department of National Defence (DND). *Defence Development Plan 1993*. Ottawa: Queen's Printer, 1993.

– *1994 Defence White Paper*. Ottawa: Canada Communications Group, 1994.

– *Peacekeeping Operations*, Vol. III of *Operations: Land and Tactical Air*. Publication B-GL-301-003/FP-001. Sept. 1995.

Canadian Government. *Towards a Rapid Reaction Capability for the United Nations*. Ottawa: Government of Canada, Sept. 1995.

Carver, Michael. "Conventional Warfare in the Nuclear Age." In Peter Paret, ed., *Makers of Modern Strategy from Machiavelli to the Nuclear Age,* Princeton, NJ: Princeton University Press, 1986.

Chaliand, Gérard. *Anthologie mondiale de la stratégie*. Paris: Robert Laffont, 1990.

– *Stratégies de la guérilla*. Paris: Gallimard, 1984.

Chandler, David. *The Campaigns of Napoleon*. New York: Macmillan, 1966.

Chiaventone, Frederick J. "Ethics and Responsibility in Broadcasting." *Military Review* (Aug. 1991), 64–76.

Chou, Eric. *Mao Tse-tung: The Man and the Myth*. London: Cassell, 1982.

Clark, Alan. *The Donkeys*. London: Cassells, 1961.

Clausewitz, Carl von. *On War*. Trans. J.J. Graham, ed. F.N. Maude. London: Kegan, Paul, Trench and Trüber Co. Ltd., 1918.

– *On War*. Trans. and ed. Michael Howard and Peter Paret. Princeton, NJ: Princeton University Press, 1976.

– *On War*. Trans. and ed. Michael Howard and Peter Paret. New York: Alfred Knopf, 1993.

- "Principles of War." In *Roots of Strategy, Book 2*. Trans. Hans W. Gatzke. Harrisburg, Penn.: Stackpole Books, 1987.
Clifford, C.M. "A Viet Nam Reappraisal." In *Fifty Years of Foreign Affairs*, ed. ‡Hamilton Fish Armstrong, New York: Praeger Publishers, 1972.
Clutterbuck, Richard. *Conflict and Violence in Singapore and Malaysia, 1945–1983*. Boulder, Col.: Westview, 1985.
Cochran, Kimberly Ann. "Press Coverage of the Persian Gulf War: Historical Perspectives and Questions of Policy beyond the Shadow of Vietnam." MA thesis, U.S. Naval Postgraduate School, 1992.
Cohen, Eliot A., and Keaney, Thomas A. *Gulf War Air Power Survey Summary Report*. Washington, DC: Government Publishing Office, 1993.
- *Gulf War Air Power Survey Summary Report* and *White Paper: Air Force Performance in Desert Storm*. Quoted on *Frontline*, WGBH Educational Foundation, on internet at www.wgbh.org.
- *Gulf War Debriefing Book*. On internet at www.nd.edu/~aleyden/contents.html.
Coletta, Paolo E. *The American Naval Heritage*. 3rd ed. Lanham, Md.: University Press of America, 1987.
Combelles, Pascale M. "Operation *Just Cause*: A Military–Media Fiasco." *Military Review*, 75 (May–June 1995), 77–85.
Coox, Alvin D. "The Effectiveness of the Japanese Military Establishment in the Second World War." In *Military Effectiveness*, Vol. III. *The Second World War*, ed. A.R. Millett and Williamson Murray, Boston: Unwin Hyman, 1988.
- "Military Effectiveness of Armed Forces in the Interwar Period." In *Military Effectiveness*, Vol. II, *The Interwar Period*, ed. A.R. Millett and Williamson Murray, Boston: Unwin Hyman, 1988.
Corum, James S. *The Roots of Blitzkrieg: Hans von Seeckt and German Military Reform*. Lawrence, Kan.: University Press of Kansas, 1992.
Coumatos, Michael J., and Poulos, Dennis D. "U.S. Must Guarantee Free Access to Space." *Aviation Week and Space Technology*, 143 (18 Sept. 1995), 60–2.
Craig, Gordon A. *Germany 1866–1945*. New York: Oxford University Press, 1978.
Creveld, Martin van. *Command in War*. Cambridge, Mass.: Harvard University Press, 1985.
- *Fighting Power*. Westport, Conn.: Greenwood Press, 1982.
Curtis, Michael, ed. *The Great Political Theories*, Vol. II. New York: Avon Books: 1981.
Dagle, Dan. "The Mobile Riverine Force, Vietnam." *Proceedings*, 95 no. 791 (1969), 126–8.
Dancocks, Daniel. *Sir Arthur Currie: A Biography*. Toronto: Methuen, 1985.
Daniel, Donald C.F., and Hayes, Bradd C., eds. *Beyond Traditional Peacekeeping*. London: Macmillan Press Ltd., 1995.
Davidson, Phillip. *Secrets of the Vietnam War*. Novato, Calif.: Presidio, 1990.
- *Vietnam at War: The History 1946–1975*. New York: Oxford University Press, 1988.
De Bary, W. Theodore. *Sources of Chinese Tradition*. New York: Columbia University Press, 1964.

DeClerq, David G. *The Stockholm Concluding Document and Exercise Observations: An Examination of Confidence and Security Building Measures.* Ottawa: DND Directorate of Nuclear and Arms Control Policy, 1991.

Delbruck, Hans. *The Dawn of Modern Warfare.* Lincoln: University of Nebraska Press, 1985.

– *History of the Art of War.* Vol. IV. Trans. Walter J. Renfroe Jr. Lincoln: University of Nebraska Press, 1975.

Deutscher, Isaac. *The Prophet Armed.* London: Oxford University Press, 1954.

Dewar, G.A.B., and Boraston, J.H. *Sir Douglas Haig's Command.* London, 1922.

Dodd, Dan. "The Mobile Riverine Force." *Proceedings*, 95 no. 796 (June 1969), 80–95.

Donnelly, Christopher. *Red Banner.* Coulsden, Surrey: Jane's Information Group, 1988.

Douhet, Giulio. *The Command of the Air.* Trans. Dino Ferrari, ed. Richard Kohn and Joseph Harahan. USAF Warrior Studies. Washington, DC: Office of Air Force History, 1983.

Doyle, Michael W. "Liberal States and War." In Lawrence Freedman, ed., *War*, Oxford: Oxford University Press, 1994.

Duffy, Christopher. *Russia's Military Way to the West.* London: Routledge and Kegan Paul, 1981.

Dugan, Michael. "The Air War." *U.S. News and World Report*, 110 no. 5 (11 Feb. 1991), 24–31.

– "First Lessons of Victory." *U.S. News and World Report*, 110 no. 10 (18 March 1991), 32–6.

Dundonald, Earl of. *My Army Life.* London: E. Arnold, 1926.

Dunnigan, James F. *How to Make War.* New York: William Morrow and Company, 1982.

Dupuy, T.N. *A Genius for War: The German Army and General Staff, 1807–1945.* New York: Prentice Hall, 1977.

Dye, Thomas R. and Ziegler, L. Harmon. *The Irony of Democracy: An Uncommon Introduction to American Politics.* 3rd ed. North Scituate, Mass.: Duxbury Press, 1975.

Eccles, Henry E. *Military Power in a Free Society.* Newport, RI: Naval War College Press, 1979.

Eddy, K.T. "Canadian Forces and the Operational Level of War." *Canadian Defence Quarterly*, 21 no. 5 (April 1992), 18–24.

Edwards, Paul N. "A History of Computers and Weapons Systems." In David Bellin and Gary Chapman, eds., *Computers in Battle*, Orlando, Fla.: Harcourt, Brace, Jovanovich, 1987.

Eisenhower, Dwight D. *Crusade in Europe.* Garden City, NY: Doubleday, 1948.

Ellis, John. *Brute Force.* London: Andre Deutsch Limited, 1990.

English, J.A. *The Canadian Army and the Normandy Campaign.* Westport, Conn.: Praeger, 1991.

– "Great War 1914–18: The 'Riddle of the Trenches'." *Canadian Defence Quarterly*, 15 no. 2 (autumn 1985), 44–7.

– *Marching through Chaos.* Westport, Conn.: Praeger, 1996.

– *On Infantry.* New York: Praeger, 1984.

Epstein, Robert. "Patterns of Change and Continuity in Nineteenth-Century War-fare." *Journal of Military History*, 56 no. 3 (July 1992), 375–88.

Fairfax, Denis. *Navy in Vietnam: A Record of the Royal Australian Navy in the Viet-nam War, 1965–1972*. Canberra: Australian Government Printing Office, 1980.

Fabyanic, Thomas A., "War, Doctrine, and the Air War College: Some Relationships and Implications for the U.S. Air Force." Reprinted in *Forces and Capabilities, Book One*, Air War College, Maxwell AFB, Alabama: Air University Press, Sept. 1990.

Fall, Bernard. *Street without Joy: Insurgency in Indochina, 1946–1963*. Harrisburg, Penn.: Stackpole Company, 1963.

– *The Two Viet-Nams: A Political and Military Analysis*. New York: Frederick A. Praeger Publishers, 1967.

Fitzsimons, B., ed. *Weapons and Warfare*. 24 vols. New York: Columbia House, 1978.

Flenley, Ralph. *Modern German History*. New York: E.P. Dutton & Co. Inc., 1964.

Fogleman, Ronald. "Air and Space Power in the 21st Century." Speech delivered 6 April 1995. On internet at *The Knowledge Warrior News Center*, http://www.acsc.au.af.mil/News.htm.

Ford, Daniel. *The Button*. New York: Simon and Schuster, 1985.

Forestier, A.M. "Into the Fourth Dimension." Royal Australian Air Force, Air Power Studies Centre, Fellowship Paper No. FP32, 1992.

Freedman, Lawrence, ed. *War*. Oxford: Oxford University Press, 1994.

French, David. *The British Way in Warfare, 1688–2000*. London: Unwin Hyman, 1990.

– "The Meaning of Attrition, 1914–1916." *English Historical Review*, 103 no. 407 (April 1988), 385–405.

Fuller, J.F.C. *The Conduct of War 1789–1961*. London: Eyre and Spottiswoode, 1961.

– *The Decisive Battles of the Western World*, Vol. III. London: Eyre Spottiswoode, 1963.

Fulton, William B. *Vietnam Studies: Riverine Operations, 1966–1969*. Washington, DC: U.S. Government Printing Office, 1973.

Funnell, Air Marshal R.G. *Royal Australian Air Force Air Power Manual*. Canberra: Australian Department of Defence, 1990.

Galvin, John. "Uncomfortable Wars: Towards a New Paradigm." In Max Manwaring, ed., *Uncomfortable Wars: Towards a New Paradigm of Low Intensity Conflict*, San Francisco, Calif.: Westview Press, 1991.

Gareev, M.A. *M.V. Frunze: Military Theorist*. London: Pergammon-Brassey's, 1988.

General Staff, War Office (United Kingdom). *Field Service Pocket Book, 1916*. London: Harrison and Sons under the authority of HMSO, 1916.

George, Alexander. *The Chinese Communist Army in Action*. New York: Columbia University Press, 1967.

Geyer, Michael. "German Strategy in the Age of Machine Warfare 1914–1945." In Peter Paret, ed., *Makers of Modern Strategy*, Princeton, NJ: Princeton University Press, 1986.

Giang, Nguyên Ken. *Les grandes dates du parti de la classe ouvrière du Viet-Nam*. Hanoi: Foreign Languages Publishing House, 1960.

Giap, Vo Nguyen. *Banner of People's War, the Party's Military Line*. New York: Praeger, 1970.

– *Big Victory, Great Task*. New York: Frederick A. Praeger Publishers, 1968.

– *The Military Art of the People's War*. New York: Monthly Review Press, 1970.

– "The Party's Military Line Is the Ever-Victorious Banner of People's War in Our Country." In *Document No. 70: Viet Nam Documents and Research Notes*. Saigon: American Embassy, 1969.

– *People's War, People's Army: The Viet Cong Insurrection Manual for Underdeveloped Countries*. New York: Praeger, 1962.

Gibson, James William. *The Perfect War: Technowar in Vietnam*. New York: Atlantic Monthly Press, 1986.

Girling, J.L.S. *People's War: The Conditions and the Consequences in China and in South-East Asia*. London: George Allen & Unwin, 1969.

Glantz, David. *August Storm: The Soviet Strategic Offensive in Manchuria*. Fort Leavenworth, Kan.: Combat Studies Institute, 1983.

– *The Soviet Airborne Experience*. Fort Leavenworth, Kan.: Combat Studies Institute, 1983.

– "Soviet Operational Formation for Battle: A Perspective." *Military Review*, 63 (Feb. 1983), 2–12.

Glantz, David, and House, Jonathan. *When Titans Clashed*. Lawrence: University Press of Kansas, 1995.

Goerlitz, W. *The German General Staff*. New York: Frederick Praeger, 1965.

Goldman, Nathan. "Transition of Confusion in the Law of Outer Space." In Daniel Papp and John McIntyre, eds., *International Space Policy*, New York: Quorum Books, 1987.

Goochman, Charles S., and Maoz, Zeev. "Militarized Interstate Disputes, 1816–1976: Procedures, Patterns and Insights." *Journal of Conflict Resolution*, 28 (Dec. 1984), 585–616.

Goodman, Glen W. "The Power of Information." *Armed Forces Journal International*, 132 (July 1995), 24.

Gourley, Scott R. "GPS: The Ultimate Dual-Use Technology?" *Defense Electronics*, 27 (Aug. 1995), 16–20.

Graham, Dominick. "Stress Lines and Gray Areas: The Utility of the Historical Method to the Military Profession." In David Charters et al. eds., *Military History and the Military Profession*, Westport, Conn.: Praeger, 1992.

Granatstein, J.L. *The Generals: The Canadian Army's Senior Commanders in the Second World War*. Toronto: Stoddart, 1993.

Gray, Colin S. *American Military Space Policy*. Cambridge, Mass.: Abt Books, 1982.

– *War, Peace and Victory*. New York: Simon & Schuster, 1990.

Greenhous, Ben, et al. *The Cruciible of War*, Vol. III of *Official History of the Royal Canadian Air Force*. Toronto: University of Toronto Press, 1994.

Guderian, Heinz. *Panzer Leader*. Ed. Basil Liddell Hart, trans. Constantine Fitzgibbon. New York: Ballantine Books, 1967.

Gulf War Debriefing Book. On the internet at www.nd.edu/~aleyden/contentents.html.

Gurr, Ted Robert. *Polity II: Political Structures and Regime Change, 1800–1986*. Inter-University Consortium for Political and Social Research No. 9263, 1990.

Halloran, Richard. "Soldiers and Scribblers: Working with the Media." *Parameters*, 25 (summer 1995), 151–60.

Hammond, Grant. "The Militarization of Space." In Daniel Papp and John McIntyre, eds., *International Space Policy*, New York: Quorum Books, 1987.

Hammond, William M. *Public Affairs*. Washington, DC: Center of Military History United States Army, 1988.

Harris, Stephen. "The Canadian General Staff and the Higher Organization of Defence, 1919–1939." In B.D. Hunt and R.G. Haycock, eds., *Canada's Defence: Perspectives on Policy in Twentieth Century*, Toronto: Copp Clark Pitman Ltd, 1993.

Hartmann, Frederick H., and Wendzel, Robert L. *Defending America's Security*. New York: Pergamon-Brassey's, 1988.

Hartmann, G. K., and Truver, S.C. *Weapons That Wait*. Annapolis, Md.: Naval Institute Press, 1991.

Hartung, William D. *And Weapons for All*. New York: HarperCollins, 1994.

Hassig, Lee, ed. *Understanding Computers – The Military Frontier*. Alexandria, Va.: Time-Life Books, 1991.

Hayward, Daniel. *The Air Defence Initiative*. Ottawa: Canadian Centre for Arms Control and Disarmament, 1988.

Henderson, William Darryl. *Why the Vietcong Fought: A Study of Motivation and Control in a Modern Army in Combat*. Westport, Conn.: Greenwood Press, 1979.

Herken, G. *Counsels of War*. New York: Oxford University Press, 1987.

Herzog, Chaim. *The Arab–Israeli Wars*. London: Arms and Armour Press, 1982.

Hirschfeld, Thomas J. *Intelligence and Arms Control: A Marriage of Convenience*. Austin: University of Texas, 1987.

Hoffman, Fred. "Review of the Panama Pool Deployment: December 1989." *Pentagon Rules on Media Access to the Persian Gulf War*. Washington, DC: U.S. Government Printing Office, 20 Feb. 1991.

Holborn, Hajo. "The Prusso-German School: Moltke and the Rise of the General Staff." In Peter Paret, ed., *Makers of Modern Strategy: From Machiavelli to the Nuclear Age*, Princeton, NJ: Princeton University Press, 1986.

Holsti, Kalevi J. *Peace and War: Armed Conflicts ad International Order 1648–1989*. Cambridge: Cambridge University Press, 1991.

Hooper, Edwin Bickford, et al. *The United States Navy and the Vietnam Conflict*. Vol. I. Washington: U.S. Government Printing Office, 1976.

Huntington, Samuel P. *The Soldier and the State*. Cambridge, Mass.: Harvard University Press, 1957.

Jablonsky, David. *The Owl of Minerva Flies at Twilight: Doctrinal Change and Continuity and the Revolution in Military Affairs*. Professional Reading in Military Strategy, No. 10, Strategic Studies Institute, U.S. Army War College, May 1994.

Jelly, Doris H. *Canada: Twenty-five Years in Space*. Montreal: Polyscience Publications, 1988.

Jockel, Joseph T. *Canada and International Peacekeeping*. Toronto: Canadian Institute of Strategic Studies, 1994.

Jones, Archer. *The Art of War in the Western World*. New York: Oxford University Press, 1987.

Jones, J. *Stealth Technology*. Blue Ridge Summit, Penn.: Tab Books Inc., 1989.

Jones, R.V. *Most Secret War*. London: Hodder and Stoughton, 1978.

Joseph, Paul, and Gladstone, Hayes. "The Strategic and Theatre Nuclear Balance." In Paul Joseph and Simon Rosenblum, eds., *Search for Sanity*, Boston: South End Press, 1984.

Kahn, H. *Thinking about the Unthinkable*. New York: Discus Books, 1962.

Kaldor, Mary. *The Baroque Arsenal*. London: Sphere Books Ltd., 1983.

Kaplan, F. *The Wizards of Armageddon*. New York: Simon & Schuster, 1983.

Karnow, Stanley. *Vietnam: A History*. New York: Penguin Books, 1984.

Karsh, Efraim. "The Causes of War." In Lawrence Freedman, ed., *War*, Oxford: Oxford University Press, 1994.

Keegan, John. *The Battle for History*. Toronto: Vintage Books, 1995.

– *A History of Warfare*. New York: Alfred A. Knopf, 1993.

Knightly, Phillip. *The First Casualty*. New York: Harcourt Brace Jovanovich, 1975.

Kolkowicz, Roman. *The Soviet Military and the Communist Party*. Princeton, NJ: Princeton University Press, 1967.

Kooistria, S.G. "The Six Rules of Soldiering." *Canadian Army Infantry Journal*, 22 (summer 1992), 10–20.

Kopp, Carlo. "A Doctrine for the Use of Electromagnetic Pulse Bombs." Royal Australian Air Force, Air Power Studies Centre, Paper No. 15, July 1993.

Koulik, Sergey, and Kokoski, Richard. *Verification of the CFE Treaty*. Stockholm: Stockholm International Peace Research Institute, 1991.

Krause, Keith, and Mutimer, David. "The Proliferation of Conventional Weapons: New Challenges for Control and Verification." In David Mutimer, ed., *Control But Verify: Verification and the New Non-Proliferation Agenda*, Toronto: York Centre for International and Strategic Studies, 1994.

Lambert, Andrew D. *The Crimean War: British Grand Strategy, 1853–56*. Manchester: Manchester University Press, 1990.

Laqueur, Walter. "The Character of Guerrilla Warfare." In Lawrence Freedman, ed., *War*, New York: Oxford University Press, 1994.

Layne, Christopher. "Kant or Cant." *International Security*, 19 no. 2 (fall 1994), 5–49.

Layton, Peter B. "Waging Tomorrow's Wars." Royal Australian Air Force, Air Power Studies Centre, Paper No. 32, May 1995.

Lehman, John F., Jr. *Command of the Seas*. New York: Macmillan Publishing Company, 1988.

Leonhard, Robert. *The Art of Maneuver*. Novato, Calif.: Presidio Press, 1991.

Liddell Hart, B.H. *The British Way in Warfare*. London: Faber and Faber, 1932.

– *The Other Side of the Hill*. London: Pan Books, 1978.

– *Why Don't We Learn from History?* New York: Hawthorn Books, 1971.

Lloyd, Clem. "The Case for the Media." In Peter R. Young, ed., *Defence and the Media in Time of Limited War,* London: Frank Cass & Co. Ltd., 1992.

Luttwak, Edward N. *Strategy: The Logic of War and Peace.* Cambridge, Mass.: Harvard University Press, 1987.

McAllister, John T., and Mus, Paul. *The Vietnamese and Their Revolution.* New York: Harper & Row, 1970.

McCaffrey, Barry R. "Human Rights and the Commander." *Joint Force Quarterly,* 9 (autumn 1995), 10–13.

McElwee, William. *The Art of War: Waterloo to Mons.* Bloomington: Indiana University Press, 1974.

MacIntosh, James. "International Verification Organizations: The Case of Conventional Arms Control." In Ellis Morris, ed., *International Verification Organizations,* Toronto: York Centre for International and Strategic Studies, 1991.

McIntyre, D.E. *Canada at Vimy.* Toronto: Peter Martin Associates Ltd, 1967.

MacIsaac, David. "Voices from the Central Blue: The Air Power Theorists." In Peter Paret, ed., *Makers of Modern Strategy,* Princeton, NJ: Princeton University Press, 1986.

Mackintosh, J. Malcolm. "The Development of Soviet Military Doctrine since 1918." In Michael Howard, ed., *The Theory and Practice of War,* New York: Praeger, 1966.

– *Juggernaut.* New York: MacMillan, 1967.

– "The Red Army 1920–1936." In Basil Liddell Hart, ed., *The Red Army,* New York: Harcourt, Brace and Company, 1956.

Macksey, Kenneth. *Guderian: Creator of the Blitzkrieg.* New York: Stein and Day, 1978.

– *The Shadow of Vimy Ridge.* Toronto: Ryerson, 1965.

Maclear, Michael. *The Ten Thousand Day War: Vietnam, 1945–1975.* New York: St Martin's Press, 1981.

McNamara, R.S. *The Essence of Security.* New York: Harper and Row, 1968.

Macphail, Andrew. *The Medical Services: Official History of the Canadian Forces in the Great War 1914–19.* Ottawa: King's Printer, 1925.

Mansfield, Edward D., and Snyder, Jack. "Democratization and the Danger of War." *International Security,* 20 no. 1 (summer 1995), 5–38.

Manstein, Field Marshal Erich von. *Lost Victories.* London: Methuen and Company, 1958.

Mao Tse-tung. "On Protracted War." In Jay Mallin, ed., *Strategy for Conquest: Communist Documents on Guerilla Warfare,* Coral Gables, Fla.: University of Miami Press, 1970.

Mao Zedong. *Chairman Mao Tse-tung on People's War.* Peking: Foreign Languages Press, 1967.

– *On Guerrilla Warfare.* Trans. Samuel B. Griffith II. New York: Anchor Press, 1978.

– *Quotations from Chairman Mao Tse-tung.* New York: Bantam, 1967.

Marsh, Alton K., et al. *Stealth and Future Military Aircraft.* Arlington, Va.: Pasha Publications, 1988.

Marteinson, John, et al. *We Stand on Guard: An Illustrated History of the Canadian Army.* Montreal: Ovale Publications, 1992.

Marx, Karl, and Engels, Frederick. *Selected Correspondence, 1846–1895.* London: International Publishers, 1935.

Meilinger, Phillips. "Ten Proposition Regarding Airpower." On internet at www.cd sar.af.mil/cc.html.

Messerschmidt, Manfred. "German Military Effectiveness between 1919 and 1939." In Allan R. Millett and Williamson Murray, eds., *Military Effectiveness*, Vol. II, *The Interwar Period*, London: Allen & Unwin, 1988.

Metcalf, Vice-Admiral J., III. "The Press and Grenada, 1983." In Peter Young, ed., *Defence and the Media in Time of Limited War*, London: Frank Cass, 1992.

Metz, Steven. *Counterinsurgency: Strategy and the Phoenix of American Capability.* Carlisle Barracks, Penn.: U.S. Army War College, 1995.

– "Insurgency after the Cold War." *Small Wars and Insurgencies*, 5 (spring 1994), 63–82.

Middlebrook, Martin. *The First Day of the Somme.* London: Penguin Press, 1971.

Millett, A.R., et al. "The Effectiveness of Military Organizations." In A.R. Millett and Williamson Murray, eds., *Military Effectiveness*, Vol. I, *The First World War*, Boston: Unwin Hyman, 1988.

Milsom, John. *AFV Weapons Profile 37: Russian BT Series.* Windsor: Profile, 1972.

Miranda, Joseph. "The Franco Prussian War." *Strategy and Tactics*, 149 (Feb. 1992), 5–18.

Moise, Edwin E. *Modern China: A History.* London: Longman, 1986.

Moltke, Helmuth von. *Essays, Speeches, and Memoirs of Field Marshal Count Helmuth von Moltke*, Vol. I. London: Harper & Brothers, 1893.

Moore, John Norton. "Government Structures: A New Paradigm in War Avoidance and International Relations." In *Globalism and Regionalism: Options for the 21st Century.* Proceedings of the 1995 Conference of the Canadian Council on International Law, 36–41.

Moorman, Thomas S. "Space: A New Strategic Frontier." *Airpower Journal*, 6 (spring 1992), 14–23.

Morgan, Sir Frederick. *Peace and War.* London: Hodder and Stoughton, 1961.

Morton, Desmond. *When Your Number's Up: The Canadian Soldier in the First World War.* Toronto: Random House, 1993.

Mott, Frank Luther. *American Journalism.* New York: Macmillan Company, 1962.

Mumford, Robert E., Jr. "Jackstay: New Dimensions in Amphibious Warfare." In Frank Uhlig, Jr., ed., *Vietnam: The Naval Story*, Annapolis, Md.: Naval Institute Press, 1986.

Myers, Kenneth A., and Tockston, John G. "Real Tenets of Military Space Doctrine." *Airpower Journal*, 2 (winter 1988), 54–68.

Naveh, Shion. "Tukhachevsky." In Harold Shukman, ed., *Stalin's Generals*, New York: Grove Press, 1993.

Neuman, Sigmund, and von Hagen, Mark. "Engels and Marx on Revolution, War, and the Army in Society." In Peter Paret, ed., *Makers of Modern Strategy from Machiavelli to the Nuclear Age*, Princeton, NJ: Princeton University Press, 1986.

Nicholson, G.W.L. *Official History of the Canadian Army in the First World War: Canadian Expeditionary Force 1914–1919*. Ottawa: Queen's Printer, 1962.

Noyes, Harry F. "Like It or Not, the Armed Forces Need the Media." *Army*, 42 (June 1992), 30–8.

O'Ballance, Edgar. *The Indo-China War 1945–1954: A Study in Guerilla Warfare*. London: Faber and Faber, 1964.

O'Connell, Robert L. *Of Arms and Men: A History of War, Weapons, and Aggression*. New York: Oxford University Press, 1989.

Ondreka, Ronald J. "Imaging Technologies." In Kosta Tsipis et al., eds., *Arms Control Verification: The Technologies That Make It Possible*, Oxford: Permagon-Brassey's International Defence Publishers, 1986.

O'Neill, Robert J. "Doctrine and Training in the German Army, 1919–1939." In Michael Howard, ed., *The Theory and Practice of War*, London: Cassell, 1965.

– *General Giap: Politician and Strategist*. Sydney: Cassell Australia Ltd., 1969.

Osgood, R.E. *Limited War Revisited*. Boulder, Col.: Westview Press, 1979.

Pakenham, Thomas. *The Boer War*. London: Futura Publications, 1982.

Palmer, David. *Summons of the Trumpet: U.S.–Vietnam in Perspective*. Novato, Calif.: Presidio Press, 1978.

Paret, Peter. "Clausewitz." In Peter Paret, ed., *Makers of Modern Strategy: From Machiavelli to the Nuclear Age*. Princeton, NJ: Princeton University Press, 1986.

– *Clausewitz and the State*. New York: Oxford Univ. Press: 1976.

– *French Revolutionary Warfare from Indochina to Algeria: The Analysis of a Political and Military Doctrine*. New York: Praeger, 1964.

Paret, Peter, and Shy, John W. *Guerrillas in the 1960's*. New York: Frederick A. Praeger Publishers, 1962.

Pearton, Maurice. *Diplomacy, War and Technology since 1830*. Lawrence: University Press of Kansas, 1984.

Perrow, C. *Normal Accidents*. New York: Basic Books Inc., 1984.

Potter, William C. *Verification and Arms Control*. Lexington, Conn.: D.C. Heath and Co/Lexington Books, 1985.

Power, John W. "Space Control in the Post–Cold War Era." *Airpower Journal*, 4 (winter 1990), 24–33.

Preston, R.A., Wise, S.F., and Werner, H.O. *Men in Arms*. London: Atlantic Press, 1956.

"Radical Sukhoi Design to Fly This Year, Says Russia." *Jane's Defence Weekly*, 8 no. 1 (Jan. 1997), 3.

Rawling, Bill. *Surviving Trench Warfare: Technology and the Canadian Corps 1914–1918*. Toronto: University of Toronto Press, 1992.

Reynolds, Clark G. *Command of the Sea*, Vol. II. Malabar: Robert E. Kreiger Publishing Company, 1983.

Rhodes, R. *The Making of the Atomic Bomb*. New York: Simon & Schuster, 1988.

Rich, Ben. *Skunk Works*. Extract from internet http://pathfinder.com@@vOGLQgUA HNz*qSN/twep/Little_Brown/Skunk_Works/Skunk1.

Richardson, Doug. *Stealth*. New York: Orion Books, 1989.

Rogers, H.C.B. *Weapons of the British Soldier*. London: Seeley Service & Co. Ltd, 1960.

Rome Laboratory. *Advanced Technology Data Sheet: Electronic Support Measurement – Bistatic Sensor Technology*. Griffiss AFB, NY: Department of the Air Force Rome Laboratory, Technology Transfer Office, 1996.

Roper, John. "A Wider Range of Tasks." In Roper, John et al., eds., *Keeping the Peace in the Post–Cold War Era: Strengthening Multilateral Peacekeeping*. New York: Trilateral Commission, 1993.

Rothenberg, Gunther. "Moltke, Schlieffen, and the Doctrine of Strategic Envelopment." In Peter Paret, ed., *Makers of Modern Strategy: From Machiavelli to the Nuclear Age*, Princeton, NJ: Princeton University Press, 1986.

Roy, Reginald. *Journal of Private Fraser, 1914–1919, The Canadian Expeditionary Force*. Victoria, BC: Sono Nis Press, 1985.

Rummel, Rudolph J. *Death by Government*. New Brunswick, NJ: Transaction Publishers, 1995.

– *Understanding Conflict and War*, Vol. IV, *War, Power, Peace*. Beverly Hills, Calif.: Sage Publications, 1979.

– *Understanding Conflict and War*, Vol. V, *The JustPeace*. Beverly Hills, Calif.: Sage Publications, 1981.

Russett, Bruce. *Grasping the Democratic Peace: Principles for a Post–Cold War World*. Princeton, NJ: Princeton University Press, 1993.

Russett, Bruce M., ed. *Peace, War and Numbers*. Beverly Hills, Calif.: Sage Publications, 1972.

Salisbury, Harrison E. *China: 100 Years of Revolution*. New York: Holt, Rinehart & Winston, 1983.

– *The Long March: The Untold Story*. New York: Harper & Row, 1985.

– *The New Emperors: China in the Era of Mao and Deng*. New York: Avon Books, 1992.

Samisch, Mark Hillel. "Comparison of the Media Coverage of the Vietnam War to the Media Coverage of the Invasions of Grenada and Panama: A Question of Legacies." MA thesis, University of Maryland, 1991.

Sassoon, Siegfried. *Counter-Attack and Other Poems*. London: Heinemann, 1918.

Savkin, V.Y. *The Basic Principles of Operational Art and Tactics*. Washington, DC: U.S. Government Printing Office, n.d.

Schreadley, R.L. "The Naval War in Vietnam, 1950–1970." *Proceedings*, 97 no. 819 (1971), 180–209.

Schreiber, Shane. "The Orchestra of Victory: Canadian Corps Operations in the Battles of the Hundred Days 8 August–11 November 1918." MA thesis, Royal Military College, Kingston, Ont., 1995.

Schurman, D.M. *Commentary on War Course – Notes on Strategy (The Green Pamphlet)*. Kingston, Ont.: Queen's University, 11 April 1980.

Scott, Harriet Fast, and Scott, William F. *The Soviet Art of War*. Boulder, Col.: Westview Press, 1982.

– *Soviet Military Doctrine*. Boulder, Col.: Westview Press, 1988.

Searle, W.F., Jr. "The Case for Inshore Warfare." In Frank Uhlig, Jr., ed., *Naval Review 1966*, Annapolis, Md.: United States Naval Institute, 1967, 2–23.

Seaton, Albert. *The Crimean War*. New York: St Martin's Press, 1977.

– *The German Army 1933–1945*. New York: St Martin's Press, 1982.

Seeckt, General Hans von. *Thoughts of a Soldier*. London: Ernest Benn, 1930.

Senger, General Frido und Etterlin von. *Neither Fear Nor Hope*. London: Greenhill Books, 1989.

Sharp, U.S.G. "Report on Air and Naval Campaigns against North Vietnam and Pacific Command-Wide Support of the War June 1964–July 1968." In *Report of the War in Vietnam* (As of 30 June 1968), i–68. Washington, DC: U.S. Government Printing Office, 1968.

Sheehan, N. *A Bright Shining Lie*. New York: Random House, 1988.

Shel, Tamir. "Stealth Aircraft Come of Age." *Defence Update*, no. 94 (March 1989), 23–37.

Shy, John, and Collier, Thomas. "Revolutionary War." In Peter Paret, ed., *Makers of Modern Strategy from Machiavelli to the Nuclear Age*, Princeton, NJ: Princeton University Press, 1986.

Sidle, Winant. "A Battle behind the Scenes: The Gulf War Reheats Military–Media Controversy." *Military Review*, 71 (Sept. 1991), 52–63.

Simpkin, Richard. *Deep Battle*. London: Brassey's, 1987.

– *Race to the Swift: Thoughts on Twenty-first Century Warfare*. London: Brassey's Defence Publications, 1985.

Singer, J. David, and Small, Melvin. *The Wages of War, 1816–1965: A Statistical Handbook*. New York: John Wiley & Sons, 1972.

Skolnik, Merrill, ed. *Radar Handbook*. Toronto: McGraw-Hill Publishing Company, 1990.

Small, Melvin, and Singer, J. David. *International War: An Anthology*. 2nd ed. Pacific Grove, Calif.: Brooks/Cole Publishing Company, 1989.

– *Resort to Arms: International and Civil Wars 1816–1980*. Beverly Hills, Calif.: Sage Publications, 1982.

Smith, Bruce A. "Milstar Balancing Cost, Mission Needs." *Aviation Week and Space Technology*, 143 (18 Sept. 1995), 50–1.

Spacecast 2020, Vol. 1. Maxwell AFB, Ala.: Air University Press, 1994.

Spires, David N. *Image and Reality: The Making of the German Officer, 1921–1933*. Westport, Conn.: Greenwood Press, 1984.

Spiro, David E. "The Insignificance of the Liberal Peace." *International Security*, 19 no. 2 (fall 1994), 50–86.

Stacey, C.P. *Canada and the Age of Conflict: A History of Canadian External Policies*, Vol. 1, *1867–1921*. Toronto: Macmillan, 1977.

– "The Staff Officer: A Footnote to Canadian Military History." *Canadian Defence Quarterly*, 3 no. 3 (winter 1973–74), 43–55.

Steadman, Stephen John. "UN Intervention in Civil Wars: Imperatives of Choice and Strategy." In Donald Daniel and Bradd Hayes, eds., *Beyond Traditional Peacekeeping*, London: Macmillan Press, 1995.

"Stealth, What Is It Really?" *Airman*, 35 no. 9 (Sept. 1991), 22–4.

Stephens, Alan. "The Transformation of 'Low Intensity' Conflict." *Small Wars and Insurgencies*, 5 (spring 1994), 141–61.

Strachan, Hew. *European Armies and the Conduct of War*. London: George Allen and Unwin, 1983.

Sully, François. *Age of the Guerrilla: The New Warfare*. New York: Parents' Magazine Press, 1968.

Summers, Harry G., Jr. *On Strategy: The Vietnam War in Context*. Carlisle Barracks, Penn.: Strategic Studies Institute, u.s. Army War College, April 1981.

Sun-Tzu. *The Art of War*. Trans. Ralph D. Sawyer. New York: Barnes & Noble Books, 1994.

Sun Zi. *The Art of War*. Ed. James Clavell. New York: Dell, 1983.

Swarztrauber, A.S. "River Patrol Relearned." *Proceedings*, 96 no. 5/806 (May 1970), 120–57.

Sweetman, Bill. "The Future of Airborne Stealth." *International Defense Review*, 27 (March 1994), 30–7.

– *Lockheed F-117A*. Osceola, Wisc.: Motorbooks International, 1990.

– "Wobbly Goblin: Not Perfect But First." *Interavia*, 44 no. 1 (1989), 28–30.

Swettenham, John. *To Seize the Victory: The Canadian Corps in World War I*. Toronto: Ryerson Press, 1965.

Tanham, George. *Communist Revolutionary Warfare: The Vietminh in Indochina*. New York: Praeger, 1961.

Thayer, Thomas C. "Patterns of the French and American Experience in Vietnam." In W. Scott Thompson and Donaldson D. Frizzell, eds., *The Lessons of Vietnam*, New York: Crane, Russak & Company, 1977.

Tilly, Charles. "Reflections on the History of European State-Making." In Charles Tilly, ed., *The Formation of National States in Western Europe*, Princeton, NJ: Princeton University Press, 1975.

Trainor, Bernard E. "The Military and the Media: A Troubled Embrace." *Parameters: Journal of the U.S. Army War College*, 20 (Dec. 1990), 2–11.

Travers, T.H.E. *How the War Was Won: Command and Technology in the British Army on the Western Front, 1917–1918*. London: Routledge, 1992.

Truong, Chinh. *Primer for Revolt: The Communist Takeover in Viet-nam*. New York: Praeger, 1963.

Tuchman, Barbara. *The Guns of August*. New York: Macmillan Company, 1962.

"Under the Skies of AAI's new MTS II Moving Target Simulator, Defending Gunners See, Hear, and Feel a Real Battle." AAI Corporation advertisement. *Armed Forces Journal International*, 127 (Oct. 1989), 84–5.

United States Army. "German Defense Tactics against Russian Breakthroughs." Washington, DC: U.S. Government Printing Office, 1951.

– *Military Operations in Low Intensity Conflicts*. FM 100–20 AF Pam. 3–20. Dec. 1990.

United States Department of the Air Force. *Legal Principles Relevant to Military Activities in Outer Space*. Office of the General Counsel, Feb. 1992.

U.S. Department of the Navy. *Naval Doctrine Publication 1: Naval Warfare (NDP-1)*. Washington, DC, 28 March 1994.

United States Marine Corps. *Small Wars Manual*. Washington, DC: U.S. Government Printing Office, 1940.

"The USAF Case for the B-2."*Air Clues*, 44 no. 10 (Oct. 1990), 364–9.

Van Loon, Richard J., and Whittington, Michael S. *The Canadian Political System: Environment Structure and Process*. 2nd ed. Toronto: McGraw-Hill Ryerson Limited, 1976.

Wallach, Jehuda L. *The Dogma of the Battle of Annihilation*. Westport, Conn.: Greenwood Press, 1986.

Waltz, Kenneth N. *Man, State and War: A Theoretical Analysis*. New York: Columbia University Press, 1954.

Webster, Charles, and Frankland, Noble. *The Strategic Air Offensive against Germany, 1939–45*. Vol. III. London: HMSO, 1961.

Weigley, Russell. *The Age of Battles*. Bloomington: Indiana University Press, 1991.

Wells, W.C. "The Riverine Force in Action, 1966–1967." In Frank Uhlig, Jr., ed., *Vietnam: The Naval Story*, Annapolis, Md.: Naval Institute Press, 1986.

West, N. *The SIGINT Secrets*. New York: William Morrow, 1988.

Westmoreland, General W.C. "Report on Operations in South Vietnam January 1964–June 1968." In *Report of the War in Vietnam* (As of 30 June 1968), 69–347. Washington, DC: U.S. Government Printing Office, 1968.

White, B.T. *Tanks and Other Armoured Fighting Vehicles of World War II*. New York: Exeter Books, 1983.

Williams, Jeffery. *Byng of Vimy: General and Governor General*. Toronto: University of Toronto Press, 1992.

Windall, Sheila. "Cooperation: Commercial Space and the United States Air Force." Remarks delivered 6 April 1995. On internet at *The Knowledge Warrior News Center*, http://www.acsc.au.af.mil/News.htm.

Winter, Denis. *Haig's Command: A Reassessment*. London: Viking, 1991.

Wirtz, James J. *The Tet Offensive: Intelligence Failure in War*. Ithaca, NY: Cornell University Press, 1991.

Worden, Simon P., and Jackson, Bruce P. "Space, Power and Strategy." *National Interest* (fall 1988).

Wright, Quincy. "A Study of War." In Lawrence Freedman, ed., *War*, New York: Oxford University Press, 1994.

Wyatt, S. "Into the Loop: A Canadian General Staff Corps." *Infantry Journal*, 29 (winter 1995), 17–21.

Ziemke, Earl. "Annihilation, Attrition and the Short War." *Parameters*, 12 no. 1 (March 1982), 23–31.

– "Strategy for Class War." In Williamson Murray, ed., *The Making of Strategy*, New York: Cambridge University Press, 1994.

Contributors

CAPTAIN NEAL ATTFIELD is a recent graduate of the War Studies program at the Royal Military College of Canada (RMC) and served as the War Studies senior during the 1995–96 academic year. His studies have focused on the changing nature of conflict within the modern nation-state. His service as an infantry officer with the Canadian Forces Reserve has included duty with the United Nations in the former Yugoslavia and command of an infantry company with the Princess of Wales' Own Regiment in Kingston, Ont. He is currently employed as a consultant at Coopers and Lybrand in Ottawa.

MERVYN BERRIDGE-SILLS was born and educated in England. He served with the British army as a territorial and as a regular, in the Royal Greenjackets and the Intelligence Corps. He came to Canada in 1972 and was a member of the Canadian Grenadier Guards until 1976. He is a computer consultant with SHL Systemhouse Limited, has been working on the Canadian Forces Supply System Upgrade project for the past four years, and is now employed on the Year 2000 project team.

LIEUTENANT-COLONEL RONALD BLANK entered the Canadian Forces in 1976 as an air weapons controller and later graduated from the University of Manitoba with a bachelor's degree in history. He has held a variety of operational, training, and staff appointments in Canada and the United States. His professional development has included studies at the Canadian Forces Command and Staff College. He is currently involved in the formulation of aerospace surveillance and command and control requirements at National Defence Headquarters (NDHQ) in Ottawa. He received an MA from RMC War Studies in 1997.

CAPTAIN EDWARD C. DENBEIGH joined the Canadian Forces in 1977 and has worked in intelligence-related positions in both the Security and Intelligence branches since 1979. He has served in a variety of staff and line positions over his career, including duty in NATO, NORAD, and NDHQ, Ottawa. From October 1990 to April 1991, during the Persian Gulf conflict, he was second-in-command of the Intelligence Section at the Canadian theatre headquarters in Al-Manama, Bahrain. From 1993 to 1996 he was a strategic analyst in the Arms Control Section within the Director General Intelligence staff at NDHQ, Ottawa. Currently, he is the J2 Operations coordinator within the Director General Intelligence staff. He holds an undergraduate degree in geography and political science from the University of Manitoba and received an MA from the RMC War Studies program in 1997.

ALLAN D. ENGLISH, the editor of this book, teaches in the War Studies and Continuing Education programs at RMC. His book *The Cream of the Crop: Canadian Aircrew 1939–45* is published by McGill-Queen's University Press.

LIEUTENANT-COLONEL J.R.D. GERVAIS is a career military engineering officer in the Canadian Forces. He enrolled in August 1973 and studied at the Collège militaire royal de Saint-Jean in Quebec and then at RMC, where he graduated with a bachelor's degree in civil engineering. He has served in various command and staff positions in combat engineering units and in facilities management both in Canada and abroad. Other posts have included UN tours to Cyprus and to Central America, NATO Headquarters in Brussels, and staff appointments at NDHQ, Ottawa. He attended senior staff college at the Collège interarmées de Défense in Paris. He has an MA in international relations from Boston University and is studying part time towards an MA in war studies with RMC and a professional master of public administration degree with Queen's University. He is currently stationed in Ottawa as director, Land Force Readiness 6 (Infrastructure and Environment), for the Chief of the Land Staff.

LIEUTENANT-COMMANDER HAROLD J. HENDERSON was commissioned as a maritime surface officer in the Canadian Forces upon graduation from Collège militaire royal de Saint-Jean with a bachelor of science degree in 1978. His Canadian naval training has included a Destroyer Weapons Electronic Warfare Officer course, the Combat Control Officers course, and an Advanced Maritime Warfare course. He has served tours at sea as ship's communications officer, anti-submarine warfare director, and combat officer of a helicopter-carrying destroyer. His service ashore has included tours of duty in Canadian Maritime Command Headquarters, Halifax, and most recently in NATO EASTLANT Headquarters at Northwood, England. There he served as a surface warfare specialist on the NATO Permanent Maritime Analysis Team, conducting operational analysis of major NATO exercises and operations. He has recently completed postgraduate training in war studies at RMC and has joined the staff of the Directorate of Maritime Force Concepts and Doctrine at NDHQ, Ottawa.

CAPTAIN PAUL JOHNSTON completed an honours BA in military and strategic studies at Royal Roads Military College in 1988. Since then, he has served in Germany, Montreal, and Kingston. Trained as an Intelligence Branch officer in 1990, he has been a CF-18 fighter squadron intelligence officer in Baden-Sollingen, Germany, and a command headquarters staff officer, and in 1994, he was the first air force intelligence officer posted into the army's 1st Canadian Division Headquarters. Having completed a year of studies at RMC towards an MA in war studies, he is now serving in the Yugoslavia Crisis Cell at NDHQ, Ottawa.

MAJOR DUNCAN C.D. MILNE graduated from RMC in 1970 with a bachelor of arts (honours history). He has served as an artillery officer in appointments in Gagetown, Shilo, Germany, Cyprus, and Fort Sill. He is a graduate of the Australian Army Command and Staff College, the Canadian Land Forces Command and Staff College, and the Instructor in Gunnery course. He currently serves as a staff officer in the Directorate of Force Concepts in the Vice Chief of Defence Staff at NDHQ, Ottawa. He commenced the RMC master of arts program on a part-time basis in 1994.

LIEUTENANT-COLONEL IAN MCCULLOCH entered the Canadian Forces as an infantry officer in the Royal Canadian Regiment and has served in a number of operational and staff appointments, including exchange duties in the British Army on the Rhine with the Royal Regiment of Fusiliers. He has also served with two Canadian reserve units, including a period as commanding officer of the Black Watch (Royal Highland Regiment) in Montreal from 1993 to 1996. He is an active free-lance journalist and military historian who has written for many magazines and journals, including *Atlantic Advocate*, *Civil War Magazine*, and *Infantry Journal*. He received as MA from the RMC War Studies program in 1997.

LIEUTENANT-COLONEL KENNETH NESBITT joined the Canadian Forces in 1976 as an air weapons controller. He has had a variety of operational assignments in NORAD and in NATO as a tactical director on AWACS, which included the Gulf War and a liaison position with the UN Headquarters UNPROFOR in Croatia. In 1993 he was assigned to NDHQ, Ottawa, as an air requirements officer and project director for modernization of the Region Operations Control Centre. Currently he is assigned to Elmendorf AFB,

Alaska, as commanding officer of the Canadian Detachment. He is a graduate of the University of Manitoba's Political Studies program. He is completing a master of arts degree in War Studies through RMC and is a student in the Air Warfare course from the USAF Air War College, Maxwell AFB, Alabama.

LIEUTENANT-COMMANDER GUY R. PHILLIPS joined the Canadian Forces as a legal officer in 1985, having previously served in the Reserves with the Grey and Simcoe Foresters and the Governor General's Foot Guards. He has held several positions at the Office of the Judge Advocate General, including posts with the directorates of law for Claims, Human Rights, Operations and Training, and International Law, and has served as deputy judge advocate at CFBs North Bay and Borden. During the Gulf War he was legal adviser to the commander of the Canadian Air Task Group Middle East in Doha, Qatar. He has a BA in political science and law from Carleton University (1979), an LLB from Osgoode Hall Law School, York University (1982), and an LLM in military law, with a specialization in international law, from the United States Army Judge Advocate General's School, Charlottesville, Va. (1993). His LLM thesis on rules of engagement was published in the *Army Lawyer*.

MAJOR ROBERT POIRIER, a field and air defence artillery officer, graduated from RMC in 1978 with a bachelor of arts (history). He has since held a variety of regimental, school, and staff appointments, including a tour as chief instructor in gunnery at the Air Defence Artillery School and attendance at the British Army Staff College, Camberly. He is currently working in the Directorate of Land Requirements, NDHQ, Ottawa. He started the RMC master of arts program as a part-time student in 1994.

MAJOR RICHARD ROY is a combat engineer who graduated from RMC in 1982 with a bachelor of engineering (civil). He has completed operational and staff tours in Cyprus and Kingston, Ont. He carried out the duties of force engineer information officer in the first rotation of UNPROFOR in the former Yugoslavia in 1992. He then returned to Land Forces Central Area Headquarters in Toronto and served there in both the Engineer and the Operations branches. He has just completed a master's degree in military history at RMC.

CAPTAIN JUSTIN SCHMIDT-CLEVER is an army officer who has held a number of positions and appointments since enrolling in 1987. Following an undergraduate degree at Bishop's University he graduated from RMC, in May 1996 with a master of arts in war studies. In addition, he was appointed War Studies administration officer for 1995–97. His interest in outer space springs from an assignment to help run the Royal Canadian Air Cadets Aerospace Sciences Course at Collège militaire royal de Saint-Jean in summer 1995. There followed the opportunity to take both the Canadian Forces' Basic Space Indoctrination Course and a course in space policy and law at RMC.

COMMANDER ROSS STRUTHERS, after graduating from Queen's University with a BA in life sciences, joined the Canadian Forces and trained as a naval officer. Over his twenty-two-year career, he has served in such diverse positions as flag lieutenant to the commander of the Canadian navy and with the UN peacekeeping force in Central America. A graduate of the Canadian Forces Command and Staff College, he is currently executive assistant to the assistant deputy minister (Policy and Communications) in NDHQ, Ottawa.

LIEUTENANT-COLONEL PAUL F. WYNNYK joined the Canadian Forces as a militiaman in 1981. Obtaining a bachelor of engineering (civil) from RMC in 1986, he was commissioned into the Canadian Military Engineers and has since served in command, staff, and peacekeeping assignments. In addition to the study of military history, he avidly pursues a number of outdoor sports. A graduate of the Canadian Forces Command and Staff College, he is currently commanding officer of 1 Combat Engineer Regiment in Edmonton.

LIEUTENANT-COLONEL RICHARD J. YOUNG is a maritime air navigator with thirty-three years of service in the RCAF and Canadian Forces. He graduated from RMC in 1967 with an honours bachelor of arts degree in economics and political science. Between his operational tours he attended the Aerospace Systems Course, Canadian Forces Command and Staff College, and the USAF Air War College at Maxwell AFB, Ala. While there, he took advantage of the cooperative educational program at Auburn University and earned a master's degree in political science. He is currently serving in Plans and Requirements at NORAD Headquarters, Peterson AFB, Col.

Index